Strategic Environmental Assessment in International and European Law

Strategic Environmental Assessment in International and European Law

A Practitioner's Guide

Simon Marsden

publishing for a sustainable future

London • Sterling, VA

First published by Earthscan in the UK and USA in 2008

Copyright © Simon Marsden, 2008

ISBN: 978-1-84407-489-1

Typeset by JS Typesetting, Porthcawl, Mid Glamorgan
Printed and bound in the UK by TJ International, Padstow
Cover design by Andrew Corbett

For a full list of publications please contact:

Earthscan
Dunstan House
14a St Cross Street
London EC1N 8XA, UK
Tel: +44 (0)20 7841 1945
Fax: +44 (0)20 7242 1474
Email: earthinfo@earthscan.co.uk
Web: **www.earthscan.co.uk**

22883 Quicksilver Drive, Sterling, VA 20166-2012, USA

Earthscan publishes in association with the International Institute for Environment and
Development

A catalogue record for this book is available from the British Library

Library of Congress Cataloging-in-Publication Data

Marsden, Simon, 1964-
    Strategic environmental assessment in international and European law : a practitioner's
guide / Simon Marsden.
        p. cm.
    ISBN 978-1-84407-489-1 (hardback)
    1. Environmental impact analysis–Law and legislation. 2. Environmental impact analysis–Law
and legislation–European Union countries. 3. Strategic planning–Environmental aspects.
4. Environmental policy. I. Title.
    K3585.M365 2008
    346.04'6714–dc22

                                                                2008015718

The paper used for this book is FSC-certified.
FSC (the Forest Stewardship Council) is an
international network to promote responsible
management of the world's forests.

Mixed Sources
Product group from well-managed
forests and other controlled sources
www.fsc.org Cert no. SGS-COC-2482
© 1996 Forest Stewardship Council

Contents

Foreword by Mikael Hildén   *vii*
Preface   *ix*
Acknowledgements   *xi*
List of Acronyms and Abbreviations   *xiii*

  1   Introduction: SEA and the Law   1

PART I – INTERNATIONAL LAW

  2   An Overview of International Law   25
  3   International Environmental Law   47
  4   The Espoo and Aarhus Conventions   73
  5   The SEA Protocol   93
  6   SEA and the Conservation Conventions   115

PART II – EUROPEAN LAW

  7   An Overview of European Law   137
  8   European Environmental Law   159
  9   The EIA and other Horizontal Directives   183
 10   The SEA Directive   205
 11   Relationship between the SEA, EIA and other Related Directives   239

 12   Comparisons and Conclusions   273

Appendix 1: SEA Protocol   287
Appendix 2: SEA Directive   299
Index   323

The development of a formalized legal basis for strategic environmental assessment (SEA) has been an important social innovation. While procedures for the assessment of various forms of impacts existed before the evolution of legislation for strategic environmental assessments, for example, in the context of land use planning, and there have been general demands on the assessment of economic effects of public policies, plans and programmes, SEA procedures are more detailed and also provide criteria by which implementation can be judged. It is therefore important to explore its roots and its connections to other legislation.

Legal innovations, especially international and European ones in the environmental field, have a complex history and carry with them a baggage of impulses, links to other pieces of legislation, and layers of negotiations and compromises. The legislation on SEA is no exception. This book explores these connections and background factors in a clear and systematic way, and thereby places SEA in context. As Simon Marsden convincingly shows: there is more to SEA than the SEA Directive and the SEA Protocol under the Espoo Convention.

Although practitioners of SEA do not have to worry about the background and wider context too much in their everyday work, it is useful to have a feeling for it. And there are occasions when the background matters, as court cases from the European Court of Justice clearly demonstrate.

The history and wider context is also important in another respect. The development of environmental assessments will not stop with the present legislation. New initiatives are under way and similar or related ideas will be taken up in other fields of legislation. The impulses for many of the ideas and initiatives can be found in examining the history that has led to the present legislation.

It took more than a decade to develop an SEA Directive that could be adopted as a piece of European legislation. One can argue that it became possible only because the ideas and practices that are embedded in the Directive had been tested, debated and developed further in pilot applications and 'gold-plated' national implementations of the environmental impact assessment (EIA) approaches that were extended to plans and programmes. Many of these developments have been documented in this book and they make interesting reading. A similar development can be foreseen with respect to, for example, broad policy assessments and evaluations, and more sophisticated regulatory impact assessment.

Thanks to the examination of SEA applications and links, this book can also be read as a source of ideas for a new generation of SEA legislation. Simon Marsden's careful review shows that there are many possible avenues and issues that can be explored and developed further. The debate on the importance of procedure versus substance has not yet been resolved and will affect how the environmental policy integration processes are taken further. The demands for broadening the assessment mandate to include not only environmental aspects but a broader sustainability agenda can also be examined in the light of the experiences with SEA. Finally, the legal support that would allow public participation to develop towards processes for social learning is also an area that should be examined. Part of the foundations have been laid in practices and legislation related to strategic environmental assessments.

Mikael Hildén
Professor, Finnish Environment Institute

Preface

The initial idea for this book arose in 2000 as a legal academic at the University of Exeter, and derived from presentations on EIA and international law to law students and to the Finnish Environment Institute. Developing academic and professional interests in the SEA Directive and SEA Protocol led to the specific focus on SEA. The book attempts to explain and develop legal concepts as clearly as possible to address an audience primarily of non-lawyers, while also building on legal and related literatures to appeal to environmental lawyers. As will readily be appreciated, the literature on international law, international environmental law, European law, European environmental law, EIA, SEA and other areas discussed (such as biodiversity conservation) is vast and complex, so the task has been substantial and challenging. While not justifying any failings to achieve these dual objectives, it may serve as a partial plea in mitigation.

Simon Marsden
Hong Kong, March 2008

Acknowledgements

I would like to thank several people for their encouragement, inspiration and assistance, many of whom are friends or former colleagues. These include the reviewers of the proposal and the final manuscript, Professor Neil Craik, Mr William Sheate, Dr Thomas Fischer, Professor Gerrit Betlem, Professor Timo Koivurova, Mr Jan de Mulder, and Professor Jeremy Rowan-Robinson. I would also like to express my appreciation to Professor Mikael Hildén of the Finnish Environment Institute for taking the time to prepare the foreword to this book at short notice, which is much appreciated. Any errors within the text, however, are mine alone. I would also like to thank my Commissioning Editor Rob West for his helpful early suggestions, Editorial Assistant Alison Kuznets and Production Coordinator Hamish Ironside. Finally, this book is dedicated to my wife Elizabeth and children Joseph and Anna.

List of Acronyms and Abbreviations

ANSEA	Analytical Strategic Environmental Assessment
ASEAN	Association of South East Asian Nations
CAP	Common Agricultural Policy
CBD	Convention on Biological Diversity 1992
CC	Compliance Committee
CEC	Commission of the European Communities
CFI	Court of First Instance
CFSP	Common Foreign and Security Policy
CITES	Convention on International Trade in Endangered Species of Wild Flora and Fauna 1975
CMS	Convention on the Conservation of Migratory Species of Wild Animals 1979
COP	Conference of the Parties
CSCE	Conference on Security and Cooperation in Europe
CSD	Commission on Sustainable Development
CTP	Common Transport Policy
DG	Directorate General
DSU	Dispute Settlement Understanding
EA	environmental assessment (EIA and/or SEA)
EAEC	European Atomic Energy Community
EAGGF	European Agricultural Guidance and Guarantee Fund
EAP	Environmental Action Programme
EC	European Community
ECE	Economic Commission for Europe
ECHR	European Convention on Human Rights
ECJ	European Court of Justice
ECSC	European Coal and Steel Community
EEA	European Economic Area
EEC	European Economic Community
EFTA	European Free Trade Association
EIA	environmental impact assessment
ELD	Environmental Liability Directive
EPBC Act	Environment Protection and Biodiversity Conservation Act 1999
EPI	environmental policy integration
EU	European Union
IA	impact assessment

IAIA	International Association for Impact Assessment
ICC	International Criminal Court
ICJ	International Court of Justice
IEL	international environmental law
IGC	Intergovernmental Conference
IGO	intergovernmental organization
ILC	International Law Commission
IMF	International Monetary Fund
IMPEL	EU Network for the Implementation and Enforcement of Environmental Law
IPPC	integrated pollution prevention and control
IUCN	International Union for the Conservation of Nature
LC	Lord Chancellor
LRTAP	Convention on Long Range Transboundary Air Pollution 1979
MEA	multilateral environmental agreement
MEP	Member of the European Parliament
MOP	Meeting of the Parties
MOS	Meeting of the Signatories
MS	Member States
NACEC	North American Commission for Environmental Cooperation
NAFTA	North American Free Trade Association
NEPA	National Environmental Policy Act 1969
NEPI	new environmental policy instrument
NGO	non-governmental organization
NRM	natural resource management
ODPM	Office of the Deputy Prime Minister, UK
OECD	Organisation for Economic Co-operation and Development
PCA	Permanent Court of Arbitration
PCIJ	Permanent Court of International Justice
PJCC	Police and Judicial Cooperation in Criminal Matters
POI	Plan of Implementation (Johannesburg Declaration)
PoM	programme of measures
PP	plan and programme
PPP	policy, plan and programme
PRC	People's Republic of China
RBMP	river basin management plan
REC	Regional Environment Center
RSPB	Royal Society for the Protection of Birds
SA	sustainability assessment/appraisal
SAC	Special Area of Conservation
SBSTTA	Subsidiary Body on Scientific, Technical and Technological Advice
SCA	Special Conservation Area
SCI	Site of Community Importance
SEA	strategic environmental assessment
SPA	Special Protection Area
STRP	Scientific and Technical Review Panel (Ramsar)
TEC	Treaty of the European Community

TEU	Treaty on European Union
TFEU	Treaty on the Functioning of the European Union
UK	United Kingdom of Great Britain and Northern Ireland
UN	United Nations
UNCED	United Nations Conference on Environment and Development 1992 (Rio de Janeiro)
UNCHE	United Nations Conference on the Human Environment 1972 (Stockholm)
UNCLOS	United Nations Convention on the Law of the Sea 1982
UNECE	United Nations Economic Commission for Europe
UNEP	United Nations Environment Programme
USSR	Union of Soviet Socialist Republics
VCLT	Vienna Convention on the Law of Treaties 1969
WHO	World Health Organization
WIPO	World Intellectual Property Organization
WSSD	World Summit on Sustainable Development 2002 (Johannesburg)
WTO	World Trade Organization

CHAPTER 1

Introduction: SEA and the Law

CHAPTER OUTLINE

This introduction first explains the objectives of and rationale for the book, and to whom it is addressed. Second, the structure and content of each chapter is outlined. Third, it provides an overview of strategic environmental assessment (SEA) by summarizing national laws, defining the concept and discussing advantages, examining its decision making context and outlining key principles used in system evaluation. Fourth, it emphasizes the importance of a legal framework, explaining the role of and difference between law and legal systems so that the relationship between international, European and national law may be understood. Matters such as the rule of law, legal interpretation and enforcement are included, together with a commentary on the need for legal requirements for SEA.

OBJECTIVES OF AND RATIONALE FOR THE BOOK

The objective of this book is to provide an overview of the current status of SEA in international and European law to assist with implementation of legal requirements and consider future developments at all levels. The book is written primarily for a non-legal audience, with practitioners responsible for environmental policy making, planning and management operating within the framework of Directive 2001/42/EC on the assessment of certain plans and programmes (the SEA Directive), and the 2003 United Nations Economic Commission for Europe (UNECE) Protocol on Strategic Environmental Assessment to the 1991 Convention on Environmental Impact Assessment in a Transboundary Context (SEA Protocol to the Espoo Convention), particularly in mind. In addition to explaining and analysing procedural and substantive law, the book is focused on explaining the context of these provisions, the underlying legal frameworks of international and European law and the relationship with each other and the national legal systems.

The transposition of the SEA Directive into the national laws of the Member States (MS) of the European Union (EU) and the ongoing ratification of the SEA Protocol by the signatories thereto, has produced the need for a greater understanding of the underlying legal frameworks, which are not always well understood despite the production of extensive guidance documentation. Wherever possible, clear explanations of the basis of international and European law are provided in plain English. The relationship between them and national law is a particular focus, providing the context for an explanation of the specific provisions analysed in detail in the following chapters.

A secondary audience for the book is environmental lawyers less familiar with the application of environmental impact assessment (EIA) and other related processes to higher levels of decision making (such as policy analysis and sustainability assessment). This audience may find some of the information in this introductory chapter useful in providing an understanding of the development of SEA and how best to conduct SEA. Environmental lawyers less familiar with international or European law, and the relationship between legal systems and the specific laws discussed, may also find much of interest in the other chapters. Synthesis and analysis of the now extensive relevant and related literatures of international and European environmental law, SEA and other areas are therefore provided for explanation and further reading, with full notes in each chapter.

STRUCTURE AND CONTENT

In addition to this introduction and a comparative concluding chapter (Chapter 12), the book is arranged into ten main chapters that are grouped into two parts. Part I first examines international law, with Chapter 2 explaining how the international legal system works as an overview for Chapters 3, 4, 5 and 6. Part II then considers European law, with Chapter 7 explaining how European law works as an overview to Chapters 8, 9, 10 and 11. Each of these chapters is summarized below.

Chapter 2 illustrates the complexities of international law from theoretical, political and legal perspectives, as well as providing an explanation of its development and structure, sources and obligations, relationship with national and supranational law, enforcement and emerging issues. Brevity and simplicity are needed to enable synthesis of a huge literature into a reasonably accessible summary. A key focus is on explaining the different types of international agreements that are commonly used (multilateral, regional and bilateral), their preparation, approval and incorporation into the domestic (and European) legal frameworks. Aside from a full explanation of treaty making, the significance of customary international law is explained as well as of the different types of 'soft law' that often develop into custom and treaties.

Chapter 3 considers international environmental law (IEL) with a focus on EIA. Three of the most important duties of IEL are outlined: prevention of harm, cooperation in transboundary situations and compensation for harm. Several general principles form part of these duties, such as the precautionary principle and the principle of sustainable development. These have been considered several times by international courts and tribunals, and this jurisprudence is analysed to see to what extent EIA at least may now be required as part of these principles. Treaty, custom and soft law provisions of relevance are also discussed, many of which make reference to EIA and SEA. In each case, reference is made to the duties of harm prevention, transboundary cooperation and liability. Finally, enforcement matters are analysed.

Chapter 4 analyses the role of the Espoo and Aarhus Conventions to explain the context for the SEA Protocol and better understand how treaty decision making works. Although the SEA Protocol is a stand alone legal instrument, understanding of the role of the sponsoring institution of both treaties (the UNECE) and the administrative function of the Meeting of the Parties (MOP) is provided because several of the treaty requirements also relate to the Protocol, and the Espoo MOP will also exercise powers in relation to the Protocol when it comes into force. As well as outlining key relevant procedural provisions of each treaty, implementation and compliance issues are therefore discussed.

Chapter 5 focuses on the SEA Protocol. The chapter considers the different legal obligations that attach to assessing different strategic proposals, with some focus on policies and legislative proposals, which takes the SEA Protocol's requirements beyond those of the SEA Directive. The SEA Protocol Guidance (UNECE/REC, 2007) is considered in depth to help explain the law and examine to what extent SEA best practice is complied with. Without commenting on the detail of the SEA Directive, the historical and structural relationship between the SEA Protocol and the SEA Directive is analysed to an extent, in part because the more extensive requirements of the SEA Protocol may result in changes in the SEA Directive in the future, but also because it is a useful way of illustrating the relationship between international and European law.

Chapter 6 considers the application of SEA to the conservation conventions, in particular the 1971 Ramsar Convention on Wetlands of International Importance (Ramsar), the 1972 Paris Convention for the Protection of the World Cultural and Natural Heritage (World Heritage), the 1979 Bonn Convention on the Conservation of Migratory Species of Wild Animals (CMS), and the 1992 Rio de Janeiro Convention on Biological Diversity (CBD). SEA has been actively encouraged by the convention secretariats as an effective means of implementing them, and the guidance documentation produced is examined to evaluate how well this is done in accordance with SEA best practice and the effect on implementation. The chapter also provides an opportunity to consider how, if new environmental treaties are drafted in the future, SEA could be incorporated as a specific requirement.

Chapter 7 explains the structure and effect of European law, including the relationship between the European Community (EC), EU, international law, MS and EU citizens. The difference between primary law (European treaties) and secondary law (mainly regulations and directives) is explained and the jurisprudence of the European Court of Justice (ECJ) on the effect of European law is analysed, including the meaning of 'direct effect' and 'indirect effect'. Enforcement matters are analysed in detail, including infraction proceedings begun by the Commission against an MS before the ECJ for failing to transpose directives into national law. Clear explanation and summary (again given the huge literature on the subject) is provided wherever possible, and topical issues are discussed.

Chapter 8 considers European environmental law, from its development to its current status. This includes an examination of the changing EC competence for environmental law making in the treaties and the policy drivers for this, such as the general principles of environmental integration and sustainable development, and the specific environmental principles of precaution, prevention and the polluter pays. Institutions of relevance are considered and the range of subject areas that have been regulated is summarized. Compliance and enforcement issues are addressed in detail with respect to the Commission and ECJ. Reference to the extensive literature on the subject is again provided with detailed analysis and citations of relevant further reading.

Chapter 9 focuses on Directive 85/337/EEC (EIA Directive, as amended by Directives 97/11/EC and 2003/35/EC) and its case law. This illustrates why the SEA Directive was needed, how it came about and likely future challenges. It also explains the relevance of Directives 90/313/EEC (Environmental Information, as amended by Directive 2003/4/EC), 2003/35/EC (Public Participation) and 2004/35/CE (Environmental Liability). The amended Environmental Information and Public Participation Directives were the means of implementing the first two 'pillars' of the Aarhus Convention, and a proposal for a directive on Access to Justice is intended to implement the third. The Environmental Liability Directive is a potential means of ensuring that compensation for environmental damage is provided, and addresses the third duty discussed in Chapter 3. Chapter 9 examines how effective these provisions are and how they relate to the SEA Directive; in examining directives implementing the Aarhus Convention, it also demonstrates the relationship between international and European law.

Chapter 10 analyses the SEA Directive, including its legal basis and effect, objectives, procedural provisions and transposition and implementation. Some brief background is given, with extensive further readings provided throughout. A thorough explanation of the key requirements is provided, with detailed discussion of the EU SEA Guidance documentation in particular (Reps of the MS/EC, 2003). Some selectivity is applied here to ensure this chapter does not dominate the book. While it is without doubt the most significant of any of the provisions in international and European law, it is not the purpose of this book to focus solely on the SEA Directive. Further discussion of the SEA Directive is provided in Chapters 5, 11 and 12.

Chapter 11 considers the relationship between the SEA and EIA Directives, and Directives 79/409/EEC (Wild Birds), 92/43/EEC (Habitats) and 2000/60/EC (Water Framework). Other relevant directives and regulations are also examined, including Directives 91/676/EEC (Nitrates), 2006/12/EC (Waste), 96/62/EC (Air Quality) and Regulations No 1260/1999 and No 1257/1999 (Structural Funds). The Habitats and Water Framework Directives contain provisions for the assessment of certain plans and programmes, and existing jurisprudence is analysed in detail. The chapter analyses these requirements and their relationship with the SEA and EIA Directives, and considers how well integrated each of the provisions are with one another.

Chapter 12 compares and contrasts the role of international and European law, including environmental protection generally, and in promulgating SEA law. The relationship between the legal systems is analysed, especially with regard to the role of the EC/EU as an international institution. The relationship between the respective competences of international tribunals and the ECJ is also analysed in the context of selected jurisprudence. Conclusions are drawn that European law provides a stronger basis for SEA because it is more easily enforceable; European law also provides a stronger basis to enforce international law when adopted by the EU. It also concludes that the SEA Directive and SEA Protocol are likely to continue to be the model for SEA legislation globally, at least where a number of countries share interests in common and have appropriate institutional structures and political will to take them forward. The chapter recommends, however, that as part of the SEA Directive Review, consideration is given to better integrating European environmental law in the area of environmental assessment (EA), which has become overly disparate and complex. In an international context, it recommends that the provisions for the assessment of policies and legislative proposals under the SEA Protocol should become a more accepted feature in national jurisdictions, although this is likely to mean that a less rigorous type of SEA takes place.

AN OVERVIEW OF SEA

SEA has been used as a term to describe the EA of strategic level proposals since the late 1980s in a draft report to the European Commission that was later published as a journal article (Wood and Djeddour, 1992). However, it was a legislative requirement, and/or practiced in an ad hoc manner from the 1970s onwards, or advocated by others thereafter (O'Riordan and Sewell, 1981; Wathern, 1988). Since 1992, it has been examined in a ballooning literature of several key texts with varying foci, (Thérivel et al, 1992; Thérivel and Partidario, 1996; Marsden and Dovers, 2002; Fischer, 2002b; Caratti et al, 2004; Thérivel, 2004a; Dalal-Clayton and Sadler, 2005; Jones et al, 2005; Schmidt et al, 2005; Fischer, 2007), a literature to which this book aims to make a further contribution.

There are numerous related terms such as policy appraisal, integrated assessment and sustainability assessment/appraisal, each of which has a different meaning (Dalal-Clayton and Sadler, 2005, pp9–14). Since the term was first used in the literature it had no official status until the SEA Protocol was explicitly so called by the UNECE. The SEA Directive is also now commonly labelled as such in guidance documentation of the MS (ODPM, 2005). This section describes the development of national SEA law, outlines the definition and advantages of SEA, explains its decision making context and outlines key principles used in system evaluation.

Development of national law and policy requirements

SEA legal provisions have been in existence since the passage of the National Environmental Policy Act (NEPA) in the US in 1969, which requires 'proposals for legislation and other major federal actions significantly affecting the environment' to include a 'detailed statement... on the environmental impact' (Sec. 102(2)(c)).[1] Typically, however, while the intention had always been that policy and legislative proposals were to be assessed, this was not forthcoming in practice, and the assessment of plans and programmes has also been slow to develop (Marsden and Ashe, 2006). Entrenched administrative discretion and underlying confidentiality of government decision making has ensured that, for the most part, political will has been lacking in this area; methodological and context constraints have also been suggested as relevant (see below). Descriptions and analysis of SEA institutional frameworks, whether legal or otherwise, are commonly cited (for example, Sheate, 1996; Tromans and Fuller, 2003; Holder, 2004; Holder and McGillivray, 2007; Ryall, 2007a) and compared in the literature (Dalal-Clayton and Sadler, 2005, pp38–39), which include provisions for the assessment of environmental impacts from all strategic levels.

Where assessment of policy or legislative proposals is required, it has, at least until recently, tended to form part of the regulatory assessment process undertaken with primarily an economic and social focus. As reported in the summary literature (see for example, de Boer and Sadler, 1996; Sadler, 2005) exceptions in part include still largely discretionary requirements in Canada (1990 and 1999), Hong Kong (1992, 1998 and 2007), Denmark (1993, 1995, 1998), the European Commission (1993), the Netherlands (1995), Finland (1998 and 1999) and under the SEA Protocol (2003). Higher level assessment has also been recommended in accordance with guidance documentation produced by the UK (1991, 1994 and 1997), or has occurred as a result of public inquiries and environmental reviews of major proposals with strategic implications, such as in Canada under the Mackenzie Valley Pipeline Inquiry (1974–1977) and in Australia under the Ranger Uranium Environmental Inquiry (1975–1977).

For the most part, therefore, legal requirements for SEA have focused on the plan and programme levels, such as in California (1970), the Netherlands (1987), New Zealand (1991 and 2003), Australia (1999) and under the SEA Directive (2001) and SEA Protocol (2003). Inevitably, SEA practice has been most extensive in this area as described (de Boer and Sadler, 1996; Thérivel and Partidario, 1996; Partidario and Clark, 2000; Fischer, 2002b; Thérivel, 2004a; Jones et al, 2005) or as summarized in the literature to date (Dalal-Clayton and Sadler, 2005, pp7–9). The ongoing need for SEA legal requirements is examined at the end of this chapter after the reasons behind a legal framework are explained.

Definition and advantages

Although commentators continue to discuss how best to describe and deploy SEA,[2] for the purposes of this book, and in line with the EIA-centred approach of the majority of SEA legal provisions (including the SEA Directive and SEA Protocol), SEA is the evaluation of the impacts of legislative, policy, plan and programme proposals upon the environment, the last three typically abbreviated as PPPs. There are, however, many detailed definitions in the relevant literature (Dalal-Clayton and Sadler, 2005, pp10–11). It is closely related to EIA, which is the evaluation of the impacts of projects on the environment.[3] Because EIA is typically applied late in the decision making process, SEA should help strengthen EIA, as it addresses impacts at a higher level or earlier stage, thereby aiming to avoid them at a lower level or later stage. It also aims to avoid later cumulative impacts[4] by carrying out an assessment at a higher level or at an earlier stage. In order to do this, a tiered planning framework and a full consideration of alternatives are needed. Assessment is therefore best carried out at the same time as the development of the strategic proposal while all options are still being discussed. Many of these matters are outlined in summarized reference works (Dalal-Clayton and Sadler, 2005, pp6–9).

Fischer (2007) points to three main functions that underlie the theoretical advantages of SEA. The first is that it provides decision makers with better information on the impacts of proposal alternatives. Although in some cases good quality information can influence decision making, in situations of conflict this may not be the case. The second is that it enables attitudes and perceptions to change as a result of participation in a transparent and systematic process. Third, it is argued that it can change established routines leading to increased environmental awareness. Some evidence is available for each of these three functions. Dusik et al (2003) point to four main benefits of SEA, which are related: it helps to achieve environmentally sound and sustainable development, it strengthens PPP processes, it saves time and money, and it improves good governance and public trust in PPP making. More detailed potential benefits have been discussed in the literature from very early on (see Wood and Djeddour, 1992, p7).

The relationship between SEA, integrated assessment and sustainability appraisal (SA) is complex and controversial (Devuyst, 1999; Nooteboom and Wieringa, 1999), with some authors suggesting that SEA should be converted into these other means of assessment that are designed to assess environmental, economic and social considerations at the same time. However, concerns remain for many that the result of this may be to dilute the environmental focus of impact assessment and that, ultimately, the decision maker will determine the balance to be struck between the various components and not the impact assessment practitioner (Smith and Sheate, 2001; Dovers, 2002; Gibson et al, 2004; Morrison-Saunders and Fischer, 2006).

Context and decision making

Given that SEA specifically advocates integrating environmental factors into decision making in order to advance sustainability, in theory, the more relevant factors that are present, the more sustainable the proposal will be. This is likely to be especially so with the assessment of the highest order proposals, as it is at the legislative and policy levels that decisions may be taken that will have the most implications for sustainability (Dovers, 2002, p26; Dalal-Clayton and Sadler, 2005, p22). Policy and legislative proposals are therefore very suitable candidates for assessment at the strategic level, although procedures and methodology applicable at this level may differ substantially from those at the plan and programme levels (Bailey and Renton, 1997, 1998; Bailey and Dixon, 1999; Renton and Bailey, 2000; Brown and Thérivel, 2000).[5] There may therefore be a need to adapt/adopt procedures and methodologies distinct from EIA-based ones at the most strategic levels. This may be more likely to gain acceptance and provide integration with different approaches to decision making that may not be so accessible to, for example, public input and lengthy documentation (Brown and Nitz, 2002).

Much of the emphasis on the assessment of plans and programmes has resulted from the perceived difficulties of assessing policy and legislative proposals, especially when rationality in decision making is questioned (Kørnøv and Thissen, 2000), or where the influence of strategic decision making depends on a much greater understanding of strategy formation (Cherp et al, 2007). Many authors have therefore recommended applying different approaches to different types of strategic proposal to take account of decision making contexts (see Marsden, 1998b; Verheem and Tonk, 2000; Hildén et al, 2004; Hilding-Rydevik and Bjarnadóttir, 2007; Runhaar and Driessen, 2007). Yet structured approaches to SEA based on EIA procedures have been defended where demands for flexibility and adaptation of SEA processes, rather than planning or policy systems, have been advocated (Fischer, 2002b, 2003).

The focus on the decision making process has been the subject of the Analytical Strategic Environmental Assessment (ANSEA) project, conducted between 2000 and 2002. ANSEA therefore considers 'the quality of the decision-making process rather than on the impacts of the decision; on describing the decision process rather than the output of the decisions and ensuring full integration of environmental values in decision making' (Thérivel, 2004b, pxv). Bina relates ANSEA to the SEA Directive, concluding that the scope of the approach will be 'wider than that required by a strict interpretation of the Directive' (2004, p112). Whether or not practitioners deploy its approach remains to be seen.

Principles and system evaluation

The SEA Directive and SEA Protocol prescribe certain procedural requirements (described and explained in detail in Chapters 10 and 5), although some flexibility is given to MS and signatories to decide exactly how to implement them, in recognition of the different contexts in which they operate. Key procedural requirements include provisions for screening, scoping, analysis in a report and subsequent review, decision making and monitoring (Morrison-Saunders et al, 2007). Consultation and participation should also form integral parts of any procedure (André et al, 2006), although there are likely to be differences in this for plans and programmes on one hand and policies and legislation on the other. SEA procedure should also be integrated with the context

---

BOX 1.1 IAIA SEA PERFORMANCE CRITERIA

A good-quality SEA process informs planners, decision makers and affected public on the sustainability of strategic decisions, facilitates the search for the best alternative and ensures a democratic decision making process. This enhances the credibility of decisions and leads to more cost- and time-effective EA at the project level. For this purpose, a good-quality SEA process:

is integrated
- Ensures an appropriate environmental assessment of all strategic decisions relevant for the achievement of sustainable development.
- Addresses the interrelationships of biophysical, social and economic aspects.
- Is tiered to policies in relevant sectors and (transboundary) regions and, where appropriate, to project EIA and decision making.

is sustainability-led
- Facilitates identification of development options and alternative proposals that are more sustainable*.

is focused
- Provides sufficient, reliable and usable information for development planning and decision making.
- Concentrates on key issues of sustainable development.
- Is customized to the characteristics of the decision making process.
- Is cost- and time-effective.

of operation wherever possible, so ideally there is one process of proposal formulation and assessment, not two separate processes. The consideration of alternatives in a tiered framework should form an integral part of this.

SEA effectiveness criteria are widely advocated in the professional literature as a means of evaluating SEA systems.[6] Based on key principles of SEA that should be generic to any SEA system (von Seht, 1999), perhaps the best known are the SEA Performance Criteria derived by the SEA Section of the International Association for Impact Assessment (IAIA, 2002) (see Box 1.1), and which followed on from the international study into the effectiveness of EA (Sadler, 1996; Sadler and Verheem, 1996).[7] These and other criteria have been widely applied to evaluate SEA systems, such as in Canada, the Netherlands and Australia (Marsden, 1998a, 1999a, 1999b). Some of the key principles include: self-assessment by the responsible authority integrated into the proposal process, application as early as possible in the decision making process, focus on the key issues at the relevant stages of proposal formulation, evaluation of a range of alternatives, provision of appropriate consultation opportunities, and application of cost effective analytical methods (UNECE/REC, 2007).

is accountable	• Is the responsibility of the leading agencies for the strategic decision to be taken.
	• Is carried out with professionalism, rigor, fairness, impartiality and balance.
	• Is subject to independent checks and verification.
	• Documents and justifies how sustainability issues were taken into account in decision making.
is participative	• Informs and involves interested and affected public and government bodies throughout the decision making process.
	• Explicitly addresses their inputs and concerns in documentation and decision making.
	• Has clear, easily-understood information requirements and ensures sufficient access to all relevant information.
is iterative	• Ensures availability of the assessment results early enough to influence the decision making process and inspire future planning.
	• Provides sufficient information on the actual impacts of implementing a strategic decision, to judge whether this decision should be amended and to provide a basis for future decisions.

Note: * That is, that contributes to the overall sustainable development strategy as laid down in Rio 1992 and defined in the specific policies or values of a country.
Source: IAIA (2002)

NEED FOR LEGAL REQUIREMENTS

Several arguments can be advanced in favour of legal frameworks for SEA, which are generally the same as those in favour of law and legal systems. Law adds legitimacy to decision making that comes from the democratic accountability that puts decision makers in office (and may likewise remove them), and ensures that laws adopted by the legislature comprising those decision makers are approved by the majority.[8] It is also about rules incorporating different values as society changes. The purpose of law is therefore to ensure objectivity, certainty, consistency and transparency in decision making. Such things typically are not possible when decisions are made arbitrarily, which is sometimes referred to as rule *by* law. The rule *of* law is somewhat different and ensures that governments are bound by the same laws as individuals, as enforced by an independent judiciary. The relationship between democracy, the rule of law and judicial review (which is a means of challenging government decision making), is therefore a close one and has been subject to extensive commentary in the legal and other literatures.[9] The relationship between the role of compliance in the rule of law, good governance (which as seen above is emphasized as an advantage of SEA) and sustainable development (an objective of SEA), has also been explored in the literature (Zaelke and Higdon, 2006; Commission of the European Communities, undated).[10]

The rule of law: separation of powers and judicial independence

The rule of law is a fundamental aspect of many legal systems, especially the common law legal system that applies in nation states such as the UK, Ireland, Australia, New Zealand, Canada and US, or jurisdictions within them.[11] It is also a key feature of continental systems and the EC, although the civil law equivalent is the notion of 'constitutional governance' (Mathiesen, 2003, pp37–38 and note 2). The rule of law has been described by an Australian High Court judge as follows (Brennan, 2005, p2):

> *There are many aspects to the rule of law and many conditions that must be satisfied before a system can be said to be entirely congruent with the rule of law. At base, there must be a separation of judicial power from the legislative and executive powers of government. Then the judges must be wholly independent – independent of government, independent of the rich and powerful, independent of pressure groups and ideologies. And the judges, whose task it must be to interpret and apply the law, must be given a sufficient leeway by the law to allow its application so as not to work injustice in particular cases or in cases of a particular kind. If the judges do not have that leeway, issues which ought properly be decided by courts are effectively determined by the will of government expressed in a law created by government. Injustice is the inevitable result, and injustice leads to an erosion of the rule of law.*

The separation of powers provides for checks and balances in government, preventing one of the branches exercising unrestrained power.[12] Together with the other prerequisite of judicial independence (Rest, 2004, pp2–3; Marsden, 2006a), it is usually provided for in constitutional provisions that form the framework to any legal and political system, outlining the powers of each branch of government and in many instances the rights of individuals governed (Street and Brazier, 1985). Constitutional law is the highest form of law with which all other law must comply, and in the European law context is found in the European treaties (see Chapter 7). If a country has more than one jurisdiction, or is subject to the law of another jurisdiction (as happened in the countries within the British Commonwealth with colonialism until full independence was granted, or with regard to the MS of the EU), the Constitution will typically explain how and in what circumstances. Australia, for example, has a federal government,[13] six states and two self-governing territories. Each of these makes laws in accordance with the powers granted under the Commonwealth Constitution (1900) (Sampford and Preston, 1996).

Common law and civil law legal systems

The common law legal system was developed in England and spread to countries or parts of countries colonized by England, such as Australia, New Zealand, South Africa, Hong Kong, Canada and the US. It is distinguished from the civil law legal system, which operates in most of the MS of the EU and jurisdictions worldwide that have adopted such systems, such as Quebec in Canada (Palmer, 2001; Glenn, 2004). In some instances a jurisdiction may also be subject to both common law and civil law elements.[14] The influence of the common law of England upon related countries is no longer as great as it was, independence and the development and application of other law, such as European and international law, have diminished its application, and it is true to say that today the common law contains influences from many other countries, especially in the areas of human rights and commercial law (Cooke, 2004, p273). However, subject to certain limitations including the existence of a written constitution,[15] several common law rights developed in England remain recognized in many of these countries, such as the right to participation in a democratic process, freedom of expression, religious freedom, the right of access to the courts and the right to a fair trial (Cooke, 2004, p277).

The common law legal system is based on legislation and the doctrine of binding precedent or *stare decisis* (stand by the decision) established by the courts, although the latter is its distinguishing feature. In civil law legal systems, legislation takes on a much greater significance and while court decisions have an important role to play they do not have the same significance as those in common law countries. Legislation in civil law systems is usually found in codes, which are consolidated legislation.[16] Judicial decision making and processes of interpretation are much more closely concerned with the wording in, and legislative intention behind, the codes rather than how previous courts have interpreted such provisions (Hartley, 2005, pp813–815).[17]

In common law legal systems, legislation comprises statutes and regulations.[18] Statutes, Acts of Parliament or ordinances are all names given to primary legislation[19] passed by the legislative branch of government in common law jurisdictions. Statutes are distinguished from regulations, which are secondary legislation prepared under delegated authority by the government department responsible for implementing both the statutes and regulations. Regulations give detail to statutory provisions but because there are less opportunities for the legislative branch to input them, the law making process for regulations is usually less rigorous than that for statutes. As such, one of the few checks on the power of the executive branch is the procedural requirement to ensure conformity of secondary legislation with primary legislation, failing which a judicial challenge may result.

The doctrine of binding precedent in a common law system ensures that judicial decisions taken by higher courts are binding on lower courts in the same hierarchy, hence decisions of the High Court of Australia are binding upon the Supreme Courts in the Australian states, and decisions of the UK House of Lords are binding upon the Court of Appeal and High Court of England and Wales (Thomson and Sarre, 2001). The doctrine of persuasive precedent enables decisions reached in different hierarchies (including in other common law jurisdictions) to be also followed by other courts if they choose to do so. Judicial decisions must be fully reasoned in order to ensure transparency and fairness, and to form a basis for higher courts to review decisions of lower courts if they are subsequently challenged on appeal. Reasoned opinions also assist in the 'development of a consistent and principled system of law' (Shelton and Kiss, 2005, pxxii).

Court challenges and legal interpretation

Decisions taken by governments can be challenged for failing to comply with the law, either on a substantive or procedural basis.[20] The first, known as a merits appeal, occurs where the law requiring something to be done, such as the prevention of pollution to a natural habitat, is not complied with, with facts or evidence presented to the court; the second, known as judicial review in common law legal systems, enables a challenge to the decision making process because of the way in which the decision was reached; for example, for failing to take relevant considerations into account or taking irrelevant ones into account (Feldman, 1990; Cane, 2000). In such cases the courts are called on to decide if the substantive or procedural law has been breached, and where individuals take such action, they must typically demonstrate a sufficient interest in the matter in order to be heard (see Chapter 9 and discussion of access to justice provisions). A breach of substantive law leads to a completely different range of court remedies to a breach of procedural ones; the former, for example, can bring monetary compensation, the latter merely an order that the decision maker take the decision again.

Judges in both common and civil law jurisdictions use a variety of techniques to interpret the law, whether it is a treaty, constitution, statute or administrative rule (Vogenauer, 2001; Lücke, 2005; Marsden, 2006a). In almost all cases, judicial decision making begins with the text of the relevant law, as the words used in any provision are always the best guide to meaning. If examining a statutory provision, for example, duties are distinguished from powers; the former is found from the use of mandatory words such as 'shall' or 'must', the latter from discretionary words such as 'may' (Bates, 2006, p100). Legislation will also commonly provide that decision makers must 'have regard to', 'take into account', or 'consider' certain objectives or criteria, although as Bates (2006, p101) comments, 'such a statutory instruction falls short of actually requiring the statutory functions to be implemented or to command decision making'. This means that provided the decision maker has adequately examined the material made available (such as an environmental report), there is often little that can be done if the conclusion reached is at odds with any recommendation in the report, especially if the decision maker is obliged to consider a range of other matters, such as social and economic effects.[21]

If after examining the legal text there is any ambiguity or uncertainty, other approaches are needed, such as a purposive or contextual approach, giving consideration to the reason for which the law was adopted. In some instances the history of the legislative provision will be considered to assist;[22] usually the legislature will itself express a preference for the approach to be used in any particular jurisdiction through statutes known as Acts Interpretation Acts, which require judges to apply particular approaches. In common law jurisdictions, a purposive approach to construction, combined with the application of the doctrine of precedent, is the favoured method.[23] Similarities and differences between approaches based on the common law and civil law systems have been examined with respect to the interpretation of the EIA Directive in England and Germany (Knill and Winkler, 2006a, 2006b).

Where legal interpretation is the responsibility of more than one legal system, however, the allocation of competences to different court systems may be complicated by unclear constitutional provisions and different techniques of legal interpretation. Legitimacy may also be questioned where interpretation falls to the competence on a non-judicial body; Hong Kong is a good example of this, with constitutional interpretation occasionally provided by a non-accountable Chinese legislative committee (Marsden, 2006a, 2006b). Ireland has also been suggested as another example, where the quasi-judicial planning review body is not a court yet makes binding decisions (Ryall, 2007a, 2007b).

Need for SEA legal requirements

With respect to the need for legal requirements for SEA, arguments in favour have tended to also emphasize the objectivity, certainty, consistency and transparency that only judicially enforceable requirements can bring (Buckley, 2000). If assessment is entirely voluntary, measures for quality assurance and enforcement are often lacking. Opponents have emphasized that legally mandated provisions are unpopular with governments, especially at the policy level, and hence if SEA is to be practised at all non-legal frameworks may be needed that can be more flexibly applied. The need to maintain collective responsibility in cabinet therefore militates against openness in Parliamentary democracies operating on the Westminster model (Street and Brazier, 1985), whether in common or civil law jurisdictions.[24]

This has resulted in a mix of instruments globally (Dalal-Clayton and Sadler, 2005, p37). The experience of Denmark is instructive as a flexible non-mandated process at the policy level later became more detailed (albeit still non-mandated), as government accepted the benefits that flowed from its use (Dalal-Clayton and Sadler, 2005, p68). Certainly at the plan and programme level opponents to the application of legal requirements tend not to be heard so much today; the adoption of the SEA Directive, SEA Protocol and the 1998 UNECE Convention on Access to Information, Public Participation and Access to Justice in Environmental Matters (the Aarhus Convention, which introduces certain information, public participation and access to justice requirements for the EU SEA process) have all been generally supported giving strength to arguments in favour of a legal basis, whatever the potential delays inherent in ensuing litigation may be.

CONCLUSIONS

SEA is a valuable contributor to environmental protection within the context of sustainable development and a legal framework is essential in providing a requirement for the assessment of plans and programmes, and potentially also its application to policies and legislation. From national laws beginning in 1969 to the development of the 2001 SEA Directive and 2003 SEA Protocol at the European and international levels, SEA today has a significant legal presence. As will be seen in more detail in the chapters that follow, in a broader legal context SEA contains both substantive and procedural legal elements, with information, participation and access to justice provisions capable of individual enforcement and remedy, and, subject to the limits of discretion, process stages binding on the decision maker in a procedural law manner.

NOTES

1   As a result of the NEPA provision, SEA has largely been limited in its application to public sector proposals, and this is true of the provisions in the SEA Directive and Protocol, unless proponents are obliged to apply SEA because they are, for example, privatized utility companies. For discussion of SEA in the private sector, see Jay (2007), Marshall and Fischer (2006) and Münchenberg (2002).
2   Some authors have questioned whether SEA is needed if EIA is applied as originally intended (see Bina, 2007), and since planners and policy analysts already incorporate environmental considerations into the assessment of strategic initiatives (Boothroyd, 1995; Wallington et al, 2007).
3   Both SEA and EIA are types of environmental assessment (EA). EA is often used to describe the assessment of environmental effects from all types of proposals, including both SEA and EIA. EA should be distinguished from impact assessment (IA), which is also used to describe and encompass all types of assessment, including those that evaluate economic and social effects and integrated processes such as sustainability assessment (SA). Care should be taken to avoid confusion, especially as EA and IA are sometimes used interchangeably.
4   The relationship between SEA and cumulative impacts has been considered by a number of authors. See, for example, Court et al (1994), James et al (2003), Thérivel (2005) and, in a transboundary context, Harty et al (2005).
5   Much has been written on SEA methods, see Fischer (2002c). For a recent example relevant to monitoring, see Donnelly et al (2007).
6   Effectiveness is a concern of many other systems, including international environmental regimes, some of which are examined in Chapter 3. Andresen (2007) defines this in terms of output, outcome and impact: output refers to rules, programmes and regulations deriving from the regime; outcome refers to changes in behaviour in the desired direction; and impact refers to environmental improvements in the relevant issue area. Andresen and Hey (2005) also examine the effectiveness of international environmental institutions (see Chapter 3).
7   See also João (2005) and Fischer (2002a).

8   Legitimacy of government or good governance is a major concern, and research indicates that legitimacy may also be closely linked with effectiveness. As noted, Andresen and Hey (2005) explore this in relation to the effectiveness and legitimacy of international environmental institutions, including the United Nations Environment Programme (UNEP), which has been responsible for the development of many international environmental agreements. They comment (p212):

> *First, the effectiveness of a regime is a factor that may contribute to a regime being perceived as legitimate. . . Secondly, a regime that is regarded as legitimate is more likely to be effective, due to, among other things, the compliance pull that it is likely to exert.*

9   The literature explores the relationship between laws passed by the legislature (when democratically elected) and laws 'made' by the judiciary when interpreting statute or case law (when not elected). Some authors question the lack of legitimacy of a judiciary to change democratically approved statute law when judges are not elected. For further discussion see Marsden (2006b, pp126–129); Cooke (2004, p275) and Feldman (1990). In some jurisdictions judges are elected, which, while perhaps providing a greater degree of democratic legitimacy may also serve to limit judicial independence and compromise the separation of powers, resulting in less rigorous checks and balances and less effective judicial scrutiny of government. See Russell and O'Brien (2001).

10   See also Johannesburg Principles on the Role of Law and Sustainable Development (2002). Zaelke and Higdon (2006, pp377–379) define each of these terms and the relationship between them as follows:

> *The term good governance includes openness, participation, accountability, predictability, and transparency. Good governance depends, in turn, on the rule of law, which is generally characterised as referring to States where conduct is governed by a set of rules that are applied predictably, efficiently, and fairly by independent institutions to all members of society, including those who govern. . . Compliance is an indivisible part of the rule of law and is defined as a 'state of conformity or identity between an actor's behaviour and specified rule.' A regulated actor, whether a State, firm, or individual, is 'in compliance' when they are acting in accordance with the law (or regulations), regardless of the motivations, or other circumstances, that may have led to that conformity. These obligations can be substantive (e.g., limit emission of a pollutant) and/or procedural (e.g., perform an EIA). Non-compliance occurs when a regulated actor fails to meet one or more of these obligations. Without compliance, the rule of law has no meaning. . . The importance of compliance, rule of law, and good governance is nowhere more important than in the field of environment and sustainable development.*

11   A nation state may have more than one jurisdiction within. Taking the complicated example of the UK, there are three separate jurisdictions of England and Wales, Scotland and Northern Ireland. A jurisdiction is simply an area covered by the same legal system, which, in the case of England and Wales may of course apply to more than one country. These jurisdictions may have different legal systems: England and Wales and Northern Ireland are common law jurisdictions, and Scotland is a civil law jurisdiction. This is further complicated by the fact that the House of Lords, the highest national court of appeal of all the jurisdictions in the UK, has to consider judicial precedents (explained in text) derived from either legal system, and, since decisions of the ECJ must also be given effect to by the House of Lords and lower courts, by the mix of legal systems in the EU. Note also that since arrangements for devolution have been put in place in the UK, the countries within the UK now have certain law making powers of their own. Although in the past the UK Parliament passed laws

for each of the jurisdictions, some which applied to all jurisdictions generally and some of specific application to each, this has now changed as a result of the law making powers held by the Scottish Parliament and, to a lesser extent, Welsh Assembly.

12 The separation of powers is a theory advanced many years ago that is, in practice, limited in some nation states by representative government and delegated legislation. Representative government means that there is no direct election of the executive branch of government (as in the UK, Australia and Canada); instead the executive branch is drawn from members of the most numerous political party in the legislature (which, if there is more than one legislative chamber, means the 'lower house', such as the House of Commons in the UK or Canada, or the House of Representatives in Australia). Delegated legislation is the same thing as secondary legislation (usually regulations), which are approved by the executive rather than the legislative branch of government (explained further in the text).

13 A federal government can be contrasted with a unitary government. In the former, there is more than one jurisdiction each with independent law making powers, and power is shared between the jurisdictions in accordance with the constitution. In the latter, with the exception of law making powers given to local government or to autonomous regions within, the national government makes law for the country as a whole. Examples of the former include Australia, Canada and the US. Examples of the latter include the UK (with exceptions for devolution and local government), New Zealand (where there are only local government law making powers or Maori treaty rights as an exception), and the People's Republic of China (PRC) (where local government also has law making powers and the special administrative regions of Hong Kong and Macau have significant autonomous powers).

14 Some common law countries have also introduced civil law elements into their legal systems. In Australia, for example, the criminal law, which is an important aspect of the common law alongside contract and tort (civil wrongs, such as negligence and nuisance), has been codified in several jurisdictions including Tasmania and the Commonwealth. This is unlikely to meet all the criteria of a civil code however (see note 16 below).

15 Most countries have written constitutions, but other than the Acts of Settlement that establish the relationship between the constituent parts of the UK, the European treaties that establish the relationship between the UK and EC/EU, and the Human Rights Act that implements the European Convention on Human Rights, the UK remains largely devoid of a written constitution, although the situation is changing. The common law constitutional rights therefore assume a greater significance in the UK than elsewhere, although other common law countries that have a written constitution are still able to apply common law constitutional principles when the written constitution is silent on certain matters. The right to be heard before a court when an individual's liberty is at stake (known as the right of *habeas corpus*) is one such right that has been applied in the Australian context and elsewhere.

16 Hartley (2005, p814) discusses the characteristics of a code as follows:

> *It is important to realize that a code is not simply a wide-ranging piece of legislation. A true code, as understood by continental lawyers, is much more than that: it embodies a different attitude towards the law, an attitude that tries to systematize the law through a hierarchy of principles that fit together to form a coherent whole. A limited number of generalized and abstract principles provide the foundation for a second level of more concrete principles. This in turn gives rise to the legal rules applicable to individual cases. This system is aesthetically pleasing; it is also easier to understand and explain. Moreover, gaps in the law can be filled by deriving new rules from existing principles, thus making the law more predictable.*

17 While the majority of civil law legal systems comply with the rule of law, there are exceptions. The PRC is commonly also referred to as a civil law legal system because it is based on

codes. However, because there is no separation of powers and the Constitution is based on communist values that fail to recognize individual freedoms in practice, legitimacy is lacking and the rule of law is not present. The PRC is also home to other legal systems that usually do uphold the rule of law however, notably Hong Kong and Macau. The former is a common law legal system (derived from former British rule and import of the English system) and the latter is a civil law system (derived from former Portuguese rule and its system). See Peerenboom (2002) and Potter (2001).

18 Regulations and *regulation* are two entirely different things, aside from the use of the words as a noun and adjective. The latter refers to any means by which a policy may be implemented by government, which can include any form of legislation including regulations (see text). Other means of implementation such as economic measures (which may or may not be required by legislation) are also types of regulation. For further information, see Gunningham and Graboski (1998).

19 Confusingly, in a European law context, primary law refers to the constitutional law found in treaties, such as the Treaty of the European Communities and the Treaty on European Union, which provides the basis for the legal competences in the EC/EU. Secondary law refers to directives and regulations.

20 The use of these words in a legal context is entirely different from their use by EIA/SEA practitioners and academics. For EIA/SEA practitioners, substantive and procedural are typically used in the context of evaluating effectiveness. Hence substantive effectiveness is concerned with whether the environment has improved as a result of applying a process. Procedural effectiveness merely considers whether a process has been applied on paper. Most evaluative criteria discussed in this chapter and applied throughout the book and elsewhere only address procedural effectiveness because of the difficulties associated with isolating the effect of a procedure on actual change. There is, however, some overlap between the use of the terms in a legal and non-legal context. Provisions for information, public participation and access to justice are substantive legal requirements as well as, in some cases, EIA/SEA procedural provisions. If breached, broader remedies may potentially be claimed than under a judicial review (see Chapters 7 and 8 in the context of European law).

21 Sometimes a decision maker is instructed to give 'due weight' to environmental factors, however, unless the decision maker is instructed as to the priority to give to them, it is a matter for the decision maker to decide (Bates, 2006, pp102–103). The application of the precautionary principle is an example, see Chapter 3.

22 The case of *Pepper v Hart* is authority for this in a common law context; see Marsden (2006a) and Cooke (2004, pp282–284).

23 Lücke (2005, p1027), however, comments that the findings of Vogenauer (2001) indicate a striking similarity between the English and continental approaches (at least to statutory interpretation), which is perhaps contrary to existing beliefs:

> *Vogenhauer has found the traditional view of the fundamental difference... to be mistaken. His counter-thesis is that there is now 'a fundamental unity in judicial approaches to statutory interpretation' in the four jurisdictions which he has examined... English law, like civilian systems, emphasises the great weight to be accorded to statutory language but permits, for valid reasons, restrictive or extensive interpretation... Vogenauer's unity thesis is his most important conclusion. He does not deny that the influence of Community law might have hastened the development, but insists that the evolution of the new style of interpretation has been an independent development within English common law.*

24 These democracies are typified by a separation of powers as explained above. Collective responsibility means that decisions taken by the executive branch in the decision making forum often known as the cabinet are, whatever the individual disagreements within,

presented as a unified whole, with no publicity given to differences of opinion. This requires secrecy, which has filtered through to the departmental structure of the executive branch and means that, in practice, requests for information on policy making are frequently denied prior to final outcomes being decided on. Public participation is usually limited in such processes.

REFERENCES

André, P., Enserink, B., Connor, D., and Croal, P. (2006) *Public Participation International Best Practice Principles*, International Association for Impact Assessment, Special Publication Series No 4, Fargo, ND

Andresen, S. (2007) 'The effectiveness of UN environmental institutions', *International Environmental Agreements*, vol 7, no 4, pp317–336

Andresen, S. and Hey, E. (2005) 'The effectiveness and legitimacy of international environmental institutions', *International Environmental Agreements*, vol 5, pp211–226

Bailey, J. and Dixon, J. E. (1999) 'Policy environmental assessment' in J. Petts (ed) *Handbook on Environmental Impact Assessment*, Blackwell, London

Bailey, J. and Renton, S. (1997) 'Redesigning EIA to fit the future: SEA and the policy process', *Impact Assessment and Project Appraisal*, vol 15, no 4, pp319–334

Bailey, J. and Renton, S. (1998) 'Environmental assessment of policies', in A. Porter (ed) *Environmental Methods Review: Retooling Impact Assessment in the New Century*, Army Environmental Policy Institute, Fargo, ND

Bates, G. (2006) *Environmental Law in Australia*, LexisNexis Butterworths, Sydney, NSW

Bina, O. (2004) 'Relating ANSEA to the European Directive on SEA' in R. Caratti, H. Dalkmann and R. Jiliberto (eds) *Analysing Strategic Environmental Assessment*, Edward Elgar, Cheltenham, pp106–114

Bina, O. (2007) 'A critical review of the dominant lines of argumentation on the need for strategic environmental assessment', *Environmental Impact Assessment Review*, vol 27, pp585–606

Boothroyd, P. (1995) 'Policy assessment' in F. Vanclay and D. Bronstein (eds) *Environmental and Social Impact Assessment*, John Wiley and Sons, Chichester

Brennan, G. (2005) 'The common law: Law for a time, law for a place', *Judicial Conference of Australia 2005 Colloquium Papers*, 3 September, Sunshine Coast

Brown, A. L. and Thérivel, R. (2000) 'Principles to guide the development of strategic environmental assessment methodology', *Impact Assessment and Project Appraisal*, vol 18, no 3, pp183–189

Brown, L. and Nitz, T. (2002) 'Applying SEA to policy making: The policy cycle model and the Queensland policy handbook' in S. Marsden and S. Dovers (eds) *Strategic Environmental Assessment in Australasia*, The Federation Press, Annandale, NSW, pp84–98

Buckley, R. (2000) 'Strategic environmental assessment of policies and plans: legislation and implementation' *Impact Assessment and Project Appraisal*, vol 18, no 3, pp 209–215

Cane, P. (2000) *An Introduction to Administrative Law*, 3rd Edition, Clarendon Press, Oxford

Caratti, P., Dalkmann, H. and Jiliberto, R. (eds) (2004) *Analysing Strategic Environmental Assessment*, Edward Elgar, Cheltenham

Cherp, A., Watt, A. and Vinichenko, V. (2007) 'SEA and strategy formation theories: From three Ps to five Ps', *Environmental Impact Assessment Review*, vol 27, pp624–644

Commission of the European Communities (undated) *Draft Handbook on Promoting Good Governance in EC Development and Co-operation*, Commission of the European Community, Brussels

Cooke, R. (2004) 'The road ahead for the common law', *International and Comparative Law Quarterly*, vol 53, pp273–286

Court, J. D., Wright, C. J. and Guthrie, A. C. (1994) *Assessment of Cumulative Impacts and Strategic Assessment in Environmental Impact Assessment*, Commonwealth Environmental Protection Agency, Barton, ACT

Dalal-Clayton, B. and Sadler, B. (2005) *Strategic Environmental Assessment: A Sourcebook and Reference Guide to International Experience*, Earthscan, London

Devuyst, D. (1999) 'Sustainability assessment: The application of a methodological framework', *Journal of Environmental Assessment Policy and Management*, vol 1, no 4, pp459–487

De Boer, J. J. and Sadler, B. (eds) (1996) *Environmental Assessment of Policies: Briefing Papers on Experience in Selected Countries*, Ministry of Housing, Spatial Planning and the Environment, Report No 54, The Hague

Donnelly, A., Jones, M., O'Mahony, T. and Byrne, G. (2007) 'Selecting environmental indicator for use in strategic environmental assessment', *Environmental Impact Assessment Review*, vol 27, pp161–175

Dovers, S. (2002) 'Too deep a SEA? Strategic environmental assessment in the era of sustainability' in S. Marsden and S. Dovers (eds) *Strategic Environmental Assessment in Australasia*, The Federation Press, Annandale, NSW, pp24–47

Dusik, J., Fischer, T. and Sadler, B. (2003) *Benefits of a Strategic Environmental Assessment*, Regional Environment Center for Central and Regional Europe/United Nations Development Programme, Szentendre

Feldman, D. (1990) 'Democracy, the rule of law and judicial review', *Federal Law Review*, vol 19, pp1–30

Fischer, T. B. (2002a) 'Strategic environmental assessment performance criteria – the same requirements for every assessment?', *Journal of Environmental Assessment Policy and Management*, vol 4, no 1, pp83–99

Fischer, T. B. (2002b) *Strategic Environmental Assessment in Transport and Land Use Planning*, Earthscan, London

Fischer, T. B. (2002c) 'Requirements of European tiered planning systems: SEA approaches and tools of general application', in S. Marsden and S. Dovers (eds) *Strategic Environmental Assessment in Australasia*, The Federation Press, Annandale, NSW, pp99–113

Fischer, T. B. (2003) 'Strategic environmental assessment in post-modern times', *Environmental Impact Assessment Review*, vol 23, pp155–170

Fischer, T. B. (2007) *Theory and Practice of Strategic Environmental Assessment*, Earthscan, London

Gibson, R. B., Hassan, S., Holtz, S., Tansey, J. and Whitelaw, G. (2004) *Sustainability Assessment: Criteria and Processes*, Earthscan, London

Glenn, H. (2004) *Legal Traditions of the World*, Oxford University Press, Oxford

Gunningham, N. and Graboski, P. (1998) *Smart Regulation: Designing Environmental Policy*, Clarendon Press, Oxford

Hartley, T. C. (2005) 'The European Union and the systematic dismantling of the common law of conflict of laws', *International and Comparative Law Quarterly*, vol 54, pp813–828

Harty, T. H., Potts, D. L., Potts, D. F. and El-Jourbagy, J. (2005) 'Handling transboundary cumulative impacts in SEA', in M. Schmidt, E. João and E. Albrecht (eds) *Implementing Strategic Environmental Assessment*, Springer-Verlag, Heidelberg, pp397–408

Hilden, M., Furman, E. and Kaljonen, M. (2004) 'Views on planning and expectations of SEA: The case of transport planning', *Environmental Impact Assessment Review*, vol 24, pp519–536

Hilding-Rydevik, T. and Bjarnadóttir, H. (2007) 'Context awareness and sensitivity in SEA implementation', *Environmental Impact Assessment Review*, vol 27, pp666–684

Holder, J. (2004) *Environmental Assessment: The Regulation of Decision Making*, Oxford University Press, Oxford

Holder, J. and McGillivray, D. (eds) (2007) *Taking Stock of Environmental Assessment: Law, Policy and Practice*, Routledge-Cavendish, Abingdon

IAIA (International Association for Impact Assessment) (2002) *Strategic Environmental Assessment: Performance Criteria*, Special Publication Series No 1, Fargo, ND, available at www.iaia.org/modx/assets/files/sp1.pdf

James, E., Tomlinson, P., McColl, V. and Fry, C. (2003) *Final Report – Literature Review / Scoping Study on Cumulative Effects Assessment and the Strategic Environmental Assessment Directive*, unpublished project report prepared for Centre for Risk and Forecasting, Environment Agency of England and Wales

Jay, S. (2007) 'Customers as decision-makers: Strategic environmental assessment in the private sector', *Impact Assessment and Project Appraisal*, vol 25, no 2, pp75–84

João, E. (2005) 'Key principles of SEA' in M. Schmidt, E. João and E. Albrecht (eds) *Implementing Strategic Environmental Assessment*, Springer-Verlag, Heidelberg, pp3–14

Jones, C., Baker, M., Carter, J., Jay, S., Short, M. and Wood, C. (eds) (2005) *Strategic Environmental Assessment and Land Use Planning: An International Evaluation*, Earthscan, London

Jones, C., Jay, S., Slinn, P. and Wood, C. (2007) 'Environmental assessment: dominant or dormant?' in Holder, J. and McGillivray, D. (eds) (2007) *Taking Stock of Environmental Assessment: Law, Policy and Practice*, Routledge-Cavendish, Abingdon, pp17–44

Knill, C. and Winkler, D. (2006a) 'Convergence or divergence of national legal and administrative structures? Europeanisation effects of the environmental impact assessment in Germany and England (part 1)', *Journal for European Environmental and Planning Law*, vol 1, pp43–51

Knill, C. and Winkler, D. (2006b) 'Convergence or divergence of national legal and administrative structures? Europeanisation effects of the environmental impact assessment in Germany and England (part 2)', *Journal for European Environmental and Planning Law*, vol 2, pp132–141

Kørnøv, L. and Thissen, W. A. H. (2000) 'Rationality in decision- and policy-making: Implications for strategic environmental assessment', *Impact Assessment and Project Appraisal*, vol 18, no 3, pp191–200

Lücke, H. K. (2005) 'Statutory interpretation: New comparative dimensions', *International and Comparative Law Quarterly*, vol 54, pp1023–1032

Marsden, S. (1998a) 'Why is legislative EA in Canada ineffective and how can it be enhanced?', *Environmental Impact Assessment Review*, vol 18, no 3, pp241–265

Marsden, S. (1998b) 'Importance of context in measuring the effectiveness of strategic environmental assessment', *Impact Assessment and Project Appraisal*, vol 16, no 4, pp255–266

Marsden, S. (1999a) 'Legislative EA in the Netherlands: The e-test as a strategic and integrative instrument', *European Environment*, vol 9, no 3, pp90–100

Marsden, S. (1999b) 'Strategic environmental assessment in Australia: An evaluation of s146 of the environment protection and biodiversity conservation act 1999', *Griffith Law Review*, vol 8, no 2, pp394–410

Marsden, S. (2006a) 'Constitutional interpretation in Hong Kong: Do common law approaches apply when the national people's congress standing committee interprets the basic law?, *LAWASIA Journal*, pp99–124

Marsden, S. (2006b) 'Regional autonomy, judicial criticism and the 2005 interpretation: Judicial independence in Hong Kong compromised again?', *Hong Kong Law Journal*, vol 36, no 1, pp117–142

Marsden, S. and Ashe, J. (2006) 'Strategic environmental assessment legislation in Australian states and territories', *Australasian Journal of Environmental Management*, vol 13, pp6–16

Marsden, S. and Dovers, S. (eds) (2002) *Strategic Environmental Assessment in Australasia*, The Federation Press, Sydney

Marshall, R. and Fischer, T. (2006) 'Regional electricity transmission planning and SEA: The case of the electricity company Scottish Power', *Journal of Environmental Planning and Management*, vol 49, no 2, pp279–299

Mathiesen, A. (2003) 'Public participation in decision making and access to justice in EC environmental law: The case of certain plans and programmes', *European Environmental Law Review*, vol 12, no 2, pp36–52

Morrison-Saunders, A. and Fischer, T. (2006) 'What is wrong with EIA and SEA anyway? A sceptics perspective on sustainability assessment', *Journal of Environmental Assessment Policy and Management*, vol 8, no 1, pp19–39

Morrison-Saunders, A., Marshall, R. and Arts, J. (2007) *EIA Follow-Up: International Best Practice Principles*, International Association for Impact Assessment, Special Publication Series No 6, Fargo, ND

Münchenberg, S. (2002) 'Strategic environmental assessment: A business perspective', in S. Marsden and S. Dovers (eds) *Strategic Environmental Assessment in Australasia*, The Federation Press, Annandale, NSW, pp182–194

Nooteboom, S. and Wieringa, K. (1999) 'Comparing strategic environmental assessment and integrated environmental assessment', *Journal of Environmental Assessment Policy and Management*, vol 1, no 4, pp441-457

ODPM (Office of the Deputy Prime Minister) (2005) *A Practical Guide to the Strategic Environmental Assessment Directive*, ODPM, London

O'Riordan, T. and Sewell, W. R. D. (1981) *Project Appraisal and Policy Review*, John Wiley and Sons, Chichester

Palmer, V. V. (2001) *Mixed Jurisdictions: The Third Legal Family*, Cambridge University Press, Cambridge

Partidario, M. and Clark, R. (2000) *Perspectives on Strategic Environmental Assessment*, Lewis Publishers, Boca Raton, Florida

Peerenboom, R. (2002) *China's Long March Toward Rule of Law*, Cambridge University Press, Cambridge

Potter, P. B. (2001) *The Chinese Legal System: Globalisation and Local Legal Culture*, Routledge Curzon, London

Renton, S. and Bailey, J. (2000) 'Policy development and the environment', *Impact Assessment and Project Appraisal*, vol 18, no 3, pp245–251

Representatives of the Member States and the Environment Directorate General of the European Commission (2003) *Implementation of Directive 2001/42/EC on the Assessment of the Effects of Certain Plans and Programmes on the Environment*, 23 September, European Commission, Brussels

Rest, A. (2004) 'Enhanced implementation of international environmental treaties by judiciary – access to justice in international environmental law for individuals and NGOs: efficacious enforcement by the Permanent Court of Arbitration', *Macquarie Journal of International and Comparative Environmental Law*, vol 1, pp1–28

Runhaar, H. and Driessen, P. P. J. (2007) 'What makes strategic environmental assessment successful environmental assessment? The role of context in the contribution of SEA to decision making', *Impact Assessment and Project Appraisal*, vol 25, no 1, pp2–14

Russell, P. and O'Brien, D. M. (eds) (2001) *Judicial Independence in the Age of Democracy*, University of Virginia Press, Charlottesville, NC

Ryall, A. (2007a) *Effective Judicial Protection and the Environmental Impact Assessment Directive in Ireland*, Hart Publishing, Oxford

Ryall, A. (2007b) 'Access to justice and the EIA directive: The implications of the Aarhus Convention', in Holder, J. and McGillivray, D. (eds) (2007) *Taking Stock of Environmental Assessment: Law, Policy and Practice*, Routledge-Cavendish, Abingdon, pp191–218

Sadler, B. (1996) *Environmental Assessment in a Changing World: Evaluating Practice to Improve Performance*, Final Report, International Study of the Effectiveness of Environmental Assessment, Canadian Environmental Assessment Agency, Ottawa

Sadler, B. (ed) (2005) *Strategic Environmental Assessment at the Policy Level: Recent Progress, Current Status and Future Prospects*, Regional Environment Centre for Central and Eastern Europe, Prague

Sadler, B. and Verheem, R. (1996) *Strategic Environmental Assessment: Status, Challenges and Future Directions*, The Netherlands Ministry of Housing, Spatial Planning and the Environment, The Hague

Sampford, C. and Preston, K. (eds) (1996) *Interpreting Constitutions: Theories, Principles and Institutions*, The Federation Press, Annandale, NSW

Schmidt, M., João, E. and Albrecht, E. (eds) (2005) *Implementing Strategic Environmental Assessment*, Springer-Verlag, Heidelberg

Sheate, W. R. (1996) *Environmental Impact Assessment: Law and Policy – Making an Impact II*, 2nd Edition, Cameron May, London

Shelton, D. and Kiss, A. (2005) *Judicial Handbook on Environmental Law*, United Nations Environment Programme, Stevenage

Smith, S. and Sheate, W. (2001) 'Sustainability appraisal of English regional plans: Incorporating the requirements of the EU strategic environmental assessment directive', *Impact Assessment and Project Appraisal*, vol 19, no 4, pp263–276

Street, H. and Brazier, R. (eds) (1985) *de Smith's Constitutional and Administrative Law*, 5th Edition, Pelican, Harmondsworth

Thérivel, R. (2004a) *Strategic Environmental Assessment in Action*, Earthscan, London

Thérivel, R. (2004b) 'Foreword' in R. Caratti, H. Dalkmann and R. Jiliberto (eds) *Analysing Strategic Environmental Assessment*, Edward Elgar, Cheltenham, ppxv–xvi

Thérivel, R. (2005) 'Strategic level cumulative impact assessment' in M. Schmidt, E. João and E. Albrecht (eds) *Implementing Strategic Environmental Assessment*, Springer-Verlag, Heidelberg, pp385–395

Thérivel, R. and Partidario, M. R. (eds) (1996) *The Practice of Strategic Environmental Assessment*, Earthscan, London

Thérivel, R., Wilson, E., Thompson, S., Heaney, D. and Pritchard, D. (1992) *Strategic Environmental Assessment*, Earthscan/RSPB, London

Thomson, J. and Sarre, R. (eds) (2001) *Introduction to Law*, Lexis Nexis Butterworths, Chatswood

Tromans, S. and Fuller, K. (2003) *Environmental Impact Assessment – Law and Practice*, Reed Elsevier, London

UNECE/REC (United Nations Economic Commission for Europe/Regional Environmental Center for Central and Eastern Europe) (2007) *Protocol on SEA: Resource Manual to Support Application of the UNECE Protocol on Strategic Environmental Assessment*, draft final, April 2007, United Nations, New York

Verheem, R. A. A. and Tonk, J. A. M. N. (2000) 'Strategic environmental assessment: one concept, multiple forms', *Impact Assessment and Project Appraisal*, vol 18, no 3, pp177–182

Vogenauer, S. (2001) *Interpretation of Statutes in England and on the Continent: A Comparative Study of Judicial Jurisprudence and its Historical Foundations*, Mohr Siebeck, Tübingen

Von Seht, H. (1999) 'Requirements of a comprehensive strategic environmental assessment system', *Landscape and Urban Planning*, vol 45, pp1–14

Wallington, T., Bina, O. and Thissen, W. (2007) 'Theorising strategic environmental assessment: Fresh perspectives and future challenges', *Environmental Impact Assessment Review*, vol 27, pp569–584

Wathern, P. (ed) (1988) *Environmental Impact Assessment: Theory and Practice*, Unwin Hyman, London

Wood, C. and Djeddour, M. (1992) 'Strategic environmental assessment: EA of policies, plans and programmes, *Impact Assessment Bulletin*, vol 10, no 1, pp3–22

Zaelke, D. and Higdon, T. (2006) 'The role of compliance in the rule of law, good governance and sustainable development', *Journal for European Environmental and Planning Law*, vol 5, pp376–384

PART I

International Law

An Overview of International Law

CHAPTER OUTLINE

In Chapter 1 national or municipal legal systems were described and distinguished on the basis of their geographical origin and political characteristics. Chapter 2 explains the structure of the international legal framework that is an important part of those systems. International law is of two types: public and private. The former, with which this book is in part concerned, deals with the international law that primarily regulates the conduct of states. The latter, sometimes known as conflict of laws,[1] regulates the conduct of individuals and business enterprises that operate between states. Public international law, or international law hereafter, regulates a huge range of activity, from humanitarian and human rights issues to resource exploitation, protection and conservation.[2]

A general understanding of the workings of international law helps provide context to the legal instruments analysed in the chapters in Part I that follow. This chapter begins by briefly discussing the historical development and structure of international law, including an explanation of the key institutions involved in the process. The next section considers the sources and obligations of international law, with a focus on explaining the different types of international agreements that are commonly used. Custom and soft law are also explained. A full explanation of treaty making is provided, from preparation and approval to incorporation of treaties (and custom) into the domestic and European legal frameworks. Compliance with international law is then examined, together with a number of topical issues considered in the recent literature. Finally, some conclusions of relevance to the specialized subject area of the book are made. As with the other chapters in this book that examine legal systems, primarily Chapters 1, 2, 7 and 12, plain English is used wherever possible.

THE DEVELOPMENT AND STRUCTURE OF INTERNATIONAL LAW

International law developed as a result of the need to regulate the acquisition of territory and, very much related, to avoid conflicts between states of the types seen in the First and Second World Wars. As such, international law has had a primary focus on the relationship between states. However, many other entities have rights and duties under international law, including international organizations such as the United Nations (UN) and the constituent Economic Commission for Europe (ECE), the latter considered in detail in Chapter 4. The rights and duties of individuals are also regulated to some extent, particularly with regard to humanitarian and human rights law. A simple definition of international law (Blay, 2005, p2) is as follows:

> *[International law is the] body of law comprising principles and rules which states recognise as legally binding and [which] regulates the conduct of subjects of the law and relates to events and issues which, transcending national boundaries, are of international concern.*

The fact that the relationship between states is the primary focus of international law also reflects their role in negotiating and approving treaties and later enforcement, and in demonstrating the state practice that allows customary norms to establish and become binding. Although individuals may be able to enforce the obligations assumed by a state, for example, under human rights agreements, individual rights will always arise from agreements between states, with interstate relations being the predominant issue.

Yet international law has changed significantly over the years and certain authors have contended that a 'new international law' has emerged 'as a patch-work of norms, institutions and actors on various overlapping levels' with the role of states, while primary, no longer exercising as comprehensive a role as in former times (Alvik et al, 2007, p1). A clear example is the role of the EC/EU in international law, as raised in the final section of this chapter and discussed in detail in Chapters 7 and 12. On many occasions therefore the ECJ has held that the EC is an independent regime where the general rules and principles of international law cannot be presumed to apply. Alongside other regimes, such as the World Trade Organisation (WTO) or specific human rights or environmental regimes therefore, while 'international law is never wholly displaced', it may be 'reduced to rules of last resort and little relevance by regime-specific rules' (Alvik et al, 2007, p8).

UN institutions

The UN was created following a number of conferences between the states that had been at war with Germany and Japan in the early 1940s. The UN Charter was adopted by these states in 1945. In future the only legitimate use of force was to be authorized by the UN Security Council to maintain or restore peace and security, or by states in self-defence. Since its creation, the UN has had a central influence on the development of international law, largely because virtually every country is a member. Article 1 of the Charter sets out the main purposes of the UN, which are to maintain international peace and security, develop friendly relations among states, achieve international cooperation in solving international problems, and coordinate and harmonize actions to achieve these ends.

The UN Charter set up a number of organs, including the Security Council, General Assembly and ICJ. As stated, the main function of the Council is to maintain international peace and security; unfortunately criticism of its failure to do so has reflected on the UN as a whole, when many matters, such as the provision of financial resources, are largely beyond its control. The general powers given to the Council to achieve this task are limited to making recommendations, which also helps to explain some of the difficulties experienced to date. Unlike the limited composition of the Council, the Assembly is constituted by all members of the UN, which, together with its broader remit, provides greater scope to bring issues of international concern before it. The role of the Assembly is essentially to consider, discuss and recommend on any matter within the scope of the Charter.

The Assembly has sponsored and promoted many of the significant developments in international law, including the adoption of the Vienna Convention on the Law of Treaties 1969 (VCLT) (discussed below) and the Convention on the Law of the Sea (UNCLOS) 1982. The International Law Commission (ILC) and Sixth Committee (Legal) of the Assembly were established in accordance with the authority given through Article 13(1) of the Charter to initiate studies and make recommendations to encourage the development and codification of international law. The ILC, in particular, has been instrumental in the development of a number of multilateral treaties of global significance. A few examples of these are given at the start of Chapter 3 where an overview of international environmental law (IEL) is presented.

The ICJ was established under its own Statute attached to the Charter. In accordance with Article 9, the membership of the Court is supposed to represent the main forms of civilization and the principal legal systems of the world, primarily common law, civil law, socialist law and Islamic law, which potentially enables it to utilize the best practice of each system in its decision making. The Court is also independent in theory,[3] with jurisdiction to decide disputes between states and to give Advisory Opinions. Despite a relatively small jurisprudence, the Court has had a significant influence on the development of international law, as Piotrowicz (2005, p29) comments:

> As the judicial arm of the UN, it exercises substantial authority. Moreover, while its decisions are binding only on the parties to a particular dispute, its influence goes very much further. It has had the opportunity to consider, and pronounce upon, some of the most significant and controversial legal issues facing the international community.

However important, the ICJ is but one method of resolving disputes between states, and although its role in enforcement is outlined later in this chapter, alternative means are also discussed. Arbitration is, in practice, one of the more important alternative methods to judicial settlement, by a tribunal set up specifically by a treaty or by the ICJ where states have consented to its jurisdiction. The Espoo Convention provides for dispute settlement either through the ICJ or by way of arbitration, for example, as discussed in Chapter 4.

International institutions

Since 1945 the role of states in international law has been supplemented by the growth in international institutions or intergovernmental organizations (IGOs), which typically have been established for a limited purpose and/or within a limited geographical area. Examples include the WTO and the institutions of the EC/EU that have responsibilities for external relations, such as the European Council and Commission. In the *Reparations* case the ICJ said that the rights and duties of an international organization such as the UN must depend on its purposes and functions, as expressed or implied by its constituent instrument and as developed in practice.[4] The ICJ said that the UN was in possession 'of a large measure of personality and the capacity to operate upon an international plane' (at 179). It also concluded that the UN 'must be deemed to have those powers which, though not expressly provided in the Charter, are conferred upon it by necessary implication as being essential to the performance of its duties'.

This doctrine of 'implied powers' is a principle of what has become known as international institutional law (Desai, 2004, pp40–42). As Desai illustrates in his book, it has grown hugely in significance, particularly in the environmental domain. Of particular importance is the relationship between treaty interpretation (see below) and the principles of international institutional law. The latter, based on custom, may well be more flexible than the former, which are derived from the Vienna Convention on the Law of Treaties (VCLT). Churchill and Ulfstein (2000, p634) discuss the relationship between the two and point out that applying international institutional law may lead to outcomes that would not be accepted under the VCLT, especially if they are applied to autonomous institutional arrangements that now exist under many treaties.[5] The institutional/procedural arrangements of IGOs are considered in the final section of this chapter, with discussion of some of the other issues arising when they form part of a self-governing regime, which in this context means distinct from that of the UN system itself, and general rules of international law that have developed thereunder.

An international institution must be comprised of states, with powers exercisable in relation to states and/or other international institutions. The powers and functions of the institution are exercisable separately from its member states. The EC/EU is an excellent example of such an 'institution', with the Council and Commission having extensive powers with regard to regulating many matters of its MS in accordance with the Treaty on European Union (TEU) and previous treaties concerning the constitution of the EC. The status of the EC/EU is considered further at the end of this chapter as an example of what is also termed a 'self-contained regime' in international law. States are of course only bound by such institutions if they are members of them, although many choose to do so, such as the members of the European Economic Area (EEA), which includes states outside the EU such as Norway. From an EC point of view, most international treaties it subscribes to are 'mixed', which means that both the EC and its member states are parties to the agreement.[6]

THE SOURCES AND OBLIGATIONS OF INTERNATIONAL LAW

The sources of international law that may become domestic law through incorporation are those listed in Article 38 of the Statute of the ICJ. This refers to (a) international conventions, (b) international custom/customary law, (c) general principles of law; and (d) judicial decisions and doctrine (the last of these assists in determining the meaning of each of the former). For the most part, states create international law by concluding agreements with one another and by established practices (customary law) that are recognized as binding. Treaties and customary law are complementary in that the latter may be of more general application than the former, although the latter may also develop into the former. General principles of law are those that are common to all the major legal systems of the world, and that often start at the national level before being adopted internationally, such as EIA (see Chapter 3 and Shelton and Kiss, 2005, p17). The jurisprudence developed by international courts and tribunals is also a very important subsidiary source of international law, which may serve to clarify certain general principles. The decisions of the Conferences or Meetings of the Parties (COPs or MOPs) established by treaties are another source of treaty law, albeit a subsidiary one. What is known as 'soft law', typically non-binding declarations of international conferences, is the other main source of international law (Pallemaerts, 2004, pp62–63), which may also develop principles later incorporated in customary law or treaty. Treaty, customary and soft law are distinguished and considered below as they reflect the differences best understood by the layman and lawyer alike. General principles of law are included in each and each is subject to judicial interpretation, which has persuasive influence on future decision making.

Treaties

Treaties are arguably the most important source of international law, which may be bilateral, multilateral or regional.[7] While customary law may be of more general application, confusion over its status compared with the relatively clearer rules applicable to treaties, together with the huge number of treaties that are now in force, suggests that treaties are today the predominant source. This is especially so in the area of IEL, given the uncertain status of many of the customary rules. As the purpose of treaties is to establish a code that can be applied generally to a particular area or issue, success is likely to be judged by the number of states that ratify the particular convention,[8] together with subsequent compliance by them.[9] The Espoo Convention may be classified as a regional treaty because it is a legal instrument derived from the UNECE, which operates primarily in a distinct region. However, because membership of the Convention and SEA Protocol will be open to all members of the UN (after both the first amendment to the Convention and the Protocol come into force), each may later develop into a multilateral environmental agreements (MEAs).

The VCLT 1969 applies to treaties entered into between states, with the VCLT between States and International Organisations or between International Organisations 1986 applying in other instances. These conventions determine how treaties are to be interpreted and applied, as supplemented by rules of custom that deal with areas that may not be covered (Kaukoranta, 2006). Articles 6–25 of the VCLT provide rules for the conclusion and entry into force of treaties, with the various stages to the treaty making process set out. To adopt a treaty text (by signature) is not the same as to be bound by it (by ratification or another means set out in Article 11 of the VCLT); both occur in various ways depending on the context of the individual country. Article 18 places an obligation on states to refrain from any act that would defeat the object and purpose of a treaty. Provided this is respected, together with acceptance by other state parties, it is quite possible for individual states to modify treaty commitments by the use of reservations and declarations, which are covered in Articles 19–23 of the VCLT and ICJ jurisprudence.[10] Only state parties to treaties will be bound; so called 'third-states' will only be affected by treaty obligations where they have also become customary law and the third state has recognized them as such.

Treaties may be amended in accordance with Articles 39–41 of the VCLT. Since these rules are inflexible, it is not surprising that, in recent years, framework conventions have emerged that contain a minimum of substantive obligations by allowing parties to enter into subsidiary, detailed agreements that are usually called protocols.[11] It is important that treaties make provision for their amendment, as without this it may be very difficult to achieve. As a result of the proliferation of multilateral treaties, there has been an increased awareness of this need, together with the provision of assistance from international organizations in treaty adoption and implementation which have provided a forum for the consideration of such amendments (Bowman, 1995, p542).

It is possible for some countries to adopt treaties through the executive branch of government (such as Australia), while in others consent of the legislature is needed. National constitutional law that sets out the powers of each branch of government will determine which is responsible for external affairs. Only when a certain number of ratifications are made and after a period of time has elapsed does a treaty usually enter into force, in accordance with the provisions of the treaty. Most common law countries that are involved in the negotiation of a new treaty will sign and later ratify, the first act indicating adoption of the treaty text, the second consent to be bound. However, it is quite possible for states to adopt a text and not become bound by it, or, where states have not been involved with the negotiations, to simply ratify at the international level. Subsequent additional approval at the national level either by the executive or legislative branch is then usually required, typically by the passage of national legislation, although in some states an international treaty will automatically apply with no need for implementing legislation.

Treaty interpretation is as complicated as constitutional or statutory interpretation, and is a primary role of the judiciary at the international and national levels. The compromises that have led to the adoption of treaty texts are one source of potential confusion; a second is the different legal system backgrounds from which judges and arbitrators are drawn. The VCLT provides some assistance with how to approach the task, Article 31 providing that a treaty is to be interpreted 'in good faith in accordance with the ordinary meaning to be given to the terms of the treaty in their context and in the light of its object and purpose'. This is essentially a combination of the literal and purposive approaches that dominate both common and civil law legal systems in a national context.[12] Where this does not assist, Article 32 provides that reference may be had to 'supplementary means of interpretation' that includes the 'preparatory work of the treaty and the circumstances of its conclusion', which is sometimes referred to as the contextual approach to interpretation (Brandon, 2002). As will be seen in Chapter 3, environmental treaties have a number of features that distinguish them from other treaties, enabling them to respond to the specific needs of environmental protection.

Article 30 sets out the rules relating to the application of treaties where there are successive treaties on the same subject matter.[13] Finally, Article 53 provides that a treaty will be void if it conflicts with a peremptory norm of general international law, essentially meaning the strongest type of customary law applies where a rule is 'accepted and recognised by the international community of states as a whole from which no derogation is permitted and which can be modified only by a subsequent norm of general international law having the same character'.[14]

Customary law

Customary international law is concerned with the acceptance by nation states of significant principles, demonstrated by state practice, which is seen in the actions, inactions and views expressed by national governments.[15] Judicial decision making is a separate but related source, complementing state practice by interpreting the current status of customary norms that may influence subsequent state practice. In a national context when court rulings are not overturned by legislation, state practice may further be demonstrated as acceptance of a ruling. According to Article 38.1(b) of its Statute, the ICJ is to apply 'international custom, as evidence of a general practice accepted by law'.

State practice must be applied consistently for it to be accepted as customary and therefore authoritative. This was concluded in the Joint Opinion in the *Fisheries Jurisdiction* case where it was stated that it was an 'essential requirement for the practice of States to acquire the status of customary law... that such State practice must be common, consistent and concordant' (at 50).[16] While state practice includes judicial opinion on the status of legal principles, it remains unclear exactly what state practice is or how custom formation works. For example, the significance to attach to what a nation state may say and what it actually does has attracted the attention of academics and jurists. Kammerhofer (2004, p526) draws attention to this, as well as to the fact that customary law is a law without authoritative texts (p552). He indicates that if international law had a dominant legal culture, such as the common law or the civil law, then the underlying contexts of that legal system may provide assistance (p552).

There is, in practice, a close relationship between treaties and customary law. Because the application of treaties is limited to the states that have signed and ratified them, and therefore falls short of achieving general acceptance, it is necessary for treaty provisions to also represent customary law if they are to bind non-parties. The three main ways in which this occurs have been set out by Greig (2005, pp62–63). The first is when the treaty rule reproduces an existing rule of customary international law, in which case the rule is often clarified in the treaty rule. The ICJ, for example, said in *Namibia* that certain provisions of the VCLT 1969, which had not at the time come into force, 'may in many respects be considered as a codification of existing customary law on the subject' (at 47).[17] The second is when a customary rule is in the process of development when its incorporation in a multilateral agreement may have the effect of consolidating or crystallizing the law in the form of the rule. This relates to the first, but as Greig (2005) points out, is limited to the extent that if the practice is less developed, the treaty provision may not be enough to crystallize customary law, as seen in the *North Sea Continental Shelf* cases.[18] The third is that if the rule is new, the drafting of the treaty provision may be the impetus for state practice.

Soft law

'Soft law' is so called because it is distinct from both treaties and customary law, which are also known as 'hard law'. Both are 'hard law' because they have a strong basis of legitimacy based on approval by the nation state and/or interpretation by the judiciary and state practice. Soft law is comprised of legal principles, action plans and detailed strategies and guidance developed in international conferences attended by member states, such as the Rio Earth Summit in 1992. They are termed soft law because they signify a lack of any legally binding aspect. Depending on their later acceptance, such principles may then develop into customary international law or treaties. The precautionary principle is a potential example, which has also been given effect to by international and national courts and tribunals, and later incorporated into several environmental treaties, including the CBD. The principle is discussed in Chapters 3 and 6, the latter with reference to biodiversity and SEA. It is also discussed in Chapter 8.

RELATIONSHIP WITH NATIONAL AND SUPRANATIONAL LEGAL FRAMEWORKS

Shelton and Kiss (2005, p12) explain the relationship between international and national law as follows:

> *The relationship between national law and international law varies considerably from one legal system to another. International law is considered the supreme body of law by international tribunals and in international relations among states. Thus, a state may not invoke a provision of its national law to excuse its violation of international law. The law of state responsibility provides that each breach of an international obligation attributable to a state automatically gives rise to a duty to cease the breach and make reparation for any injury caused, irrespective of national law.*

Unless it has 'direct effect', international law must be implemented by national or supranational (for example, EC/EU) law before it is binding.[19] In many instances this requires the enactment of new legislation, in other cases when dealing with either treaties or custom courts recognize that international law must be applied regardless of domestic implementation as a result of 'indirect effect' or what is called the practice of 'consistent interpretation', that is interpreting existing national or supranational legislation in conformity with international law.[20] After explaining the theoretical bases for international law that distinguish these two positions, this section considers the different ways in which international law is incorporated into the national framework of individual states or the supranational framework of an international institution such as the EU through the propositions of direct and indirect effect.

Customary law

Two doctrines have influenced the development of international law and its incorporation into national law. Proponents of the 'natural law' doctrine view international and natural law as part of the same universal normative order, with national law deriving its binding force as a result of delegation from international law. As such, these proponents are termed 'monists' and believe that international law is automatically applicable in the domestic legal context, without the need for further implementing legislation. This can also be termed 'direct effect', a term with very specific meaning in a European law context (see Chapters 7, 8 and 9). Lord Talbot LC took this view in stating that 'the law of nations... in its fullest extent... [is] part of the law of England' (cited in Balkin, 2005, p116). Proponents of the positivist doctrine view international and national law as two entirely separate legal orders. They are termed 'dualists' and believe that each rule of international law must be incorporated into national law before it can have effect, especially on individual rights. This would occur either as a result of judicial pronouncement under the common law, or by the passage of statutes.

Monism and dualism are most relevant to customary international law, although they are also relevant to treaty law (Shelton and Kiss, 2005, pp12–15). The constitutions of some countries specify that custom is part of the municipal law of the state without the need for national legislation; examples include Italy, Germany and the Netherlands. Most common law countries consider customary law to be part of the common law and also automatically binding on the state. In *Trendtex Trading Corporation v Central Bank of Nigeria*[21] the English Court of Appeal reaffirmed the view expressed by Lord Talbot above that international law in its fullest extent is automatically incorporated as part of the law of the land in the UK. While the common law legal system operates a system of applying previous judicial precedents, between common law states such precedents are usually only persuasive, meaning that other countries are free to follow previous decisions in other common law countries or to decide the law for themselves.

Such has been the experience of Australia, for example, which has decided that the view of the English Court of Appeal was 'without foundation', and that the 'true view' was that international law is not a part but is one of the sources of Australian law. Each rule of international law therefore has to be individually examined to decide whether it has been received into national law (see Balkin, 2005, p117). If it has, then there is an obligation to interpret national law consistently with it. This has also been the experience of the US, where 'courts adhere to the "Charming Betsy" rule, named after the case in which the Supreme Court announced that courts must interpret and apply statutes consistent with international law, unless it unmistakably appears on the face of a statute that Congress intends to modify or reject an international obligation' (Shelton and Kiss, 2005, p14).

Treaties

Once a treaty is in force it is 'binding upon the parties to it and (it) must be performed by them in good faith.' This has been termed the 'fundamental rule of treaty law' by Lacey (2005, p99) and is set out in Article 26 of the VCLT. Article 27 provides that a state 'may not invoke the provisions of its internal law as justification for its failure to perform a treaty'. In some states, constitutions specify that ratified treaties are automatically part of the law of the land and must be applied by judges in relevant cases. Many national legal systems, however, require a domestic act of ratification to bring into effect treaty commitments, in which case a failure to introduce, amend or modify such domestic law could leave a state in breach of its international obligations, with potential liability as a result.[22] Other states, such as the US, distinguish between self-executing treaties that judges can apply and non-self-executing treaties that require domestic ratification first (Shelton and Kiss, 2005, p13). Once a treaty has been incorporated and made binding 'it may rank at the level of constitutional law, or be superior, equal or inferior to legislation, according to the hierarchy of legal sources, generally stipulated in the constitution' (Shelton and Kiss, 2005, p13; see Marks, 2000). What this means is that it is ultimately a matter for each individual state to decide on the weight to attach to international law, which, of course, suggests that some states may breach their international legal obligations.

Where a division of responsibility exists between national and regional government, federal states such as Australia have, in the past, had difficulty fulfilling the obligation of ensuring compliance. However, the High Court in the *Tasmanian Dam* case expressly rejected the domestic legal relevance of federalism requiring the national government to implement its international obligations fully.[23] While Australian law therefore still requires implementing legislation for treaties, once Australia has ratified a treaty it has no choice but to bring this into effect to comply with international law. Other federal states, such as Germany have had similar issues, although Article 25 of the Constitution of Germany states clearly that once a treaty has been ratified or approved it ranks above ordinary legislation.

In order to comply with Article 31(1) of the VCLT, Australian courts have had to interpret treaty provisions to give primacy to their ordinary meaning in terms of their context and in the light of their object and purposes.[24] The courts have also favoured a construction of a statute that accords with Australia's treaty obligations.[25] Other states have taken similar approaches, applying international norms and standards to the interpretation of domestic law where definitions are unclear or ambiguous (Shelton and Kiss, 2005, pp13–14). Focusing on the role of Dutch courts, statutory interpretation in conformity with international (and European obligations) has been discussed by Betlem and Nollkaemper (2003). Dutch courts have followed the undeveloped doctrine concerning the invocability of treaties in national courts as set out by the predecessor of the ICJ, the Permanent Court of International Justice (PCIJ),[26] and as followed by states such as Australia, Israel and the UK. They argue that in certain legal contexts, the reception of international law 'looks much like that of EC law' (p570), meaning it has direct effect without the need for implementing legislation. This is considered in detail in Chapters 7, 8 and also in Chapter 12 when the relationship between international law and European law is analysed in detail.

Betlem and Nollkaemper (2003) emphasize the need to distinguish between direct effect as understood by European lawyers (see Part II of this book) and consistent interpretation. The latter is more akin to 'indirect effect' since under it rules of international law are interpreted via a rule of national law, whereas direct effect means a national court can apply international law regardless of a lack of transposing legislation. In the Netherlands, the practice is backed up by national constitutional law, as Article 94 of the Dutch Constitution requires that all directly effective provisions of international law take precedence over national law, with the Dutch Supreme Court taking decisions to fill gaps in Dutch law to comply with international law (pp583–584). Betlem and Nollkaemper (2003, p588) conclude:

> ... *through the practice of consistent interpretation, national courts play a major role in the application of international law. This is true where a treaty has not been implemented, but also when the legislature has transposed a rule of international law, giving rise to questions as to its proper application.*

ENFORCEMENT OF INTERNATIONAL LAW

International law is fundamentally different from national law in that, unlike, for example, the criminal law of individual states, there is no police force to oversee compliance and bring charges before relevant courts or tribunals. There is also no compulsory judicial means for the consideration of any charges brought, nor are there binding ways of ensuring court judgments are carried out. States have to agree to be subject to a court's jurisdiction, and often do not.

International Court of Justice

The origins of the ICJ were briefly described above. As the successor to the PCIJ, it is important to be aware that the jurisprudence of the PCIJ remains of persuasive influence on the ICJ. However as the President of the ICJ, Higgins (2003, p3) indicates, [the ICJ's] symbiotic relationship to the UN is even closer than was that of the Permanent Court to the League [of Nations]. This section is designed to illustrate further the work of the Court, which, for the purposes of this book, is the most important of the UN organs.[27] The relationship between the ICJ and the European Courts of Justice (ECJ) is discussed further in Chapter 12 as part of the analysis between the relationship between international and European law.

The ICJ has power to hear matters under three different heads: contentious jurisdiction, advisory jurisdiction and incidental jurisdiction. The first arises when a dispute is brought to the Court by the parties involved, the second allows the Court to provide a detailed opinion when requested by the UN General Assembly or other international institution such as the World Health Organization (WHO), and the third permits it to make interim orders. Article 36 of the Statute of the ICJ outlines the ways in which the Court obtains jurisdiction or competence to hear matters brought before it. The most straightforward way is for a state to forward a declaration to the UN Secretary General that it accepts the authority of the Court. Provided the states in dispute have each made a declaration, the Court is competent to act, with the only exception being their ability to make reservations to declarations, which may limit the scope or subject matter of disputes that may go to the ICJ. As an example, France's declaration includes nuclear testing. Alternatively, states can consent to the Court's jurisdiction in a number of other ways, including with respect to particular treaties.

Third parties can intervene in proceedings if their interests are affected, subject to the Court giving consent. Once it has decided it has jurisdiction to hear a case, the

ICJ functions much as other courts do, with the possibility of making interim measures as appropriate. Enforcement of judgments is the most difficult issue for the ICJ, as although Article 94 of the UN Charter calls upon states to carry out orders of the Court, this is essentially subject to the goodwill of a state (Kaye, 2005, pp151–152). States have mostly been compliant with orders of the Court, however, for the reasons given by Kaye (p152) below:

> *The Court is seen not merely as an arbiter of disputes, but as a significant source of international law, and to reject a decision made by it would confirm that the state involved was acting contrary to international law. Although many states will often behave in a manner inconsistent in some way with international law, few are prepared to have their continuing conduct labelled as improper by so respected a body as the ICJ. The desire to be seen as a good international citizen is a strong motivator for states to comply. Further, states have to consent to have the ICJ involved in the dispute in the first place. Participation in the process would be rendered rather meaningless if it were likely that a loser would refuse to obey the order of the Court, and so consenting to jurisdiction is usually accompanied with a commitment to comply.*

Another judge of the ICJ, Guillaume (1995) discusses the role of the Court in an article that considers the increase in the Court's activity in more recent times and concerns expressed by states about its role in dispute settlement. The increased caseload and procedural delays (writing in 1995, potentially three to six months for an advisory opinion, two to three years for a judgment), cost of proceedings and composition of the Court have all been raised as concerns (pp851–852). Improvements suggested to judicial practice are that the UN Secretary General could have the right to request advisory opinions, the Court could settle disputes to which international organizations are parties and that if chambers were established, it would be possible for more cases to be dealt with simultaneously. Procedural improvements could be made in limiting the number of written arguments and shortening the time for oral arguments. Judgments could also be shorter (Guillaume, 1995, pp853–854).

In a recent article, Paulson (2004) examines compliance with the final judgments of the ICJ since 1987. Compliance is defined as acceptance of the judgment as final and reasonable performance in good faith of any binding obligation. The latter includes a duty to give effect to the judgment with a view to avoiding its superficial implementation or otherwise circumventing it. Fourteen contentious cases that resulted in final judgments on the merits before the ICJ are examined. One, concerning non-compliance, is of particular interest. This is the decision on the *Gabcikovo-Nagymaros Project*, which discusses the concept of sustainable development in international law, and whether it has the significance of a customary international rule.[28] At the time of writing, Paulson indicated that the parties to the dispute were apparently not fulfilling their duty of good faith negotiation and that they 'have been unable to use the Judgment to resolve their differences' (2004, p449).

Arbitration

Arbitration is, in practice, the most significant of the alternative methods of dispute resolution. The ILC (1958) has defined it as a procedure for the settlement of disputes between states by a binding award, on the basis of law and as a result of a voluntarily accepted undertaking. The dispute is decided on by a third party, whether an individual or a panel of arbitrators. This is the key distinguishing feature of arbitration, for all other non-judicial means of dispute resolution are ultimately decided by the parties themselves. Arbitration is also limited to legal issues, with political, economic or other considerations, in theory at least, to play no part. The parties also agree to be bound by the decision. In most cases, arbitrators are appointed in accordance with treaty provisions, although in some instances states make use of the Permanent Court of Arbitration (PCA), which was set up under the Hague Conventions on Pacific Settlement of International Disputes and is located in the same building as the ICJ.[29]

There is far greater control for the parties in arbitration, despite many similarities with the judicial process. States can usually set the terms of reference and can set limitations on the judgment reached. Even though an arbitrators ruling is binding, it is quite possible for disputes to occur over interpretation, implementation and enforcement. It may also be possible for a state to challenge the legality of an arbitrator's award if the arbitrator has acted improperly or has breached some rule of procedure, such as a party having insufficient time to present its case. The Espoo Convention (see Chapter 4) sets out 18 detailed articles in its Appendix VII on the procedure of the arbitral tribunal to which parties must comply.

Negotiation, mediation, conciliation and inquiry[30]

Negotiation, mediation, conciliation and inquiry may also be available to the parties. Together with arbitration and judicial settlement, each is referred to in Article 33(1) of the UN Charter, with respect to resolving disputes that threaten peace and security. In other instances, there is no obligation to solve disputes in any of these ways, although in practice many are utilized. Each of the methods of dispute resolution can be seen in a continuum, with arbitration and judicial settlement the most structured and formal and negotiation, mediation, conciliation and inquiry (in that order) less structured to begin with but progressively more so. Negotiation will therefore take place on an ad hoc basis, unless issues are raised in a particular forum such as through the Group of 8 meetings of the largest western economic powers. It is by far the most common method used. It is particularly important given the emphasis in international law on the peaceful resolution of disputes.

Mediation will involve a third party in the dispute, albeit not in an adjudicative capacity as with arbitration. The UN Secretary General will often take on such a role, or other world leaders. Conciliation lies between mediation and arbitration and is a formalized version of mediation with an advisory decision being reached that is not binding on the parties. Conciliation mechanisms have been included in many treaties including UNCLOS 1982 and the Vienna Ozone Convention 1985. Finally, inquiry is the most formal of the above methods before arbitration and judicial settlement. Again, a third party is involved in the dispute, in this case to make a ruling with regard to a question of fact. States can agree to be legally bound by the decision, but do not have to. Together with conciliation, inquiries are rarely used, usually because states prefer either the informality of negotiation or mediation, or the formality of arbitration and judicial settlement. The Espoo Convention inquiry procedure (see Chapter 4) is, however, an important exception.

TOPICAL ISSUES

A number of topical issues have featured in recent international law journals that have relevance to the subject matter of this book. The first is whether international law has a constitutional basis or not. Constitutionalism is closely associated with transparency in governance and as such requirements for assessment of strategic level proposals that are required by international law may gain greater acceptance if the international legal system has strong claims to legitimacy. The second is the interest that has developed in self-contained regimes in international law, which allows some initial discussion concerning the links between international law generally and European law, although Chapter 12 examines the relationship in detail. The proliferation of international courts and tribunals and their relationships with one another are an important part of these regimes, as are the procedural arrangements of individual treaties that supplement general international law. An understanding of the practical working arrangements of individual COPs/MOPs is important partly because they pass resolutions that result in changes to treaties and practice.

A constitutional basis to international law?

As discussed in Chapter 1, constitutional law provides a framework for the relationship between the three branches of government and individuals who have dealings with them. At the international level, the three 'branches of government' in this context are loosely perceived to be the UN Security Council (executive), the General Assembly (legislature) and the ICJ (judiciary). As to the existence of a constitution, the Statute of the UN is often pointed to as a possible example. There are many difficulties with respect to such an analogy, however, including the fact that while the Assembly contains representatives of all states, it is not responsible for treaty making and its resolutions are not legally binding. Treaty making falls to the states themselves, and resolutions passed by the COPs/MOPs of treaties thereafter may make changes to the treaties. Discussions of legitimacy of international law-making inevitably raise the subject of the potential for a constitutional basis for international law (Kumm, 2004). In particular relation to the role of national courts in enforcing an international value system, De Wet (2006), a Professor of International Constitutional Law suggests that legitimacy of that value system is of upmost importance. She comments (p71):

> *In the current context, legitimacy should be understood as the extent to which the international value system is accepted as being representative of the values of the domestic legal order. For many authors such legitimacy is closely connected to the process by means of which the respective value system came into being and, in particular, the democratic quality of that process.*[31]

De Wet (2006, p51) argues for an international constitutional order consisting of an 'international community, an international value system and rudimentary structures for its enforcement'. All of these aspects are present to some extent. She examines the development of constitutionalism in nation states and argues that there is no reason why the term constitution should be reserved for the supreme law of sovereign states since federal states such as Germany and the US recognize constitutions at the state level. The constituent documents of international institutions such as the UN, World Trade Organization (WTO) and WHO are also often described as 'constitutions'. However, it is the development of the EU and its former draft constitution that provides particular strength to the arguments she puts forward, given that it 'envisages the co-existence of national constitutional orders within a supra-national constitutional order in the form of the EU' (De Wet, 2006, p52). While the theory of the argument is certainly sound, the practice has failed to meet it given the reluctance of the EU MS to accept the draft constitution. As sovereignty has progressively been handed over to the EC/EU during its historical development, the recent rejections of the draft constitution may have had as much to do with timing as principle.[32] The adoption of the 2007 Lisbon Reform Treaty has, however, put an end to the constitutional project, so the matter may be regarded as now settled (see Chapter 7).

Self-contained regimes

Many treaties contain regimes that are largely self-governing, and as such reference to the general law of the UN is often limited. The EU is an excellent example, and the relationship between international and European law is therefore much discussed. As this is the subject of Chapter 12, other than with regard to the proliferation of courts, this section is limited to some general remarks, with European law as an example. In 1985 Simma, a judge at the ICJ raised the question of whether self-contained regimes in the area of state responsibility were conceivable (Simma, 1985).[33] Over 20 years later he returned to the subject in a co-authored article (Simma and Pulkowski, 2006) that concludes that while the general rules on state responsibility are to apply residually to these self-contained regimes, they nonetheless remain applicable. The EU, WTO, human rights and diplomatic law are the regimes suggested that are largely autonomous because they operate to the significant exclusion of general international law in both content and procedure, including dispute settlement. Tailor made rules on the legal consequences of breach therefore limit the application of state responsibility as understood in customary international law, although where those rules fail to provide comprehensive solutions, custom is available to fill the gaps in the treaty regimes.

The proliferation of international courts and tribunals

Related to the above, one of the most notable developments in international law in recent times has been a proliferation of international courts and tribunals (Guillaume, 1995, pp854–860). Several treaties now have designated forums to which the parties can or must refer disputes. These include the dispute settlement panel system of the WTO and the tribunal under the UNCLOS. Two main problems arise as a result of this. The first is that different courts and tribunals may apply individual interpretations of substantive rules of international law,[34] which may produce conflicting jurisprudence. The second is that it can result in the creation of overlapping or competing jurisdictions, leading to 'forum shopping' by which states pick and choose the court that is most likely to favour their point of view.[35] Brown (2003) gives as examples the Southern Bluefin

Tuna dispute (ICJ and UNCLOS tribunal), the Swordfish dispute (UNCLOS tribunal and WTO panel) and the MOX Plant case (UNCLOS tribunal and ECJ). The last of these cases is considered in Chapters 8 and 12.

As raised by Simma (1985; Simma and Pulkowski, 2006) the other controversy resulting from the proliferation of courts and tribunals is whether the rules of these bodies are of a specialist nature to such an extent that states that submit disputes to them are able to 'opt out' of the substantive rules of international law developed in part by the ICJ. Higgins (2003, pp16–17) highlights the role of WTO panels and Appellate Body, which has had 'great difficulty, in particular, in dealing with competing obligations in other treaties- whether those on energy law, environmental law, the IMF or the WIPO Conventions'. Rather simplistically, Higgins believes the best way forward in the face of the difficulties experienced to date may be for the judiciary of each of the courts and members of the tribunals to keep themselves well informed of the jurisprudence of the other. There do not appear to be any clear cut answers to the problems that have arisen and, while inevitably a source of frustration for those that would prefer greater certainty, she hopes that 'friendly mutual respect will remain the order of the day' (Higgins, 2003, p19).

Autonomous procedural arrangements

Also part of any self-contained regime is the application of self-governing procedural rules that limit the need for recourse to the general body of international law. The establishment of COPs/MOPs are often replete with procedural regulation. Churchill and Ulfstein (2000) identifed this growing phenomenon some years ago, with regard to MEAs. They indicate that the institutional arrangements usually consist of a COP or MOP with decision making powers, a secretariat and one or more specialist subsidiary bodies. Multilateral examples include the Ramsar Convention, CMS and CBD (see Chapter 6). Regional examples include treaties concluded by the UNECE such as the Convention on Long Range Transboundary Air Pollution 1979 (LRTAP) and the Convention on the Protection and Use of Transboundary Watercourses and International Lakes 1992 (Watercourses and Lakes). While the ad hoc nature of the arrangements does not bring with it the status of an IGO (as outlined above), nonetheless Churchill and Ulfstein (2000, p625) argue that:

> The phenomenon we have chosen to call 'autonomous institutional arrangements' is one that we believe to be significant, as in comparison to traditional IGOs, it marks a distinct and different approach to institutionalised collaboration between states, being both more informal and more flexible, and often innovative in relation to norm creation and compliance.

The article discusses the scope of the decision making powers of the arrangements with regard to internal matters, substantive obligations, implementation and compliance and external capacity. As outlined, a COP/MOP has a number of functions. First, it acts in relation to internal matters by establishing subsidiary bodies, deciding on arrangements for meetings and rules of procedure and promulgating guidance. Second, it may amend the treaty or adopt new protocols to it. Third, it supervises implementation and compliance. Finally, it may adopt arrangements with international organizations and states. As will be seen in Chapter 4, all of these functions have been carried out by the Espoo and Aarhus Convention MOPs.

CONCLUSIONS

This brief overview of the international legal framework sets the scene for the other chapters in Part I. It demonstrates the complexities of international law from theoretical, political and legal perspectives, as well as providing an explanation of the development and structure, sources, relationship with national and supranational law, enforcement and the emerging issues that are impacting upon it. Many of the issues and themes outlined are developed further throughout the book, especially the relationship between international and European law that forms the subject of Chapter 12 and which allows analysis of the effectiveness of each legal system to be compared and contrasted. It is suggested that the reader of the chapters that follow in Part I especially refer to Chapter 2 as needed to better understand technicalities of process, of which the referenced literature provides a wealth of further reading if required.

NOTES

1   Conflict of laws is an unfortunate description for private international law. While it accurately describes one of the main issues to be determined – which law of which country applies in the event of any dispute – many laws come into conflict in many other ways. For example, public international law is also riven by conflicts when it is not clear which treaty applies, or which court or tribunal has jurisdiction to hear a dispute.

2   There are numerous standard texts on international law. One of the better known and recommended is Brownlie (2003).

3   Note the comments by Piotrowicz (2005, p29) concerning this, primarily with respect to composition of the Court, where he suggests that the practice of appointing a judge from each of the permanent members of the Council limits the potential independence of the Court.

4   *Reparations for Injuries Suffered in the Service of the United Nations (Advisory Opinion)* [1949] ICJ Reports 174.

5   The example given is that under the doctrine of implied powers a state can be expelled from an IGO even in the absence of an express provision in its constitution, if the party's behaviour prevents the organization from carrying out its functions. Under the VCLT the only basis for expulsion would be a material breach of the treaty.

6   The relationship between the EU and EC with regard to participation in international negotiations and agreements is extremely complex. The EU has not replaced the EC as the competent body in this regard; the EC retains legal power and the EU has not been given this power. For an explanation see Delreux (2006) and Chapter 12 for discussion.

7   Bilateral treaties are between two parties and multilateral are between more than two parties. Regional treaties are limited by geographical area, usually developed by an institution with functions in that region, and are typically only open to states within that region that are members of the institution. Multilateral treaties are commonly open to all states that are members of the UN. The VCLT does not distinguish between them.

8 Ratify has different meanings in international and national law, see Lacey (2005, p90) and discussion below.

9 Compliance also has a number of different elements as discussed below, and should be distinguished from enforcement. All are ways of illustrating effectiveness.

10 See the *Reservations to the Convention on the Prevention and Punishment of the Crime of Genocide (Advisory Opinion)* [1951] ICJ Reports 15.

11 An example of this is the 1985 Vienna Convention on the Protection of the Ozone Layer, UKTS 1 (1990) and the 1987 Montreal Protocol on Substances that Deplete the Ozone Layer, UKTS 19 (1990). While the Espoo Convention provides some structure to the SEA Protocol, it cannot be termed a framework convention because it contains obligations just in regard to transboundary EIA, most of which are procedural only. Both are considered in Chapters 4 and 5 respectively.

12 See Marsden (2006a and 2006b) for an explanation of these approaches with examples.

13 See Sadat-Akhavi (2003) on methods of resolving conflicts between treaties.

14 See *Case Concerning Military and Paramilitary Activities in and against Nicaragua (Nicaragua v United States of America (Merits)* [1986] ICJ Reports 14.

15 The distinction between these is used as a means of drawing a distinction between 'traditional and modern approaches to customary international law' by Roberts (2001), who argues that while one may be in decline, the other has become an increasingly significant source.

16 *Fisheries Jurisdiction Case (United Kingdom v Iceland) (Merits)* [1974] ICJ Reports 3.

17 *Legal Consequences for States of the Continued Presence of South Africa in Namibia (South West Africa) notwithstanding Security Council Resolution 276 (1970) (Advisory Opinion)* [1971] ICJ Reports 16.

18 *North Sea Continental Shelf Cases (Federal Republic of Germany v Denmark; Federal Republic of Germany v Netherlands)* [1969] ICJ Reports 4.

19 For examples of countries where international law has direct effect, see Brandon (2002).

20 Much research has been done into the role of international law, and especially IEL, in national courts. See, for example, Anderson and Galizzi (2002), Brandon (2002), Brunnée and Toope (2004), and De Marco and Campbell (2004). The general conclusion is that application has been limited thus far although the courts have contributed to dispute resolution and implementation in individual cases. See also Chapter 4.

21 *Trendtex Trading Corporation v Central Bank of Nigeria* [1977] 1 QB 529.

22 Some states require domestic legislation to be introduced *before* taking any binding action internationally, in which case this should not be an issue.

23 See *Commonwealth of Australia and Another v The State of Tasmania and Others* (1983) 158 CLR 1, which considered the Convention for the Protection of the World Natural and Cultural Heritage.

24 See *Commonwealth of Australia and Another v The State of Tasmania and Others* (1983) 158 CLR 1.

25 See *Minister for Immigration and Ethnic Affairs v Teoh* (1995) 128 ALR 353, where the High Court held that entry into a treaty by the executive government, even if not subsequently incorporated into domestic law, created a 'legitimate expectation' in administrative law that the executive government would act in accordance with the treaty provisions.

26 See *Jurisdiction of the Courts of Danzig* [1928] PCIJ Series B, No 15, pp17–18.

27 For a detailed analysis, see Meyer (2002).

28 *Gabcikovo-Nagymaros Project (Hungary/Slovakia)* 1997 ICJ Rep 1, 37 ILM 162 (1998). This is considered further in Chapter 3.

29 This section is largely taken from Kaye (2005, pp146–148), where further details are provided.

30 This discussion is also taken from Kaye (2005).

31   The absence of a democratic basis for the international legal system causes difficulties for
     many writers. De Wet (2006) uses the overlap in content between the international and
     domestic value systems with regard to human rights as an example of where representative
     values lie even in the absence of democracy (p74). That some jurisdictions have advanced
     human rights regimes in the absence of democracy – for example, Hong Kong – while some
     jurisdictions do not that are supposedly democratic, such as Singapore, lends strength to her
     argument. It must also be remembered that democracy is not an absolute and is subject to
     significant interpretation.
32   The expansion of the EU with a large number of accession countries together with procedural
     changes in EU governance are suggested as possibilities. These issues are briefly explored in
     Chapter 7. In Chapter 12, concerning the relationship between EU and international law,
     the arguments of Kumm (2004) with regard to legitimacy are explored in more detail.
33   State responsibility deals with the consequences of a states breach of international law. This
     is discussed at the start of Chapter 3 on IEL.
34   The difference between substantive and procedural law was discussed in Chapter 1.
35   See generally Yuval (2003).

REFERENCES

Alvik, I., Emberland, M. and Eriksen, C. (2007) 'Polycentric decision-making structures and
     fragmented spheres of law: what implications for the new generation of international legal
     discourse?', paper presented to the New International Law Conference, Oslo, March 2007,
     www.jus.uio.no/forskning/grupper/intrel/nil-conference/
Anderson, M. and Galizzi, P. (2002) *International Environmental Law in National Courts*, British
     Institute of International and Comparative Law, London
Balkin, R. (2005) 'International law and domestic law' in S. Blay, R. Piotrowicz and M. Tsamenyi
     (eds) *Public International Law: An Australian Perspective*, Oxford University Press, Melbourne,
     Vic, pp115–140
Betlem, G. and Nollkaemper, A. (2003) 'Giving effect to public international law and European
     Community law before domestic courts. A comparative analysis of the practice of consistent
     interpretation', *European Journal of International Law*, vol 14, no 3, pp569–589
Blay, S. (2005) 'The nature of international law' in S. Blay, R. Piotrowicz and M. Tsamenyi (eds)
     Public International Law: An Australian Perspective, Oxford University Press, Melbourne, Vic,
     pp1–19
Bowman, M. J. (1995) 'The multilateral treaty amendment process - a case study', *International
     and Comparative Law Quarterly*, vol 44, pp540–559
Brandon, E. (2002) 'Does international law mean anything in Canadian courts?, *Journal of
     Environmental Law and Practice*, vol 11, no 3, pp397–443
Brown, C. (2003) 'Book review: Shany, Yuval. The competing jurisdictions of international courts
     and tribunals', *European Journal of International Law*, vol 14, no 5, pp1045–1047
Brownlie, I. (2003) *Principles of Public International Law*, 6th Edition, Clarendon Press, Oxford
Brunnée, J. and Toope, S. J. (2004) 'A hesitant embrace: The application of international law
     in Canadian courts' in D. Dyzenhaus (ed) *The Unity of Public Law*, Hart Publishing, Oxford,
     pp357–388
Churchill, R. and Ulfstein, G. (2000) 'Autonomous institutional arrangements in multilateral
     environmental agreements: A little-noticed phenomenon in international law', *American
     Journal of International Law*, vol 94, no 4, pp623–659

Delreux, T. (2006) 'The European Union in international environmental negotiations: A legal perspective on the internal decision-making process', *International Environmental Agreements*, vol 6, pp231–248

Desai, B. (2004) *Institutionalising International Environmental Law*, Transnational Publishers, Ardsley

De Marco, J. V. and Campbell, M. L. (2004) 'The Supreme Court of Canada's progressive use of international environmental law and policy in interpreting domestic legislation', *Review of European Community and International Environmental Law*, vol 13, no 3, pp320–332

De Wet, E. (2006) 'The international constitutional order', *International and Comparative Law Quarterly*, vol 55, pp51–76

Greig, D. (2005) 'Sources of international law' in S. Blay, R. Piotrowicz and M. Tsamenyi (eds) *Public International Law: An Australian Perspective*, Oxford University Press, Melbourne, Vic, pp52–84

Guillaume, G. (1995) 'The future of international judicial institutions', *International and Comparative Law Quarterly*, vol 44, pp 848–862

Higgins, R. (2003) 'The ICJ, ECJ and the integrity of international law', *International and Comparative Law Quarterly*, vol 52, pp1–20

Kammerhofer, J. (2004) 'Uncertainty in the formal sources of international law: Customary international law and some of its problems', *European Journal of International Law*, vol 15, no 3, pp523–553

Kaukoranta, P. (2006) 'The treaty-making process and basic concepts of treaty law' in M. Berglund (ed) *International Environmental Law Making and Diplomacy Review 2005*, UNEP Course Series 2, University of Joensuu, Joensuu, pp53–58

Kaye, S. (2005) 'Peaceful settlement of disputes in international law' in S. Blay, R. Piotrowicz and M. Tsamenyi (eds) *Public International Law: An Australian Perspective*, Oxford University Press, Melbourne, Vic, pp141–153

Kumm, M. (2004) 'The legitimacy of international law: A constitutionalist framework of analysis', *European Journal of International Law*, vol 15, no 5, pp907–931

Lacey, W. (2005) 'The law of treaties' in S. Blay, R. Piotrowicz and M. Tsamenyi (eds) *Public International Law: An Australian Perspective*, Oxford University Press, Melbourne, Vic, pp85–114

Marks, S. (2000) *The Riddle of all Constitutions, International Law, Democracy, and the Critique of Ideology*, Oxford University Press, Oxford

Marsden, S. (2006a) 'Constitutional interpretation in Hong Kong: Do common law approaches apply when the National People's Congress Standing Committee interprets the Basic Law?, *LAWASIA Journal*, pp99–124

Marsden, S. (2006b) 'Regional autonomy, judicial criticism and the 2005 interpretation: Judicial independence in Hong Kong compromised again?', *Hong Kong Law Journal*, vol 36, no 1, pp117–142

Meyer, H. (2002) *The World Court in Action: Judging Among the Nations*, Oxford, Rowman and Littlefield Publishers Inc, New York, NY

Pallemaerts, M. (2004) 'An introduction to the sources, principles and regimes of international environmental law' in M. Berglund (ed) *International Environmental Law Making and Diplomacy*, *UNEP Course Series 2*, University of Joensuu, Joensuu, pp61–96

Paulson, C. (2004) 'Compliance with final judgments of the International Court of Justice since 1987', *American Journal of International Law*, vol 98, no 3, pp434–461

Piotrowicz, R. (2005) 'The structure of the international legal system' in S. Blay, R. Piotrowicz and M. Tsamenyi (eds) *Public International Law: An Australian Perspective*, Oxford University Press, Melbourne, Vic, pp20–51

Roberts, A. (2001) 'Traditional and modern approaches to customary international law: a reconciliation', *American Journal of International Law*, vol 95, no 4, pp757–791

Sadat-Akhavi, S. (2003) *Methods of Resolving Conflicts between Treaties*, Martinus Nijhoff Publishers, Leiden/Boston MA

Shelton, D. and Kiss, A. (2005) *Judicial Handbook on Environmental Law*, United Nations Environment Programme, Stevenage

Simma, B. (1985) 'Self-contained regimes', *Netherlands Yearbook of International Law*, vol XVI, p111–135

Simma, B. and Pulkowski, D. (2006) 'Of planets and the universe: Self-contained regimes in international law', *European Journal of International Law*, vol 17, no 3, pp483–529

Yuval, S. (2003) *The Competing Jurisdictions of International Courts and Tribunals*, Oxford University Press, Oxford

CHAPTER 3

International Environmental Law

CHAPTER OUTLINE

The purpose of this chapter is to provide more specific context for the analysis of the Espoo and Aarhus Conventions in Chapter 4 and the SEA Protocol in Chapter 5. The present chapter therefore outlines the development of international environmental law (IEL), initially from a soft law historical perspective, but later with particular emphasis on the customary rules for resolving transboundary disputes and the other relevant treaty provisions, many of which make direct or indirect reference to EIA. The customary rules partly mirror the national development of EIA, which from an international perspective may be of relevance either to transboundary issues between states or to international and shared areas.[1] The chapter builds on the previous chapter on international law by making reference, with examples, to differences between treaty and custom development as applicable to the natural environment, and especially EIA. Three duties are emphasized to organize the discussion: harm prevention, transboundary cooperation and liability for harm. Enforcement is examined in the final section.

INTERNATIONAL ENVIRONMENTAL LAW

IEL is today one of the largest constituent parts of international law, illustrative of the growth of global concern for the environment. It has its own specialized literature describing and analysing a huge range of regimes for environmental conservation and protection that have been incorporated in treaties, custom and soft law.[2] The development through treaties has been particularly significant, and there are now hundreds containing provisions related to various aspects of the environment. Together with the UNECE conventions of relevance to the SEA Protocol considered in Chapter 4, several others will be examined in Chapter 6, especially the CBD,[3] Ramsar,[4] CMS[5] and World Heritage[6] Conventions, which recommend utilization of, or have potential to utilize, SEA in treaty implementation. IEL has also developed significantly through the resolutions, recommendations and declarations of international conferences and IGOs, what was described in the previous chapter as 'soft law' because of its lack of binding status.[7] The remainder of this section provides an overview of the recent historical development of IEL with a focus on the soft law policy development of EIA with which readers may be most familiar, interpretation of environmental treaties and the difference between principles and rules, which form the basis of the hard law of international custom and treaties.

IEL from a historical perspective

The UN Conference on the Human Environment (UNCHE) 1972 was the beginning of a long history of the development of IEL through soft law mechanisms. It resulted in the *Stockholm Declaration on the Human Environment*,[8] which sets out numerous principles relating to the use and protection of the natural environment, including its relationship to economic development. For the first time the importance of air, water, flora and fauna as natural resources was recognized, in addition to oil and minerals that had traditionally been viewed differently. As well as leading to the creation of the UN Environment Programme (UNEP), several other principles were developed, such as the duty to safeguard and manage resources for future generations (inter- and intra-generational equity), to be expounded in later UN declarations and resolutions (Sands, 1999).

The *World Conservation Strategy* 1982, as developed by the International Union for the Conservation for Nature (IUCN) and sponsored by UNEP, was the next significant example of soft law development; its calls for the protection of biological diversity were an early influence on later treaty law. It is often referred to as the *World Charter for Nature*, paragraphs 11(b) and (c) of which support the 'exhaustive examination' and 'assessment' of activities likely to pose a significant risk to nature or which may disturb nature, requiring that activities should not proceed or should minimize potential adverse effects on the basis of the findings of the assessment or examination.[9]

The Brundtland Report 1987, *Our Common Future*, was the main output of the UN Commission on Environment and Development,[10] and the first time sustainable development was specifically recommended in IEL. In the same year, UNEP adopted general goals and principles for EIA to ensure that 'environmentally sound and sustainable development' of planned activities take place. Since that time, the relationship between EIA and sustainable development has been intricately linked.[11] The UNEP principles have three related objectives: to ensure that environmental effects are taken into account before decisions are taken to allow activities to be carried out; to provide for the implementation of national EIA procedures; and to encourage reciprocal procedures for notification, information exchange and consultation on activities likely to have significant environmental effects.

The UN Conference on Environment and Development 1992 (UNCED) in Rio de Janeiro was established by the General Assembly to encourage further development of IEL since Stockholm, with particular reference to the needs of developing states. Known as the 'Earth Summit', in addition to the CBD and the Climate Change Convention,[12] the main soft law outputs were the *Rio Declaration on Environment and Development*,[13] the *Declaration on Forest Principles*,[14] and *Agenda 21*.[15] Sands (1995, p581) points out that in particular the last of these has many references to EIA, which call on all countries to 'assess the environmental suitability of infrastructure of human settlements', ensure that 'relevant decisions are preceded by environmental impact assessments' and integrate environmental considerations in decision making at all levels.

Ten years after the Earth Summit in Rio, the World Summit on Sustainable Development 2002 (WSSD) was held in Johannesburg to review progress. Outputs were the *Johannesburg Declaration on Sustainable Development*, reaffirming the commitment to sustainable development made earlier, and the *Plan of Implementation* (POI). The POI establishes targets, endorses the strengthening of UNEP and better coordination of environmental issues through the UN generally, as well as improving links with financial institutions such as the World Bank and WTO.

Andresen (2007a) compares and examines the effectiveness of UNCHE, UNCED and WSSD. As to the similarities between them, all had a preparatory phase and a focus on soft political declarations that resulted in a declaration and plan of action. Differences are largely seen in terms of outputs, with the Rio Summit regarded as the most productive with three declarations, two legally binding conventions and one new institution created, the Commission on Sustainable Development (CSD). Stockholm resulted in two declarations and one new institution (UNEP),[16] and Johannesburg only produced two declarations. Overall, he concludes that the Rio Earth Summit was the most effective of the three, and that thereafter 'attention gradually shifted from the creation of institutions and adoption of ambitious goals, to implementation and necessary behavioural change on the ground' (Andresen, 2007a, p322). Part of the reason for this was the increased importance given to the social dimension of sustainable development in Johannesburg, under the principle of 'common but differentiated responsibilities' (see below), which saw poverty eradication assume a greater priority than environmental protection. Another reason was the different perspectives taken by the key state actors in UN environmental governance, especially the US, EU and China (Andresen, 2007b).

Interpretation of environmental treaties

Shelton and Kiss (2005, pp15–16) indicate that environmental treaties are different from other treaties as they have particular characteristics that respond to the needs of environmental protection. These include interrelated provisions or cross referencing of instruments, the widespread use of framework agreements, interim application of treaties, specified means of modification or amendment, and the application of either self-executing or non-self-executing provisions.

With regard to the first feature, environmental treaties often cross reference other international instruments. Shelton and Kiss (p15) refer to the example of recent marine environmental treaties, which often cite the rules of UNCLOS[17] or what is termed 'generally accepted international standards', in some instances incorporating such rules by reference. As a result, a state that is party to the environmental treaty may also be bound or have to have regard to the other treaty, to which it may not be a party.

With respect to the second, the use of framework conventions, such as the CBD or the Climate Change Convention, ensures that a treaty with general scope is adopted, setting out basic principles on which consent can be granted. The parties to such treaties envisage that additional protocols will be later adopted setting out more detailed obligations; these are usually separately ratified but usually interpreted and applied in order to carry out the aims of the main agreement. The Cartagena[18] and Kyoto[19] Protocols are respectively protocols to the CBD and Climate Change Conventions, for example.[20]

The third feature of environmental treaties identified is the technique of approving interim application pending entry into force (for example, on ratification). As a means of responding to urgent problems that must be dealt with quickly, Shelton and Kiss indicate that it was used with the 1995 Agreement for the Implementation of the Provisions of UNCLOS relating to Article 41 of the Conservation and Management of Straddling Fish Stocks and Highly Migratory Fish Stocks.[21] As they comment, 'This allows judges to apply the agreements even before the participating state has ratified them or they have entered into force' (p16).

The fourth feature is the technique of drafting treaties that establish stable general obligations but allow for the addition of flexible specific provisions, which are likely to include technical norms. This allows for effective responses to rapid advances in scientific knowledge, so that detailed listings of prohibited substances or protected species can be included in annexes that can be changed easily without having to amend the principal treaty. Since these annexes will be legally binding, it will be necessary for the modification procedure to be expressly included in the treaty's provisions.

The last feature enables environmental treaties to contain both self-executing and non-self-executing provisions. As discussed in Chapter 2, and in common with other treaties, this ensures that the former provisions are capable of immediate judicial application without the need for national legislation, while in the latter instance legislation (or approval by the executive branch of government) will be required. The CMS, for example, contains provisions that oblige state parties to enact and enforce penal sanctions (which apply the criminal law) against those in breach, and unless a state brings such provisions into effect, the judiciary will have limited ability to remedy the breach. Shelton and Kiss (2005, p16) refer to a case where it was not possible to prevent permission for oil development in a Ramsar wetland because the national legal framework (the non-self-executing provision) had not been brought into effect under the treaty.

Duties and principles

Rayfuse (2005, pp358–362) outlines three of the most important 'duties' of IEL: prevention of environmental harm,[22] cooperation in transboundary situations and compensation for environmental damage. While these duties have no status as such in IEL, they are a useful means of organizing the discussion that follows. Several general principles of law form part of these duties. For example, the precautionary principle (or approach) relates to harm prevention, the participatory principle (or principle of non-discrimination) relates to cooperation, and the polluter pays principle relates to compensation. The principle of common but differentiated responsibilities has also acquired recent significance given the focus since the Rio Earth Summit on the position of developing countries, which are typically permitted greater flexibility in implementation (Pallemaerts, 2004, pp64–69). Several authors have also argued that EIA (which also relates to harm prevention and cooperation) is itself a principle of international law (for example, Sands, 1995, 2003). Shelton and Kiss (2005, p17) comment:

> *The requirement to conduct environmental impact assessment of proposed activities...*
> *started as the law of a component unit of a federal state, was adopted at the federal level,*
> *and was then progressively accepted by other countries and by regional organizations*
> *and regional treaty systems.*

Pallemaerts (2004, p63) explains that the relationship between general principles of law, such as the precautionary principle and the sources of international law, such as international custom, has traditionally been 'derived by induction from the national legal systems of the so-called civilized nations'. He cites Article 38(1) of the Statute of the ICJ, which as seen in Chapter 2 refers to 'the general principles of law recognized by civilized nations' as one of the sources of international law. However, in accordance with a more modern view, the principles have been derived from positive rules of international law, as a reflection of 'a general legal conviction of the international community'. A combination of the two views would therefore 'hold that general principles emerge from both national law, and soft and hard international law'. Clearly such principles have no legal status unless they become customary norms or are incorporated into treaty regimes or national law, when they become *rules* of law.[23] In referring to De Sadeleer (2002), Pallemaerts (2004, p64) distinguishes rules and principles as follows:

> *Rules are precise prescriptions for specific factual situations. They determine specific*
> *action by clearly identifiable subjects. Rules have a determinate content and provide*
> *a specific behavioural prescription, thus guaranteeing legal certainty. Principles,*
> *however, are flexible norms which help orient decision-making. There is a high degree*
> *of abstraction and a low measure of determinacy in principles and no automatic*
> *legal consequences can be derived from them. A principle can be seen as a kind of*
> *rule with indeterminate content, as addressees enjoy a wide margin of discretion in*
> *its implementation. The difference between rules and principles, in this view, appears*
> *more like a question of degree of determinacy rather than a clear-cut dichotomy.*

CUSTOMARY LAW

The first two duties of prevention of environmental harm and cooperation in transboundary situations have become accepted as customary norms and are of particular relevance to EIA, even though EIA lacks a specific obligation to prevent harm, which would be needed for the third duty to be enforceable. As concluded below, the third duty of compensation for environmental damage is unlikely to be a customary norm, but is also related to EIA. This section considers the customary position of these duties and analyses the relationship between each and the principles that form part of them.

Prevention of environmental harm

Three of the earliest IEL cases, the *Trail Smelter Arbitration*,[24] the *Corfu Channel* case[25] and the *Lac Lanoux Arbitration*,[26] established the rule that states must not cause harm to others and must not allow their territory to be used in such a way as to do harm.

They demonstrate the importance of judicial decisions and doctrine as a source of international law, which also, in many instances, 'are considered as the affirmation or the revelation of customary international rules' (Shelton and Kiss, 2005, p17). In the first case, concerning a claim for compensation by the US for air pollution caused by Canada, the Tribunal held that 'under the principles of international law... no state has the right to permit the use of its territory in such as manner as to cause injury by fumes in or to the territory of another... when the cause is of serious consequence and the injury is established by clear and convincing evidence'. As such, once a state knows, or ought to know, that activities are being undertaken on its territory that are causing or may cause environmental harm, it is obliged to take measures to prevent the harm. This requirement of foreseeability is established by the *Corfu Channel* case, and more recent case law in national jurisdictions has discussed the duty further (Shelton and Kiss, 2005, p21).

The duty to prevent environmental harm has therefore led to the development of the precautionary principle, which is now often discussed by international and national lawyers, despite its uncertain status in customary law (see, for example, Freestone and Hey, 1999); it is also an important consideration for the judiciary involved in the development of environmental law (Shelton and Kiss, 2005, pp21–22). The principle originated in Germany in the mid 1960s and at the international level in the 1980s. Although the *Trail Smelter Arbitration* required 'clear and convincing evidence' of actual or threatened injury before the obligation to prevent harm arose, as Rayfuse indicates (2005, p360):

> developing awareness of the uncertainty of scientific information and prediction, and the possible catastrophic effects of this uncertainty and inaccuracy for humankind, particularly in the areas of marine and atmospheric pollution and overexploitation, has led to the development of the precautionary principle.

Because definitions vary and some important states have refused to give effect to it, assessing whether the precautionary principle is now a customary rule of international law is difficult (Burns, 2005, p1; Rayfuse, 2005, p360; Ellis, 2006, pp447–450). In reviewing a book by Trouwborst (2002), and with reference in large part to EIA, Ellis (2006, p448) comments that 'there is little doubt that these forms of action are compatible with the precautionary principle and further its aims: indeed it may well be that they were deliberately adopted as precautionary measures'.[27] Ellis (p462) concludes her review with the following comment on the relationship between precaution and the law, and the difficulties of encapsulating the former into the latter:

> Precaution certainly poses challenges to law on a number of levels. Law seeks to impose boundaries; to bring certainty and clarity to situations that are ambiguous, confused and in flux; to assess responsibility for events and actions that occurred in the past, and to allow people to project themselves into an uncertain future and to impose limits on the limitless chain of events unleashed by human action. Precaution seems destined to defeat these attempts with its fluidity and flexibility, the amorphous nature of the boundaries that are meant to identify and constrain the scope of its application, and with its injunction to keep changing the rules of the game as new knowledge and understandings are accumulated.

The inability of the law to adequately capture scientific principles has been commented on by others. Dawson (2004) has written recently on this in relation to biodiversity conservation (see also Raffensperger and Tickner, 1999; Morris, 2000; Cooney, 2005), where she concludes that the tendency to assume that science can provide clear, objective goals for biodiversity conservation that can provide a foundation for law and policy is a false assumption. Much of the transposition of principles and also practice therefore fails to relate the depth and complexity when reduced to a dialogue between policy maker and legislative draftsperson.[28]

The ICJ had the opportunity to consider the precautionary principle in both the second *Nuclear Tests* case of 1995 and the *Gabcíkovo-Nagymaros* case of 1997. In the first, New Zealand requested the ICJ to examine France's decision to resume underground nuclear testing, arguing that France was under an obligation in customary international law to conduct an EIA before carrying out the tests, and in doing so to apply the precautionary principle to show that they would not result in the introduction of radioactive material to the environment. In response, Judge Weeramantry described EIA as an ancillary part of the broader precautionary principle.[29] In the second, where a dispute arose between Hungary and Slovakia over Hungary's unilateral suspension of the construction of a dam on the River Danube due to concerns about the environmental impact of the project, the Court decided to express the principle (alongside the polluter pays principle) in terms of the concept of sustainable development requiring that two of the important values of international society be reconciled.[30] In discussing the legal status of the principle, Koivurova (2002, pp143–146) suggests its main function is to provide guidance to the national environmental protection systems of the countries of the world. The general nature of the principle is therefore such that it cannot be thought of as a customary norm of international law. The failure of the Court to decide conclusively whether the precautionary principle is now an accepted customary norm has only served to maintain uncertainty, despite recent efforts to clarify the role of the principle (IUCN, 2007).

Cooperation in transboundary situations

The *Lac Lanoux Arbitration* also sets out the duty to cooperate in transboundary situations, such as the use of a shared natural resource. In this case the Tribunal held that in preparing a water diversion scheme that would impact upon Spain, France had a duty to advise Spain and take into account Spain's interests. Proper observance of the duty requires states to undertake EIA, give prior notice, and consult and negotiate with any state whose interests may be affected. However there are limitations on this, as under the doctrine of state sovereignty states only have to negotiate in good faith. They are not required to obtain the prior consent of states potentially affected by intended activities in their own jurisdiction. In relation to emergency situations and accidents, the duty to notify is enhanced by a need to take timely action if they might cause harm to others. The *Corfu Channel* case set out this rule, under which it was held that Albania was under a duty to warn British warships of the existence of mines in the Corfu Channel, part of Albanian waters. Connected with the duty to notify is the duty to assist others, which, while a feature of some treaty regimes, is unlikely to exist as a customary norm.

In the second *Nuclear Tests* case in 1995, Judge Sir Geoffrey Palmer commented on the status of EIA in the following terms:

> *As the law now stands it is a matter of legal duty to first establish before undertaking an activity that the activity does not involve any unacceptable risk to the environment. An EIA is simply a means of establishing a process to comply with that international legal duty.*[31]

Later, in the *Gabcíkovo-Nagymaros* case of 1997, separate judicial opinion supported the view that EIA had assumed the status of a principle of customary international law. Judge Weeramantry therefore referred to the need for 'continuing environmental impact assessment', acknowledging the significance of ongoing assessment and continual monitoring of a project while in operation. He stated that a duty of EIA is to be read into treaties whose subject can reasonably be considered to have a significant impact on the environment.[32] The comments of Judges Palmer and Weeramantry (which were in the minority in each case, and therefore cannot be given much weight), tend to suggest that while the status of the precautionary principle in customary international law may be uncertain, the status of EIA is a little clearer. However that is not to say that EIA has yet attained the status of a customary norm, with Judge Palmer's comment only establishing that 'EIA is a means of establishing a process to comply' rather than the legal duty itself. Yet state practice since then may suggest otherwise, with growing compliance with the Espoo Convention as an example (see Chapter 4).

Connected generally with the duty to cooperate is the participatory principle, or principle of non-discrimination, which has developed as a result of the expansion of procedural environmental rights as most clearly outlined in the Aarhus and Espoo Conventions (see below for both). State practice and judicial opinion have ensured that the participatory principle is widely accepted by the international community, largely as a result of national law preceding developments at the international level, as several countries have had such provisions in their national law for some time. The participatory principle, also termed the principle of non-discrimination, is discussed further with respect to the Espoo Convention in Chapter 4. Shelton and Kiss (2005, pp27–30) discuss the full range of environmental rights, including participation, access to information and access to justice. They also consider human rights (pp28 and 31), environmental justice and equity (pp23–24), and discuss case law in a national context where challenges to EIA procedures have been upheld on the basis of failure to comply with various aspects of the duty to cooperate, which sometimes may include transboundary elements (2005, p39).

Compensation for environmental damage

The duty to compensate for environmental damage has an extensive literature of its own in connection with international liability regimes (see, for example, Bowman and Boyle, 2002; Hanqin, 2003), and incorporating a substantive duty to avoid harm has sometimes been considered in relation to EIA.[33] Although it effectively falls outside the scope of EIA procedures, which are directed towards prevention (through information provision) and cooperation in order to *avoid* damage and hence liability,[34] it is analysed in relation to custom, treaties and soft law to explain the full potential scope of IEL and perhaps the missing component of EIA in environmental protection. Brunnée (2004) has explored this in a recent article in which she reflects on whether liability regimes are an appropriate tool for international environmental protection. Customary law is governed by the law of state responsibility, under which there is an obligation not only to refrain from the conduct complained of, but also to repair the harm caused. Although the legal position concerning liability for that harm is not yet settled, there is now some agreement on draft articles for a UN Convention on State Responsibility, which has taken over 50 years since the General Assembly first requested the ILC to consider the issue. Yet there is little state practice and limited jurisprudence, alongside the uncertain status of related norms, especially the polluter pays principle, which while well understood may not always be well applied.

The fact that the polluter pays principle has not received the same attention as the precautionary principle in international and national courts suggests it is even less likely to have acquired the status as a customary norm than the precautionary principle. Nonetheless, it is recognized in judicial guidance as a method for internalizing externalities, which can be applied most easily in a geographic region subject to uniform environmental law (Shelton and Kiss, 2005, pp22–23). It has, however, been downplayed in relation to the customary law of state responsibility and the draft ILC Convention as a result of the need to move away from notions of strict liability (which require only proof of a wrongful action without proof of wrongful intention),[35] and which are unpopular with states who do not wish to be legally responsible for the full extent of transboundary harm. Nonetheless, as will be seen, it has a significant profile in soft law instruments, with some incorporation in treaties, although considerable discretion as to interpretation is permitted where it is included.

The current position with respect to a Convention on State Liability was reported on by Crawford and Olleson (2005), with the ILC recommending the deferral of the question of an international conference to consider whether a treaty should be concluded. This would give time for the draft articles prepared to 'exert an influence on the crystallisation of the law of state responsibility through application by international courts and tribunals and state practice' (Crawford and Olleson, 2005. p960).

TREATIES

Much of the earliest treaty development in IEL was in relation to the use of international watercourses. Although early treaties such as the Boundary Waters Treaty 1909 in North America[36] aimed at the prevention of pollution of such waters, the management of the resource generally rather than environmental protection specifically, was the predominant objective. This section considers treaties of relevance to the two underlying general duties of international EIA, prevention of environmental harm and cooperation in transboundary situations, together with the related principles. For completeness, compensation for environmental damage is also briefly discussed, although treaty provision here is limited.

Prevention of environmental harm

As Rayfuse (2005, p354) indicates, it was only later in the development of IEL that there was recognition of the need to regulate transboundary matters and the global commons[37] from exploitation, for example, through development of treaties for marine protection, such as UNCLOS, and in relation to nuclear hazards. The principle of harm prevention as developed in customary law therefore provided much of the inspiration behind later decisions to promote and bring into effect treaties aimed at preventing transboundary impacts, such as Article 2 of the UNECE Convention on Long-Range Transboundary Air Pollution 1979 (LRTAP),[38] Article 194 of UNCLOS, and Article 3 of the CBD.

Pollution of the marine environment was one of the most significant areas in which EIA was given early prominence in harm prevention, as indicated in Munro and Lammers (1986, p59). Alongside the inclusion of specific EIA provisions in UNCLOS (see below), Pallemaerts (2004, p67) illustrates how the precautionary principle has also been applied by the International Tribunal for the Law of the Sea in disputes concerning the management of fish stocks,[39] radioactive pollution of the marine environment[40] and land reclamation works.[41] He also indicates (p67), how the position of the parties to such disputes is not always consistent. Malaysia in the land reclamation case argued that its rights were protected by the precautionary principle, when it had in the past opposed recognition of precaution as a general principle. Burns (2005, p1) summarizes the international and national reach of the precautionary principle as follows:

> *Since its first explicit incorporation in an international document in 1987, the concept has been 'included in virtually every recent treaty and policy document related to the protection and preservation of the environment', as well as in national legislation and regulations in many States and applied by many domestic courts.*

Shelton and Kiss (2005) give examples of a wide range of environmental treaties that today incorporate the precautionary principle. These attempt to deal with the following matters: the likelihood and extent of environmental harm, the level of scientific uncertainty or uncertainty needed for precautionary action, whether cost-effectiveness of measures is relevant, whether precaution applies to individual parties or one of the treaty's institutions, and whether precaution is being applied in an environmental context to encourage action (p21). These include the CBD (in the Preamble, and subsequently related work on marine and coastal biodiversity, invasive alien species and sustainable use of wild living resources). The CBD's Cartagena Protocol on Biosafety 2000 also strongly affirms the role of the principle. The Convention on International Trade in Endangered Species of Wild Flora and Fauna (CITES) is another good example to have taken measures in this regard.[42] While other treaties such as Ramsar and CMS predate the development of the principle and therefore do not include it in their treaty texts, it has been incorporated into various resolutions and related agreements.[43]

As stated, prevention of environmental harm to the marine environment is reasonably well developed under UNCLOS. Section 4 concerns monitoring and environmental assessment, with Article 206 requiring EIA. This is, however, limited, given the addition of 'as far as practicable' to the obligatory 'shall'. This is set out in full below, as similar provisions are present elsewhere, for example, Article 14(1) of the ASEAN Agreement,[44] which uses the same wording to introduce a discretionary element:

Article 206 – Assessment of potential effects of activities

When states have reasonable grounds for believing that planned activities under their jurisdiction or control may cause substantial pollution of or significant and harmful changes to the marine environment, they shall, as far as practicable, assess the potential effects of such activities on the marine environment and shall communicate reports of the results of such assessments in the manner provided by article 205.

Similarly Article 3 of the Convention on the Protection and Use of Transboundary Watercourses and International Lakes 1992[45] requires the application of EIA in order to prevent, control and reduce transboundary impacts. This is also set out below:

Article 3 – PREVENTION, CONTROL AND REDUCTION

1. *To prevent, control and reduce transboundary impact, the Parties shall develop, adopt, implement and, as far as possible, render compatible relevant legal, administrative, economic, financial and technical measures, in order to ensure, inter alia, that:*

   (h) *Environmental impact assessment and other means of assessment are applied...*

Cooperation in transboundary situations

The customary, duty to cooperate is also seen in a number of international agreements, for example Articles 8 and 12 of the Convention of the Law of Non-Navigable Uses of International Watercourses 1997.[46] One of the earliest, with specific reference to transboundary EIA would appear to be found in the 1974 Nordic Environmental Protection Convention,[47] which requires an assessment of the effects in the territory of one party of activities carried out in the territory of another party. Emergency situations have received particular emphasis in treaties, for example, the Convention on Early Notification of a Nuclear Accident 1986,[48] prepared in response to the failure of the USSR to notify the international community in a timely or adequate manner about the Chernobyl incident in the same year.

Together with the Espoo Convention, which is specifically focused on the subject (see Chapter 4), there are many MEAs with provisions for EIA that incorporate both the duties to prevent harm and to cooperate. These include Article 7 of LRTAP 1979, Articles 4 and 10 of the Convention on the Control of Transboundary Movements of Hazardous Wastes and their Disposal 1989 (Basel),[49] the EIA Annex to the Protocol on Environmental Protection to the Antarctic Treaty 1991,[50] Articles 3 and 9 of the Convention on the Protection and Use of Transboundary Watercourses and Lakes 1992, Article 4 of the UN Framework Convention on Climate Change 1992, Articles 7 and 14 of the CBD and Article 12 of the UN Convention on the Law of the Non-Navigable Uses of International Watercourses 1997.[51]

Article 9 of the 1992 Watercourses and Lakes Convention deals with bilateral and multilateral cooperation, and requires states to enter into agreements to prevent, control and reduce transboundary impact. Such agreements must provide for the establishment of joint bodies to serve as a forum for information exchange and in order to participate in the implementation of EIA. Article 12 of the 1997 International Watercourses Convention requires notification of planned measures with possible adverse effects before implementation, including the results of any EIA carried out. Article 14(1) of the CBD is a wide-ranging provision that includes a requirement for SEA in sub-paragraph (b). Because of its comprehensive nature, this is cited in full below, with the SEA provision discussed later in Chapter 6:

Article 14 – Impact Assessment and Minimizing Adverse Impacts

1. *Each Contracting Party, as far as possible and as appropriate, shall:*

    (a) *Introduce appropriate procedures requiring environmental impact assessment of its proposed projects that are likely to have significant adverse effects on biological diversity with a view to avoiding or minimising such effects and, where appropriate, allow for public participation in such procedures;*

    (b) *Introduce appropriate arrangements to ensure that the environmental consequences of its programmes and policies that are likely to have significant adverse impacts on biological diversity are duly taken into account;*

    (c) *Promote, on the basis of reciprocity, notification, exchange of information and consultation on activities under their jurisdiction or control which are likely to significantly affect adversely the biological diversity of other States or areas beyond the limits of national jurisdiction, by encouraging the conclusion of bilateral, regional or multilateral arrangements, as appropriate;*

    (d) *In the case of imminent or grave danger or damage, originating under its jurisdiction or control, to biological diversity within the area under jurisdiction of other States or in areas beyond the limits of national jurisdiction, notify immediately the potentially affected States of such danger or damage, as well as initiate action to prevent or minimise such danger or damage; and*

    (e) *Promote national arrangements for emergency responses to activities or events, whether caused naturally or otherwise, which present a grave and imminent danger to biological diversity and encourage international cooperation to supplement such national efforts and, where appropriate and agreed by the States or regional economic integration organisations concerned, to establish joint contingency plans.*

The participatory principle, or the principle of non-discrimination, is a significant part of the duty to cooperate, especially where a transboundary EIA procedure is envisaged. As will be seen in the next chapter, the Espoo and Aarhus Conventions feature this prominently and are therefore two of the best examples of its inclusion in treaty law. Pallemaerts (2004, p69) cites the 1985 ASEAN Agreement on the Conservation of Nature and Natural Resources[52] as the first regional agreement to give effect to the principle, and more recently, the African Union's 2003 African Convention on the

Conservation of Nature and Natural Resources.[53] He defines the principle as follows, including reference to the role of strategic proposals (p69):

> *The participatory principle essentially calls for environmental information to be made public and disseminated as widely as possible, for public participation to be guaranteed in decision-making on projects, plans and programmes with significant environmental implications, and for access to justice to be granted to the public in environmental matters.*

Compensation for environmental damage

What is understood generally by environmental damage in international law remains uncertain (Bowman, 2002; Boyle, 2002; De La Fayette, 2002; Brunnée, 2004). While states may be required to prevent environmental damage, there is little threat of sanction should they fail to do so, limiting the effectiveness of treaty provisions in most instances. In regard to existing liability regimes, the only treaties that require costs to be borne directly by those that cause them are in relation to 'ultra-hazardous activities', such as those that deal with oil pollution, nuclear incidents or, more recently, hazardous wastes,[54] where damage is likely to be far more than basic pollution. This is largely because of the presence of a substantive prohibition of harm contained within. The standard of care here is one of strict liability, under which states are liable for all damage caused by them, regardless of where it occurs and regardless of fault.

In most cases, however, states are expected to exercise 'due diligence', meaning that they should have in place measures to control public and private acts that may result in harm. Article 194 of UNCLOS, for example, merely obliges states to take measures to prevent, reduce and control pollution using 'the best practicable means available to them and in accordance with their capabilities'. Article 6 of the CBD requires states to develop strategies and integrated programmes and policies 'in accordance with particular conditions and capabilities', therefore establishing the notion of common but differentiated standards of responsibility for what amounts to due diligence. Little guidance is typically available for what is reasonably required, and in common with other provisions, Article 6 of LRTAP just requires states to use the 'best available technology'. Article 6 of the CBD is supplemented by Article 14(2), which follows the provisions for prevention and cooperation that are found in Article 14(1). As such, while not requiring compensation, it consolidates those provisions by indicating the linked nature of the three underlying duties of IEL. Article 14(2) is therefore cited in full:

> *The Conference of the Parties shall examine, on the basis of studies to be carried out, the issue of liability and redress, including restoration and compensation, for damage to biological diversity, except where such liability is a purely internal matter.*

With regard to the polluter pays principle, Pallemaerts (2004, p65) points to Europe as the driving force for its early development in hard law, with the 1986 Single European Act amending the EEC Treaty to insert specific provisions on environmental policy.[55] Article 130R(2) of the Treaty includes the polluter pays principle as one of the general principles of the Community's environmental policy. Outside Europe, Pallemaerts (2004, p65) highlights that there has been 'scant recognition of the principle in universal hard law instruments', with incorporation mostly in the preambles of the various multilateral environmental agreements (MEAs), which means that it is merely to be used as an aid in interpreting what the substantive provisions require, not a substantive provision in itself. He cites the 1990 IMO Convention on Oil Pollution Preparedness, Response and Cooperation,[56] where it is referred to in the preamble as 'a general principle of international environmental law'. The strongest example of its inclusion appears to be in the 1992 Convention for the Protection of the Marine Environment of the North-East Atlantic (OSPAR Convention),[57] which requires in Article 2(2)(b) that 'Contracting Parties shall apply the polluter pays principle'. Most other instruments merely state that parties should be 'guided by' or 'take into account' the principle (p66).

Recent research has focused on the incorporation of the principle at a national and supranational level. Of particular interest here is the incorporation of the principle as part of the European Directive on Environmental Liability (see Betlem and Brans, 2006). Larsen (2005, p559) examines this in depth and concludes:

> *The new environmental liability regime aims at making the polluter pay for remediating the damage that he has caused. Environmental regulation aims at establishing norms and procedures through which the environment is preserved, and it will allow the European Community to challenge potential polluters to comply, or to restore and compensate for, the damage that they have caused according to the polluter pays principle.*

This is examined in detail in Chapter 9.

SOFT LAW

An overview of the soft law developments was presented in the early part of this chapter, with reference to some of the principles of IEL including EIA. For completeness, this section considers how the three duties of harm prevention, cooperation and compensation have been explicitly included in soft law instruments.

Prevention of environmental harm

Principle 21 of the *Stockholm Declaration* provides that states have 'the sovereign right to exploit their own resources pursuant to their own environmental policies, and the responsibility to ensure that activities within their jurisdiction or control do not cause damage to the environment of other States or of areas beyond the limits of national jurisdiction'. The principle has been a starting point for much customary and treaty law development since, and has been cited as the 'cornerstone of IEL' by Sands (1995, p186). The principle has been interpreted to mean that states have the right to exploit their own resources provided that they ensure that activities within their jurisdiction or control do not harm the environment beyond their territory (Knox, 2002, p293).

However, as Knox identifies on the same page, Principle 21 has the major problem that 'it does not enjoy the necessary support in state practice' for it to have become a principle of customary international law.

Judicial opinion in itself would therefore appear to not be enough, for although the ICJ has said that: 'The existence of the general obligation of States to ensure that activities within their jurisdiction and control respect the environment of other States or of areas beyond national control is now part of the corpus of international law relating to the environment',[58] the reality would appear somewhat different. This is because if it had become a principle of customary international law, then the transboundary harm that is a frequent occurrence would not exist. Knox believes the key term 'respect' is so vague that it fails to provide the clarity that is needed, including whether Principle 21 emphasizes resource exploitation or protection (2002, p295).

Woodliffe (2002) emphasizes the role of the Organisation for Economic Co-operation and Development (OECD) in its work on transboundary issues in the 1970s as also being a significant driver for harm prevention. He states that 'Prevention of future environmental deterioration was viewed as the most important way of realizing environmental policy goals, in the implementation of which "prior assessment of the environmental consequences of significant public and private activities" assumed an essential part' (p135). Transfrontier pollution issues occupied the OECD initially but in 1979 it recommended that EIA be introduced for all situations where there might be significant transboundary effects (OECD, 1979).

The failure to clarify Principle 21 at the Rio Conference further suggests that states do not wish to be bound by a more substantive duty to prohibit all environmental harm, with Principle 2 of the *Rio Declaration* being in virtually identical terms to the original Principle 21. Principle 21 must therefore be seen for what it is, which is a soft law provision requiring significant or substantial damage before it can be enforced and even then with the defence of due diligence available in most cases; it therefore remains to develop fully into customary law, primarily as a result of the absence of state practice.

Principles 14 and 15 of the *Declaration* are also relevant because of the focus on planning. This is because whether in relation to land use, transport or related sectors, planning has traditionally been the framework within which assessment of proposals has been undertaken. Principle 14 therefore states that 'rational planning constitutes an essential tool for reconciling any conflict between the needs of development and the need to protect and improve the environment'. Principle 15 states that 'planning must be applied to human settlements and urbanization with a view to avoiding adverse effects on the environment and obtaining maximum social, economic and environmental benefits for all'.

The soft law relating to harm prevention also includes the precautionary principle, with the *World Charter for Nature* in 1982 holding that 'where potential adverse effects are not fully understood, the activities should not proceed'.[59] Principle 15 of the *Rio Declaration* in 1992 recognized the principle more explicitly, albeit in relation to the principle of common but differentiated responsibilities,[60] stating that 'in order to protect the environment, the precautionary approach shall be widely applied by states according to their capabilities'.

Cooperation in transboundary situations

There are many references to EIA in soft law instruments, some which concern both harm prevention and cooperation. Following Principle 24 of the *Stockholm Declaration* 1972, one of the earliest is found in Article 11 of the *World Charter for Nature* 1982, which is set out in full:

> *Activities which might have an impact on nature shall be controlled, and the best available technologies that minimise significant risks to nature and other adverse effects shall be used; in particular;*
>
> (a)   *Activities that are likely to cause irreversible damage to nature shall be avoided;*
>
> (b)   *Activities that are likely to pose a significant risk to nature shall be preceded by an exhaustive examination; their proponents shall demonstrate that expected benefits outweigh potential damage to nature, and where potential adverse effects are not fully understood, the activities shall not proceed;*
>
> (c)   *Activities which may disturb nature shall be preceded by assessment of their consequences, and environmental impact studies of development projects shall be conducted sufficiently in advance, and if they are to be undertaken, such activities shall be planned and carried out so as to minimise potential adverse effects*

The *Rio Declaration* 1992 is one of the most significant soft law instruments as it sets out numerous principles that have become customary norms or part of treaty law, or indeed are already such, reaffirming their significance. Principle 10 of the *Rio Declaration* is also a classic exposition of the participatory principle in soft law. This calls for environmental information to be made public and distributed as widely as possible for the public to be permitted to participate in environmental decision making and for access to justice to be granted to the public.[61] Without setting out any substantive obligations, Principle 17 sets out the requirement for EIA:

> *Environmental impact assessment, as a national instrument, shall be undertaken for proposed activities that are likely to have a significant adverse impact on the environment and are subject to a decision of a competent national authority.*

Sands (1995, p579) indicates that the language of this principle is such that EIA could, in certain circumstances, be required as a matter of customary international law. However, as he points out, it is described as a 'national instrument' that could arguably preclude transboundary impacts from consideration. Significance is also not defined, and it suggests that activities that are not subject to decisions by competent authorities are excluded.

Compensation for environmental damage

Knox (2002) also considers liability issues consequent upon his examination of the efficacy of Principle 21 of the *Stockholm Declaration*. As he says, 'normally, the law of state responsibility would suggest that in the event of a violation of the principle (however characterized), the state of origin would be bound to make good any resulting harm to the affected state' (p294). However, the ILC has considered whether liability should be strict, so that even if due diligence is exercised, there should be an obligation to make good any resulting damage. The present position with respect to a potential convention on state responsibility (as discussed in Chapter 2) suggests that this is unlikely.

De Mulder (1996) therefore rightly indicates that there is a heavy emphasis on the use and application of national law when it comes to implementation of international obligations, whether in hard or soft law. He refers to Principle 13 of the *Rio Declaration* that says 'States shall develop national law regarding liability and compensation for the victims of pollution and other environmental damage' (p2). Clearly the relevance of this to transboundary impacts, given the restrictions on national jurisdiction is limited, but together with Principle 17 (above) and the likely fate of the ILC draft articles, it would appear that the preference of the international community is for harm to be dealt with by the state responsible for it, rather than for international solutions to be found.

ENFORCEMENT OF IEL

Chapter 2 provided an overview of existing UN institutions, explaining the role of the ICJ and the enforcement methods available to it and other bodies in international law; it also discussed the proliferation of international courts and tribunals, several of which are today active in environmental matters. Enforcement of environmental matters raises a number of issues for consideration (see Faure and Lefevere, 1999; Brunnée, 2005; Stroll and Wolfrum, 2006) that have been a focus of recent international conferences (where priority has been given to the implementation of existing treaties, rather than the development of new agreements), and of the COPs/MOPs (which have also been concerned to ensure the effective application of treaty provisions, including those that deal with dispute settlement). Enforcement of the duties established in IEL between one state and another has been examined above in this chapter.

Rest (1998, 1999, 2004) comments on the need for the international judiciary to enforce IEL. There are several reasons for this. First, the behaviour of states must fall within judicial control as states themselves may commit or allow environmental destruction; second, only an independent judiciary can scrutinize the implementation of treaty law; third, the protection of the global commons (such as the high seas, seabed and Antarctica) is dependent on the actions of an international judiciary, and possibly also that of a human right to a decent environment (although this has also been enforced by national courts); and fourth, for political and economic reasons, states may also be reluctant to take action to protect their own citizens if another state has been responsible for transboundary pollution.

Rest specifically examines the role of individuals and NGOs in accessing the judiciary,[62] reviewing the full range of international courts and tribunals established to ensure enforcement of treaties and custom, some specific to the environment but most not. These include the ICJ, the International Tribunal for the Law of the Sea (established by UNCLOS), the International Criminal Court (ICC, which includes jurisdiction to examine 'crimes against the environment') and the Permanent Court of Arbitration (PCA), which he believes may be the best institution to take forward individual complaints (see 2004, pp20–22). One recent case, albeit concerning state action, and which is examined in detail in Chapter 12, dealt with proceedings taken by Ireland against the UK in the PCA in relation to the *MOX plant*.

Rest refers to Principle 10 of the Rio Declaration and the development of the Aarhus Convention (see Chapter 4) in examining whether individuals have (or should have) access to the courts and tribunals currently in existence, or whether an alternative forum is needed to ensure that they do. He concludes (not surprisingly) that at present the structure of the international court system favours states, although individuals and NGOs may now seek redress with regard to national matters in national courts. However, 'as soon as *transboundary or transnational effects* and objectives of international environmental law are at stake, national jurisdiction may be deficient or even fail' (Rest, 2004, p5). He refers to German case law to substantiate his argument, which 'reflect the general tendency that in cases of transboundary/transnational pollution, the injured individual victims have no prospect of success and only a limited opportunity to bring an action against a foreign polluter, and specifically against a foreign polluter-state or its organs before national courts' (2004, p6). This is a matter that will be considered further in Chapter 12 with regard to the differences between international and European law.[63]

CONCLUSIONS

This chapter has provided an overview of IEL; it has also given a detailed analysis of the custom, treaty and soft law duties that are of relevance to EIA. What it has not done is consider issues of effectiveness of international regimes, which is a topical matter well examined elsewhere and that is largely demonstrated 'in the international relations domain' (see, for example, Zovko, 2006, p109). Matters of enforcement and judicial compliance with international law generally were examined in Chapter 2, together with the role of international law in a domestic context. The subject of effectiveness is of course concerned with much more than procedural compliance, as emphasized in Chapter 1. Since the Rio Earth Summit and the Johannesburg meeting, much greater emphasis has been placed on the enforcement and effectiveness of IEL regimes. In part this is explained by the lack of political will for further MEAs and, related, the financial constraints that many environmental regimes are operating under. Chapter 4 considers the question of effectiveness to some extent with regard to the Espoo Convention, and Chapter 6 with respect to the conservation conventions, which have cooperated significantly with one another in recent times through the medium of EA.

This chapter has demonstrated the similarities between the underlying duties and principles in IEL in customary, treaty and soft law and those found in the familiar EIA procedure that operates on a national level. It has also explained and analysed provisions of relevance to the Espoo and Aarhus treaties that assist an understanding of the SEA Protocol. The overall conclusion of this chapter is that despite the development of national EIA to some extent mirroring the development of the principles of customary law of relevance to it, it may also be true to say that national EIA has spread around the world largely on its own merits, rather than specifically as a result of international law.[64] To ignore the relevance of international law to national EIA procedure is, however, to ignore the benefits that any legal framework can bring. Providing opportunities for the enforcement of procedural (and potentially substantive) legal obligations, is uppermost among these. Chapter 4 examines the Espoo and Aarhus conventions and Chapter 5 the SEA Protocol. In each case the influence of the duties and principles of IEL can be seen.

NOTES

1   Please see Bastmeijer and Koivurova (2008) and Craik (2008), which fill a significant gap in the literature. See also Mallepree (2005).
2   Recommended texts include Birnie and Boyle (2002) and Sands (1995, 2003). For an overview, see Pallemaerts (2004) and Weiss (1999), the latter now somewhat dated. See also Bodansky et al (2007).
3   Convention on Biological Diversity (Rio de Janeiro, 5 June 1992), 31 ILM (1992) 818; in force 29 December 1993; for background and analysis, see McConnell (1996) and Nagle and Ruhl (2002).
4   Convention on Wetlands of International Importance, Especially as Waterfowl Habitat (Ramsar, 2 February 1971), 11 ILM (1972) 963; in force 21 December 1975; Amended 1982 and 1987.
5   Convention on the Conservation of Migratory Species of Wild Animals (Bonn, 23 June 1979), 19 ILM (1980) 15; in force 1 November 1983.
6   UNESCO Convention Concerning the Protection of the World Cultural and Natural Heritage, (Paris, 1972), 11 ILM (1972) 1358; in force 17 December 1975.
7   International conferences such as the UN Conference on the Human Environment 1972 in Stockholm (UNCHE) and the UN Conference on Environment and Development 1992 in Rio (UNCED) are examples of these international conferences, which must not be confused with the COPs or MOPs established under treaty regimes, the decisions of which are binding.
8   Declaration of the United Nations Conference on the Human Environment (Stockholm, 16 June 1972), UN Doc A/CONF/48/14/REV.1; B & B Docs 1.
9   United Nations General Assembly Resolution 37/7 and Annex: World Charter for Nature (28 October 1982), UN Doc A/ 37/51 (1982).
10 United Nations Commission on Environment and Development, *Our Common Future* (1987); see generally Soroos (1999).
11 UNEP/United Nations Environment Programme Governing Council (1987) *Goals and Principles of Environmental Impact Assessment*, Dec 14/25, UN Doc. UNEP/GC/DEC/14/25 (1987).
12 Framework Convention on Climate Change, 31 ILM (1992), 851; in force 21 March 1994.
13 Declaration of the United Nations Conference on Environment and Development, UN Doc A/CONF.151/26/Rev.1, *Report of the UNCED*, vol 1 (New York); B&B Docs 9, 1992.
14 Non-Legally Binding Authoritative Statement of Principles for a Global Consensus on the Management, Conservation and Sustainable Development of all Types of Forests, 31 ILM (1992) 881.
15 UNCED, *Report*, I (1992); see Bryner (1999).

16 The effectiveness and legitimacy of UNEP and other environmental institutions is also evaluated by Andresen (2007a) and Andresen and Hey (2007). Alongside the United Nations Development Programme (UNDP) it scores highly in terms of legitimacy, but is regarded as less effective than financial institutions such as the World Bank.

17 United Nations Convention on the Law of the Sea (Montego Bay, 10 December 1982), 21 ILM (1982) 1261; in force 16 November 1994.

18 Protocol on Biosafety (Cartagena), 39 ILM (2000), 1027; not in force.

19 Protocol to the Framework Convention on Climate Change (Kyoto), 37 ILM (1998), 22.

20 Note that the SEA Protocol, while concluded under the auspices of the Espoo Convention is a largely self-contained agreement providing for SEA at the national level. Although it also contains a provision for transboundary SEA and is subject to certain procedural provisions of the Espoo Convention, it is not primarily concerned with transboundary EA.

21 UN Agreement Relating to the Conservation and Management of Straddling Fish Stocks and Migratory Fish Stocks, 34 ILM 1542 (1995) 6 *YbIEL* 841; not in force.

22 Some authors controversially dispute whether the duty is a customary norm to prevent transboundary harm or is in fact a customary norm *allowing* transboundary harm. This is evidenced by some judicial comment, but mainly by state practice whereby pollutants commonly travel across state boundaries with little or no objection by other states. See Roberts (2001) who cites Bodansky (1995). See also Knox (2002).

23 Note that here Pallemaerts (2004) is referring to legislation or judicial precedent with hard law, binding effect. Rules of law should also not be confused with the *rule of law*, which was explained in Chapter 1 and distinguished from *rule by law*, the former meaning that everyone (including the government) is bound by the legitimate laws of society, the latter that the government abuses its authority in the name of the law.

24 *Trail Smelter Arbitration (United States of America v Canada)* (1938) RIAA Volume 3, 1905; 9 ILR 315.

25 *The Corfu Channel Case (United Kingdom v Albania) (Merits)* [1949] ICJ Reports 4.

26 *Lac Lanoux Arbitration (France v Spain)* 24 ILR 101.

27 For examples of how the precautionary principle has filtered down to the national level, see Gustavson (2003) and Stein (2000).

28 The author's own experience of this in relation to a policy maker attempting to explain to a legislative draftsperson the difference between the saturated and unsaturated zones that can be encapsulated into wording for site contamination law is instructive.

29 See Separate Opinion of Judge Weeramantry, *Request for an Examination of the Situation in Accordance with Paragraph 63 of the Court's Judgement of 20 December 1974 in Nuclear Tests (New Zealand v France)* (1995) ICJ Reports 288.

30 *Case Concerning the Gabcíkovo-Nagymaros Project (Hungary/Slovakia)*, ICJ Reports 1997, 7 (see also (1998) 37 ILM 162).

31 *Request for an Examination of the Situation in Accordance with Paragraph 63 of the Court's Judgment of 20 December 1974 in Nuclear Tests (New Zealand v France)* (1995) ICJ Reports 288.

32 See Separate Opinion of Judge Weeramantry, *Case Concerning the Gabcíkovo-Nagymaros Project (Hungary/Slovakia)*, ICJ Reports 1997, 1, 15 (see also (1998) 37 ILM 162).

33 Because of the limitations of EIA to force decisions, some authors question the effectiveness of EIA. Knox (2002, p317) refers to the calls by some to amend NEPA in the US to provide for a substantive prohibition on environmental harm, for example.

34 Knox concludes (2002) that the reason for the criticism is largely a misunderstanding of the purpose of EIA, which is to improve decisions. In his words 'it aims not so much at increasing environmental protection as at improving decision making with environmental effects' (p318).

35 Under the criminal law, liability may be absolute, strict or fault based. To secure a conviction for a crime, certain things must be proved by the prosecution. Absolute liability requires

no evidence of a wrongful action or intention, merely that an event has happened, even if committed by someone else (such as a former polluter on land currently held by the accused); strict liability requires evidence only of a wrongful action, with no need to prove intention; and fault based liability requires evidence of both a wrongful action and intention. For further information (including examples), see Waite (2005).

36 Treaty between the United States and Great Britain Respecting Boundary Waters between the United States and Canada (Washington, 1909), 4 AJIL (Suppl) 239; in force 5 May 1910.

37 The global commons are areas beyond the territorial jurisdiction of any state. They include the high seas, deep seabed, outer space and arguably Antarctica, despite the territorial claims already made there. In the last of these especially, this is sometimes referred to as the common heritage of (hu)mankind. See second part of Bastmeijer and Koivurova (2007).

38 UNECE Convention on Long-Range Transboundary Air Pollution (Geneva, 13 November 1979), 1302 UNTS 217; in force 16 March 1983; Protocols of 1984, 1985, 1988, 1991, 1994 and 1998.

39 International Tribunal for the Law of the Sea, Order of 27 August 1999, *Southern Bluefin Tuna Cases (New Zealand v Japan, Australia v Japan)*, www.itlos.org/start2_en.html at para 80.

40 International Tribunal for the Law of the Sea, Order of 3 December 2001, *The MOX Plant Case (Ireland v United Kingdom)*, www.itlos.org/start2_en.html Note this case is discussed in Chapters 8 and 12 concerning European environmental law and the relationship between international and European law.

41 International Tribunal for the Law of the Sea, Order of 8 October 2003, *Case Concerning Land Reclamation by Singapore in and around the Straits of Johor (Malaysia v Singapore)*, www.itlos. org/start2_en.html at paras 95-99.

42 Convention on International Trade in Endangered Species of Wild Fauna and Flora (Washington), 12 ILM 1085 (1973); in force 1 July 1975; see Resolution Conf. 9.24 (Rev. COP13).

43 See Ramsar Guidelines on Management Planning for Wetlands (Resolution VIII.14 Chapter VI) and the Resolution on Allocation and Management of Water (Resolution VIII.1 Article 10.1), the CMS resolution on Wind Turbines and Migratory Species (Resolution 7.5), and the Agreement on the Conservation of Albatrosses and Petrels 2001.

44 ASEAN Agreement on the Conservation of Nature and Natural Resources (Kuala Lumpur, 1985); not in force.

45 UNECE Convention on the Protection and Use of Transboundary Watercourses and International Lakes (Helsinki, 17 March 1992), 31 ILM 1312; in force 6 October 1996. Note also the Protocol on Water and Health 1999 to the 1992 Convention; Article 4(6) requires EIA.

46 UN Convention on the Law of the Non-Navigable Uses of International Watercourses (New York, 21 May 1997), 36 ILM (1997) 719; not in force.

47 Nordic Convention on the Protection of the Environment (Stockholm, 1974), 13 ILM (1974) 511; in force 5 October 1976.

48 Convention on Early Notification of a Nuclear Accident (Vienna, 1986), 25 ILM (1986) 1370; in force 27 October 1986; see also Convention on Nuclear Safety (Vienna, 20 September 1994), 33 ILM (1994) 1518; in force 24 October 1996.

49 Convention on the Control of Transboundary Movements of Hazardous Wastes and their Disposal (Basel, 22 March 1989), 28 ILM (1989) 657; in force 24 May 1992.

50 Protocol to the Antarctic Treaty on Environmental Protection (Madrid, 4 October 1991), 30 ILM (1991), 1461; in force 14 January 1998.

51 For others, see footnote 4 in Ebbesson (1999, p48).

52 See note 44 above.

53 African Convention on the Conservation of Nature and Natural Resources (Maputo, 11 July 2003); not yet in force.

54 See the International Convention on Civil Liability for Oil Pollution Damage (Brussels, 1969), 9 ILM (1970), 45; in force 19 June 1975. Note also Convention on Third Party Liability in the Field of Nuclear Energy (Paris, 1960), UKTS 69; in force 1 April 1968, amended 1964; in force 7 October 1988. Finally, the Protocol on Liability and Compensation for Damage Resulting from Transboundary Movements of Hazardous Wastes and Their Disposal (Basel, 10 December, 1999). Note that the ILC draft convention on environmental harm also includes provisions for transboundary EIA.

55 The status of European law is analysed in Chapter 7 and the relationship between it and international law in Chapter 12. For now, it is sufficient to comment that European law is for many international lawyers an example of a self-contained regime in international law terms. While it operates largely autonomously therefore it has a basis of treaties made between the member states that can appropriately be referred to as examples of treaty law.

56 International Convention on Oil Pollution Preparedness, Response and Cooperation 1990, London 30 November 1990, in force 13 May 1995, 30 ILM (1991) 735.

57 Convention for the Protection of the Marine Environment of the North East Atlantic 1992, Paris, 22 September 1992; in force 25 March 1998, 32 ILM (1993) 1072. This convention is considered in Chapter 12 concerning the relationship between international and European law in the MOX Plant case.

58 ICJ Advisory Opinion, *Legality of the Threat or Use of Nuclear Weapons*, 1996, ICJ Reports 226, pp241–42.

59 *World Charter for Nature*, para 11. GA Res. 37/7, 28 October 1982.

60 For further exposition of this principle, see Pallemaerts (2004, pp67–68).

61 Other soft law pronouncements on the participatory principle include the World Charter for Nature (above) and the *Malmö Ministerial Declaration*, 31 May 2000.

62 See generally, McCormick (1999).

63 Note that MEAs often include compliance mechanisms that parties (and in some instance individuals and NGOs) can access. The Aarhus Convention is a very good example of this, which is considered in the next chapter.

64 See Robinson (1993, p679) as cited in Knox (2002, p297).

REFERENCES

Andresen, S. (2007a) 'The effectiveness of UN environmental institutions', *International Environmental Agreements*, vol 4, no 7, pp317–336

Andresen, S. (2007b) 'Key actors in UN environmental governance: Influence, reform and leadership', *International Environmental Agreements*, vol 4, no 7, pp457–468

Andresen, S. and Hey, E. (2005) 'The effectiveness and legitimacy of international environmental institutions', *International Environmental Agreements*, vol 5, pp211–226

Bastmeijer, K. and Koivurova, T. (eds) (2008) *Theory and Practice of Transboundary Environmental Impact Assessment*, Martinus Nijhoff, Leiden and Boston, MA

Betlem, G. and Brans, E. (eds) (2006) *Environmental Liability in the EU: The 2004 Directive Compared with US and Member State Law*, Cameron May, London

Birnie, P. and Boyle, A. (2002) *International Law and the Environment*, 2nd Edition, Oxford University Press, Oxford

Bodansky, D. (1995) 'Customary (and not so customary) international environmental law', *Indiana Journal of Global Legal Studies*, vol 3, pp105–119

Bodansky, D., Brunnée, J. and Hey, E. (2007) *The Oxford Handbook of International Environmental Law*, Oxford University Press, Oxford

Bowman, M. (2002) 'The definition and valuation of environmental harm: An overview' in M. Bowman and A. Boyle (eds) *Environmental Damage in International and Comparative Law: Problems of Definition and Valuation*, Oxford University Press, Oxford, pp1–15

Bowman, M. and Boyle, A. (2002) *Environmental Damage in International and Comparative Law: Problems of Definition and Valuation*, Oxford University Press, Oxford

Boyle, A. (2002) 'Reparation for environmental damage in international law: Some preliminary problems' in M. Bowman and A. Boyle (eds) *Environmental Damage in International and Comparative Law: Problems of Definition and Valuation*, Oxford University Press, Oxford, pp17–26

Brunnée, J. (2004) 'Of sense and sensibility: Reflections on international liability regimes as tools for environmental protection', *International and Comparative Law Quarterly*, vol 53, pp351–368

Brunnée, J. (2005) 'Enforcement mechanisms of international law and international environmental law', in D. Zaelke, D. Kaniaru and E. Kruziková (eds) *Making Law Work: Environmental Compliance and Sustainable Development*, Cameron May, London

Bryner, G.C. (1999) 'Agenda 21: Myth or reality?' in N. J. Vig and R. S. Axelrod (eds) *The Global Environment: Institutions, Law and Policy*, Earthscan, London, pp157–189

Burns, W. (2005) 'Introduction to special issue on the precautionary principle and its operationalisation in international environmental regimes and domestic policymaking', *International Journal of Global Environmental Issues*, vol 5, no 1/2, pp1–9

Cooney, R. (2005) 'From promise to practicalities: The precautionary principle in biodiversity conservation and sustainable use' in R. Cooney and B. Dickson (eds) *Biodiversity and the Precautionary Principle: Risk and Uncertainty in Conservation and Sustainable Use*, Earthscan, London, pp3–17

Craik, N. (2008) *The International Law of Environmental Impact Assessment: Process, Substance and Integration*, Cambridge University Press, Cambridge

Crawford, J. and Olleson, S. (2005) 'The continuing debate on a UN convention on state responsibility', *International and Comparative Law Quarterly*, vol 54, pp959–972

Dawson, F. (2004) 'Analysing the goals of biodiversity conservation: Scientific, policy and legal perspectives', *Environmental and Planning Law Journal*, vol 21, pp6–26

De La Fayette, L. (2002) 'The concept of environmental damage in international liability regimes' in M. Bowman and A. Boyle (eds) *Environmental Damage in International and Comparative Law: Problems of Definition and Valuation*, Oxford University Press, Oxford, pp149–189

De Mulder, J. (1996) 'The legal environment of (environmental and social) impact assessment in the development process' in *Integrating Environmental Assessment and Socio-Economic Appraisal*, EIA Centre, University of Manchester and University of Bradford

De Sadeleer, N. (2002) *Environmental Principles: From Political Slogans to Legal Rules*, Oxford University Press, Oxford

Ebbesson, J. (1999) 'Innovative elements and expected effectiveness of the 1991 EIA convention', *Environmental Impact Assessment Review*, vol 19, pp47–55

Ellis, J. (2006) 'Overexploitation of a valuable resource? New literature on the precautionary principle', *European Journal of International Law*, vol 17, no 2, pp445–462

Faure, M. and Lefevere, J. (1999) 'Compliance with international environmental agreements' in N. J. Vig and R. S. Axelrod (eds) *The Global Environment: Institutions, Law and Policy*, Earthscan, London, pp138–156.

Freestone, D. and Hey, E. (1999) *The Precautionary Principle and International Law: The Challenge of Implementation*, Kluwer, London

Gustavson, K. (2003) 'Applying the precautionary principle in environmental assessment: The case of reviews in British Columbia', *Journal of Environmental Planning and Management*, vol 46, no 3, pp365–379

Hanqin, X. (2003) *Transboundary Damage in International Law*, Cambridge University Press, Cambridge

IUCN (International Union for the Conservation of Nature) (2007) *Guidelines for Applying the Precautionary Principle to Biodiversity Conservation and Natural Resource Management*, IUCN, Gland

Knox, J. (2002) 'The myth and reality of transboundary environmental impact assessment', *American Journal of International Law*, vol 96, no 2, pp291–319

Koivurova, T. (2002) *Environmental Impact Assessment in the Arctic: A Study of International Legal Norms*, Ashgate, Aldershot

Larsen, E. (2005) 'Why environmental liability regimes in the US, European Community and Japan have grown synonymous with the polluter pays principle', *Vanderbilt Journal of Transnational Law*, vol 38, pp541–575

Mallepree, V. (2005) 'Trans-boundary EIA provisions and initiatives in selected regional and multilateral environmental agreements, a comparative review', UNECE, unpublished Secretariat document

McConnell, F. (1996) *The Biodiversity Convention: A Negotiating History*, Kluwer, London

McCormick, J. (1999) 'The role of environmental NGOs in international regimes' in N. J. Vig and R. S. Axelrod (eds) (1999) *The Global Environment: Institutions, Law and Policy*, Earthscan, London, pp52–71

Morris, J. (2000) *Rethinking Risk and the Precautionary Principle*, Butterworth-Heinemann, London

Munro, R. D., and Lammers, J. G. (1986) *Environmental Protection And Sustainable Development*, Experts Group on Environmental Law of the World Commission on Environment and Development, Graham and Trotman/Martinus Nijhoff Publishers, London

Nagle, J. and Ruhl, J. (2002) *The Law of Biodiversity and Ecosystem Management*, Foundation Press, New York

OECD (Organisation for Economic Cooperation and Development) (1979) *The Assessment of Projects with Significant Impact on the Environment*, Recommendation C(79), OECD, Paris, p116

Pallemaerts, M. (2004) 'An introduction to the sources, principles and regimes of international environmental law' in M. Berglund (ed) *International Environmental Law Making and Diplomacy*, *UNEP Course Series 2*, University of Joensuu, Joensuu, pp61–96

Raffensperger, C. and Tickner, J. (1999) *Protecting Public Health and the Environment: Implementing the Precautionary Principle*, Island Press, Washington DC

Rayfuse, R. (2005) 'International environmental law' in S. Blay, R. Piotrowicz and M. Tsamenyi (eds) *Public International Law: An Australian Perspective*, 2nd Edition, Oxford University Press, Melbourne, Vic, pp352–378

Rest, A. (1998) 'The indispensability of an international environmental court', *Review of European Community and International Environmental Law*, vol 7, no 1, pp63–67

Rest, A. (1999) 'An international court for the environment: The role of the Permanent Court of Arbitration', *Asia Pacific Journal of Environmental Law*, vol 4, pp107–129

Rest, A. (2004) 'Enhanced implementation of international environmental treaties by judiciary – access to justice in international environmental law for individuals and NGOs: Efficacious enforcement by the Permanent Court of Arbitration', *Macquarie Journal of International and Comparative Environmental Law*, vol 1, pp1–28

Roberts, A. (2001) 'Traditional and modern approaches to customary international law: a reconciliation', *American Journal of International Law*, vol 95, no 4, pp757–791

Robinson, N. (1993) 'EIA abroad: the comparative and transnational experience' in S. Hildebrand and J. Cannon (eds) *Environmental Analysis: The NEPA Experience*, Lewis Publishers, Florida

Sands, P. (1995) *Principles of International Environmental Law*, Manchester University Press, Manchester

Sands, P. (1999) 'Environmental protection in the twenty-first century: Sustainable development and international law' in N. J. Vig and R. S. Axelrod (eds) *The Global Environment: Institutions, Law and Policy*, Earthscan, London, pp116–137

Sands, P. (2003) *Principles of International Environmental Law I: Frameworks, Standards and Implementation*, 2nd Edition, Cambridge University Press, Cambridge

Shelton, D. and Kiss, A. (2005) *Judicial Handbook on Environmental Law*, United Nations Environment Programme, Stevenage

Soroos, M. S. (1999) 'Global institutions and the environment: An evolutionary perspective' in N. J. Vig and R. S. Axelrod (eds) *The Global Environment: Institutions, Law and Policy*, Earthscan, London, pp27–51

Stein, P. (2000) 'Are decision-makers too cautious with the precautionary principle?', *Environmental and Planning Law Journal*, vol 17, no 1, pp3–21

Stroll, P. T. and Wolfrum, R. (eds) (2006) *Ensuring Compliance with Multilateral Environmental Agreements: A Dialogue between Practitioners and Academia*, Martinus, Nijhoff

Trouwborst, A. (2002) *Evolution and Status of the Precautionary Principle in International Law*, Kluwer, Dordrecht

Waite, A. (2005) 'The quest for environmental law equilibrium', *Environmental Law Review*, vol 7, pp34–62

Weiss, E. B. (1999) 'The emerging structure of international environmental law' in N. J. Vig and R. S. Axelrod (eds) (1999) *The Global Environment: Institutions, Law and Policy*, Earthscan, London, pp98–115

Woodliffe, J. (2002) 'Environmental damage and environmental impact assessment' in M. Bowman and A. Boyle (eds) (2002) *Environmental Damage in International and Comparative Law: Problems of Definition and Valuation*, Oxford University Press, Oxford, pp133–147

Zovko, I. (2006) 'International law-making for the environment: A question of effectiveness' in M. Berglund (ed) *International Environmental Law Making and Diplomacy*, UNEP Course Series 2, University of Joensuu, Joensuu, pp109–128

CHAPTER 4

The Espoo and Aarhus Conventions

CHAPTER OUTLINE

This chapter is concerned with the Espoo[1] and Aarhus[2] Conventions, which are considered in detail where relevant to the SEA Protocol (see generally Marsden, 2002; Marsden and De Mulder, 2005). The chapter builds on the previous two chapters on international law by further explaining the role of IGOs in the context of the UNECE and examining the self-governing provisions of the conventions. In doing so, it discusses the relevance of the three duties of IEL outlined in Chapter 3 and considers compliance and enforcement issues. All of these matters have relevance for the SEA Protocol, which is the subject of Chapter 5.

UNITED NATIONS ECONOMIC COMMISSION FOR EUROPE

As Connelly indicates (1999, p38), the UNECE was established as a key UN organization for ongoing dialogue and improved relationships among eastern and western European countries, Canada and the US at a time of high political tension in the early 1970s. The signature of the Final Act of the Conference on Security and Cooperation in Europe (CSCE) in 1975, with two references to the environment therein, led to a referral to the UNECE of an examination of two transboundary environmental issues, long-range transmission of air pollutants and the concept of EIA, including its later application to PPPs (see, for example, UNECE, 1991, 1992). The former was motivated by concerns about acid rain, the latter in part as a result of the US promulgation of NEPA in 1969 and development of EIA globally thereafter, together with Principle 21 of the *Stockholm Declaration*.

Reflecting its original purpose, it has since been responsible for a significant amount of treaty development in a transboundary context. As seen, the Convention on LRTAP was adopted in Geneva on 13 November 1979 and came into force on the 16 March 1983, and the Convention on the Protection and Use of Transboundary Watercourses and International Lakes was adopted in Helsinki, 17 March 1992, and came into force on 6 October 1996.[3] The 1991 Espoo and 1998 Aarhus Conventions are examples of its recent work in the area of procedural environmental provisions, so called because they focus on contributing to the prevention of harm and transboundary cooperation rather than the substantive obligations of attributing liability resulting from harm and resolving claims for damage. This section explains briefly the context and content of the Espoo and Aarhus Conventions, with a focus on their relevance for the SEA Protocol.

THE ESPOO CONVENTION

The Espoo Convention came into force on the 27 June 1997 after adoption in Espoo, Finland on 25 February 1991 by 27 countries and the EC, the first major treaty to specify in detailed terms transboundary EIA procedures.[4] It has been described as the 'highwater mark in the internationalization of EIA' (Woodliffe, 2002, p137). Since then, other treaties have also provided for transboundary EIA, notably in North America under the auspices of the North American Commission for Environmental Cooperation (NACEC).[5] The Espoo Convention remains the most significant of any of the regional agreements because of the large number of parties that have ratified the Convention. These parties include most of the member states of the UNECE[6] and the EU, as well as the EEA.

Historical development

The Espoo Convention drew on other international and European requirements that dealt with transboundary and procedural provisions, notably the 1974 Nordic Convention[7] and the 1985 EIA Directive.[8] Connelly (1999) traces its historical development, highlighting Principle 21 of the *Stockholm Declaration*, and indicating that the first work internationally on the concept of EIA in a transboundary context occurred in January 1987 under the auspices of the UNEP Group of Experts on Environmental Law with the elaboration of principles on transboundary EIA. He also draws attention to the influence of the Brundtland Report, *Our Common Future*, which recommended that governments should support the development of regional and subregional cooperative arrangements for the protection and sustained use of transboundary ecological systems, with joint action programmes to combat common problems. However the Nordic Convention and EIA Directive undoubtedly also influenced the work of the UNECE in the development of the Espoo Convention.

Connelly (1999) discusses the six meetings of the Working Group responsible for preparation of the text that would form the basis of the final Convention. He discusses the debate over the provisions included, and indicates that at the third meeting the document 'began to bear the resemblance of an international agreement' (pp41–42). His observations and conclusions (pp44–46) on the significance of the EIA Convention in particular draw attention to the following matters of relevance to the SEA Protocol:

- *The political environment was conducive to the development of the Convention, given the attention being paid internationally to environmental issues and the growing desire for cooperation between eastern and western countries;*
- *The Convention was innovative and far from the 'lowest common denominator' – the content and obligations were, in many instances, beyond what was in*

> *existence in many countries at the time and its reference to the possible application*
> *to policies, plans and program[s] was forward looking;*
> ● *The Convention has influenced the development of EIA legislation in a number*
>   *of countries through the content and nature of its obligations;*
> ● *The Convention has served as a model in the development of regional and bilateral*
>   *agreements on EIA in a transboundary context, eg, the Arctic Environmental*
>   *Protection Strategy and the EIA Agreement being developed in North America*
>   *under the North American Free Trade Agreement.*

Of particular note is the attention drawn to the reference to SEA in the Convention, and related, the need for a welcoming political environment to take such matters forward. Clearly the political environment under which the SEA Protocol has developed moved on sufficiently for the Protocol to gain acceptance at the time of its adoption. At the time of writing, the same may also be the case for its final ratification, and as experience is gained, potentially the mandatory application to policies and legislation.

The influence on other legislative developments is also of general interest. In the same way that the Convention was itself influenced by other international and national legal developments, so the Convention has in turn influenced the development of the law, particularly in the EU and its member states. It has also had an influence on other international legal developments, several of which have links with the Espoo Convention, such as the Convention on the Transboundary Effects of Industrial Accidents (Schrage, 1999, p95). The relationship between international and European law (see Chapter 12) is therefore such that ratification of international treaties brings an obligation to introduce/amend existing law to ensure compliance. The changes to the original EIA Directive and transposition in the MS required by ratification of the Espoo Convention are an example of this (see Chapter 9).

Procedural provisions

Briefly, the following procedural provisions make up the Espoo Convention,[9] which deal primarily with prevention of harm and cooperation. The Preamble sets out the objective to 'ensure environmentally sound and sustainable development' and to 'enhance international cooperation'. Article 1 contains the definition section with terms such as 'party of origin', 'affected party', 'proposed activity', 'environmental impact assessment', 'impact', 'transboundary impact', 'competent authority' and 'public' explained. Article 2 then contains general provisions for the management of effects, legal measures required, anticipation and notification, consultation and participation, reference to SEA, exemptions and requirements for more stringent measures. The detailed specific provisions of the agreement then follow. For example, Article 3 deals with notification, Article 4 with documentation, Article 5 with consultation, Article 6 with the final decision, Article 7 with post project analysis and Article 8 with bilateral and multilateral cooperation.

Other provisions of interest include Article 2(10) that states that 'the provisions of this Convention shall not prejudice any obligations of the Parties under international law with regard to activities having or likely to have a transboundary impact'. This indicates that other causes of action that may be available to states, such as any customary rules of international law relating to environmental harm, international cooperation or liability, and/or other treaty obligations, remain applicable, despite the requirements, or absence thereof, in the Espoo Convention. Another is Article 6(1) that, notwithstanding the vagueness of the wording, contains the substantive obligation to give 'due account' to the outcome of the EIA, and in Article 6(2) the substantive requirement for provision of reasons and considerations on which the EIA is based.

Compensation for environmental harm

Chapter 3 considered three broad duties of IEL: prevention of environmental harm, cooperation in transboundary situations and compensation for environmental damage, and stated that while the first two are of particular relevance to EIA, the third is also related because it deals with situations of failure to comply with the first two duties. As also seen in Chapter 3, invoking a liability provision depends on the existence of a substantive prohibition of harm. In common with national (and European) EIA law, the Espoo Convention does not contain such a prohibition. Knox (2002, p302) comments on the relationship between the Convention and Principle 21 of the *Stockholm Declaration* in the following terms:

> *The Espoo Convention requires its parties to assess the transboundary environmental effects of certain actions within their jurisdiction and to notify and consult with potentially affected states about those effects. It may therefore appear to provide the procedural corollaries to Principle 21, and it has been cited in support of the mythic view of transboundary EIA. But its limited coverage and lack of a substantive prohibition against transboundary harm are inconsistent with the myth. Instead, in these respects and in its procedural provisions, the Espoo Convention reflects and extends its signatories' pre-existing EIA laws.[10]*

While the procedural provisions of the Convention outlined above are directed towards harm prevention and cooperation, Article 2(1) is of interest to liability. This stipulates that Parties 'shall, either individually or jointly, take all appropriate and effective measures to prevent, reduce and control significant adverse transboundary environmental impact from proposed activities'. Woodliffe (2002) cites Barboza (1994, p398) and discusses the implications of this with respect to liability or compensation for environmental damage, which, as seen in Chapter 3 is of uncertain status because of definition and enforcement difficulties. He comments (p141), with my emphasis:

> *Barboza, while accepting that the Espoo Convention is 'not a liability convention', invokes the above Article and the definition of impact... in support of the view that the Convention deals with 'environmental damage and reparation'. The relationship between EIA and liability regimes has frequently been the subject of doctrinal discussion. If carried out in accordance with the letter and spirit of the procedure, EIA ought to serve as a **liability suppressant**... It would in any event be obtuse of the state making a final decision pursuant to the full panoply of notification, assessment and consultation requirements under the Espoo Convention not to take account of the broader international legal duties incumbent on it.*

Woodliffe (2002, p142) discusses the work of the ILC on international liability (2001) (considered in the previous chapter) and indicates that the articles of the 2001 ILC draft Convention on the Prevention of Transboundary Harm from Hazardous Activities 'at many points replicate the terminology and formal structure of rights and duties found in the Espoo Convention'. Members of the Commission have acknowledged the impact of the Espoo Convention on its work, and the Espoo Convention is highlighted as a guide to the procedure and content of the risk assessment. Since the draft articles are directed at activities that are not prohibited under international law (because of the lack of a substantive prohibition), if the draft convention is ever adopted it may mean that any harm resulting from activities assessed in accordance with the Espoo Convention may have remediation consequences, even if there is no admission of liability. Liability matters are deliberately avoided under the draft convention because of the wider implications entailing judicial claims. The ILC general commentary states that 'prevention... as a procedure or as a duty, deals with the phase prior to the situation where significant harm or damage has actually occurred' (2001, para 1). Woodliffe (2002, p142) states that this is 'the point at which obligations to repair, remedy or compensate take over'.

Woodliffe (p143) also considers the issue of legal challenge for a failure to carry out an assessment in a procedurally correct manner, which in a national context may provide a remedy in judicial review.[11] This has of course been an important part of the history of the implementation of the EIA Directive, which, in a national context, has been subject to significant challenge as a result of procedural failings. The UK has certainly generated a broad jurisprudence on this (Tromans and Fuller, 2003). This is something that others have previously considered in a situation where a transboundary EIA has indicated that there will be no risk of significant harm yet nonetheless harm does result. In such a situation, is a legal claim possible? The answer is in the affirmative because the procedure operates in the form of a national instrument in which the affected state has an interest. If the assessment is flawed procedurally or the decision failed to give sufficient weight to it, then a challenge is quite possible. Such challenges may also be available to individuals or NGOs if they could demonstrate sufficient interest in the case. Woodliffe refers to the Institut de Droit International (1997), which had earlier adopted a Resolution on Responsibility and Liability under International Law for Environmental Damage in which the issue was addressed. Woodliffe (202, p143) states:

> The relevant draft article attached to the Resolution declares that submission of a proposed activity to EIA 'under environmental regimes, does not in itself exempt from responsibility for harm alone or civil liability if the assessed impact exceeds the limit judged acceptable.' The same article then proposes that an 'EIA may require that a specific guarantee be given for adequate compensation should the case arise'.

Innovative elements, including SEA

The Espoo Convention contains a number of innovative substantive elements. Sands (1995, pp588–591) draws attention to the detailed information to be submitted to the competent authority of the party of origin, for onward transmission to the affected party which, before revision of the EIA Directive (see Chapter 9) was more comprehensive than European law required. Provisions for post-project analysis and follow-up (monitoring) are also good examples, as are references to human health and safety (Schrage, 1999, p88); the former is also emphasized in the SEA Protocol.

Although Ebbesson (1999, p48) and Knox (2002, p301) emphasize that many previous treaties have made provision for transboundary assessment and that many of the core concepts of the Convention are drawn from these, Ebbesson in particular focuses on its innovative elements and the expected effectiveness of the Convention. He indicates that because it operates to change the behaviour of 'non-state actors' as well as states (such as individuals and business organizations), formal compliance with the Convention is dependent upon the establishment of implementing provisions in domestic law. It is also dependent upon the right of the public in one state to participate in the administrative and judicial procedures established in another state, which is known as the principle of non-discrimination in international law. Gray (2000, pp101–102) emphasizes this and comments: 'The novel provisions of Espoo relate to public participation. The public in the affected area has a right to be informed of and to participate in the EIA procedure, even though the procedure takes place in another country'.

Making reference to the EIA Directive, where such a provision is absent, Knox (2002, p303) identifies this as the 'principal innovation of the Convention', with Ebbesson (1999, p50) commenting that if the affected public is not given the opportunity to participate, 'the state in question does not comply with international law'. Schrage also draws attention to this feature, commenting that the Convention 'reflects new trend in international environmental law, which allow all those who are likely to be affected by an environmental impact to be involved in the decision-making process' (1999, pp96–97). Ebbesson (1999) identifies two other innovative elements: it provides more specific procedures for notification and consultation regarding transboundary effects, and it advances the use and meaning of EIA in international law.

As Sheate indicates (1994, p188), in 1990 the UNECE established a task force led by the US to examine the application of EIA principles to PPPs. It recommended to the member governments of the UNECE that EIA should be considered on a par with economic and social issues in the development of and decisions on PPPs (UNECE, 1992). It therefore recognized that EIA for PPPs should reflect EIA principles as applied to projects, and encouraged the passage of legislation for both. Article 2(7) of the Espoo Convention also encourages parties to the Convention to carry out EIA for PPPs, as cited below:

> *Environmental impact assessments as required by this Convention shall, as a minimum requirement, be undertaken at the project level of the proposed activity. To the extent appropriate, the Parties shall endeavour to apply the principles of environmental impact assessment to policies, plans and programmes.*

Schrage (1999, p90) draws attention to this SEA provision in the Espoo Convention, commenting that although the wording clearly indicates that there is no obligation on a party to apply SEA, a number of countries had already introduced legislation for this. Schrage acknowledges that the principles of EIA could be relevant at these higher levels and that in order to avoid the significant environmental impacts from PPP at all levels of government, SEA should be carried out.

Implementation and compliance

The provisions of the Espoo Convention have been incorporated into the amended EIA Directive (see Chapter 9); subject to transposition by each MS as appropriate, this has in general ensured legal implementation with the Convention in the EU, albeit with reference to the Commission and ECJ where necessary. Non-EU Parties have needed to introduce domestic legislation where not already compliant. Practical matters are to a large extent dealt with by the MOP. Article 11(2)(c) requires the MOP to 'prepare, where appropriate, protocols to th[e] Convention', which provided it with competence to prepare the SEA Protocol. Article 15 on dispute settlement is of particular interest with relevance to the SEA Protocol. Article 15(1) permits the application of any method of dispute settlement, but parties who ratify the Convention and fail to reach agreement (presumably under the non-judicial means of settlement – see Chapter 2), are obliged to submit the dispute either to the ICJ or to arbitration, depending on their stated wishes, and in accordance with the procedure set out in Appendix VII of the Convention. This is significant because the same dispute settlement mechanisms will apply under the terms of the SEA Protocol (see Article 20 of the SEA Protocol).

Koivurova (2007, p218) indicates that since the Convention came into force in 1997, the MOP has met several times and has adopted many significant decisions with respect to the institutional structure of the Convention (see also Hallo, 2007). It has also established a Bureau of the Convention to coordinate the work programme between the MOPs. Although secretariat tasks are dealt with by the UNECE in Geneva, the MOP is also assisted by the Working Group on EIA and the Implementation Committee. The first assists the MOP in the implementation of the Convention and management of the work programme and the second develops the reporting system and considers individual cases of non-compliance. All of these bodies have similar roles with respect to the SEA Protocol.

Koivurova (2007) focuses on the dispute resolution, compliance control and enforcement procedures of the Convention as a means of examining the substantive provisions. He comments (p220) favourably on these provisions in relation to provisions elsewhere in MEAs in the following terms:

> The substantive obligations of the Espoo Convention and SEA Protocol set out clear obligations and rights for the States parties. This approach stands in direct contrast to that found in many other international environmental treaties, for example the Convention on Biological Diversity, whose primary rules are so loose and open-ended that their legal status can be questioned.

Despite the Convention failing to contain a prohibition on environmental harm as suggested by Knox (2002), as an example of one of the many provisions of the type discussed by Bodansky (1995), the substantive obligations that are present in the Convention are viewed favourably by international environmental lawyers. Koivorova (2007, p220) in particular indicates that 'substantial consensus exists on the content and scope of the primary rules, which greatly facilitates the creation of a compliance control system'. One of the dispute settlement features of the Espoo Convention does not apply to the SEA Protocol; this is the inquiry commission procedure that applies where a dispute centres on whether the state of origin is required to initiate the transboundary procedure or not (Koivurova, 2007, pp222–226).

Koivurova (2007, p227) also distinguishes between the requirements for compliance control under the Espoo Convention and SEA Protocol, the latter of which imposes reporting obligations on the parties, while the former has not to date but may, if amendment to the Convention is approved by the parties. The only existing requirement under the Espoo Convention is Article 11(2), which indirectly sets out the terms of reference of the MOP to require parties to continuously review implementation in the ways stated. A new Article 14 *bis* concerning review of compliance by regular reporting arrangements, will be applicable to the SEA Protocol (see 14(1)) and Convention if approved at the next MOP and ratified by the parties thereafter in accordance with the procedure specified in the existing Article 14.4 (see Koivurova, 2007, p228).

Implementation of the Espoo Convention has been reviewed twice by the UNECE, following detailed reports submitted to the secretariat by the parties to the Convention in response to a standard questionnaire. The most recent were prepared by the parties for the period mid-2003 to the end of 2005, which resulted in a draft of 17 April 2007 of the review of implementation submitted by the Secretariat (UNECE, 2007). The 2007 review reveals a number of weaknesses in the implementation of the Convention, including deficiencies in information exchange, public participation and reporting obligations, and a lack of monitoring. Many of these issues are also common to the enforcement of other treaties (De Mulder, 2006, p270). There also remains a continuing need for bilateral and multilateral agreements to identify contacts, and address differences in procedural steps, timing of participation, the interpretation of certain terms and the content of the EIS. With respect to the clarity of the Convention, for example (p48), Switzerland considered there to be a large margin for interpretation, the meaning of the word 'likely' was not clear to Hungary, and the terms 'major', 'large' and 'close to an international frontier' were also not clear to Kyrgyzstan. The Czech Republic further sought guidance on post-project analysis.

Other documentation on the UNECE website (unece.org) includes the Final Report of the Taskforce on Legal and Administrative Aspects of the Practical Application of Relevant Provisions of the Convention, and a report on Bilateral and Multilateral Cooperation submitted by the delegation of the Netherlands. The Finnish Environment Institute has also prepared a final report of a workshop on the Practical Application of the Convention, and several academic articles have been published on application with respect to bilateral agreements (De Boer, 1999) and other application challenges (Tesli and Husby, 1999; Hildén and Furman, 2001; Schrage, 2004). Koivurova (2007, pp229–234) also reports on the work of the Implementation Committee with examples of failures of implementation.

THE AARHUS CONVENTION

The Aarhus Convention on Access to Information, Public Participation in Decision-Making and Access to Justice in Environmental Matters was adopted on 25 June 1998, and entered into force on 30 October 2001 following ratification by the required number of signatories. Since then, it has been subject to significant comment in the literature (see, for example, Brady, 1998; McCracken and Jones, 2003; Koester, 2007b). It has had an influence on the development of both the SEA Directive and SEA Protocol, particularly in the area of public participation (Davies, 2002; Lee and Abbot, 2003). It has also been influential in contributing to the development of democratic and constitutional principles in the Eastern European members of the UNECE (Jendroska and Stec, 2001; Zschiesche, 2002, p21; Wates, 2005) and indeed beyond the nation state (Petkova and Veit, 2000), or where democracy may not be attainable at the international level, it may well provide significant assistance to 'enhanced transparency, participation, more balanced voting procedures and effectiveness of decisions as possible ways of making decisions more legitimate' (Andresen and Hey, 2005, p221). It has also served to link the environment and human rights in international law (Morgera, 2005, p139; McAllister, 1998).

Historical development[12]

As Palerm indicates (1999, p229), public participation was the driving force behind the development of EIA in the US, the country where greater involvement in political decisions was demanded from the modern environment movement in the 1960s and 1970s, and which was a strong contributor to the development of NEPA in 1969. Palerm's examination of the literature concludes that demands for public participation were motivated by redefinitions of the concept of democracy, widespread education, greater access to information through the expansion of the media, and the growth of bureaucracy (1999, p231).

International and European developments took the concept further in the 1980s and 1990s, with the *World Conservation Strategy* (IUCN/WWF/UNEP, 1980), EIA Directive (85/337/EC), Brundtland Report, *Our Common Future* (WCED, 1987), UNEP's *Goals and Principles of EIA* (UNEP, 1987), Access to Environmental Information Directive (90/313/EEC),[13] 1990 establishment of the European Environmental Agency, the UNECE recommendations on EIA (UNECE, 1991), Principle 10 of the *Rio Declaration* 1992, and *Fifth Environmental Action Plan (1993–2000): Towards Sustainability*, collectively recognizing the importance of all of the procedural aspects: access to information, public participation in environmental decision making, access to justice and links with sustainable development.[14] All of the above developments at national, international and European levels had a significant influence on the three procedural pillars of the Aarhus Convention.

In 1991 the Environment for Europe Process was begun in Dobris, which eventually led to the Aarhus Convention (Stanners and Bordeau, 1995). The Process was established with the objective of agreeing on ways to improve the environment at the pan-European level. The second meeting in Lucerne in 1993 resulted in the *Lucerne Declaration* that called for proposals by the UNECE for legal, regulatory and administrative mechanisms to encourage public participation. The third Ministerial Conference in Sofia in 1995 endorsed *Guidelines on Public Participation in Environmental Decision Making* (UNECE, 1996). The negotiation process for these guidelines lasted several years, and as Zschiesche (2002, pp21–22) indicates 'was in particular pushed by European non-governmental organisations, the responsible Directorate-General of the European Commission as well as by the Regional Environment Centre (REC) in Budapest. This framework document paved the way for negotiations on an international agreement'. From 1996 to 1998, there were ten meetings at which NGOs were involved from the start until the finish, when the final text was ready for signature. At the fourth conference, in Aarhus, the Convention was finally adopted by 36 countries and the EC.

Procedural provisions

As indicated by its title, the Convention is concerned above all with three matters: access to information, public participation in decision making and access to justice in environmental matters.[15] The lengthy preamble is made up of some 23 paragraphs recognising earlier legal and policy developments relating to environmental protection and the procedural rights enshrined in the Convention. The UNECE has prepared an Implementation Guide (UNECE, 2000) on the Convention generally, and on the access to justice provisions specifically (Stec, 2003). As with all procedural guidance on legal instruments discussed in this book, the guides have no legal status, as authoritative interpretations of the law can only be given by the judiciary. However, they have been prepared by experienced senior lawyers and are therefore of great value in understanding the Convention. With regard to the preamble, for example, the main Implementation Guide (p11) helpfully indicates its legal status, in that it may be relied upon for implementation purposes but that it does not in itself contain binding obligations.[16]

Article 1 indicates that the objective of the Convention is to guarantee procedural rights in order to contribute to protection of the right of current and future generations to live in an environment adequate for health and well being. Article 2 contains the definition section, with terms such as 'Party', 'public authority', 'government', 'environmental information', 'the public' and 'the public concerned' set out. The Implementation Guide also helpfully considers terms not defined in the Convention (pp30–31), which include 'in the framework in accordance with national legislation', which may permit flexibility in implementation. Article 3 contains general provisions that apply to the Convention as a whole. These include that public authorities should assist and guide the public, that environmental education and awareness be promoted, that environmental NGOs should be supported and recognized, that Parties have the right to introduce more stringent measures (and should not derogate from existing rights), and that the Convention should be promoted in the international arena. Anti-harassment and anti-discrimination provisions are an important part of Article 3 also.

The Convention deals with access to and collection of environmental information in Articles 4–5,[17] public participation in decision making in Articles 6–8 and access to justice in Article 9.[18] Articles 5–8 (which have implications for SEA) are examined in the paragraph on innovative elements below. The access to justice provisions of the Aarhus Convention deal with three situations: where the right of access to environmental information is impaired (Article 9(1)), where the right to public participation is impaired (Article 9(2)), and access to justice where acts and omissions of public authorities or private persons are in breach of the law (Article 9(3)). Zschiesche (2002, pp27–28) comments on the weakening of the last provision:

> *Initially, it was intended by this provision to grant everybody the broadest possible access to justice in environmental matters. The provision as it stands now has been*

weakened during the last negotiation rounds and now unfortunately is considerably restricted by making reference to the national criteria.

Innovative elements, including SEA

Aside from the compliance mechanism outlined below, another of the innovative elements of the Aarhus Convention is the Article 3(7) obligation placed on Parties to promote the application of the principles of the Convention in international decision making processes and within the framework of international organizations where relating to the environment, such as UNEP, or in COPs and MOPs of other treaties. Morgera (2005, pp145–146) explains how at the first MOP in 2002 the possibility of considering guidelines on the issue was discussed. Following a preliminary study prepared by the Working Group of the Parties, it was stressed that there was a need for 'improved access to fair and transparent proceedings, allowing the public to review access to information and for public participation and the review of the rules of international organizations in this regard' (p145). An ad hoc working group was subsequently established, and in May 2005 the resulting guidelines were due to be discussed at the MOP. Morgena comments on their significance (2005, pp145–146):

> *The purpose of the draft guidelines is of global interest. They will be applied not only by the State parties to the Aarhus Convention, acting individually or in a collective way, but also possibly serve as a 'source of inspiration' to other interested States, the secretariats of international fora, as well as other concerned actors such as NGOs and members of the public... Interestingly, the guidelines focus not only on negotiation, implementation and other decision making relating to MEAs, but also include an indicative list of other MEAs, and connected dispute resolution processes, whose decisions or projects have, or may have, a significant impact on the environment... Potentially, the scope of the guidelines extends to all stages of any given international policy process from initiation and pre-negotiation, to the decision making and implementation phases.*

Article 5(3) of the Convention requires each party to ensure that environmental information progressively becomes available in electronic databases, which are easily accessible to the public through public telecommunication networks. Information in this form should include texts of legislation on or relating to the environment (Article 5(3)(b)), and, 'as appropriate', PPPs on or relating to the environment and environmental agreements (Article 5(3)(c)). The Implementation Guide (UNECE, 2000, p76) comments on the latter that:

> *In this case 'as appropriate' means that Parties have additional flexibility in determining which policies, plans and programmes would be most usefully accessible through electronic databases because of a public interest in assessing them. For example, this can be a useful tool for implementing article 7 on public participation in decisions concerning plans, programmes and policies. It is very important for the public and for public authorities to have easy access to existing plans, programmes and policies when commenting on proposals.*

Article 5(5)(a) contains measures for the dissemination of legislation and policy documents, such as strategies, policies, programmes and action plans relating to the environment, and progress reports on their implementation, prepared at various levels of government. The Implementation Guide (UNECE, 2000, p78) comments on the extensive information disclosure and reporting obligations contained in this section and how it relates to public participation in respect of similar documents:

> *Paragraph 5(a) requires Parties to develop a legal system to disseminate legislation and policy documents that concern the environment. This provision should be considered also in the context of articles 7 and 8, which concern public participation in plans, programmes, policies, law-making and rule making. Parties are required to actively disseminate the texts of strategies, policies, programmes and action plans relating to the environment. In addition to the texts of these law and policy documents, the Convention requires Parties to disseminate progress reports on their implementation. The term 'relating to the environment' is used here instead of 'environmental information'. 'Relating to the environment' arguably includes a broader range of information such as policies on transport, energy, agriculture or mining as these relate to the environment through their impacts or otherwise.*[19]

Article 5(7) requires Parties to publish information that will help the public, public authorities and other Parties understand the content of government decisions, monitor their implementation and make more effective contributions to decision making. Article 5(7)(a) requires publication of the facts and analyses of facts 'which it considers relevant and important' in framing major environmental policy proposals. Although there is discretion given to the state party here, the Implementation Guide (UNECE, 2000, p80) states that: 'Since article 7 provides for public participation during the preparation of policies, article 5, paragraph 7, is intended to ensure that the public will be properly equipped with the information necessary to take advantage of this opportunity'.

The Convention distinguishes between three areas of environmental decision making for which public participation is required: specific activities in Article 6,[20] plans, programmes and policies in Article 7, and executive regulations and/or generally applicable legally binding normative instruments in Article 8, meaning environmental legislation. There is no definition of PPPs in the Convention, but the Guidance indicates that the meaning is likely to be the same as when considered under the other UNECE legal instruments, the Espoo Convention and SEA Protocol (see UNECE, 2000, p113). It also indicates that the experience of the Espoo MOP 'may be relevant in interpreting the meanings of 'plans, programmes and policies' (p113).

As indicated in note 19, and as stated by the Implementation Guide (p114):

> *While the Convention does not oblige Parties to undertake assessments, a legal basis for the consideration of the environmental aspects of plans, programmes and policies is a prerequisite for the application of article 7... Thus, proper public participation procedures in the context of strategic environmental assessment (SEA) is one method of implementing article 7.*

The Guide justifies this by indicating that since due account must be taken of the outcome of public participation there is an implication that there must be a legal basis to take environmental considerations into account in PPPs. Furthermore, the obligations in Article 7 are capable of enforcement through the access to justice provisions in Article 9, provided states already have guarantees of such rights (in which case they cannot go back on them as a result of the principles in Article 3(5) and (6)) or because they decide to adopt such guarantees.

Article 7 distinguishes between plans and programmes on one hand and policies on the other; the more specific the decision, the greater the procedural guarantees are available, hence the application of Article 6(3), (4) and (8) to plans and programmes, which set timeframes, require participation at an early time in decision making and ensure that due account is taken of the participation in the decision.[21] With regard to plans and programmes, Article 7 therefore states:

> *Each party shall make appropriate practical and/or other provisions for the public to participate during the preparation of plans and programmes relating to the environment, within a transparent and fair framework, having provided the necessary information to the public. Within this framework, article 6, paragraphs 3, 4 and 8, shall be applied. The public which may participate shall be identified by the relevant public authority, taking into account the objectives of this Convention.*

With respect to policies there is no express incorporation of the provisions of Article 6, although a state is free to include those provisions in domestic law if it wishes. Again, 'policies' are not defined in the Convention, although this does not mean that Parties lack an understanding of their meaning or that their preparation should not also be subject to public input. Article 7 therefore suggests that 'to the extent appropriate' each Party 'shall endeavour' to provide opportunities for public participation in the preparation of policies relating to the environment. Similarly, Article 8 in providing that the public shall be involved in the law making process uses the wording that a state should 'promote' or use its best efforts to allow public input, establishing elements of participation procedures (such as appropriate timeframes and publication of draft rules) and requiring Parties to ensure that participation is taken account of in decision making.

Palerm (1999, p240) concludes overall on the role of the Aarhus Convention in relation to SEA:

> *The Aarhus Convention does not venture to be as detailed for the SEA process as it is for EIA. The only provisions it makes regarding SEA are that reasonable time frames for the different phases are to be established, that sufficient time should be allowed for informing the public so that it can prepare and participate effectively, that early participation should occur when options are still open, and that the decision must take into account the outcome of the public participation.*

Even if the public participation provisions for SEA are not as comprehensive as those for project level decision making, they do represent an important step in establishing binding provisions to allow for participation in the definition of policies, plans and programmes.

Implementation and compliance

The provisions of the Aarhus Convention have been incorporated into the EIA Environmental Information, Public Participation[22] and SEA Directives (see Chapters 9 and 10; Ziehm, 2005; Jendroska, 2005, 2006). They have also been incorporated into an EU Regulation that is applicable to EC institutions and bodies[23] and are the subject of a proposed Directive on Access to Justice.[24] Aside from this European and MS transposition (see Lavrysen, 2007), Article 10 of the Convention deals with the procedure applicable to the MOP, including the ability to establish subsidiary bodies (Article 10(2)(d)) as necessary, such as the Working Group of the Parties.[25] Article 15 is concerned with review of compliance, and Article 16 with settlement of disputes. Annex II of the Convention deals with arbitration; the Implementation Guide (UNECE, 2000, pp167–170) explains the role of arbitration in relation to the dispute settlement provision in the Convention, which is almost identical to that found in the Espoo Convention.[26] These provisions are of notable interest in examining implementation and compliance with the Convention to date.

Koester (2005, 2007a) examines the role of the Compliance Committee (CC) in relation to the Aarhus Convention (see also Morgera, 2005, pp140–143). At the first MOP in October 2002, a decision on review of compliance was adopted, which established the CC, later to hold its first meeting in March 2003. Koester (2007a, p83) indicates that by the end of 2006, the CC had held 13 meetings and had concluded nine cases between state Parties and/or third parties. The procedures adopted by the CC are innovative, permitting wide access to meetings and documentation. In its work it has addressed a number of interpretative issues relating to the Convention, and therefore has contributed significantly to its developing jurisprudence; it has also made recommendations to the MOP, which may result in changes to the Convention in the future.[27] Most of the cases have related to Article 6 or 9, although one case (see Koester, 2007a, pp88–89) found a provision of Article 7 not to be complied with, and also considered a potential breach of Article 8. As such, those interested in the application of the Aarhus Convention to SEA should watch the developing jurisprudence of the CC, as it may serve to clarify some of the terms of relevance in the Convention. The MOP has adopted most of the recommendations made by the CC, although as Koester concludes (2007a, p93), 'It still remains to be seen to what extent recommendations will be implemented [by the state Party] in practice'.

CONCLUSIONS

This chapter has explained the institutional and procedural basis for the SEA Protocol, found in two of the most important of the recent treaties on IEL, the Espoo and Aarhus Conventions. It has explained how and why the Espoo Convention includes only two of the most important duties of IEL that have attained customary status, the principle of harm prevention and cooperation. It has also shown how and why it fails to include the third duty, that of compensation for environmental damage, but how it nonetheless addresses it in some way. It has also explained how the Aarhus Convention addresses the three pillars of access to information, public participation in decision making and access to justice in environmental matters. Each of these matters is incorporated to some extent within the SEA Protocol, which is the subject of the next chapter.

The most significant achievement of both the Espoo and Aarhus Conventions concerns project level decision making, although some emphasis is also placed on decision making for PPPs in both. Since the Aarhus Convention has a much broader horizontal scope than the Espoo Convention, it is perhaps not surprising that its contribution to international jurisprudence is already regarded as greater than that of the Espoo Convention, in part because of the greater substantive obligations imposed, and because of the ability of individuals to take action in a public international law world dominated by states. The implementation of its provisions by European directives (see Chapter 9) are testament to the influence of its provisions in particular.

NOTES

1 Convention on Environmental Impact Assessment in a Transboundary Context (Espoo, 25 February 1991), 30 ILM (1991) 802, in force 27 June 1997.
2 Convention on Access to Information, Public Participation in Decision-Making and Access to Justice in Environmental Matters (Aarhus, 25 June 1998), 38 ILM (1999) 517, in force 30 October 2001.
3 Another example is the Convention on the Transboundary Effects of Industrial Accidents (Espoo, 1992), 31 ILM (1992) 1333, in force 19 April 2000.
4 The Nordic Environment Protection Convention preceded it to some extent; this came into force in 1976, see Koivurova in Bastmeijer and Koivurova (2008) and Dzidzornu (2001).
5 See Knox (2002, pp305–308), Craik (2008) and Bastmeijer and Koivurova (2008). Other international agreements are also analysed in the last of these books, notably the Mekong River Basin Agreement and developing systems in Central America. Knox (p301) also indicates that the ILC draft convention on environmental harm also requires transboundary EIA.
6 Woodliffe (2002, p137) indicates there are 55 member states of the UNECE. There are now 56; see unece.org
7 Ebbesson (1999, p49) draws attention both to the Nordic Convention and also the 1977 OECD Recommendation on the Implementation of a Regime of Equal Right of Access and Non-Discrimination in Relation to Transfrontier Pollution.
8 On the relationship between the Espoo Convention and EIA Directive, see McHugh (1994).
9 Those interested in the Espoo Convention generally are referred to Garcia-Ureta (1993), Schrage (1999) and Koivurova (2007) for further and more detailed descriptions and analysis.
10 The main substantive provision in the Convention is the requirement for the state of origin to take 'due account' of the EIA and the comments received from the public and the affected state. There are no requirements to prohibit proposed activities or minimize adverse transboundary effects (see Knox, 2002, p304-305).
11 Judicial review is a procedural claim for a failure to have carried out the decision making process correctly. It is not directed to the merits of a case but the way in which the process considering those merits was performed. For illustrations in a common law context, see Cane (2000) and Chapter 1 of this book.
12 Much of this section is taken from Palerm (1999). Interested readers are referred to the references cited there in for further information, particularly on the theory of participation,

which is the focus of the article. For further background on the development of the concepts embodied by the Aarhus Convention, especially in the context of European environmental law, see Mathieson (2003) and the Aarhus Implementation Guide (UNECE, 2000, pp1–4).

13   See Kimber (1998) for discussion of the proposed Directive. The differences between the 1990 Directive and the Aarhus Convention Pillar I that deals with access to information are set out in the Aarhus Implementation Guide (UNECE, 2000, pp65–66). The 1990 Directive was replaced by a new Directive in 2003 to ensure compliance with the Aarhus Convention (see Chapter 9).

14   See also Ebbesson (1997).

15   For a general overview, see McCracken (2003).

16   Article 31, paragraph 2 of the 1969 VCLT, states that the preamble is part of the context and is the primary source of interpretation (see Chapter 2).

17   There is much useful interpretative guidance in the Implementation Guide (UNECE, 2000). For example, assistance is provided on the meaning of 'too general' in Article 4(3)(b), 'materials in the course of completion' in Article 4(3)(c), the importance of the public interest test, and what amounts to a 'legitimate economic interest' in Article 4(4)(d).

18   Again, there is much useful interpretive guidance in the Implementation Guide in relation to the third pillar (access to justice). For example, 'sufficient interest' in relation to the issue of standing is examined in relation to the domestic law of England and Wales. More detailed information is also available in Stec (2003); and see Ebbesson (2002), Lavrysen (2007) and Zodrow and Zengerling (2007) for application in the EU.

19   With respect to plans and programmes that relate to the environment, the Implementation Guide (UNECE, 2000, p115) indicates that this should be determined with reference to the implied definition of 'environment' within the definition of 'environmental information' found in Article 2(3). It therefore concludes (p115):

> Plans and programmes relating to the environment may include land-use and regional development strategies, and sectoral planning in transport, tourism, energy, heavy and light industry, water resources, health and sanitation, etc., at all levels of government. They may also include government initiatives to achieve particular policy goals relating to the environment, such as incentive programmes to meet certain pollution reduction targets or voluntary recycling programmes, and complex strategies such as national and local environmental action plans and environmental health action plans. Often such strategies are the first step in action to reach environmental protection goals, followed by the development of plans based on the strategies. Integrated planning based on river basins or other geographical features is another example.

20   The Implementation Guide (UNECE, 2000, pp90–91) indicates at length that whether public participation during decision making on specific activities is required depends on whether the decision making itself may have a potentially significant impact on the environment, not on whether the procedure requires EIA. The Guide comments (p91) 'Even if the Aarhus Convention does not establish an EIA regime per se, its article 6 does establish a kind of review of the environmental impacts of particular activities, where decision making in relation to them takes place'. Further detailed information on the obligations under Article 6 can be found on pp92–113 of the Implementation Guide. Note also UNECE (1996).

21   Clearly, certain paragraphs of Article 6 are not applicable to the implementation of Article 7. The Implementation Guide (UNECE, 2000, p 117) discusses these and the reasons why they are not applicable in the case of PPPs.

22   This also relates access to justice to public participation.

23   Regulation (EC) No 1367/2006 of 6 September 2006 of the European Parliament and of the Council on the application of the provisions of the Aarhus Convention on Access to

Information, Public Participation in Decision Making and Access to Justice in Environmental Matters to EC institutions and bodies. See Rodenhoff (2002).

24 Proposal for a Directive of the European Parliament and of the Council on access to justice in environmental matters, COM (2003) 624 final.

25 During its sixth meeting in April 2006, the Working Group agreed to hold a workshop on public participation in strategic decision making, which would focus on participation in PPPs and also laws with environmental impact (i.e. covering both Articles 7 and 8 of the Convention). The workshop was aimed at providing an opportunity for a broad exchange of views among experts involved with the Aarhus and Espoo Conventions and the SEA Protocol. The workshop was due to be held in December 2007, with information available on the Aarhus website: www.unece.org

26 The Implementation Guide (UNECE, 2000, p168) indicates that the scope of the arbitration provision is limited to disputes between the Parties, so arbitration with third parties, such as NGOs, is not covered. Parties remain free to enter into arbitration with third parties, it is just that the arbitration provision is not automatically applicable in such instances. The Implementation Guide (p168) goes on to emphasize that the Permanent Court of Arbitration (PCA) regularly settles disputes between states and private parties (see Rest, 2004), which has its own procedures that are followed in such cases.

27 Morgera (2005, p141) emphasizes that the MOP is ultimately responsible for deciding upon issues of compliance and may take appropriate measures to ensure the Convention is complied with. This includes assistance to individual parties, recommendations, declarations of non-compliance and cautions. It can also request a party to submit to the CC a time-limited strategy on the achievement of compliance and to report on the implementation of the strategy.

REFERENCES

Andresen, S. and Hey, E. (2005) 'The effectiveness and legitimacy of international environmental institutions', *International Environmental Agreements*, vol 5, pp211–226

Barboza, J. (1994) 'International liability for the injurious consequences arising from acts not prohibited by international law and protection of the environment' 247 *Recueil des Cours* (1994 III), pp291–406

Bastmeijer, K. and Koivurova, T. (eds) (2008) *Theory and Practice of Transboundary Environmental Impact Assessment*, Martinus Nijhoff, Leiden/Boston MA

Bodansky, D. (1995) 'Customary (and not so customary) international environmental law', *Indiana Journal of Global Legal Studies*, vol 3, pp105–119

Brady, K. (1998) 'The new convention on access to information, public participation and access to justice in environmental matters', *Environmental Policy and Law*, vol 28, no 2, pp69–75

Cane, P. (2000) *An Introduction to Administrative Law*, 3rd Edition, Clarendon Press, Oxford

Connelly, R. (1999) 'The UN convention on EIA in a transboundary context: A historical perspective', *Environmental Impact Assessment Review*, vol 19, no 1, pp37–46

Craik, N. (2008) *The International Law of Environmental Impact Assessment: Process, Substance and Integration*, Cambridge University Press, Cambridge

Davies, P. (2002) 'Public participation, the Aarhus convention, and the European Community' in D. N. Zillman, A. R. Lucas and G. Pring (eds) *Human Rights in Natural Resource Development: Public Participation in the Sustainable Development of Mining and Energy Resources*, Oxford University Press, New York, pp155–185

De Boer, J. J. (1999) 'Bilateral agreements for the application of the UN-ECE convention on EIA in a transbounday context', *Environmental Impact Assessment Review*, vol 19, no 1, pp85–98

De Mulder, J. (2006) 'The expansion of environmental assessment in international law: The Protocol on Strategic Environmental Assessment to the Espoo Convention', *Environmental Law and Management*, vol 18, pp269–281

Dzidzornu, D. (2001) 'Environmental impact assessment procedure through the conventions', *European Environmental Law Review*, vol 10, no 1, pp15–26

Ebbesson, J. (1997) 'The notion of public participation in international environmental law', in 8 *Yearbook of International Environmental Law*, Oxford University Press, Oxford

Ebbesson, J. (1999) 'Innovative elements and expected effectiveness of the 1991 EIA convention', *Environmental Impact Assessment Review*, vol 19, pp47–55

Ebbesson, J. (ed) (2002) *Access to Justice in Environmental Matters in the EU*, Kluwer Law International, The Hague

Garcia-Ureta, A. (1993) 'A comment on some provisions of the United Nations convention on EIA in a transboundary context', *Environmental Liability*, vol 1, pp101–112

Gray, K. R. (2000) 'International environmental impact assessment: Potential for a multilateral environmental agreement', *Colorado Journal of International Environmental Law and Policy*, vol 11, no 1, pp83–128

Hallo, R. (2007) 'The Aarhus Convention in operation: EEB survey initial results', *Environmental Law Network International Review*, no 2, pp2–4

Hildén, M. and Furman, E. (2001) 'Assessment across borders: Stumbling blocs and options in the practical implementation of the Espoo Convention', *Environmental Impact Assessment Review*, vol 21, pp537–551

Institut de Droit International (1997) *Resolution on Responsibility and Liability under International Law for Environmental Damage*, adopted on 4 September 1997 (1998) ILM 1474

IUCN/WWF/UNEP (1980) *The World Conservation Strategy*, International Union for the Conservation of Nature, World Wildlife Fund and United Nations Environment Programme, Gland, Switzerland

Jendroska, J. (2005) 'Public information and participation in EC environmental law: Origins, milestones and trends' in R. Macrory (ed) *Reflections on 30 Years of EU Environmental Law: A High Level of Protection*, Europa Law Publishing, Groningen, pp62–86

Jendroska, J. (2006) 'Public participation in environmental decision making: Implementation of the Aarhus Convention requirements in EC law' in T. Ormond, M. Führ and R. Barth (eds) *Environmental Law and Policy at the Turn of the 21st Century*, Lexxion, Berlin, pp37–50

Jendroska, J. and Stec, S. (2001) 'The Aarhus Convention: Towards a new era in environmental democracy', *Environmental Liability*, vol 9, pp140–151

Koester, V. (2005) 'Review of compliance under the Aarhus Convention: A rather unique compliance mechanism', *Journal for European Environmental and Planning Law*, vol 2, no 1, p33

Koester, V. (2007a) 'The compliance committee of the Aarhus Convention – An overview of procedures and jurisprudence', *Environmental Policy and Law*, vol 37, no 2, pp83–96

Koester, V. (2007b) 'The Convention on Access to Information, Public Participation in Decision Making and Access to Justice in Environmental Matters (Aarhus Convention)' in G. Ulfstein, T. Marauhn and A. Zimmermann (eds) *Making Treaties Work: Human Rights, Environment and Arms Control*, Cambridge University Press, Cambridge

Kimber, C. (1998) 'Understanding access to environmental information: The European experience' in T. Jewell and J. Steele (eds) *Law in Environmental Decision Making*, Clarendon, Oxford, pp139–160

Knox, J. (2002) 'The myth and reality of transboundary environmental impact assessment', *American Journal of International Law*, vol 96, no 2, pp291–319

Koivurova, T. (2007) 'The convention on environmental impact assessment in a transboundary context' in G. Ulfstein, T. Marauhn and A. Zimmermann (eds) *Making Treaties Work: Human Rights, Environment and Arms Control*, Cambridge University Press, Cambridge, pp218–241

Lavrysen, L. (2007) 'Presentation of Aarhus-related cases of the Belgium Constitutional Court', *Environmental Law Network International*, no 2, pp5–8

Lee, M. and Abbot, C. (2003) 'The usual suspects? Public participation under the Aarhus Convention' *Modern Law Review*, vol 66, no 1, pp80–108

Marsden, S. (2002) 'SEA and international law: An analysis of the effectiveness of the SEA protocol to the Espoo convention, and of the influence of the SEA directive and Aarhus convention on its development', *Environmental Law Network International Review*, vol 2, pp1–10

Marsden, S. and De Mulder, J. (2005) 'Strategic environmental assessment and sustainability in Europe: How bright is the future?', *Review of European Community and International Environmental Law*, vol 14, no 1, pp50–62

Mathiesen, A. (2003) 'Public participation in decision making and access to justice in EC environmental law: The case of certain plans and programmes', *European Environmental Law Review*, vol 12, no 2, pp36–52

McAllister, S. T. (1998) 'Human rights and the environment: The Convention on Access to Information, Public Participation in Decision Making, and Access to Justice in Environmental Matters', *Colorado Journal of International Environmental Law Yearbook*, vol 9, p187

McCracken, R. (2003) 'The Aarhus Convention: From Technocratic Paternalism to Participatory Democracy', paper presented to Aarhus Convention Conference, Environmental Law Foundation, Lincoln's Inn, London, 27 May

McCracken, R. and Jones, G. (2003) 'The Aarhus Convention', *Journal of Planning and Environmental Law*, vol 7, pp802–811

McHugh, P. (1994) 'The European Community Directive – An alternative environmental impact assessment procedure?', *Natural Resources Journal*, vol 34, pp589–600

Morgera, E. (2005) 'An update on the Aarhus Convention and its continued global relevance', *Review of European Community and International Environmental Law*, vol 14, no 2, pp138–147

Palerm, J. (1999) 'Public participation in environmental decision making: Examining the Aarhus convention', *Journal of Environmental Assessment Policy and Management*, vol 1, no 2, pp229–244

Petkova, E. and Veit, P. (2000) *Environmental Accountability Beyond the Nation State: The Implications of the Aarhus Convention*, World Resources Institute, Washington, DC

Rest, A. (2004) 'Enhanced implementation of international environmental treaties by judiciary – access to justice in international environmental law for individuals and NGOs: Efficacious enforcement by the Permanent Court of Arbitration', *Macquarie Journal of International and Comparative Environmental Law*, vol 1, pp1–28

Rodenhoff, V. (2002) 'The Aarhus Convention and its implications for the "institutions" of the European Community', *Review of European Community and International Environmental Law*, vol 11, no 3, p343

Sands, P. (1995) *Principles of International Environmental Law*, Manchester University Press, Manchester

Schrage, W. (1999) 'The convention on environmental impact assessment in a transboundary context' in Petts, J. (ed) *Handbook of Environmental Impact Assessment*, Blackwell Science, Oxford, vol 2, pp85–97

Schrage, W. (2004) 'The UN-ECE Convention on EIA in a trans-boundary context', *Environmental Liability*, vol 12, no 4, p151

Sheate, W. R. (1994) *Making an Impact Law and Policy: Making an Impact*, Cameron May, London.

Stanners, D. and Bordeau, P. (ed) (1995) *Europe's Environment: The Dobris Assessment*, European Environment Agency, Copenhagen

Stec, S. (ed) (2003) *Handbook on Access to Justice under the Aarhus Convention*, UNECE, New York and Geneva

Tesli, A. and Husby, S. (1999) 'EIA in a transboundary context: Principles and challenges for a coordinated Nordic application of the Espoo convention', *Environmental Impact Assessment Review*, vol 19, no 1, pp57–84

Tromans, S. and Fuller, K. (2003) *Environmental Impact Assessment - Law and Practice*, Reed Elsevier, London

UNECE (1991) *Policies and Systems of Environmental Impact Assessment*, United Nations, New York

UNECE (1992) *Application of Environmental Impact Assessment Principles to Policies, Plans and Programmes*, ECE/ENVWA/27, United Nations, New York

UNECE (1996) *Guidelines on Public Participation in Environmental Decision Making*, UNECE, Geneva

UNECE (2000) *The Aarhus Convention: An Implementation Guide*, United Nations, New York and Geneva

UNECE (2007) *Convention on Environmental Impact Assessment in a Transboundary Context Review of Implementation 2003*, Draft of 17 April 2007 submitted by the Secretariat for Consideration by the Respondents to the Questionnaire and by the Working Group on EIA, 21–23 May 2007

UNEP (1987) *Goals and Principles of Environmental Impact Assessment*, UNEP Res. GC14/25, 14th Sess., United Nations Environment Programme

Wates, J. (2005) 'The Aarhus Convention: A driving force for environmental democracy', *Journal for European Environmental and Planning Law*, vol 2, no 1, pp1–11

WCED (The World Commission on Environment and Development, or 'Brundtland Commission') (1987) *Our Common Future*, Oxford University Press, New York

Woodliffe, J. (2002) 'Environmental damage and environmental impact assessment' in M. Bowman and A. Boyle (2002) *Environmental Damage in International and Comparative Law: Problems of Definition and Valuation*, Oxford University Press, Oxford, pp133–147

Ziehm, C. (2005) 'Legal standing for NGOs in environmental matters under the Aarhus Convention and under Community and national law', *Journal of European Environmental and Planning Law*, vol 4, pp287–300

Zodrow, I. and Zengerling, C. (2007) 'Opening the doors to justice – the challenge of strengthening public access', *Environmental Law Network International Review*, no 2, pp20–23

Zschiesche, M. (2002) 'The Aarhus convention – more citizens' participation by setting out environmental standards?', *Environmental Law Network International*, vol 1, pp21–29

CHAPTER 5

The SEA Protocol

CHAPTER OUTLINE

This chapter analyses the procedural and substantive provisions of the SEA Protocol in detail, the latter of which are concerned primarily with access to information and public participation as influenced by the Aarhus Convention.[1] Without venturing too far into the content of Chapters 10 and 12, it also makes some comparisons with the SEA Directive.[2] It builds on Chapter 4 and the discussion of the two UNECE Conventions that provide institutional and procedural background and grounding to the Protocol; as such it should be read in close conjunction with Chapter 4. This is particularly so with respect to the substantive obligations of the Espoo Convention in Articles 14 and 15 (compliance and dispute settlement) and those of the Aarhus Convention in Articles 5(3)(b), 5(3)(c), 5(5)(a) and 5(7) (access to environmental information), and Articles 7 and 8 (public participation in the preparation of strategic proposals).

SEA PROTOCOL

The SEA Directive was adopted almost two years before the SEA Protocol, and as there is a close relationship between the membership of the UNECE and the membership of the EU, inevitably the SEA Directive had a significant influence on the development of the SEA Protocol. However, as indicated in Chapter 4, the SEA Protocol has also been developed in the context of the Aarhus and Espoo Conventions, the former to a greater extent than the latter, despite the Protocol being allied to the Espoo Convention. As De Mulder (2003) indicates, the SEA Protocol focuses almost entirely on establishing procedural SEA requirements in a national context, whereas the 'mother' agreement, the Espoo Convention, deals almost exclusively with procedural issues for EIA in a transboundary context.[3] Despite dilution of its early drafts, the adopted Protocol is undoubtedly the most significant of the international legal instruments that requires the assessment of certain strategic proposals and encourages the assessment of others. It was adopted in Kiev on 21 May 2003 at an extraordinary meeting of the Espoo Convention MOP, during the fifth Ministerial Meeting, 'Environment for Europe', and will come into force when 16 of the signatories ratify the Protocol.[4]

The Protocol followed on from the recommendation in Article 2(7) of the Espoo Convention that the parties 'endeavour to apply the principles of environmental impact assessment to policies, plans and programmes'. Although it is quite possible to evaluate the Protocol against SEA evaluative criteria to find out to what extent it demonstrates best practice, Jendroska and Stec (2003, p107) suggest that the key to evaluating the SEA Protocol is 'to measure it against the existing level of advancement of the UNECE member states'. It is therefore necessary to see to what extent the Protocol takes forward existing provisions found in the Aarhus Convention and SEA Directive, both of which are applicable to a large number of countries in the EU, EEA[5] and UNECE region.

Although some comparisons with the SEA Directive are therefore inevitable, readers are referred to Chapters 10 and 12 in this respect for further detailed analysis and comparison.[6] In making comparisons between provisions in legal instruments in both international and European law it must be remembered that if states are bound by each law then they must give effect to each, subject only to any reservations that have been validly made. The relationship between each legal instrument should be considered carefully, especially if they are linked, and any tendency to interpret the effect of a provision in isolation, either within the instrument or from linked instruments, should be avoided.[7] While there is discretion as to the means of implementing both treaties and European directives, and it is quite possible for one national law to implement the requirements of a combination of international and European law, this is also not always a straightforward matter. States that do not wish to 'gold plate' supranational or international legal requirements must at the same time be very careful not to transpose requirements inadequately and risk court or other action as a result.[8]

Historical development

Jendroska and Stec (2003) and De Mulder (2006) outline the historical development of the SEA Protocol.[9] Both indicate that while the issue had been discussed during negotiations for the Espoo Convention, Article 2(7) was as far as the parties were prepared to go at the time. Since the adoption of the Espoo Convention, however, state practice (and in some instances national legislative provisions) provided impetus to the development of the Protocol. The long discussions surrounding the SEA Directive in the EU, and the eventual decision in 1995 for an SEA Directive to proceed (see Chapter 10), were also instrumental in keeping the issue alive in the UNECE region (see also UNECE, 1992). The Espoo ratification process and the development of the Aarhus Convention were prioritized over the Protocol's development, which resulted in some delay in the period to 2000. The references to SEA in Articles 7 and 8 of the Aarhus Convention (as discussed in Chapter 4) illustrated that the matter had not been forgotten however.

In June 1999 at the third Ministerial Conference on Environment and Health in London, a proposal was tabled to begin work on the SEA Protocol under the Aarhus Convention. At Cavtat during the second Meeting of the Signatories (MOS) to the Aarhus Convention,[10] the proposal was hotly debated. In the meantime the Espoo Convention bodies had discussed the SEA issue during the initial work plan, and the decision was therefore taken at Cavtat that work on the SEA Protocol should begin under the auspices of the Espoo Convention and not the Aarhus Convention. The Aarhus Implementation Guide (UNECE, 2000, note 149) indicates that having the Protocol under either convention raised problems, 'to the Aarhus Convention because SEA is not only about public participation, to the Espoo Convention because SEA should not relate only to transboundary issues'. Jendroska and Stec (2003, p106) discuss this and the possibility of a protocol being developed jointly under both Conventions,[11] and suggest the reason why the Espoo Convention was ultimately chosen as the best vehicle for its development:

> *A main factor was that the Aarhus Convention had not yet entered into force (although steady progress was being made). The option of having a joint Protocol under the two Conventions – which at that very time was being arranged within the UNECE in another context – was also considered. However, the fact that the Aarhus Convention had not yet entered into force again made this premature.*[12]

The MOS to the Aarhus Convention eventually made a decision to ask the UNECE Committee on Environmental Policy to address the MOP of the Espoo Convention to take into account the need for involvement of the Aarhus Convention in the work plan on the SEA Protocol. The Aarhus MOS also decided to begin its own work to facilitate the integration of public participation and health issues into SEA, requesting the Regional Environment Centre for Central and Eastern Europe (REC) in cooperation with the World Health Organization (WHO) to organize international workshops to discuss such issues.[13] The final decision to begin the negotiations for the SEA Protocol was taken at the second MOP to the Espoo Convention on 26–27 February 2001 in Sofia, with a Working Group established to negotiate the instrument ready for adoption at the Fifth Ministerial Conference in May 2003 in Kiev. The Working Group held seven meetings from May 2001 to November 2002 when the final agreed text was prepared.

The January 2002 draft Protocol

One of the drafts of the Protocol was prepared by the Working Group of the Economic and Social Council of the UNECE in January 2002 (UNECE, 2002), with a view to its possible adoption. This is evaluated in Marsden (2002b) against the SEA performance criteria prepared by the IAIA (2002), which are outlined in Chapter 1. Such drafts are not just of academic importance to the final version; historically they are of interest because of the more far-reaching provisions originally contained within, which may point to future development;[14] legally such drafts are also preparatory documents, which when provisions in a final instrument are unclear may be used as an aid to interpretation.[15] The January 2002 draft included a general definition of 'strategic proposals' to include PPPs and legislation, rather than distinguishing between plans and programmes and policies and legislation.

A draft Article 3 also included a requirement for each party to 'modify the planning and decision-making frameworks to facilitate the integration of SEA, environmental and environment-related health considerations and public concerns into strategic decisions'. As Marsden comments (2002b, p5), 'this is significant, because the majority of the SEA literature strongly advocates *SEA* adapting to existing decision- and policy-making contexts' (my emphasis). Another provision originally included was that each party must 'apply the provisions of this Protocol [to changes] to existing strategic decisions'. This is also significant because the SEA Directive only applies to minor modifications and only to existing plans and programmes. Other original provisions that were more far reaching than in the final adopted Protocol were the requirements for public participation in Article 4, which were based substantially on the Aarhus Convention. As Marsden (2002b, p6)[16] comments:

> *The Article is potentially very significant indeed... because if approved in its broadest form, it may require public participation not only in the assessment process, but also in the decision-making process. This is phrased as 'participation in [procedures for making strategic decisions for which strategic environmental assessment is required under this Protocol, including] the strategic assessment procedure [itself].' There is no provision of this kind in the SEA Directive.*

Another provision of potential significance that was not included in the adopted version was the original Article 16 entitled 'Access to Justice'. Again derived from the Aarhus Convention, it required parties to ensure that the public has access to a review procedure before a court of law or other independent and impartial body established by law that must have the ability to challenge the substantive and procedural legality of the decisions on screening and scoping, and the preparation and content of the documentation produced. This would enable members of the public with a sufficient interest to challenge the legality of the strategic decision. Although the provision is not included in the adopted version, given that the Aarhus Convention is now in force and its requirements must be implemented, the absence of the original Article 16 from the Protocol does not mean that these opportunities of challenge are no longer available for individuals of states that have ratified both legal instruments. They should be seen as additional to the provisions for dispute settlement that are included in the adopted Protocol.

Context and objectives[17]

The adopted Protocol contains 8 recitals, 26 articles and 5 annexes. The first recital recognizes the importance of integrating environmental, including health, considerations into the preparation and adoption of plans and programmes, and to the extent appropriate, policies and legislation. The second recital commits the parties to promoting sustainable development, based in particular upon the conclusions of UNCED, especially Principles 4 and 10 of the *Rio Declaration* and *Agenda 21*, together with the outcome of the third Ministerial Conference on Environment and Health and the WSSD. These developments arguably provide the policy framework needed because they place the objective of the Protocol within a sustainable development context agreed by the international community, including the emphasis placed by the Protocol upon environmental health. The third and fifth recitals recognize the importance of the Espoo and Aarhus Conventions respectively, with the sixth emphasizing the importance of public participation. The fourth recital stresses the role of SEA:

> *Recognising that strategic environmental assessment should have an important role in the preparation and adoption of plans, programmes, and, to the extent appropriate, policies and legislation, and that the wider application of the principles of*

*environmental impact assessment to plans, programmes, policies and legislation will
further strengthen the systematic analysis of their significant environmental effects.*

The objectives of the SEA Protocol are found in Article 1, which states:

*The objective of the Protocol is to provide for a high level of protection of the environment,
including health, by:*

(a) *Ensuring that environmental, including health, considerations are thoroughly
taken into account in the development of plans and programmes;*
(b) *Contributing to the consideration of environmental, including health, concerns
in the preparation of policies and legislation;*
(c) *Establishing clear, transparent and effective procedures for strategic environmental
assessment;*
(d) *Providing for public participation in strategic environmental assessment;*
(e) *Integrating by these means environmental, including health, concerns into
measures and instruments designed to further sustainable development.*

De Mulder (2006, p271) believes that it is only Article 1(c) of the above objectives that
is really required, as supplemented by Article 1(d) that emphasizes the requirement for
transparency. The other objectives are not directed at the establishment of procedures,
or 'technical means' but at the decision making process, which is largely discretionary.
With regard to the role of the SEA Protocol in 'further[ing] sustainable development',
outlined in Article 1(e), De Mulder (2003, p13; 2006, p272) is highly critical. He states
that:

*Although the considerations in the preamble refer to the WSSD outcome (Johannesburg,
2002), the objectives of the SEA Protocol are not clearly situated within a policy
framework aimed at sustainable development. Given the absence of SEA in the meagre
WSSD Plan of Implementation, perhaps one should not be surprised.*

This is significant, because while some international instruments with a clear sustainable
development focus recognize the importance of SEA (such as the CBD, see Chapter
6), and while the SEA Directive is clearly situated in a sustainability framework of the
Treaty and Action Programmes of the EU, which recognize the role of SEA in taking the
agenda forward (see Chapters 7–11), this may not be the case with the SEA Protocol.
This is especially the case given the much criticized WSSD outcomes that include
diluting environmental protection in favour of economic development and a lack of
concrete proposals for action, such as new MEAs.

Strategic proposals covered

As also seen in the first, fourth and eighth recitals, of immediate note is that while the
Protocol is directed primarily at plans and programmes (see Article 4), Article 13(1)
also provides that it applies to policies and legislation, taking it beyond the provisions
of the SEA Directive in this significant area. It states:

> *Each Party shall endeavour to ensure that environmental, including health, concerns are considered and integrated to the extent appropriate in the preparation of its proposals for policies and legislation that are likely to have significant effects on the environment, including health.*

Article 13(2) emphasizes that in applying the above, each Party shall consider 'principles and elements' of the Protocol. The SEA Protocol Guidance (UNECE/REC, 2007a, p120) suggests that this means something other than 'an SEA process similar to that for plans and programmes', which, while it may be consistent with the majority view held by SEA academics and practitioners, is not apparent from a reading of either the legal text or its context. Rather, in referring to '*appropriate* principles and elements' of the Protocol, there is discretion given to the Parties to decide on the 'practical arrangements' as indicated in Article 13(3). Furthermore, the definition of SEA in Article 2(1)(6) does not distinguish between different types of strategic proposals, indicating that all of the procedural elements included therein are also applicable to the assessment of policies and legislative proposals, at least to some extent. Despite the discretionary nature of the provisions in Article 13(1), (2) and (3), they are given weight because of the obligation contained within Article 13(4), which requires that: 'Each Party shall report to the Meeting of the Parties to this Convention serving the Meeting of the Parties to this Protocol on its application of this article'.

De Mulder (2003, p9; 2006, p276) comments on Article 13(4) that it: 'is intended to push parties towards the implementation of this article'. The title and objectives of the Protocol give additional substance to this conclusion. While plans and programmes are strategic decisions, they are not *as* strategic as policies and legislation, as they are not the highest levels of decision making and are therefore rather more limited in the extent to which they can provide a 'high level of protection of the environment'. In Dovers' terminology (2002, p26), they are 'shallow' rather than 'deep' targets for SEA. The SEA Protocol Guidance (UNECE/REC, 2007a, p121) recognizes the greater role the assessment of policy and legislative proposals can play in commenting: 'the potential for furthering sustainable development is substantial when environmental concerns can be considered and integrated into decision-making at these more strategic levels'. The Guidance (p125) also makes reference to Articles 7 and 8 of the Aarhus Convention, which provides for public participation in the preparation of policy and legislative proposals (see Chapter 4).

The SEA Protocol therefore takes assessment of strategic decision making a stage further, albeit on a discretionary basis, as it can be applied to policies and legislation.[18] Commentators differ on how much further, with pessimism not uncommon (see, for example, De Mulder, 2006, p276); Jendroska and Stec (2003 p108), however, draw particular attention to the potential assessment of policies and legislation, commenting:

> *by covering, even in a soft way, policies and legislation, the Protocol adds something in comparison with the SEA Directive of 2001, which does not mention policies and legislation. Worth noting here in particular is the fact that the Protocol covers legislation. While policies have already been mentioned in the context of environmental assessment in other documents (for example in the Espoo Convention itself) the Protocol is to be arguably the first binding international instrument to mention (though in a*

rather recommendatory fashion) the need for environmental assessment in relation to legislation.

Definitions and general provisions

Article 2 is the definition section and follows the definitions in the Espoo Convention wherever possible. In a transboundary context, for example, 'party of origin' is used to refer to the contracting party responsible for the strategic decision and 'affected party' refers to the contracting party whose environment may be impacted upon by the decision. Of particular importance is the definition of 'strategic environmental assessment', which fails to state categorically whether it is limited to plans and programmes or includes policies and legislation, as indicated above. This therefore concerns a much greater range of decisions than the SEA Directive, which is presently limited to plans and programmes.

Procedural provisions of the SEA Protocol are very similar if not identical to those of the SEA Directive. The definition of plans and programmes (Article 2(5)) is identical, and the definition of SEA in the Protocol is very similar to that of EA in the Directive, although the Protocol goes further and includes the evaluation of likely environmental and health effects (Article 2(6)). The definition of 'the public' in Article 2(8) is discussed at length in the section on public participation because it fails to accord with the definition of 'the public concerned' in the Aarhus Convention (see also Chapter 4). General provisions of the Protocol are outlined in Article 3 and include that 'Each Party shall take the necessary legislative, regulatory and other appropriate measures to implement the provisions of this Protocol within a clear, transparent framework' (Article 3(1)). Assistance from authorities to the public (Article 3(2)) and support to NGOs (Article 3(3)) is also an important part of the Protocol.

Screening

The SEA Protocol Guidance (UNECE/REC, 2007a) explains the legal obligations that determine whether SEA is required under the Protocol through ten key tests (pp52–62), which are set out in the form of questions in a flowchart reproduced here as Figure 5.1. Because of the almost identical provisions, the Protocol Guidance refers extensively to the SEA Directive Guidance (Reps of the MS/EC, 2003), which is outlined in detail in Chapter 10; as such, cross references will be omitted here.

Tests 1 and 2 deal with the definition of a plan or programme, and ask first whether the plan or programme (or modification) is required by legislative, regulatory or administrative provisions (Article 2(5)(a)), and second whether the plan or programme is subject to preparation and/or adoption by an authority for adoption, through a formal procedure, by parliament or a government (Article 2(5)(b)). Not surprisingly, the label of the strategic proposal is not relevant to whether it is classed as a plan or programme, although no definition is provided by the Protocol itself, which also treats plans and programmes identically. The SEA Protocol Guidance (UNECE/REC, 2007a, p49) comments:

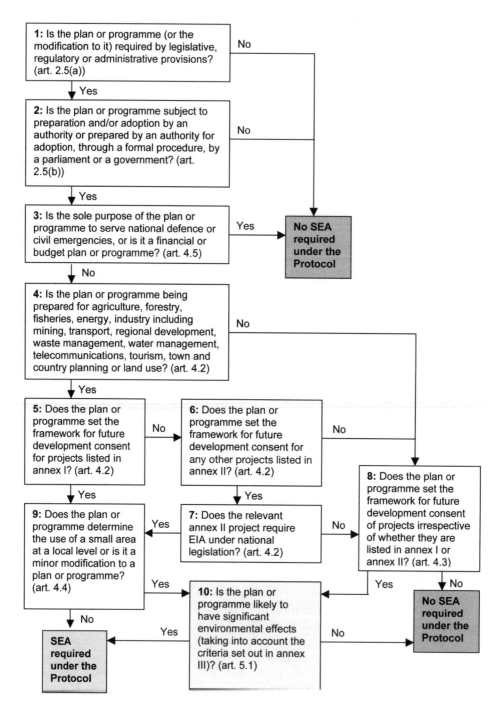

Figure 5.1   *Guide to determining whether a particular plan or programme should be subject to SEA under the Protocol*

Some so-called policies, strategies and concepts that have the features of plans or programmes defined by the Protocol will require SEA. It is even possible that some laws and regulations might fall within the field of application of the Protocol, again provided that they meet its conditions.

Article 2(5) clearly ensures, however, that there is a need for a plan or programme to be formally required or prepared through the broad range of mechanisms outlined. Test 3 contains an exemption for plans and programmes where the sole purpose of their preparation is to serve national defence or civil emergencies, or they are financial or budget plans or programmes.

Tests 4, 5, 6 and 7 concern the mandatory application of the SEA Protocol (Article 4(2)). Test 4 asks whether the plan or programme is being prepared for agriculture, forestry, fisheries, energy, industry including mining, transport, regional development, waste management, water management, telecommunications, tourism, town and country planning or land use. Test 5 asks whether the plan or programme sets the framework for future development consent for any project listed in Annex I, which is broadly similar to the relevant list for the SEA Directive (which is Annex I of the EIA Directive, see Chapter 9). Test 6 asks whether the plan or programme sets the framework for future development consent for any other project listed in Annex II, and Test 7 whether the relevant Annex II project requires EIA under national legislation.

The key legal issue in respect of the mandatory application of the SEA Protocol is the meaning of 'set the framework for future development consent', which is discussed in detail in Chapter 10. The SEA Protocol Guidance (UNECE/REC, 2007a, p58) suggests that Tests 6 and 7 can be considered together. It also highlights that the Annex II list in the Protocol is not identical to the Annex II list of the EIA Directive, which is relevant to the SEA Directive. It further emphasizes that:

Test 7 introduces an important difference between the Protocol and Directive: those projects listed in annex II to the Protocol that do not require EIA under national legislation do not need to be included. In contrast, all projects in the corresponding list for the SEA Directive are included, irrespective of whether national legislation requires EIA.

Tests 8 and 9 concern the non-mandatory application of the Protocol. Test 8 asks whether the plan or programme sets the framework for future development consent of projects irrespective of whether they are listed in Annex I or Annex II (Article 4(3)), which includes projects in sectors that are not listed in Article 4(2) and projects that are not listed in Annexes I and II. Test 9 asks whether the plan or programme determines the use of a small area at a local level or is a minor modification to a plan or programme (Article 4(4)). There is a need for interpretation of the terms in Article 4(4) as the Protocol does not define them; the SEA Directive Guidance (Reps of the MS/EC, 2003) (see Chapter 10) again provides suggestions. Where Tests 8 and 9 apply, Test 10 must also be applied (Article 5(1)). This asks if the plan or programme is likely to have significant environmental effects, which is determined in accordance with the criteria set out in Annex III (which is similar to Annex II of the SEA Directive).

The SEA Protocol Guidance (UNECE/REC, 2007a, pp60–61) cautions against making judgments not to carry out SEA where uncertainty is present, concluding that in relation to the word 'likely', 'it is only required to show that an effect can be expected with a reasonable degree of probability'.[19] Annex III(5) provides that where there is discretion as to whether plans or programmes are to be assessed, one of the criteria for determining likely significant effects is 'the nature of the environmental, including health, effects such as probability, duration, frequency, reversibility, magnitude and extent'. Annex III(6) cites 'the risks to the environment, including health'.

The Protocol must therefore be applied to the same plans and programmes as the Directive, with the addition of regional development and mining (as part of the industry sector), and with the change that the Protocol does not specify that SEA is required for plans and programmes prepared at all levels of government, which may result in different interpretations (Jendroska and Stec, 2003, p108). Sectoral plans and programmes must set the framework for future development consent of projects for which an EIA is required under national or international law; Annex I (based on Appendix I of the Espoo Convention) and Annex II (based on Annex II of the EIA Directive) set out relevant projects. Similar provisions to the SEA Directive allow for discretionary SEA under the Protocol in the case of plans and programmes that determine the use of small areas at local level and minor modifications to plans and programmes. Jendroska and Stec (2003, pp105–110) state that even minor modifications to supplement the obligations envisaged in the SEA Directive were not accepted by the EU MS negotiators during the work on the draft Protocol; it was also not accepted that the Protocol could avoid the need for plans and programmes to set the framework for development consent of projects, which was another possibility under the January 2002 draft.

Scoping

Article 6(1) of the Protocol states that each Party shall establish arrangements for the determination of the relevant information to be included in the environmental report in accordance with Article 7(2). There is no obligation to prepare a scoping report that would set out the terms of reference, although this is recommended by the SEA Protocol Guidance, which gives some examples in a European context (UNECE/REC, 2007a, pp79–80). There is no indication in the Protocol of who is responsible for preparing the environmental report, but the SEA Protocol Guidance suggests it is likely to be the authority responsible for preparing the draft plan or programme (p71). Article 7(1) only requires an environmental report to be prepared if plans and programmes are determined to need SEA. Article 7(2) outlines the terms of reference for the report and states:

> *The environmental report shall, in accordance with the determination under article 6, identify, describe and evaluate the likely significant environmental, including health, effects of implementing the plan or programme and its reasonable alternatives. The report shall contain such information specified in annex IV as may reasonably be required, taking into account:*

(a)   Current knowledge and methods of assessment;
(b)   The contents and the level of detail of the plan or programme and its stage in the decision-making process;
(c)   The interests of the public; and
(d)   The information needs of the decision-making body.[20]

Health effects are a significant addition to be considered in the environmental report, and as such, health authorities have the same procedural rights as environmental authorities (see next section). However, Jendroska and Stec (2003, p110) indicate that health effects may cause one of the greatest interpretation issues with the Protocol because the lack of agreement between the negotiators over what types of health effects are covered (for example, human health, animal health, environmental health generally). Despite the production of guidance documentation from WHO (Breeze and Lock, 2001) and now also UNECE/REC (2007b), the status of this is that it will not be legally binding and hence interpretation will remain a matter for the courts in all cases.

Alternatives form a significant part of the overall determination and several pages of the SEA Protocol Guidance are devoted to this (UNECE/REC, 2007a, pp69–71 and p81). Although the term 'alternatives' is not defined, the Protocol treats the draft plan or programme and the alternatives as the same, so the report must cover all reasonable alternatives fully. The Guidance suggests that alternatives may include an alternative plan or programme, or alternative elements within the plan or programme. They may also include alternative locations, land uses, technologies, timing, development paths or sets of objectives (p71). The consideration of alternatives should ideally form part of an iterative process, as indicated (p72), which should include the elaboration of objectives established at international, national and other levels (p73). Consideration of the benefits of a tiered approach should also be given despite, in contrast to the SEA Directive, the absence in the Protocol of an explicit reference to tiering (p75). This is no doubt in part explained by the difference in European environmental law that there is a clear procedural link between project and plan and programme level assessment with respect to the EIA and SEA Directives. The link between the Espoo Convention (concerned with transboundary EIA) and the SEA Protocol (concerned with national SEA) is rather different and as seen, was more a matter of convenience than practicality.

Article 7(3) emphasizes that each Party must 'ensure that environmental reports are of sufficient quality to meet the requirements of this Protocol'. What this means is explained by the SEA Protocol Guidance with examples (UNECE/REC, 2007a, pp82–85). This indicates that there is flexibility as to the body responsible for ensuring quality control, there being no obligation to ensure independence from the authority responsible for the preparation of the draft plan or programme, and/or the environmental report, which is undoubtedly a disadvantage when contrasted with national traditions whereby independent bodies may evaluate reports or procedures, such as in the Netherlands with the EIA Commission and Canada with an Environmental Commissioner (Marsden, 1998, 1999).[21] It also indicates that a failure to ensure sufficient quality in report preparation 'may call into question the validity of any decision taken as a result of the SEA' (p83), which potentially can result in a legal challenge.

Consultation, participation and information provision

There are several provisions in the SEA Protocol that deal with consultation with authorities (including of a transboundary nature), public participation and the provision of information. The general legal obligations are found in Article 9 (consultation with environmental and health authorities), Article 10 (transboundary consultations) and Article 8 (public participation). Other obligations deal with various matters, such as screening. Article 5, for example, introduces mandatory and discretionary provisions for the involvement of environmental and health authorities and the public in the significance determinations, with the SEA Protocol Guidance setting out some practical arrangements for making publicly available the determination of significant effects (UNECE/REC, 2007a, p63), and commenting (pp59–60):

> *Whereas the earlier tests (1–9 – field of application) may be carried out internally, within an authority, Test 10 (determination of significant effects) requires at least the consultation with the environmental and health authorities. Test 10 also explicitly provides for public participation, but this provision is not mandatory (and is not a requirement of the SEA Directive...). The Protocol requires that the results of any determination of significant effects be made publicly available, again in contrast with the earlier tests.*

In accordance with Article 9(1) it is up to each Party to designate the authorities that must be consulted and to whom the draft plan or programme and environmental report shall be made available (Article 9(2)). This can be done explicitly by including them in legislation implementing the Protocol, or implicitly, providing for their appointment on a case by case basis (UNECE/REC, 2007a, p96). Although the documents must be given in an 'early, timely and effective manner', in order that they may have an opportunity to express their opinion, the detailed arrangements are left to the discretion of each Party. Article 10 draws a close link between the SEA Protocol and Espoo Convention, requiring transboundary consultations between Parties of origin and affected Parties, at the initiation of either, 'as early as possible before the adoption of the plan or programme' (Article 10(1)). Notifications are to include the draft plan or programme and the environmental report, and information on the decision making procedure. The public concerned in either country are able to express their opinions within a reasonable timeframe, subject to agreement between each Party as to the detailed arrangements (Article 10(4)). Bilateral and multilateral arrangements may be established for this purpose (UNECE/REC, 2007a, p99).[22]

Article 8(1) requires 'early, timely and effective opportunities for public participation, when all options are open'. De Mulder (2006, p274) discusses the meaning of this, concluding that 'the public participation referred to in paragraph 1 must be situated earlier in the SEA process [than under the SEA Directive, which comes after the report is finished]'.[23] The SEA Protocol Guide (UNECE/REC, 2007a, p93) suggests utilizing experience with EIA consultation procedures to establish when this may be, 'but care should be taken to allow enough time for opinions to be properly developed and formulated on lengthy, complex, contentious or far-reaching plans and programmes' (p93).

Article 8(2) contains an information provision, such that each Party shall ensure the 'timely public availability of the draft plan or programme and the environmental report'. This is to be done 'using electronic media or other appropriate means', suggesting that 'timely' is to be interpreted in an expedious manner. There is no explicit requirement that the draft plan or programme and the environmental report must be made available together in the Protocol, unlike the SEA Directive (in Article 6(2)). The public concerned (including relevant NGOs) must be identified (Article 8(3)) and must have an opportunity to express its opinion on the draft plan or programme and the environmental report within a 'reasonable time frame' (Article 8(4)). The detailed arrangements for informing and consulting the public must be decided on and also made publicly available (Article 8(5)).

There are several other provisions. Article 6(3) allows for public participation in deciding on the terms of reference for the environmental report, 'to the extent appropriate', which contrasts with the obligation in Article 6(2) to ensure that environmental and health authorities are consulted at this stage. Although Article 6(3) is apparently a weak discretionary provision (of which there is no comparable provision in the SEA Directive), it is possible that this may be interpreted more expansively because the wording of Article 8(1) applies to 'the strategic environmental assessment of plans and programmes', which would certainly include scoping the terms of reference of the environmental report because of the definition of SEA in Article 2(6). Article 7(2)(c) also requires the interests of the public to be taken into account in the environmental report.

Both the Protocol and the Directive (see Chapter 10) have failed to implement an important requirement of the Aarhus Convention, as despite the use of the words 'the public concerned' in Article 8(3) and 8(5) of the Protocol, the definition of this is absent from Article 2 (De Mulder, 2006, p272). Article 2(8) only defines the public but not the public concerned, although the inclusion of 'associations, organizations and groups' takes it beyond the Aarhus definition of 'the public' as follows: '"The public" means one or more natural or legal persons and, in accordance with national legislation or practice, their associations, organizations or groups'. Although the Aarhus Convention had not entered into force at the time the decision was taken to proceed with the Protocol under the Espoo Convention, there was no obvious reason why its provisions should not have been transferred to the SEA Protocol. To remedy the deficiency, the SEA Protocol Guidance suggests, rather than recommends, that 'Parties might choose to employ this definition' (UNECE/REC, 2007a, p91), which, for Parties to the Protocol who are also Parties to the Aarhus Convention, or who are bound by its provisions as a matter of EC law, is likely to result in non-compliance with the Convention.

Jendroska and Stec (2003, p108) discuss the absence of other substantive provisions in the SEA Protocol that should also have been transferred from the Aarhus Convention:

> The final version of the Protocol, unlike the initial draft, does not in general terms address the issue of rights of the public in the preparation of plans, programmes, policies or legislation (i.e., in terms of the broadly formulated rights granted under Articles 7, 8 and 9 of the Aarhus Convention). While there are references to the Aarhus Convention in the Preamble, subparagraph (d) of Article 1 sets the stage when it states that one of the objectives of the Protocol is to provide, 'for public participation

> *in strategic environmental assessment.' As distinct from public involvement in the whole complex process of decision-making from start to finish, the Protocol provisions concerning rights of the public are limited to the SEA element itself and the documents produced under it, except for Article 8.4 which, following the SEA Directive, provides an option to comment upon the draft plan or programme, not only upon the relevant environmental report.*

Further, as mentioned above, the original draft Article 16 on access to justice is absent from the adopted Protocol. De Mulder (2003, p10) comments pessimistically on this that 'if the unwillingness to agree on a provision that could have been a cornerstone for the effectiveness of a national SEA system is symbolic for the future, then the SEA Protocol remains an open question'. What is included, however, is the reference to discrimination in Articles 3(6) and 3(7), which is relevant to the third pillar of the Aarhus Convention. The question of the full implementation of the Aarhus Convention is also discussed with regard to the SEA Directive and Public Participation Directive in Chapter 9, the latter of which has been comprehensively analysed by Mathieson (2003).

Reporting, decision making and monitoring

Under Article 5(4), the results of the screening process must be made available, 'by public notice or other appropriate means, such as electronic media'. Jendroska and Stec (2003, p109) indicate that while this still falls short of the Aarhus obligation of actively informing a targeted public, it still requires some 'affirmative action'. They state that the term 'appropriate' refers back to the requirement of 'timely' availability, 'which should be interpreted in the context of further stages of the process'. This would allow for the possibility of questioning the results of screening or influencing scoping.

As already stated, reasonable alternatives must be considered in the environmental report under Article 7(2), and Annex IV(8) emphasizes the importance of this. Both of these provisions are almost identical to provisions in the SEA Directive. When the decision is taken to adopt the plan or programme, Parties must ensure that due account is taken of the conclusions of the environmental report, the measures to prevent, reduce or mitigate the adverse effects identified, and the comments received (Article 11(1)). In accordance with Article 11(2) notice of the decision must be given to the public and authorities (including any consulted affected Party), together with the adopted plan or programme, with a statement of how the environmental and health considerations and comments received have been integrated/taken into account, as well as the reasons for adopting it 'in the light of the reasonable alternatives considered'. This is very similar to Annex I(h) of the SEA Directive, and there is no provision for confidentiality.

With regard to monitoring, the Protocol and Directive provisions are almost identical. Article 12(1) of the Protocol requires each Party to monitor effects 'to identify, at an early stage, unforeseen adverse effects and to be able to take appropriate remedial action'. Monitoring measures must be stipulated in the environmental report in accordance with Annex IV(7) and results are to be made available to the authorities and the public in accordance with Article 12(2). Overall, the provision is scant, with an absence of detail, as indicated by the SEA Protocol Guidance. Given that follow-up is the weakest link of EA, it is therefore perhaps unsurprising, that the Guidance is impliedly critical (UNECE/REC, 2007a, p102):

> *The Protocol does not suggest the who, what, where, when or how of monitoring – who is to undertake it, who is to make results available, what to monitor (except, in general terms, the significant environmental effects of the plan or programme), what to make available (raw results or analyses thereof), where to monitor, what frequency and for how long, when to make results available, and how to monitor (methods) and to make results available.*

In relation to this, a further weakness of the Protocol is the quality control procedure in Article 7(3), which is considered weaker than the provision in the SEA Directive, as it fails to stipulate any mechanism at all for achieving it. This is surprising given that the Commission's representative admitted during the negotiations that this requirement in the Directive could have been stronger, and the five year review of the EIA Directive demonstrated the need for such a provision (Commission of the European Communities, 2003; De Mulder, 2006, pp273–274). Jendroska and Stec (2003, p108) refer to this weakness, suggesting that some countries were not prepared to take on responsibility for a stricter quality control mechanism.

Implementation and compliance

The questions of implementation and compliance with the SEA Protocol are largely academic until the Protocol enters into force,[24] yet it is still surprising that the SEA Protocol Guide (UNECE/REC, 2007a) makes no reference to the administrative and judicial provisions governing these important matters, as they may serve to influence the extent to which a Party is prepared to 'gold plate' the provisions of the Protocol to take greater account of, for example, the Aarhus Convention. In this regard, the omission of an access to justice provision has been commented on already as a weakness of the Protocol (De Mulder, 2003).

The Protocol is, however, subject to review by the Parties under Article 14, in accordance with the procedures for the Espoo MOP (see Chapter 4). There are a number of elements to this, outlined in paragraph 4, which include the need to improve procedures, exchange information and consider and adopt proposals for amendment. Jendroska and Stec (2003, p110) identify the importance of this and hope 'that a strong procedure for review of compliance will be established at the first Meeting of Parties'. Yet a crucial factor in the success of this will be whether there is sufficient funding for the process and the political will to provide the information as well as consider reform options. The effectiveness of MEAs have been demonstrated to be closely linked to both of these things. De Mulder (2003, p11) cites Wettestad (1999) in this respect, who comments on the crucial role of a convention secretariat in the following terms:

> *Regimes with secretariats which have financially strong and relatively autonomous and active positions (up to a certain optimal point) tend to be more effective than regimes with less financially strong and active secretariats; however the importance of the role of the secretariat may be seen as conditional upon the administrative capacities of the parties themselves.*

As to dispute settlement, Article 20 of the SEA Protocol states that the Espoo dispute settlement procedures apply also to the SEA Protocol (see Chapter 4). Referring to the views of other commentators, De Mulder (2006, p276) describes this as 'no worse than similar provisions in other MEAs', although the reality is that Parties usually prefer non-judicial means of settling their disputes, which is likely to entail political compromise. Whether this is possible where individuals are able to utilize access to justice provisions in respect of situations that are also governed by the third Aarhus pillar requirements remains to be seen. In relation to transboundary disputes, De Mulder (2006, pp276–277) outlines the recent application of Article 3 of the Espoo Convention, which is designed to prevent disputes occurring in the first place, with reference to an inquiry commission, and also to the role of a compliance commission, neither of which are applicable in the context of the SEA Protocol, although the approval of the Espoo compliance procedure will become binding on Parties to the SEA Protocol in the future (see Chapter 4), as Article 14 *bis*, paragraph 2 states that: 'The compliance procedure shall be available for application to any protocol adopted under this Convention'.

In response to a decision of the Protocol MOS in June 2004, the UNECE and REC prepared a draft Resource Manual in 2006 to support the application of the SEA Protocol; this was later finalized (2007a) and as considered above includes information on both the application of the Protocol and a trainers' guide.[25] The information contained within is largely directed to practical issues, with legal matters mainly confined to two chapters, A3 and A4, which cover screening and other procedural stages as discussed. While the information contained within has no legal status, it is intended to assist in the practical implementation of the Protocol, which includes help in explaining the intention and meaning of the law set out in the Protocol, albeit as heavily influenced by the SEA Directive Guidance (Reps of the MS/EC, 2003).

The intention is that the Manual will be revised and developed as decided by the signatories and later parties to the Protocol. In referring to the SEA Directive Guidance it is made clear, however, that the Manual 'does not serve as formal interpretative guidance for the SEA Protocol or for the SEA Directive' (p3). In highlighting the main requirements of the Protocol, outlining the key issues for applying it in practice,and providing materials for training and capacity building, several suggestions are made for 'gold plating' the requirements of the Protocol in accordance with best practice, which overall are to be recommended.[26] Until the Protocol comes into force, guidance and capacity building activity within the context of the UNECE is likely to be ongoing.[27]

CONCLUSIONS

The SEA Protocol is unquestionably the most significant of the international legal instruments making provision for the assessment of strategic proposals. Its entry into force and future development will likely encourage preparation of national SEA laws globally, many of which may choose to 'gold plate' its existing requirements and require application to policies and legislation as well as plans and programmes, just as a few enlightened countries have already done regarding the SEA Directive. The Protocol will also result in changes to the SEA Directive when it comes into force, as the EC is a signatory and will, on ratification, be bound to bring into effect the changes between the Protocol and Directive outlined, including changes needed as a result of ratification of the Aarhus Convention also, of which both the SEA Protocol and Directive are currently not compliant.

That the Protocol is a product of the heavyweights at the negotiating table and reflects their views is not surprising. Where the Protocol fails to take account of existing legally binding obligations and incorporate them fully (such as the Aarhus requirements) it is likely to be the subject of initial resolutions of the MOP when it commences business. Similarly, the Protocol is likely to continue to change and develop over time to reflect the majority position, which may bring it more into line with the aspirations of those who were disappointed by the watering down of many of its early provisions. Chapter 6 considers other MEAs that relate to SEA. While these typically do not require SEA as a matter of convention law, resolutions of COPs and MOPs have encouraged its use in implementing treaty provisions, and therefore illustrate practice that may develop when the SEA Protocol MOP begins its own work.

NOTES

1   See Chapter 1 where it was explained how the use of the terms 'procedural' and 'substantive' in the context of legal provisions is in a completely different sense to their use in evaluating the effectiveness of EA systems.
2   The decision where to place this chapter in the book was not an easy one. While it may have been easier to discuss the individual provisions of the SEA Protocol if it had followed a chapter on the SEA Directive, the overall structure of the book would have been compromised, as dealing with international law first in its entirety makes sense for several reasons: much IEL has influenced European environmental law, especially the soft law of sustainable development and the precautionary principle, and the general principle of EIA; explaining the structure of international law also assists in understanding the treaty based nature of European law; and the analysis of the SEA Protocol is also best followed on from an examination of UNECE treaties. Similarly, the SEA Directive is best placed in the context of European law as it relates to the EIA and other directives explained in Chapters 9 and 11. To overcome the difficulties of immediate comparative analysis that come from the placement of Chapters 5 and 10 therefore, Chapter 12 provides a final opportunity to consider and emphasize key differences, which are in any event very few.
3   As seen, this language is common in international and European law. Framework conventions or directives are often referred to as 'mother' conventions/directives, with 'daughter' protocols or directives, containing more specific content, related to them. Unlike these framework conventions/directives, the relationship between the Espoo Convention and SEA Protocol is somewhat different, the first being focused on transboundary EIA, the second on national SEA. Examples of more typical mother conventions/directives and related daughter protocols/directives include the Framework Convention on Climate Change and related Kyoto Protocol, and the Waste Framework Directive and the Hazardous Waste Directive; for detail on both see Davies (2004, pp217–305).
4   Jendroska and Stec (2003, p108) indicate that the Protocol was negotiated with a view to its being signed and ratifed by the European Commission on behalf of the EC. This means that its provisions will apply to EU institutions as well as the MS within; the same is also the case for the Aarhus Convention, which has already been implemented by Regulation (EC) No 1367/2006 of 6 September 2006 of the European Parliament and of the Council

on the application of the provisions of the Aarhus Convention on Access to Information, Public Participation in Decision Making and Access to Justice in Environmental Matters to EC institutions and bodies. To date (January 2008) there are seven parties to the Protocol; for the current ratification status, see unece.org

5   To recap, the EEA also comprises countries outside the EU but which bind themselves to EU law, such as members of the EFTA, including Norway. The EEA is not the same as the ECE region, which includes countries outside of the European continent, particularly Canada and the US.

6   The reason the provisions of the Protocol are so closely related to the Directive is because of the reluctance of the European Commission and many MS of the EU to consider substantial changes to the Directive so soon after it came into effect. This was reflected in the turbulent discussions in the SEA Working Group, which are outlined by De Mulder (2003), a Belgium delegate to the negotiations and later Chair of the MOS to the SEA Protocol (see below), who comments: 'the overall feeling is that the EU has been able to obtain what it wanted'.

7   Jendroska and Stec (2003, p109) comment on the relationship between the SEA Directive, Espoo and Aarhus Conventions as follows:

> *[It] must be remembered that States which are Parties to both the SEA Protocol and the Aarhus Convention may find some further elaboration of the standards relevant to public participation in strategic decision-making in the latter instrument. The Protocol takes the unusual step of referring to both the parent convention and the Aarhus Convention in an article on the relationship of the Protocol to other international agreements, Article 15. That article provides that the Protocol shall apply without prejudice to those two conventions.*

The last sentence means that there is an obligation to implement the requirements of all relevant provisions.

8   'Gold plating' refers to doing more than the provision requires. States are always free to do this if they wish and many do. Compliance with the basic provisions of international and European law is typically referred to as a 'write-out', which simply copies the exact wording into national law; while it may on paper be the safest way of ensuring legal compliance, the complexities of the legal traditions of each state may still cause difficulties needing contextualization.

9   Professor Jendroska served as the Vice-Chair of the Working Group negotiating the SEA Protocol and as the Head of the Polish delegation, and, at least at the time of publication, was the Chair of the Aarhus Convention MOP. The Chair of the SEA Working Group was Terje Lind.

10 An MOS denotes that a convention has been adopted by the states involved in its preparation but not ratified by those eligible to join. It is only after ratification that an MOP or COP can be held.

11 This is not uncommon practice. Jendroska and Stec (2003) (endnote 5) refer to the joint Protocol on Civil Liability that was negotiated under two other UNECE conventions: the Convention on the Protection and Use of Transboundary Watercourses and International Lakes, and the Convention on the Transboundary Effects of Industrial Accidents. The Aarhus Implementation Guide (UNECE, 2000, note 149, p177) also makes reference to this, but states that 'the success of this approach is not yet apparent, however'. It goes on to state, perhaps controversially, that: 'It would seem to be most appropriate for SEA to be the subject of a new convention' (note 149, p177).

12 Note that the Aarhus Convention now has a protocol of its own, the Protocol on Pollutant Release and Transfer Register, which was adopted at the same extraordinary meeting of the MOP as the SEA Protocol in Kiev on 21 May 2003, during the Fifth Ministerial Conference. See Morgera (2005, pp143–144).

13   The REC has played an active role in SEA development, especially in the areas of practice and guidelines. For examples see the SEA Handbook that emerged from the First International Conference on SEA held in Prague 2005 (Sadler et al, 2008), *SEA Resource Manual to Support Application of the UNECE Protocol on SEA* (UNECE/REC, 2007a) and *SEA at the Policy Level: Recent Progress, Current Status and Future Prospects* (Sadler, 2005).

14   In referring to the provision encouraging parties to apply environmental assessment to policies and legislation, Jendroska and Stec (2003, p109) illustrate this and comment: 'Taken as a whole, while obviously falling short of the expectations of many as to the potential for addressing these issues under the Protocol, Article 13 creates a significant framework upon which to build in the future'.

15   This is discussed in Chapter 2 paragraph 2.3.1 with reference to Article 32 of the VCLT 1969.

16   The square brackets in the quotation contain an expanded version of the draft for the potential signatories of the Protocol to consider.

17   This section is drawn largely from Marsden and De Mulder (2005).

18   SEA provisions in some countries do this already; see Chapter 1, Sadler (2005) and Marsden (1998, 1999, 2002a).

19   By contrast, for the mandatory application of the Protocol (under Article 4(2), if Tests 4, 5, 6 and 7 are satisfied), it is assumed that the proposal will have significant environmental effects.

20   The SEA Directive does not include (c) and (d) of these criteria.

21   The SEA Protocol Guidance (UNECE/REC, 2007a, p83) acknowledges that the Protocol provides only a 'minimum standard' in this regard, commenting 'there are many options for going further, e.g. independent assessments, guidelines on procedural or substantive requirements, review by an independent institution, reliance on complaints or legal appeals'.

22   The Espoo Convention has prepared guidance on public participation in a transboundary context, available at www.unece.org/env/eia/publications.html

23   De Mulder (2006, note 40) also compares the wording of Article 8(1) with Article 8(4), concluding that because of the differences, 'in my opinion, the use of "early" in para 1 of Article 8 has a very general but far-reaching meaning'.

24   For example, Stoeglehner and Wegerer (2006, p586) have compared the potential implementation of the SEA Protocol with the SEA Directive regarding spatial planning in Austria. They conclude that the Protocol will 'generate comparatively modest additional benefits that might be accompanied by quite high additional expenses'. Whether this occurs remains to be seen. Further comparisons between the SEA Directive and SEA Protocol are made in Chapters 10 and 12.

25   See also Dusik et al (2006)

26   See, for example, (p25) the suggestions made about considering the conclusions of the environmental report during the development of the plan or programme as well as during the adoption of the plan or programme, which exceed the requirements of Article 11.

27   At the 'Environment for Europe' Ministerial Conference held in Belgrade in October 2007, a side event was organized to review implementation of the Protocol and discuss the Resource Manual.

REFERENCES

Breeze, C. and Lock, K. (2001) *Health Impact Assessment as Part of Strategic Environmental Assessment*, World Health Organization, Regional Office for Europe, Copenhagen

Commission of the European Communities (2003) *Five-Year Report to the European Parliament and Council on Application and Effectiveness of the EIA Directive*, Commission of the European Communities, Brussels

Davies, P. (2004) *European Union Environmental Law*, Ashgate Publishing Ltd, Aldershot

De Mulder, J. (2003) 'The new UNECE protocol on strategic environmental assessment', *Environmental Law Network International Review*, vol 1, pp1–11

De Mulder, J. (2006) 'The expansion of environmental assessment in international law: The Protocol on Strategic Environmental Assessment to the Espoo Convention', *Environmental Law and Management*, vol 18, pp269–281

Dovers, S. (2002) 'Too deep a SEA? Strategic environmental assessment in the era of sustainability' in S. Marsden and S. Dovers (eds) *Strategic Environmental Assessment in Australasia*, The Federation Press, Annandale, NSW, pp24–47

Dusik, J., Cherp, A., Jurkeviciute, A., Martinakova, H. and Bonvoisin, N. (2006) *Capacity Development for Implementing the UNECE SEA Protocol in the Former Soviet Union Countries in Eastern Europe, Caucasus and Central Asia*, UNDP, REC and UNECE, Bratislava, Szentendre and Geneva

IAIA (International Association for Impact Assessment) (2002) *Strategic Environmental Assessment: Performance Criteria*, Special Publication Series No 1, Fargo ND

Jendroska, J. and Stec, S. (2003) 'The Kyiv Protocol on strategic environmental assessment', *Environmental Policy and Law*, vol 33, no 3/4, pp105–110

Marsden, S. (1998) 'Why is legislative EA in Canada ineffective and how can it be enhanced?', *Environmental Impact Assessment Review*, vol 18, no 3, pp241–265

Marsden, S. (1999) 'Legislative EA in the Netherlands: the E-test as a strategic and integrative instrument', *European Environment*, vol 9, no 3, pp90–100

Marsden, S. (2002a) 'An international overview of strategic environmental assessment, with reference to world heritage areas globally and in Australian coastal zones', *Journal of Environmental Assessment Policy and Management*, vol 4, no 1, pp31–66

Marsden, S. (2002b) 'SEA and international law: An analysis of the effectiveness of the SEA protocol to the Espoo convention, and of the influence of the SEA directive and Aarhus convention on its development', *Environmental Law Network International Review*, vol 2, pp1–10

Marsden, S. and De Mulder, J. (2005) 'Strategic environmental assessment and sustainability in Europe: How bright is the future?', *Review of European Community and International Environmental Law*, vol 14, no 1, pp50–62

Mathieson, A. (2003) 'Public participation in decision making and access to justice in EC environmental law: The case of certain plans and programmes', *European Environmental Law Review*, vol 12, no 2, pp36–52

Morgera, E. (2005) 'An update on the Aarhus Convention and its continued global relevance', *Review of European Community and International Environmental Law*, vol 14, no 2, pp138–147

Reps of the MS/EC (Representatives of the Member States and the Environment Directorate General of the European Commission) (2003) *Implementation of Directive 2001/42/EC on the Assessment of the Effects of Certain Plans and Programmes on the environment*, 23 September, Commission of the European Communities, Brussels

Sadler, B. (ed) (2005) *Strategic Environmental Assessment at the Policy Level: Recent Progress, Current Status and Future Prospects*, Regional Environment Centre for Central and Eastern Europe, Prague

Sadler, B., Partidario, M., Fischer, T. B. and Dusik, J. (eds), (2008) *Strategic Environmental Assessment Handbook*, Earthscan, London

Stoeglehner, G. and Wegerer, G. (2006) 'The SEA-directive and the SEA-protocol adopted to spatial planning – similarities and differences', *Environmental Impact Assessment Review*, vol 26, pp586–599

UNECE (1992) *Application of Environmental Impact Assessment Principles to Policies, Plans and Programmes*, ECE/ENVWA/27, United Nations, New York

UNECE (2000) *The Aarhus Convention: An Implementation Guide*, United Nations, New York and Geneva

UNECE (2002) *Draft Protocol on SEA*, Ad Hoc Working Group on the UNECE Protocol on Strategic Environmental Assessment, Fourth Session, Warsaw, 11–13 February

UNECE/REC (UNECE/ Regional Environmental Center for Central and Eastern Europe) (2007a) *Protocol on SEA: Resource Manual to Support Application of the UNECE Protocol on Strategic Environmental Assessment*, draft final, April 2007, United Nations, New York

UNECE/REC (2007b) *Protocol on SEA: Health chapter/annex - Resource Manual to Support Application of the UNECE Protocol on Strategic Environmental Assessment*, draft final, United Nations, September 2007, United Nations, New York

Wettestad, J. (1999) *Designing Effective Environmental Regimes – the Key Conditions*, Edward Elgar, Cheltenham

CHAPTER 6

SEA and the Conservation Conventions

CHAPTER OUTLINE

Chapter 5 examined the SEA Protocol, which is the only international legal instrument to regulate the assessment of strategic proposals, albeit largely in a national context and currently not in force. This chapter considers other MEAs that, while not requiring SEA, suggest its use as a means of implementing treaty provisions. In most cases SEA is recommended as a significant aspect of EA, which has been shown to have benefits generally in protecting biodiversity through the application of the precautionary principle. The role of EA has also had positive benefits in developing collective approaches to the implementation of these conventions, the most significant of which have had a focus on conservation. As such, the chapter first considers the relationship between the precautionary principle, EA and biodiversity conservation, before examining the role of treaties in promoting the use of SEA to conserve biodiversity. The remainder of the chapter analyses the place of SEA within four specific conventions, before conclusions are drawn.

THE PRECAUTIONARY PRINCIPLE, ENVIRONMENTAL ASSESSMENT AND BIODIVERSITY CONSERVATION

The precautionary principle was discussed in Chapter 3, where it was concluded that there remains uncertainty about whether it has become part of customary international law. It was also concluded, with reference to Ellis (2006, p448), that EIA is compatible with the precautionary principle, furthers its aims and may even have been deliberately adopted as a precautionary measure.[1] As such, it is not surprising that practitioners have been keen to explore the links between EA and the precautionary principle. The reason for this interest is because of the significance of the principle in biodiversity conservation (Cooney, 2005).

Tucker and Treweek examine this in an international review (2005, pp73–93). Because EA is widely applied to predict the effects of proposed activities on the environment, they rightly argue that it 'can be an important component in a precautionary approach' (p73). There are many ways in which this can happen, 'not least by providing information about environmental effects and their likely significance'. They point to the following, including the role of SEA, and refer to EA as IA (impact assessment), which is often the preferred terminology of the international treaties (p73):

> *It forces proponents of new developments and activities to provide evidence that their proposals will be environmentally acceptable and provides a framework for discussion of possible harm and uncertainty. If properly applied IA provides opportunities to redesign proposals to avoid possible harm to sensitive biodiversity and promote alternatives that reduce risks. New developments in strategic environmental assessment will provide additional opportunities to avoid environmental harm at source, and to implement the precautionary approach for the benefit of biodiversity.*

In stricter formulations, the precautionary principle may shift the burden of proof to the proponent of an activity to resolve the uncertainty over potential impacts (Cooney, 2005, p7; Raffensperger and Tickner, 1999). Cooney, in a review of the international literature including international and European law, refers to the *Earth Charter* (2000), a soft law instrument, which states in Article 6: '[W]hen knowledge is limited, apply a precautionary approach... Place the burden of proof on those who argue that an activity will not cause significant harm'. She indicates that usually reversing the burden of proof is limited to situations that 'by their nature or context appear likely to be harmful' (Cooney, 2005, p7), such as endangered species or within protected areas.[2] Cooney also indicates that disputes over the principle and its different formulations are disputes 'about how competing interests should be balanced' (p8); the stronger forms of the principle will 'weigh the environmental interest above these other interests' (p10).

This is the essential 'action-forcing' requirement in both EIA and SEA. In both cases information needs depend on the likely impacts, of which those on biodiversity may be significant. If potential negative impacts cannot be avoided and it is nonetheless decided that the proposal should go ahead, then mitigation measures will be required to minimize or manage the effects or to provide compensation (where biodiversity is to be lost), by typically ensuring that habitats or species are protected elsewhere. This is the approach of many procedures including the Habitats Directive in European law as examined in Chapter 11.

Tucker and Treweek (2005) give five international examples of the application of the precautionary principle, which illustrate the application of both international and European law, which often both apply in many situations.[3] The examples are the Alvão Wind Farm in Portugal, located in an area proposed for designation under the Habitats Directive; Voisey's Bay Mine and Mill in Canada, which considered the *Rio Declaration;* the new Quito International Airport in Ecuador; an application for consent to use poisoned bait to control predators of an endangered bird in New Zealand; and the proposed port development at Dibden Bay in the UK, parts of which were designated under the Ramsar Convention and the Habitats and Wild Birds Directives (pp82–87).

The case study examples 'reinforce the relevance of the precautionary principle in EIA decisions where risks and uncertainty are high' and also 'reinforce the need for the precautionary principle to be firmly embedded in policy and law and for clear guidance to be given about its interpretation' (Tucker and Treweek, 2005).[4] In a provincial context, Gustavson (2003, pp376–377) considers the application of the precautionary principle in EIA with regard to the procedures in British Columbia deployed in the

Salmon Aquaculture and Burns Bog Ecosystem Reviews.[5] In conclusion, he highlights three considerations: clear communication of the various ways to interpret and apply the principle, avoidance of separating the policy and management decision making from EIA, and making interpretations in accordance with the limits imposed by existing laws and policy.[6]

Byron and Treweek (2005a, p4) indicate that while EA procedures are in place and applied in many countries, biodiversity considerations are often poorly addressed. The reasons given for this include: attaching a low priority to biodiversity; a lack of awareness of biodiversity values and importance; a lack of capacity to plan for biodiversity, carry out, commission or review EIAs; and a lack of up to date and easily accessible information. As a result of this, the IAIA established a Capacity Building for Biodiversity in Impact Assessment project to assist in supporting decisions of the CBD and comparable decisions of the Ramsar Convention and CMS.[7]

THE ROLE OF STRATEGIC ENVIRONMENTAL ASSESSMENT IN THE CONSERVATION CONVENTIONS

Given the relevance of EIA to the precautionary principle, it is not surprising that SEA has been viewed as having significant additional benefits for biodiversity conservation (Thérivel and Thompson, 1996; Treweek et al, 2005), especially in the context of the conservation conventions, not least because addressing potential negative impacts from highest level proposals is the best way to consider the full range of alternatives while they are still available. The most significant of the conservation conventions are undoubtedly the 1971 Wetlands Convention (Ramsar), the 1972 World Heritage Convention (Paris), the 1979 CMS (Bonn) and the 1992 CBD (Rio); others also include provisions for EA in other, broader contexts.[8] As a result of clear synergies and growing links between the conservation conventions, it is increasingly appropriate to consider them as an informal 'regime' of IEL (Pallemaerts, 2004) because despite their differences, they are all focused on ensuring conservation of aspects of the natural environment, particularly of habitats and species.[9]

Aside from the Espoo Convention and SEA Protocol and the clear role for EIA especially being set out in several MEAs or encouraged by COPs or MOPs (see Chapter 4), in the words of Pritchard (2005, p9) 'for the greater part of the history of both the conventions and EIA, there has been a striking separateness of these two worlds in terms of their processes and the people involved'. This is true not only of those involved internationally with EA and biodiversity conservation, who may, until recently, have been unaware of the benefits to be gained from closer cooperation, but also between those involved with EA and biodiversity conservation and the wider legal community of international law and governance, especially IEL. Legal advice and assistance for NGOs, for example, has, until recently, been regarded as a luxury beyond the limited means of such groups, which have usually been reliant on the free services provided by legal practitioners with expertise and willingness to act. Today, there is not only a greater knowledge among NGOs of the importance of the law generally in advancing an agenda, but also often procedural provision for legal standing to take action and improved funding provision to obtain legal advice.[10]

Since the UNCED called on each contracting party to the 1992 CBD to 'introduce appropriate arrangements to ensure that the environmental consequences of its programmes and policies that are likely to have significant adverse impacts on biological diversity are duly taken into account',[11] there has been a significant amount of research undertaken into the benefits that can be gained from applying EA to the implementation of the conservation conventions. This was taken up by the *Journal of Environmental Assessment Policy and Management* and by *Impact Assessment and Project Appraisal* in 2005 in special issues devoted specifically to the topic. The guest editors of both journals, Byron and Treweek, emphasize the significance as follows with respect to the international law of treaties (2005a, p4):

> *Impact assessment is an important tool for 'mainstreaming' biodiversity into the planning and realisation of development and has been identified as having an important role in implementing the biodiversity-related global conventions, including the Convention on Biological Diversity (CBD), the Convention on Wetlands of International Importance (Ramsar Convention) and the Convention on Migratory Species (CMS). Impact assessment is widely applied throughout the world and can help to ensure that development is planned and implemented with biodiversity in mind.*

Although the initial work of the Capacity Building for Biodiversity in Impact Assessment project was directed to EIA, the focus later turned to SEA. Byron and Treweek (2005b, pviii) give examples of this, which include: work commissioned by the CBD for the Netherlands EIA Commission to produce guidelines on SEA and biodiversity (Slootweg and Kolhoff, 2003), and the production of guidance on SEA and biodiversity in the UK prompted by the requirement in the SEA Directive to address impacts on biodiversity (South West Ecological Surveys et al, 2004). Conferences held by the IAIA in Vancouver (2004) and Prague (2005) also held special sessions on biodiversity and SEA, and other work since has included the results of an NGO questionnaire survey by the European Environmental Bureau (2005), focused on the quality of national transposition and application of the SEA Directive. NGOs generally have had a significant role to play in drawing links between EA and the conservation conventions. Pritchard (2005) points to the early work of the IUCN and BirdLife International, and his own initiatives. With respect to the latter, following a session on EIA at the Ramsar COP6,[12] a recommendation was adopted addressing good practice principles and the question of guidelines, followed by a similar session at the 1997 IAIA annual meeting. He comments (p9):

> *Since then, a series of liaison processes, joint work programmes and substantive agenda debates have developed in the conventions, with involvement from IAIA, IUCN and BirdLife International. This has included analyses of treaty requirements, awareness-raising events at conferences, provision of resource materials and adoption of resolutions and guidance materials on EIA. Elements have also been included in joint work plans and other arrangements that link together the conventions themselves. Among EIA professionals, there is a growing awareness of conventions as a policy context for significant parts of their work.*

The remainder of this section examines each of the four conservation conventions that arguably have the greatest potential to incorporate SEA provisions in order to implement treaty obligations, the Ramsar, World Heritage, CMS and CBD. In each case an overview of the principal requirements are first set out before the role of SEA is analysed in detail with respect to the recommendations of the treaty COPs and MOPs.

Ramsar Convention

The Convention on Wetlands of International Importance, Especially as Waterfowl Habitat 1971 entered into force on 21 December 1975. Concluded in the year before the landmark Stockholm Conference in 1972 it 'constituted the first attempt by the international community to establish a legal instrument providing comprehensive protection for a particular ecosystem type' (Bowman, 1995a, p2). It has been amended twice, in 1982 and 1987. As at September 2006, 153 nations had joined the Convention as Contracting Parties and more than 1600 wetlands globally had been designated for inclusion in the List of Wetlands of International Importance (Ramsar Convention Secretariat, 2006b).

The most important requirements of the Convention in relation to biodiversity conservation concern its obligations to record key wetlands on a List of Wetlands of International Importance, 'promote' their conservation, and 'promote', as far as possible, the 'wise use' of all wetlands within the territory of the parties (Bowman, 1995a; Ramsar Convention, 1993). Birnie and Boyle (2002, p617) comment that 'the general nature of its provisions has given rise to problems of interpretation and weakness of obligations. It was not clear, for example, whether parties had an obligation to promote conservation of listed sites in all state parties or only of their own sites'.

Although the requirement of 'wise use' is not defined in the Convention, COP1 subsequently recommended that it be interpreted as involving 'maintenance of their ecological character, as a basis not only for conservation, but for sustainable development'. COP2 redefined it to mean 'their sustainable utilization for the benefit of human kind in a way compatible with the maintenance of the natural properties of the ecosystem'. Farrier and Tucker (2000) discuss the 'wise use' concept with reference to the position of the Convention in Australia, arguing that until the time of writing it had 'been largely neglected' and that Australia's response has been 'minimalist' (p22).[13]

The absence of amendment provisions has caused difficulties, with Birnie and Boyle commenting (2002, p619) 'The lack of amendment procedures is a serious defect in a wildlife conservation convention since it inhibits its flexibility in adapting it to changed perceptions and needs, including the need to conserve biodiversity, now considered vital to successful conservation in general.' Bowman (1995b) has considered the Ramsar Convention amendment process in detail, concluding that although it took a significant length of time to 'remedy the structural deficiencies which have handicapped it from the outset... the Ramsar experience amply demonstrates the importance, as well as the inherent complexity, of effective utilisation of the multilateral treaty amendment process' (p559).

Although the Ramsar Convention itself does not adopt a precautionary approach to the 'wise use' of wetlands, as will be seen, subsequent COPs have taken on board the need for EA requirements, with the promulgation of guidance in the area. Related to this, the Ramsar Convention has been operating closely with the CBD COP, with a

Memorandum of Cooperation concluded between the CBD Secretariat and the Ramsar Convention and subsequent approval of a joint work plan.[14] The Ramsar parties have also recognized that it is appropriate for them to play a leading role in the conservation of wetland biodiversity.[15] The Ramsar Convention Secretariat (2006a) has recently produced the 4th edition of *The Ramsar Convention Manual*, a general guide to the operation of the Convention, which provides a brief introduction to the Convention and its processes alongside a detailed series of handbooks for the wise use of wetlands, of which volume 13 on EA is considered below.

Application of SEA

Bowman (1995a, p10) discusses the impact on Ramsar wetlands of development proposals as they are 'particularly vulnerable to the dam-building and irrigation schemes traditionally so favoured by the development agencies'. As such, the 1987 Regina COP adopted a recommendation that all agencies with a significant role in funding such development were urged to adopt policies directed at sustainable utilization, wise management and conservation of wetlands, together with the development of guidelines to ensure the integration of environmental aspects in all stages of the project cycle, with particular reference to prior EIA. It also called on the parties themselves to require their own agencies to adhere to the strategy.[16] Bowman (1995a, p10) comments: 'The obligation in respect of listed sites can therefore quite readily be interpreted to impose upon all parties a duty to avoid positively causing them harm'.

Pritchard (2005) refers to Article 3.2 of the Ramsar Convention as an example of an 'implied' EIA requirement, which requires the contracting parties to detect and then take action in response to change or likely change in the ecological character of wetlands. He states (p9): 'This implies a need to have the capability to anticipate and predict the effects of actions on wetland ecosystems, and, it could be argued, a need to go through a process of the kind typically embodied by EIA'. Although not required to do so specifically therefore, several parties have enacted legislation to require EIA that might affect listed sites. Australia is an example, and the Environment Protection and Biodiversity Conservation Act 1999 (EPBC Act) states that an EIA is to be carried out for activities that may impact on Ramsar wetlands as a 'matter of national environmental significance' (McGrath, 2005).[17] With respect to SEA, Pritchard (2005, p14) cites Article 3.1, which requires parties 'to formulate and implement their planning so as to promote the conservation of wetlands', as having scope for 'defining the need for SEA, for example requiring environmental assessment of programmes, plans and policies (as well as projects) potentially having a negative impact on attempts to conserve wetlands or use them wisely'.

Farrier and Tucker (2000, pp36–40) discuss the role of EIA in implementing the 'wise use' concept, pointing to developments in the Australian states in the lead-up to the coming into force of the EPBC Act. They indicate that EIA requirements are 'clearly a vital component of wise use' (p40), citing the Convention's *Additional Guidance for the Implementation of the Wise Use Concept* (1993) as indicative, where the Wise Use Working Group advocates EIA 'to determine if a proposed project is compatible with the general requirements of wise use and the maintenance of the ecological character of the wetlands concerned'. Without specifying it, they suggest (on p40) the application of a broader tool such as SEA when they comment on the inadequacies of a project based assessment approach, although at the same time they perhaps fail to appreciate that alternative approaches are in fact available:

Activities outside the wetland which may have a significant effect on it should also be assessed. In theory at least, environmental impact statements provide fuller information to decision-makers about likely environmental impact. But they deal badly with cumulative effect because they are generated by, and necessarily focus on, proposals involving specific projects.

Since the 1993 guidance was produced, there have been significant revisions. Pritchard (1996) described the need for greater attention to EIA in wetland policy and included a set of potential guidelines on the use of EIA 'as an aid to the wise use of wetlands' for the consideration of COP6 in Brisbane. At that time the COP adopted Recommendation 6.2 entitled 'Environmental impact assessment' requesting the Standing Committee and the Scientific and Technical Review Panel (STRP) to examine relevant existing EIA guidelines and, if necessary, to pursue the question of drafting Ramsar guidelines. The Convention's first Strategic Plan, for 1997–2002 was adopted in 1996, with Operational Objective 2.5 'intended to increase the visibility of EIA issues in the Convention's processes' (Ramsar Convention Secretariat, 2006b, p6).[18]

At COP7 in Costa Rica, Bagri and Vorhies (1999) took this further, dealing specifically with the need for SEA also. The conclusion and priorities of the presentation were embodied by the Parties in their Resolution VII.16, entitled 'The Ramsar convention and impact assessment: strategic, environmental and social'. The Ramsar Convention Secretariat (2006b, p6) comments on this as follows:

Resolution VII.16 calls upon the Contracting Parties to strengthen their efforts to ensure that any projects, plans, programmes and policies with the potential to alter the ecological character of wetlands in the Ramsar List, or impact negatively on other wetlands within their territories, will be subjected to rigorous impact assessment procedures, and it urges them to formalize such procedures with policy, legal, institutional and organizational arrangements.

There is a handbook on the convention devoted specifically to EA, updated as at 2006 (Ramsar Convention Secretariat, 2006b), which includes copies of all of the above Convention documents. The 2002 'Guidelines for incorporating biodiversity related issues into EIA legislation and/or processes and in SEA' contained within the Handbook was adapted from the CBD guidance (see below) in order to place it within a Ramsar context. These guidelines were adopted in full as the Annex to Resolution VIII.9 at COP8 in Valencia in 2002. Section I of the Handbook contains an introductory section prepared by the Secretariat on EA and the Ramsar Convention; Section II contains the CBD 2002 Guidelines; and Section III deals with SEA specifically, reproducing as an extract the Bagri and Vorhies paper (1999).

As indicated at the beginning of this chapter, the recommendations and resolutions made at the Ramsar COPs are not generally obligatory on the state parties, and as such while the COP can produce hard law by amending a convention and/or utilizing obligatory provisions, the Ramsar COP has not, in these instances, chosen to do so.[19]

Recommendation 6.2 paragraph 5 from COP6, for example, merely 'calls on' the contracting parties to integrate etc., and recommendation 6.2 paragraph 6 only 'invites' the contracting parties to submit EIA guidelines to the Ramsar Bureau. Resolution VII.16 paragraph 10 from COP7 only 'calls on' the contracting parties to reinforce and strengthen their efforts etc., with later paragraphs only 'encouraging' and 'requesting' certain behaviour. None of this language produces obligatory effect.

World Heritage Convention

The Convention Concerning the Protection of the World Cultural and Natural Heritage 1972 entered into force on 17 December 1975. Article 4 requires states to conserve and protect elements of World Heritage, which can include natural and cultural heritage, such as habitats of 'threatened species of animals and plants of outstanding universal value'. As with the Ramsar Convention, with which it has a Memorandum of Understanding, it also provides for a list of sites to be protected.[20] The IUCN reviews the sites after they are nominated by a state party and submitted to the Secretariat. It is possible for transboundary properties to be nominated under the Convention, which are jointly submitted in accordance with Article 11.3. The Convention establishes a World Heritage Committee and provides procedures for evaluating and designating such sites in a World Heritage List, as well as establishing a fund for assisting conservation. Operational Guidelines (UNESCO, 2005) provide a means of evaluating nominations (see Annex 6), as well as dealing with other implementation matters.

The Convention recognizes that the international community has a duty to conserve heritage of universal value. Articles 4 and 5 contain the conservation obligations. Parties must do all they can to ensure identification, protection, conservation, preservation and transmission of the natural and cultural heritage for future generations. They must adopt protective policies, set up management services for conservation, conduct relevant research to remove threats, take other appropriate measures and institute training. For listed sites, the Convention provides real protection (Birnie and Boyle, 2002, pp622), with the High Court of Australia deciding in the case of *Australia v The State of Tasmania* in 1983[21] that there is a legal duty on parties to the Convention such as Australia to protect its listed areas, despite the generality of the expressions used in the articles and the degree of discretion left to states concerning the precise measures to be taken. Despite the significance of the decision in an Australian context, as Birnie and Boyle comment in 2002 (p621), 'as no other such cases have arisen, so far as the authors are aware, it is impossible to say whether other states' courts would hold otherwise'. While the decision is persuasive on other common law courts therefore, it has no binding effect, and indeed while the High Court of Australia would be likely to follow its previous decisions, it has no obligation to do so.

Because of the significance of a listing, listing has therefore on occasion been challenged. However, the Convention obligations also apply to non-listed sites that are 'natural heritage' in accordance with the Convention's definitions and that are located within the territory of the state party concerned. In the Australian context again, the High Court held in the case of *Richardson v Forestry Commission* (Bates, 2006, pp64, 191–192) that the potential for a site to be listed under the Convention had to be taken into account in decisions to allow development to proceed. While the fact of designation does not prevent development, it should also not impact adversely on the qualities of the area designated, which may be located some distance away from the development planned. This was the situation in *Minister for the Environment and Heritage v Queensland Conservation Council Inc* (McGrath, 2005, pp36–38). A List of World Heritage in Danger is maintained as a means of monitoring non-compliance, the threat of a listing often serving to ensure that parties do more to protect listed sites, which helped ensure greater protection was given to the Kakadu World Heritage Area following development proposals. Birnie and Boyle (2002, p621) conclude on the significance of the World Heritage Convention (see also comments on p622), including its relationship with other conservation conventions (of which the Convention on International Trade in Endangered Species 1973 (CITES) is also mentioned) as follows:

> *the increasing number of sites of outstanding natural heritage now listed, including marine sites, does represent an important contribution to the network of conventions relevant to biodiversity conservation, and the Secretariat of the Biodiversity Convention has participated in a project to harmonize the reporting requirements of this Convention, as well as those of the CITES, Ramsar and CMS Conventions and has developed joint work programmes.*

Application of SEA

Article 5 of the Convention contains provisions that have potential to set the framework for and also to require SEA, without making this explicit (Marsden, 2002a, p48). These include the requirement for state parties 'to adopt a general policy which aims to give the cultural and natural heritage a function in the life of the community and to integrate the protection of that heritage into comprehensive planning programmes'. There is also a requirement 'to develop scientific and technical studies and research and to work out such operating methods as will make the State capable of counteracting the dangers that threaten its cultural or natural heritage'. Finally, states must 'take the appropriate legal, scientific, technical, administrative and financial measures necessary for the identification, protection, conservation, presentation and rehabilitation of this heritage'. Pritchard (2005, p9) comments that the World Heritage Convention:

> *has an implied requirement in Article 5 that addresses, among other things, the integration by states of heritage protection into comprehensive planning programmes (relevant therefore to SEA) and the development by states of studies and research to enable them to counteract threats to the heritage.*

The Operational Guidelines deal with matters of protection and management (UNESCO, 2005, pp24–28), stating in paragraph 97 that 'All properties inscribed on the World Heritage List must have adequate long-term legislative, regulatory, institutional and/or traditional protection and management to ensure their safeguarding'. Although there is no specific reference to EA, paragraph 110 states that 'An effective management system... may incorporate traditional practices, existing urban or regional planning instruments, and other planning control mechanisms, both formal and informal', which would include EA. Annex 5 of the Operational Guidelines that must be used for all nominations submitted, requires detailed information to be given concerning the protection and management of the property in accordance with paragraph 132, which should include an appropriate management plan and is also likely to include details of national EA procedures, possibly with a transboundary element. This is given added obligation by the requirement in the explanatory notes to section 5.c of the proforma to 'describe how the protection afforded by its legal, regulatory, contractual, planning and/or traditional status indicated... actually works'.

Article 11(4) sets out factors that may cause a World Heritage Area to be listed as 'in danger', and, as such, highlights environmental impacts of which the drafters of the Convention were particularly concerned (as related to the other conventions, see also Meynell, 2005). These are:

> *the threat of disappearance caused by accelerated deterioration, large scale public or private projects or rapid urban or tourist development projects; destruction caused by changes in the use or ownership of the land; major alterations due to unknown causes; abandonment for any reason whatsoever; the outbreak or the threat of an armed conflict; calamities and cataclysms, serious fires, earthquakes, landslides, volcanic eruptions, changes in water level, floods and tidal waves.*

Each of these could be considered in any SEA prepared.

Marsden (2002a) gives examples of the application of SEA to World Heritage Areas globally and in Australia. In Australia some aspects of SEA have since also been applied to the defence activities in the Great Barrier Reef Marine Park (URS Australia Pty Ltd, 2006) and in waters surrounding Heard Island and McDonald Islands (Ashe and Marsden, in press). Marsden (2002a, p54) comments that:

> *SEA should be applied to the designation and management of all coastal protected areas in Australia... Australia's coastal WHAs, such as Shark Bay and the Great Barrier Reef should certainly be subject to SEA. World Heritage listing does not prevent development, so it would be preferable if all interested parties knew in advance what the generic environmental implications of future development would be.*

Convention on Migratory Species

The Convention on the Conservation of Migratory Species of Wild Animals 1979, or the Bonn Convention/CMS, entered into force on 1 November 1983. It conserves habitat as well as aiming to protect the species during migration across national boundaries. The Convention provides for cooperation in scientific research, restoring habitat and removing obstacles to species migration. Appendix I lists the species that are endangered, either with extinction over all or a significant part of their range, the taking of which must be prohibited by range state parties. Formal conservation AGREEMENTS[22] are provided for with respect to other species listed in Appendix II, which, as Birnie and Boyle (2002) indicate, are the key to the success of the Convention. They comment (p622):

They are to be concluded among range states of particular migratory species listed on the Convention's Appendix II as having 'unfavourable conservation status' and requiring an international agreement for their conservation and management, or as having a conservation status that would significantly benefit from international cooperation achieved by international agreement.

It is also possible for species to be listed in Appendix I and II even if they are also dealt with by other treaties, including fishery and mammal treaties. Other types of agreements can be concluded under Article IV.4 of the Convention, which encourages parties to conclude them for any population or geographically separate part of the population of any species, which can include those not listed in Appendix I or even those that are not defined as migratory, the aim of which is to protect species that do not fulfil the Appendix I criteria or have not yet resulted in a listing. One of the major problems of the Convention as identified by Birnie and Boyle (2002, p624) is the lack of precision concerning definitions. While COP2 went some way to further define migratory species in guidelines adopted, 'practical application by conclusion of AGREEMENTS is the best clarifier of its inadequacies'. The other major problem has been the overlap between the provisions of the Convention and other conservation conventions, some of which deal specifically with certain of the listed species. As Birnie and Boyle comment (p624), 'there is clearly a need to improve coordination and cooperation between these conventions on the grounds of both efficiency and the need for a more holistic approach'. The use of EA is obviously one of the ways in which this has been happening, as the next section illustrates.

Application of SEA

Some of the AGREEMENTS entered into between states refer to the application of EA, and in common with developments under the Ramsar and CBD especially, the CMS has recently recommended the application of EA further. As with the other conservation convention recommendations, no substantive obligations are required as a result, merely encouragement as a means of implementation. In 2002, therefore, COP2 adopted Resolution 7.2 that relates the use of EIA and SEA to the Convention's provisions, promotes the cooperation with other conservation conventions that had previously been absent and urges the parties to make use of the CBD guidelines on EA. The CMS also has a Memorandum of Understanding and a joint work plan with the Ramsar Convention, the Memorandum identifying EA as a matter for institutional cooperation, especially with regard to future guidelines. As Pritchard comments (2005, p12): 'Thus, three global conventions have now formally endorsed effectively the same single source of principles and advice: in this respect, EIA has been the focus of pioneering endeavours'.

Convention on Biological Diversity

The Convention on Biological Diversity 1992 was opened for signature at the Earth Summit in Rio in 1992 and it entered into force on 29 December 1993. It emphasizes the importance of biodiversity to people worldwide. The key objectives of the CBD are the conservation of biodiversity, the sustainable use of the components of biodiversity and the fair and equitable sharing of benefits arising from the use of genetic resources. In 2004 a Strategic Plan was adopted, committing the Parties to a more effective and coherent implementation of these objectives, which were designed in particular to result in a significant reduction of the rate of biodiversity loss by 2010. The CBD fails to define obligations precisely because it operates as a framework convention,[23] with detailed substantive provisions on specific areas outlined elsewhere. Yet the CBD has been instrumental in bringing together the conservation conventions. Bowman (1995a, p2) comments that:

> *through the signature at the Rio Earth Summit of the 1992 Convention on Biological Diversity... [the international community has established] a basic conceptual framework to underpin the various conservation initiatives embodied in the now substantial number of international treaties for the protection of wildlife. This framework, which was arguably already emerging in customary international law, emphasises a broad, threefold obligation regarding the conservation of ecosystems, of species and of genetic diversity within species. As each species, and indeed each individual member of that species, exists not in isolation but as a functioning unit within a wider ecosystem, it is axiomatic that the protection of natural habitats must continue to play a particularly crucial role in the global conservation effort.*

Birnie and Boyle (2002, p571) would appear to agree that the CBD provides some assistance in 'organizing' or 'integrating' related conventions, of which Ramsar, the World Heritage and CMS outlined above are good examples. While its provisions 'afford only vague guidance', institutions established by the CBD provide 'opportunities for effective cooperation'. Andresen (2007) also discusses coordination among what he refers to as the 'biodiversity conservation cluster' of agreements, which also takes in CITES. He comments (para 2.3):

> *Various formal co-ordination activities take place within the biodiversity conservation cluster. There is a Joint Web Site involving the CBD, CITES, CMS, WHC and Ramsar; and several memoranda of understanding have been signed between the CBD and the other conventions. Also, the seventh conference of the parties to the CBD in 2004 established the Biodiversity Liaison Group, including the CBD, CITES, Ramsar, CMS and WHC.*

Articles 6–20 of the CBD set out the commitments of the parties for conservation and sustainable use of biological diversity, including incentives to do so, research and training, public awareness and education, EA, regulating access to genetic resources, access to and transfer of technology and the provision of financial resources. Many of these provisions lack substantive obligation, with extensive use of discretionary language. As such the implementation of the treaty is of far greater importance than the wording of many of the provisions themselves. The inclusion of a weak formulation of the precautionary principle is an example of this, the Preamble to the CBD merely noting that 'where there is a threat of significant reduction or loss of biodiversity, lack of full scientific certainty should not be used as a reason for postponing measures to avoid or minimise such threat'. Despite this, as Birnie and Boyle (2002, p574) comment, 'the failure to cite the precautionary principle explicitly is to some extent offset by the Convention's provisions on environmental impact assessment'.

Application of SEA

Article 14 of the CBD calls for Parties to introduce both EIA and SEA procedures to ensure the effects of development on biodiversity are adequately assessed and that due consideration is given to them. Article 14 is set out in full in Chapter 3 of this book, with Article 14(b) stating that:

> *Each Contracting Party, as far as possible and as appropriate, shall... introduce appropriate arrangements to ensure that the environmental consequences of its programmes and policies that are likely to have significant adverse impacts on biological diversity are duly taken into account.*

While the CBD is hard law and its requirements must therefore be given effect to by those that have ratified it, there are elements of discretion here. Although the word 'shall' means that parties must comply, 'as far as possible and as appropriate' provides much scope for the extent and nature of this compliance. Furthermore, in accordance with all EA provisions, reference to 'significant adverse impacts' means not only that there is no absolute prohibition on harm, and 'duly taken into account' means only that the decision maker has to have regard to such impacts; the weighting to attach to them is a matter left to the decision maker to decide.

Other articles of the CBD relate to the EA provisions in Article 14. For example, although Article 8(j) does not refer specifically to EA, Byron and Treweek (2005b, pvi) indicate that EA tools are being developed to ensure that traditional knowledge is used and taken into account when evaluating development proposals, and decisions relating to incentive measures to be adopted under Article 11 have directly referenced the importance of EA tools in developing and implementing incentives for biodiversity conservation and sustainable use. Pritchard (2005, p9) also cites Article 3, which is designed to prevent transboundary harm.

Since the CBD came into force, the convention law has been supplemented by decisions of the COP. As such, they must also be given effect to, although the language of such decisions means that they are not substantive obligations, providing much room for discretion. Byron and Treweek (2005a, p5) summarize the key decisions of COPs 4, 5 and 6 of relevance to EA (all of which are based on Article 14) up to the date of their editorial as follows:

> *Decision IV/10-C of the 4th COP*
> *Invited parties, governments, national and international organisations and indigenous and local communities embodying traditional lifestyles to exchange information and share experiences on impact assessment and strategic environmental assessments that consider environmental effects and interrelated socio-economic aspects relevant to biological diversity.*

Decision V/18 of the 5ᵗʰ COP
Requested the Subsidiary Body on Scientific, Technical and Technological Advice
(SBSTTA) further to develop guidelines for incorporating biodiversity-related
issues into legislation and/or processes on strategic environmental assessment and
impact assessment, in collaboration with the scientific community, the private sector,
indigenous and local communities, non-governmental organisations and relevant
organisations, inter alia, the IAIA, and further elaborate the application of the
precautionary approach and the ecosystem approach, taking into account the needs
for capacity building.

Decision VI/7 of the 6ᵗʰ COP
Endorsed guidelines for incorporating biodiversity-related issues into impact assessment
legislation and/or processes, and into SEA and called for further elaboration of the
guidelines. (The draft guidelines were developed by IAIA through the activities of an
ongoing action programme managed by IAIA's Biodiversity and Ecology Section.)

Decision VI/7 [also of COP6]
Also requested the Executive Secretary to compile and disseminate current experiences in
impact assessment and SEA procedures that incorporate biodiversity-related issues and
experiences of parties in applying the guidelines. Also, in the light of this information,
to prepare, in collaboration with the relevant organisations, in particular the IAIA,
proposals for further development and refinement of the guidelines, particularly to
incorporate all stages of the impact assessment and the SEA processes, taking into
account the ecosystem approach, and to provide a report of this work to SBSTTA prior
to the 7ᵗʰ COP of the CBD.

None of the decisions impose any substantive obligations on the contracting parties,
being designed primarily to exchange information and develop guidance to improve
the capacity of the parties to better implement the CBD. Examples of the application of
the guidance to the parties given by the Convention on Biological Diversity Secretariat
(2007) concerned with EIA include the work programmes related to agricultural
biodiversity (Decision V/5 paragraph 23, Annex B paragraph 2.2(b)); forest biological
diversity (Decision VI/22 Annex Programme element 2, Goal 1, Objective 3(h));
biological diversity of inland water ecosystems (Decision VII/4); marine and coastal
biological diversity (Decision VII/5); and mountain biological diversity (Decision
VII/27).

At COP7 it was recommended that the parties endorse the guidelines prepared,
which was duly done in decision VII/10. COP7 also requested the contracting parties
and governments to use the *Akwé: Kon* voluntary guidelines for the conduct of cultural,
environmental and social impact assessments regarding developments proposed to
take place on, or which are likely to impact on, sacred sites and on lands and waters
traditionally occupied or used by indigenous and local communities (Decision VII/16,
Part F), in conjunction with the guidelines for incorporating biodiversity related issues
into EIA legislation and/or processes and in SEA (Decision VI/7, Part A).

At COP8 in Curitiba in 2006, Decision V/18 was adopted, entitled 'impact
assessment, liability and redress'. Part I, which deals with EA, continues its invitation
to the parties to integrate EA into the work programmes on thematic areas, adding

biological diversity of dry and sub-humid lands and others to those already cited. Paragraph 1(c) interestingly invites parties, governments and other relevant organizations to also 'consider biological diversity concerns from the early stages of the drafting process, when developing new legislative and regulatory frameworks', which shows the concern of SEA with the highest levels of decision making, and the growing interest of international law with the assessment of legislative and policy proposals as encouraged particularly by the SEA Protocol.

SEA is specifically referred to in paragraph 2(a) that encourages Parties, governments and other relevant organizations 'to use strategic environmental assessments to assess not only the impact of individual projects, but also their cumulative and global effects, incorporating biological diversity considerations at the decision-making and/or environmental planning level'. Paragraph 3 requests from the parties 'information on practices, systems, mechanisms and experiences in the area of strategic environmental assessment and impact assessment'. Paragraph 4 requests the SBSTTA to 'further develop' the guidelines for incorporating biodiversity related issues into legislation and/or processes on SEA, in collaboration with a wide range of specified interested Parties including the parties, private sector, related convention bodies, NGOs and IGOs. It also includes a request for further elaboration of the precautionary approach and the ecosystem approach in this regard, ensuring the maintenance of the close connection between the precautionary principle and EA.

Given the earlier discussion in Chapters 3 and 4 with respect to the role of EIA not only in harm prevention and cooperation but also in compensation for environmental damage, it is perhaps not surprising that the subject is of increasing significance to many treaty regimes, including those that include linked substantive provisions for EIA, such as the CBD. Article 14.2 of the CBD therefore states that 'the Conference of the Parties shall examine, on the basis of studies to be carried out, the issue of liability and redress, including restoration and compensation, for damage to biological diversity, except where such liability is a purely internal matter'. This suggests that liability for transboundary harm to biological diversity, where the harm originates in one state and is transferred to another by, for example, air, soil, water or migratory species of plant or animal, is a matter of concern to the Convention, although in line with other regimes, there is no substantive obligation to prevent such harm. Decision V/18, Part II renews an earlier invitation to the parties, governments and relevant international organizations (originally contained in Decision IV/10C, paragraph 8), 'to provide the Executive Secretary with information on national, international and regional measures and agreements on liability and redress applicable to damage to biological diversity', which is designed to give effect to Article 14.2.

CONCLUSIONS

This chapter illustrates the potential for SEA to assist in implementing treaty obligations, especially in the context of the conservation conventions analysed. While none of the examples given is contained within a mandatory provision, it is open to the contracting parties of each treaty to make decisions that would have this effect, provided the relevant treaty gives such powers. Typically substantive obligations will be contained in the treaty itself (if at all) and not in resolutions and recommendations, but again this option is available to parties should they so wish. The chapter has also shown how EA can produce a cooperative dynamic between different treaty administrations, especially when a treaty is focused on harm prevention and cooperation itself.

The acceptance of the benefits of utilizing SEA in implementing the conservation convention requirements suggests that other regimes of IEL may well decide to pursue similar avenues, especially when a substantive EIA obligation is already present. UNCLOS and the Antarctic Protocol come readily to mind given the extensive potential for harm to the high seas and the last great wilderness. It may only be a matter of time before we will begin to see similar recommendations made as part of such treaty regimes, which are ultimately designed to ensure harm prevention and international cooperation in order to avoid the more controversial issue of liability and compensation for harm that could well have been avoided.

NOTES

1   For an example of the clear links between the two, see Gustavson (2003).
2   Note the work of the Precautionary Principle Project, which recently held a workshop on the relationship of the principle to biodiversity conservation and natural resource management (NRM) (2005). See also IUCN (2007) and for protected areas management generally see Lockwood et al (2006).
3   For an example of overlapping legislative competences involved in protecting heritage in wetlands, see Marsden (2002b).
4   See also Dawson (2004), who has raised concerns about how well the law has responded to the science of the precautionary principle. Note that the Voisey's Bay Mine and Mill example illustrates that it is not just scientists that have a role with regard to the principle. Indigenous peoples such as the Innu Nation took a different approach to the interpretation of the principle, arguing that the adaptive management favoured for the project relies on a monitoring and mitigation approach that would violate both the precautionary and sustainability principles (Tucker and Treweek, 2005, p84).
5   Canada is a federal jurisdiction with national, provincial and territorial governments; each has different legislative and judicial functions as set out in the constitution.
6   For an example of how biodiversity considerations are included at the national level in Australia under current legislation, see Marsden (2000).
7   For example, the IAIA is a formally invited permanent observer to the Scientific and Technical Review Panel (STRP) in accordance with Resolution VIII.28 and has been contributing to its work since the establishment of the STRP Working Group on IA in 1999. See also IAIA (2005).
8   The UN Framework Convention on Climate Change 1992, 31 ILM (1992) 851, in force 21 March 1994, also provides for EA of measures taken to mitigate or adapt to climate change, which could involve SEA as well as EIA.
9   The Ramsar Convention has a sectoral approach unlike the ecological approach of the CBD, for example. Yet Ramsar and the CMS are each concerned with the protection of water birds, and all of the conventions adopt a list approach to protecting habitats and species.
10 Procedural provisions present in the Aarhus Convention and related legal instruments have improved the position of NGOs in obtaining access to the courts. All three pillars of the Aarhus Convention have strengthened the position of environmental groups significantly.

For a detailed discussion, see Zschiesche (2002, pp26–27), which makes reference to the transposition of the convention into the national law of Germany, and Chapters 4 and 9 of this book.

11 Article 14.1(b), Impact Assessment and Minimising Adverse Impacts, see Chapter 3.

12 International lawyers and NGOs often abbreviate terminology so that, for example, the sixth Conference of the Parties becomes COP6.

13 Wise use was redefined further in a 2005 Resolution of the COP; see www.ramsar.org/res/key_res_ix_01_annexa_e.htm. Note that the contents and conclusions of the Farrier and Tucker (2000) article have been subject to significant criticism in a review solicited by the Secretary General of the Ramsar Convention, provided by Phillips (2000), the former Deputy Secretary-General of the Convention and Australian expert, and subsequently published in the same journal. Phillips argues that the original article fails to include significant developments in the Convention as well as pre-dating some recent happenings in Australia, especially matters that evidence an ecosystem approach and recognize wetlands for all of their functions, values and benefits. None of this addresses the concerns regarding the role of EA.

14 Decision IV/13, para 2. The Ramsar Convention Secretariat (2006b, p 6) comments on this cooperation as follows: 'Through the Ramsar Convention's Joint Work Plans with the CBD, the members of both secretariats and subsidiary scientific bodies... have contributed to each other's progress'. Note that at COP9 in Kampala, Resolutions IX.22 on systems of protected areas and Resolution IX.5 on synergies with other international organizations were adopted. Both improve opportunities for collaboration between relevant treaties substantially.

15 Resolution 5.1, COP5, Kashiro, 1993.

16 Recommendation C. 3.4 (Rev), Regina, 1987.

17 Note that in the case of *Minister for Environment and Heritage v Greentree*, a successful prosecution of a farmer was achieved when the defendant in question cleared acres of Ramsar listed wetlands protected under the EPBC Act. See McGrath (2005, pp29–30). For details on arrangements in the UK, see Marsden (2002b).

18 The current Strategic Plan for 2003–2008 urges Parties to 'develop and implement EIA legislation so as to ensure that an EIA is carried out, as appropriate, in wetlands, including Ramsar sites, where adverse impacts may occur due to a proposed development, change in land/water use, invasive species, etc.'. The wording 'as appropriate' permits considerable discretion to parties to decide on this.

19 A distinction was drawn in Chapter 3 between international conferences such as Stockholm and Rio that produced soft law documentation such as the *Declarations* of each, and the COPs and MOPs of international treaties that can produce hard law. Strictly speaking international conferences and COPs/MOPs can do both. International conferences can produce new treaties as well as declarations. COPs and MOPs can produce treaty amendments as well as recommendations and resolutions. The powers of a COP/MOP are set out in the relevant treaty, and although it would appear that a recommendation is non-binding and a resolution is binding, the effect of each depends on the wording contained within and not what it is called. See Churchill and Ulfstein (2000, p634) on this point; note also the position of IGOs and the contentious matter of whether the doctrine of 'implied powers' is applicable to COPs/MOPs as well as the law of treaties (see Chapter 3).

20 The World Heritage Convention has links with many other related conservation conventions, which are outlined in the Operational Guidelines (UNESCO, 2005, pp10-12). Guidelines on the inscription of specific types of properties on the World Heritage List have also been prepared that include wetland and marine protected areas, and protected areas of particular importance for biodiversity (p90).

21 *Commonwealth of Australia v The State of Tasmania*, 46 ALR (1986), at 625.

22 These are in upper case to differentiate them from a second type of agreement explained below. Some state parties refused to conclude such AGREEMENTS initially because they were considered a form of treaty for which national legislative approval was needed.

23 This is defined by Birnie and Boyle (2002, p571) as:

> *one that lays down various guiding principles at the international level which states parties are required to take into account in developing national law and policy to implement its objectives, but to which can also be added subsequent ad hoc protocols on related issues laying down more specific and detailed requirements and standards.*

REFERENCES

Andresen, S. (2007) 'The effectiveness of UN environmental institutions', *International Environmental Agreements*, vol 7, number 4, pp317–336

Ashe, J. and Marsden, S. (in press) 'Strategic environmental assessment in Australia' in B. Sadler, M. Partidario, T. B. Fischer and J. Dusik (eds) *Strategic Environmental Assessment Handbook*, Earthscan, London

Bagri, A. and Vorhies, F. (1999) 'The Ramsar Convention and Impact Assessment', paper presented to the Technical Session of the 7th Meeting of the Conference of the Contracting Parties to the Ramsar Convention, San José, 10–18 May, www.ramsar.org/cop7/cop7_doc_19.1_e.htm

Bates, G. (2006) *Environmental Law in Australia*, Butterworths, Sydney

Birnie, P. and Boyle, A. (2002) *International Law and the Environment*, 2nd Edition, Oxford University Press, Oxford

Bowman, M. J. (1995a) 'The Ramsar convention comes of age', *Netherlands International Law Review*, vol XLII, pp1–52

Bowman, M. J. (1995b) 'The multilateral treaty amendment process – a case study', *International and Comparative Law Quarterly*, vol 44, pp540–559

Byron, H. and Treweek, J. (2005a) 'Editorial', *Impact Assessment and Project Appraisal*, vol 23, no 1, pp4–6

Byron, H. and Treweek, J. (2005b) 'Guest editorial: Strategic environmental assessment – great potential for biodiversity?', *Journal of Environmental Assessment Policy and Management*, vol 7, no 2, ppv–xiii

Churchill, R. and Ulfstein, G. (2000) 'Autonomous institutional arrangements in multilateral environmental agreements: A little-noticed phenomenon in international law', *American Journal of International Law*, vol 94, no 4, pp 623–659

Convention on Biological Diversity Secretariat (2007) *Impact Assessment Background*, www.biodiv. org/programmes/cross-cutting/impact/background.asp

Cooney, R. (2005) 'From promise to practicalities: The precautionary principle in biodiversity conservation and sustainable use' in R. Cooney and B. Dickson (eds) *Biodiversity and the Precautionary Principle: Risk and Uncertainty in Conservation and Sustainable Use*, Earthscan, London, pp3–17

Dawson, F. (2004) 'Analysing the goals of biodiversity conservation: Scientific, policy and legal perspectives', *Environmental and Planning Law Journal*, vol 21, pp6–26

Ellis, J. (2006) 'Overexploitation of a valuable resource? New literature on the precautionary principle', *European Journal of International Law*, vol 17, no 2, pp445–462

European Environmental Bureau (2005) *Biodiversity in Strategic Environmental Assessment: Quality of National Transposition and Application of the Strategic Environmental Assessment Directive*, European Environmental Bureau, Brussels

Farrier, D. and Tucker, L. (2000) 'Wise use of wetlands under the Ramsar convention: A challenge for meaningful implementation of international law', *Journal of Environmental Law*, vol 12, no 1, pp21–42

Gustavson, K. (2003) 'Applying the precautionary principle in environmental assessment: The case of reviews in British Columbia', *Journal of Environmental Planning and Management*, vol 46, no 3, pp365–379

IAIA (International Association for Impact Assessment) (2005) *Biodiversity in Impact Assessment*, Special Publication Series No 3, IAIA, Fargo ND

IUCN (International Union for the Conservation of Nature) (2007) *Guidelines for Applying the Precautionary Principle to Biodiversity Conservation and Natural Resource Management*, IUCN, Gland

Lockwood, M., Worboys, G. L., and Kothari, A. (eds) (2006) *Managing Protected Areas: A Global Guide*, Earthscan, London

Marsden, S. (2000) 'Biodiversity', Subtitle 14.7, 11pp – Commonwealth chapter on terrestrial protected areas, *The Laws of Australia*, Law Book Company, Sydney

Marsden, S. (2002a) 'An international overview of strategic environmental assessment, with reference to world heritage areas globally and in Australian coastal zones', *Journal of Environmental Assessment Policy and Management*, vol 4, no 1, pp 31–66

Marsden, S. (2002b) 'Protecting archaeological heritage in wetlands: The muddied waters of international, European, English and Australian law', *Environmental Law Review*, vol 4, no 1, pp26–50

McGrath, C. (2005) 'Key concepts of the Environment Protection and Biodiversity Conservation Act 1999', *Environmental and Planning Law Journal*, vol 22, no 1, pp20–39

Meynell, P. J. (2005) 'Use of IUCN Red Listing process as a basis for assessing biodiversity threats and impacts in environmental impact assessment', *Impact Assessment and Project Appraisal*, vol 23, no 1, pp65–72

Pallemaerts, M. (2004) 'An introduction to the sources, principles and regimes of international environmental law' in M. Berglund (ed) *International Environmental Law Making and Diplomacy*, *UNEP Course Series 2*, University of Joensuu, Joensuu, pp61-96

Phillips, B. (2000) 'A review of the paper: Wise use of wetlands under the Ramsar convention: a challenge for meaningful implementation of international law', http://ramsar.org/w.n.wise_use_article_response.htm

Precautionary Principle Project and Traffic (2005) *The Precautionary Principle in Biodiversity and Natural Resource Management*, Workshop Summary Report, Precautionary Principle Project and Traffic, Quito

Pritchard, D. (1996) 'Environmental impact assessment: towards guidelines for adoption under the Ramsar convention', paper presented to a Technical Session of the 6th Meeting of the Conference of the Contracting Parties to the Ramsar Convention, Brisbane, http://ramsar.org/archives/archives_pritchard.htm

Pritchard, D. (2005) 'International biodiversity-related treaties and impact assessment – how can they help each other?', *Impact Assessment and Project Appraisal*, vol 23, no 1, pp7–16

Raffensperger, C. and Tickner, J. (1999) *Protecting Public Health and the Environment: Implementing the Precautionary Principle*, Island Press, Washington DC

Ramsar Convention (1993) *Additional Guidance for the Implementation of the Wise Use Concept*, 5th Meeting of the Conference of the Contracting Parties, Kushiro

Ramsar Convention Secretariat (2006a) *The Ramsar Convention Manual: A Guide to the Convention on Wetlands*, 4th Edition, Ramsar Convention Secretariat, Gland

Ramsar Convention Secretariat (2006b) *Impact Assessment: Guidelines for Incorporating Biodiversity-Related Issues into Environmental Impact Assessment Legislation and/or Processes and in Strategic Environmental Assessment*, 3rd Edition, vol 13, Ramsar Convention Secretariat, Gland

Slootweg, R. and Kolhoff, A. (2003) 'A generic approach to integrate biodiversity considerations in screening and scoping for EIA', *Environmental Impact Assessment Review*, vol 23, pp657–681

South West Ecological Surveys, Levett-Therivel Sustainability Consultants and Oxford Brookes University (2004) *Strategic Environmental Assessment and Biodiversity: Guidance for Practitioners*, Countryside Council for Wales, English Nature, Environment Agency, Royal Society for the Protection of Birds, Oxford

Thérivel, R. and Thompson, S. (1996) *Strategic Environmental Assessment and Nature Conservation*, Report to English Nature, Peterborough

Treweek, J., Therivel, R., Thompson, S. and Slater, M. (2005) 'Principles for the use of strategic environmental assessment as a tool for promoting the conservation and sustainable use of biodiversity', *Journal of Environmental Assessment Policy and Management*, vol 7, no 2, pp173–199

Tucker, G. and Treweek, J. (2005) 'The precautionary principle in impact assessment: An international review' in Cooney, R. and Dickson, B. (eds) *Biodiversity and the Precautionary Principle: Risk and Uncertainty in Conservation and Sustainable Use*, Earthscan, London, pp73–93

UNESCO Intergovernmental Committee for the Protection of the World Cultural and Natural Heritage (2005) *Operational Guidelines for the Implementation of the World Heritage Convention*, World Heritage Centre, Paris

URS Australia Pty Ltd (2006) *Strategic Environmental Assessment of Defence Activities in the Great Barrier Reef World Heritage Area*, URS Australia Pty Ltd, East Perth

Zschiesche, M. (2002) 'The Aarhus convention – more citizens' participation by setting out environmental standards?', *Environmental Law Network International*, vol 1, pp21–29

PART II

European Law

CHAPTER 7

An Overview of European Law

CHAPTER OUTLINE

This chapter provides an overview of European law as a means of giving context to the specific laws analysed in the other chapters in Part II that follow. Where possible, the structure of the chapter is similar to Chapter 2 to enable comparisons to be more readily made with the international legal framework in Chapter 12. It begins with a historical summary of the development of the European Community and Union, outlining the jurisdiction given by the treaties.[1] The current difference between the EC and EU is explained, together with the relationship between the EC/EU and the international community, which is a recurring theme. The chapter next considers the major institutions in the legal process, the Council, Commission, Parliament and ECJ, as well as the MS and citizens of the EU.

The following section explains the sources of European law, particularly the treaties and principles on which they are based, and regulations and directives. A detailed analysis of the nature of the obligations imposed by European law[2] and of the relationship between EC law and national and international law is included, with a focus on the national law relationship in this section. The final section of the chapter examines enforcement, (with particular attention given to the role of the Commission and ECJ), discusses the draft European Constitution and its replacement, the Reform Treaty, before some conclusions are presented.[3]

THE DEVELOPMENT AND STRUCTURE
OF EUROPEAN LAW

Until the 2007 Lisbon Reform Treaty is ratified by the MS, 'European law' is strictly speaking EC not EU law. Thereafter, the EU will acquire a separate legal personality and EU law will replace EC law (see also note 7). The EU is based on the three original European Communities, the ambit of each of which is outlined by separate treaties: the European Coal and Steel Community (ECSC), the European Economic Community (EEC) and the European Atomic Energy Community (EAEC).[4] It is impossible to discuss the development and structure of European law without reference to the role of the European treaties concerning European integration, especially the EEC; the treaties are the primary source of European law and must be considered in all law making and interpretation. Treaties are developed by Intergovernmental Conferences (IGC) of the European Council and later signed by the MS, some of which require referenda of their citizens prior to their ratification.

An outline of the treaties

The original EEC Treaty was signed in Rome in 1957 and was designed to establish a common market with free movement of goods, persons, services and capital. The signing of the Single European Act of 1986 gave new competences to the EEC.[5] Decision making was made more flexible by the introduction of qualified majority voting in the Council, and it also provided for greater involvement of the Parliament by the introduction of the cooperation procedure (now Article 252, see section on institutions below).

In 1992 the Treaty on European Union (TEU) was signed at Maastricht, and thereafter the EEC became the EC to better describe the competences that had expanded beyond the economic sphere;[6] the objectives of the EC were also expanded, which are now included in Articles 2, 3 and 4 of the TEC. Qualified majority voting of the Council was extended further, and the co-decision procedure was introduced giving the Parliament greater involvement (now Article 251, see section on institutions below), which was supplemented by greater application of the cooperation procedure and procedures that permitted the Parliament to give its assent or provide advisory opinions (Article 192).

The Treaty of Amsterdam in 1997 added further new objectives to the EC, provided some new competences to it, and renumbered the TEC. The Treaty of Nice in 2001 further reformed the institutions to assist with the enlargement process, which would see membership of the EU expand considerably to 27 members. A draft Treaty establishing a Constitution for Europe and intended to replace the TEC and TEU was agreed in 2004 but was subsequently abandoned after it failed to get support in the MS. A new Treaty of Lisbon was adopted in 2007 and is designed to introduce constitutional reforms on a far less extensive, though not insignificant basis; this was formally signed by the members of the European Council on 13 December 2007, subject to approval of the citizens of certain MS thereafter. The constitutional reforms of 2004 and 2007 are discussed briefly at the end of this chapter.

Relationship between the EC and EU

The Treaties of the European Communities (TEC) and the TEU regulate the relationship between the institutions of the EC, the MS and as stated citizens of the EU, and outline the powers of the institutions; the role of each is explained in the next section. The TEU aimed at consolidating the role of the EC with the relationships entered into between MS on matters that fell outside the EC's sphere of operation, thereby combining the 'integration paths' pursued by the EC on one hand and the MS independently of it on the other. Lenaerts and van Nuffel (2005) distinguish between these paths as a means of distinguishing between the status of the EC and EU, which while the labels are often used interchangeably in common usage, have clear, distinct meanings in law. According to Lenaerts and van Nuffel (2005, p23) in the broader context of the political status of the EU therefore, 'the post-war history of European integration is made up of a succession of co-operation groupings set up to prepare for, or in parallel to, integration in the context of the Communities'. Such developments include the international law of the European Convention on Human Rights (ECHR) under the auspices of the Council of Europe, and the cooperation that led to the single currency and transfrontier aspects of justice and migration.[7]

The TEU therefore did not bring to an end the EEC (thereafter termed the EC), and as stated reference to EC law remains accurate and appropriate, as it is only the legislative acts of the European institutions based on the European treaties that constitutes a source of 'Community law'. EC law will only be replaced by EU law when the Reform Treaty, the Treaty of Lisbon, is adopted by the MS, and thereafter the distinction between Community and non-Community action will no longer exist.[8] As such, until that time, reference to 'European law' in this book should be read as, and is used interchangeably with, EC law or 'Community law.' Further, as will be seen below, the role of the EC and EU in external relations (at the level of international law) also currently remains distinct. Lenaerts and van Nuffel (2005, p50) comment on some of the constitutional changes brought by the TEU:

> The EU Treaty establishes a legal link between the Communities and the supplementary policies and forms of co-operation: henceforward, there is to be one procedure for acceding to the Union, supplanting the various accession procedures provided for in the ECSC, EEC and EAEC Treaties (EU Treaty, Art. 49) and one procedure for amending the various Treaties on which the Union is founded (EU Treaty, Art. 48). Yet the EU Treaty has not conferred legal personality on the Union as a whole.[9]

Relationship between the EC/EU and the international community

Chapter 3 briefly considered the position of the EC/EU as a 'self-contained regime' in international law, concluding generally that despite many similarities, the legal basis of the EC regime in particular excluded the operation of many aspects of international law. It is therefore important to understand that the European treaties are, despite the similarities, of an entirely different nature to international law treaties.[10] While they provide the framework for law making and interpretation in much the same way as the Charter of the UN and VCLTs do in the international law domain,[11] they operate as horizontal constitutional documents of the EC and EU, establishing and regulating the institutions, relationships between the institutions, MS and citizens. It is only with respect to the external relations of the EC/EU that international law has competence to decide disputes between the EC/EU and non-MS.[12] For all internal matters, EC law governs relationships between the European institutions, MS and citizens of the EU.

Lenaerts and van Nuffel (2005, pp12–16) point to four principal characteristics of the EC that demonstrate its 'supranational' context, removing it from the realm of international law. The first is that the EC has institutions that act independently of the MS; the second is that although the EC can take majority decisions, they bind all the MS; the third is that the institutions implement and are responsible for supervision of those decisions; and the fourth is that the TEC and case law gives rise to individual rights and obligations that are directly enforceable by the MS courts, even if national law is in conflict. The entry into force of the TEC and TEU (and subsequent amendments) was and is conditional on their ratification by all of the contracting parties, for example, and apart from the ECSC Treaty, all of the treaties were concluded for an unlimited period. The significance of the autonomous regime created and the distinction with international law generally, is clearly explained by Lenaerts and van Nuffel (2005, p341) as follows:

> *The fact that a Community, having its own institutions and powers, was established for an unlimited duration demonstrates that the Member States intended to create a new legal order, which binds both their subjects and themselves. In order to bring about the abrogation of the Treaties and, with them, the Communities or the Union, the Member States may not rely unconditionally on the rule of international law that a treaty may be terminated if the parties conclude a subsequent treaty between them. It appears to be contrary to Community law for the Member States simply to bring an end to European integration by means of an amendment to the Treaties or in some other manner.*[13]

EUROPEAN INSTITUTIONS, MEMBER STATES AND CITIZENS

In accordance with the first paragraph of the TEU, the EU has an 'institutional framework which shall ensure the consistency and the continuity of the activities carried out in order to attain its objectives while respecting and building upon the *acquis communautaire* [body of Community law]'. As such, laws passed by the institutions must give effect to the principles laid down by the TEC. There are five institutions within the EU, the first four of which are of relevance to this book: the Council of Ministers or the Council of the European Union (Council), Commission, Parliament, Court of Justice (primarily the ECJ) and Court of Auditors. Each institution is regulated by the treaties, which define and limit their powers and relationship with the other European actors, the MS and EU citizens (see Obradovic and Lavranos, 2007).

Analogies with national separations of power between the legislative, executive and judicial branches of government, broadly positions the Parliament as the legislature, Council as the executive (with the Commission as the related civil/public service) and ECJ as the judiciary. However, this is in many ways inaccurate, and the institutions exercise many distinct and overlapping roles. While the Council 'as executive' decides on the broad policy direction of the Union, the Commission exercises significant autonomy in its responsibilities for the formulation of legislative proposals. The Council is also largely responsible for approving legislative proposals, not the Parliament, although the latter's decision making role has recently increased. Fundamentally, the Commission (in conjunction with the judicial powers of the ECJ) has an important supervisory power as the 'guardian of the treaties', which, in a national context, is usually given solely to the judicial branch. The role of the ECJ is, however, particularly important for the purposes of this book, as it is the primary body that decides on disputes between the institutions, between the MS, between the institutions and the MS, and on the interpretation of primary and secondary law. While the Commission may be instrumental in bringing actions before the Court, it may also be subject to actions if it fails to perform its own responsibilities. The related position of the ECJ and the Commission is explored further in the section concerned with enforcement.

Council

The Council of Ministers (or Council) is, as its name suggests, comprised of one minister from each state appropriate to the subject under discussion, the most important of which are the meetings relating to economic issues, foreign affairs and agriculture, which meet monthly. Its powers are defined by Article 202 of the TEC as coordination, decision making and implementing tasks carried out in order to 'ensure that the objectives set out in this Treaty are attained'. The Council should not be confused with the unofficial European Council of the EU or the Council of Europe, which is unrelated to the EU. The European Council is comprised of the Heads of State or Government of the MS (and others including the foreign ministers and the President of the Commission), and meets at least twice a year under the leadership of the MS that holds the Presidency. Its decisions are expressed as Conclusions or Declarations and it is responsible for development of the European Treaties. The Council of Europe has no connection with the EU at all; its membership comprises 41 countries and its best known achievement is the ECHR.

EC decision making is almost always carried out via the Council, which adopts legislation on the basis of Commission proposals, some of which may be subject to a co-decision/cooperation procedure of the Parliament (see below). The Council also decides on the budget of the EU, mostly together with the Parliament, and concludes international agreements that have been negotiated by the Commission on its behalf. Decisions concerning pillars two and three of the EU (CFSP and PJCC) are its responsibility. The Council also appoints members of the Commission, Court of Auditors and may alter the number of members of each and of Advocates General of the ECJ, which allows it some influence over each institution.

Commission

Article 211 of the TEC sets out the powers of the Commission, which are granted: 'in order to ensure the proper functioning and development of the common market'. Particular attention is given to implementation of the provisions of the Treaties and the measures taken in accord with them. As mentioned, it therefore operates as the 'guardian of the Treaties', which is an important check on the powers of the Council and Parliament, which is unusual from a national perspective. These powers are explained in detail in the enforcement section towards the end of this chapter. The Commission also has the power to formulate recommendations or deliver opinions on treaty matters, which includes its participation in contributing to the measures taken by the Council and Parliament under Article 211 of the TEC. It can also submit proposals on non-Community matters in the same way as the MS. The Commission represents the

EC in dealings with the MS and also in international transactions. Each MS is entitled to have one of its nationals as a member of the Commission, although enlargement of the EU will result in a situation where this will no longer be possible, yet in accordance with the principle of equality there will be fair representation from the MS. Commissioners are, however, expected to be completely independent in the performance of their duties, weighing the interests of different MS and groups against the interests of the Community.

Above all, the Commission has the power to propose legislation, giving it the ability to decide whether the EC should act, and, if so, on what legal basis and in what legal form. The articles of the treaties provide the legal bases for action, to which proposals must refer and, as will be seen in Chapter 8, in some instances more than one may be applicable. The legal form of a legislative proposal refers to the type of act that is deemed most appropriate, for example, a regulation or a directive. The Parliament must usually be notified before any proposal is made,[14] and widespread consultation typically underlies all new proposals; this is a requirement under the Protocol on the application of the principles of subsidiarity and proportionality (see below), and which involves the publication of consultation documents justifying proposals. EA may also be applied to all major legislative proposals, which has produced much interest in the academic literature and NGO world.[15] Once formulated, the Commission publishes it in the *Official Journal*. Proposals that have already been approved by the Commission are referred to as 'COM documents'. They are forwarded to national parliaments to allow time for discussion; six weeks must be allowed prior to its being placed on the Council agenda for a decision, which will either result in it being adopted by the Council or in a common position (by a qualified majority vote) being agreed under Articles 251 or 252 of the TEC (see below).

Parliament

The Parliament, originally the Assembly of the ECSC, the EAEC and the EEC, has undergone many changes during its history. Its powers are to advise, take part in EC and EU decision making, pronounce on external relations matters, adopt the budget and supervise other institutions of the EU, particularly the Commission. The Parliament represents the interests of EU citizens through the election of Members of the European Parliament (MEPs) and in permitting them to directly petition the Parliament in accordance with Articles 21 and 194 of the TEC.[16] Each MS has a number of representatives in accordance with its population size, although arrangements have changed to an extent as a result of enlargement of the EU.

Articles 251 and 252 of the TEC outline the co-decision and cooperation procedures, which enable the Parliament to contribute to the decision making process. The cooperation procedure under Article 252 begins with the Commission submitting its proposal, the Parliament delivering its opinion and the Council adopting a common position, which is a draft act published in the *Official Journal*. The Parliament must next take one of three decisions on the common position: it may approve it, although if it does not within three months it is deemed approved; it may propose amendments to it, to which the Council must give its unanimous assent; or it may decide to reject it, which may result in the Council still adopting it by a unanimous vote. The co-decision procedure provides greater power to the Parliament to submit amendments directly to the Council and prevent approval of draft acts to which it is opposed. Under it both institutions must give their approval, but if each does so by a qualified majority then it may be adopted. The first stage is the same as for the cooperation procedure and ends with the publication of the draft act, which the Parliament may approve, adopt amendments or reject. If the adopted amendments are approved by the Council then the act is adopted in that form; if not, a Conciliation Committee is appointed of members of both the Parliament and Council to try and reach agreement, failing which the act is not adopted. The Commission is also entitled to withdraw the proposal before this time, but not thereafter.

The Parliament can also give its assent on various matters including international agreements, and provide advisory opinions if appropriate under Article 192 of the TEC. As mentioned, any legislative proposal submitted by the Commission must have a legal basis in the TEC or TEU before the Parliament can take action.[17] The ECJ held in the case of *Roquette Frères* that participation by the Parliament in EC decision making is an essential procedural requirement with which other institutions must comply, failing which the act adopted can be annulled.[18] However, since there are no general rights to initiate and participate in decision making, the Parliament does not operate as a national legislature does, with much of the control falling to the Council.

ECJ

The ECJ plays a very important role in compliance with EC law, which is examined in the enforcement section at the end of this chapter. For now, the structure of the Court and its interpretation approach is outlined very briefly. Since 1989, there have in fact been two courts, the Court of First Instance (CFI) and the ECJ itself, which operate in accordance with a Protocol on the Statute of the Court of Justice.[19] Both the CFI and ECJ ensure that the interpretation and application of the treaties are observed under Article 220 of the TEC. The ECJ consists of one judge from each MS, as assisted by a number of Advocates General and a Registrar. The Advocates General make reasoned submissions before the Court makes its own deliberations. The CFI has at least one judge from each MS and a Registrar. Each judge is appointed by the governments of the MS, who are to be selected for their independence.

Treaty interpretation is, in practice, an important role of the ECJ, and the Court is required to provide interpretations of how acts of the European institutions such as directives are to be interpreted with reference to Treaty principles, or to what extent national implementing laws are compliant with both, when national courts exercising the highest appellate functions request them. Dhondt (2003, p15) explains the interpretative approach of the ECJ, which is, in practice, similar to that utilized by national and international courts.[20] She therefore refers to the literal, contextual and teleological (purposive) methods of interpretation. The literal approach is often complemented by a comparative examination of different language versions of EC law, which if the language is clear may result in a particular conclusion being reached. The contextual approach involves interpreting a provision in relation to other provisions of EC law, and the purposive approach focuses on the reason for the provision and its relationship to the Treaty objectives.

Member states and citizens of the Union

This subsection examines the role of the MS and citizens of the EU and relationship between them. In many MS, legislative approval was needed for the TEC and TEU, in some cases by referendum; approval of all constituent parts in a federal MS is often also required. Applicant MS have also frequently held referenda before making final decisions to join the EU. The reason why some MS needed legislative approval is because the principle of the primacy of EC law (see below) is not automatically applied, but depends on whether the MS is a monist or dualist system. This was discussed in Chapter 2 with respect to international law and is equally relevant regarding EC law.[21]

Once part of the EU, government ministers who are members of the Council take the main decisions on new legislative proposals, subject to the restrictions outlined above. Once legislative acts have been approved in the EU, if they take the form of directives, national parliaments have the obligation to transpose the requirements into national law in accordance with the requirements of Article 249 TEC (see below). National parliaments also exercise some control in relation to the democratic character of the EU, with their own members of the Council usually being answerable to them as representatives of the national parliament also. A Protocol to the Treaty of Amsterdam provides for all Commission consultation documents to be promptly forwarded to the national parliaments.[22] Together with national legislatures, national courts play a significant role in relation to EC law. This is discussed below in the section concerned with the enforcement of EC law.

As will be seen in the next section, both primary and secondary EC law is directly applicable and confers rights on individuals who are able to bring actions before national courts against other persons or authorities in their own or another MS.[23] Certain types of action can also be brought before the CFI. Such rights are of clear relevance given increased opportunities to participate in decision making at all levels. Articles 17–22 of the TEU conferred specific rights on nationals of MS as citizens of the EU. Citizenship of the EU complements national citizenship and includes the right not to be discriminated against on the grounds of nationality and to equal treatment within the scope of EC law. Articles 18 to 21 of the TEC codify the rights in existence before the TEU, such as the rights to reside, move and vote. In the Charter of Fundamental Rights of the EU, the rights of citizens of the EU are enshrined in the chapter entitled 'citizenship'; this will gain legal force after the Lisbon Reform Treaty is ratified by the MS. Aside from this, fundamental rights and freedoms of EU citizens are not listed, and in accordance with Article 6(2) of the TEC, reference must be made to the European Convention for the Protection of Human Rights and Fundamental Freedoms, the human rights case law of the ECJ relating to Article 220 of the TEC, and national provisions. Specific directives concern rights to move and reside freely within the territory of an MS.[24]

THE SOURCES AND OBLIGATIONS OF EUROPEAN LAW

The first two sections of this chapter examined the role of the TEC and TEU in establishing the EC and EU, their internal and external relationships, and the different actors in European law making, primarily the institutions of the EC, with the Commission formulating legislative proposals, the Council approving them subject to Parliamentary input, and (as will be seen in more detail later) the Commission and ECJ ensuring implementation. This third section looks at the sources and obligations of European law[25] that are the treaties and specific acts of the EC institutions (primarily regulations and directives), together with the case law of the ECJ and the national courts when applying and interpreting EC law as a whole.[26] Another source is the international law beyond the European treaties, which may be applicable in the EU when the EC or EU is a party to international agreements. The relationship with national and international law is also analysed in this section, specifically the legal questions of direct and indirect effect, the first dealing with the obligations of EC law in the national legal framework, the second the obligations of international law in the EC legal framework, which in turn impact on the national laws of the MS.

Treaty principles

The TEC and the TEU contain the powers of the EC and EU and outline several general principles, notably the principles of subsidiarity, proportionality, integration, sincere cooperation and cooperation in good faith and equal treatment, which apply to all law making (see, for example, Tridimas, 1999). Reference to these principles will be made from time to time in this part of the book, especially to the principle of integration. Other recent principles are also of general effect, including the principles of democracy, liberty, respect for human rights and fundamental freedoms and the rule of law, which are recognized by Article 6(1) of the TEU.[27] As the historical development of the treaties has already been outlined, and without downplaying the significance of the TEU principles, this subsection is limited to briefly outlining the longstanding principles found in the TEC that must also be taken account of in making, applying and interpreting acts of the institutions, notably directives and regulations.

   Under Article 5 of the TEC, the principle of subsidiarity provides that whenever the EC does not exercise exclusive competence, it is only able to take action 'if and in so far as the objectives of the proposed action cannot be sufficiently achieved by the Member States and can therefore, by reason of the scale or effects of the proposed action, be better achieved by the Community'.[28] The principle of proportionality (also in Article 5) requires a balance to be struck between the means used and intended aim or result, and applies to both the MS and the EC institutions.[29] Both the principles of subsidiarity and proportionality are the subject of a Protocol annexed to the TEC.[30] The integration principle is found in Article 6 of the TEC and requires that 'environmental protection requirements must be integrated into the definition and implementation of the Community policies and activities referred to in Article 3, in particular, with a view to promoting sustainable development'.[31] The cooperation principle(s) are found in Article 10 of the TEC and are expressions of Community solidarity.[32] As such, Lenaerts and van Nuffel (2005, p115) comment that they are 'not the same as the principle of international law that States are required to implement in good faith the treaties which they conclude'. Finally, the principle of equal treatment is designed to avoid discrimination at all levels and is found in many Treaty provisions, including Article 12.

Regulations and Directives

Article 249 of the TEC permits the EC institutions to make regulations and issue directives. A number of formal requirements apply, including an obligation to state reasons on which they are based, and publication in the *Official Journal.* Regulations are directly applicable and are therefore binding without the need for transposition within the national legal system. Directives are binding on the MS as to the results to be achieved, with the form and methods by which they are to be incorporated into the law of the MS left up to the national authorities, although a time limit is set for transposition. The reality tends to be somewhat different, partly as a result of the detail that, at least other than framework directives, is included, and also because of the likelihood of infraction proceedings should directives fail to be implemented correctly. Many MS therefore tend to 'write-out' the text of directives in national implementing legislation rather than risk a legal challenge, which may also come from an individual as well as an EC institution or another MS. However, if the matter covered by the directive is already one that is subject to national law(s), those laws may need to be substantially amended or indeed rewritten in their entirety in order for EC law to be accurately transposed and hence fully complied with. Lenaerts and van Nuffel (2005, p609) express the complexities of this as follows, with reference to the principle of direct effect, which is considered below:

> *The need to ensure that Community law is fully applied requires Member States not only to bring their legislation into conformity with Community law but also to do so by adopting rules of law capable of creating a situation which is sufficiently precise, clear and transparent to allow individuals to know the full extent of their rights and rely on them before the national authorities.*[33]

Decisions, recommendations and opinions

Decisions, recommendations and opinions are also provided for under Article 249 TEC. A decision is binding in its entirety on those to whom it is addressed, although it will always be addressed to specific legal persons. Those addressed to the MS are binding on all the institutions of the state, including the judiciary, which are under a duty to refrain from applying conflicting provisions of national law. In some circumstances, a provision within a decision may have direct effect so that an individual can rely on it in a dispute with a public authority (see below). Recommendations and opinions have no binding force and do not create any rights for individuals. However, national courts must take recommendations into account in deciding on disputes, especially where they contribute to an interpretation of whether national provisions are in conformity with binding EC law.

Case law of the Court of Justice and Court of First Instance

The case law of the ECJ and CFI is an important additional source of EC law, albeit formally limited to applying and interpreting the other sources of law. The interpretation of the Courts defines the meaning and scope of the EC norms, thereby providing assistance for later courts and national authorities in deciding what action should be taken. Interpretative techniques are similar to those of national and international courts as outlined previously.

International law

Article 307 of the TEC makes it clear that it is the intention of the EC to comply with international law. The ECJ has therefore held that the EC must respect international law in the exercise of its powers, including respect for the principles of the UN Charter. The ECJ takes principles of customary international law into account in its judgments and applies the VCLT. International agreements entered into by the EC under Article 300 of the TEC are binding on the EC institutions and MS and form part of the EC legal order from when they enter into force. This is because the EC is considered to be a monist legal system, there being no need to transpose the requirements into internal provisions of EC law. It is also possible for individuals to rely on provisions in international agreements if the provision satisfies the requirements for 'direct effect' (see below for discussion, and Lenaerts and van Nuffel, 2005, pp742–743 for further detail). Incorporated norms of international law take precedence over acts of the institutions, which must be interpreted in conformity with them. Similarly, agreements entered into by the EC take precedence over conflicting national provisions of MS.

Principles of primacy and full effectiveness of EC law

In connection with the relationship between EC and national law (and the distinction between EC law and international law), the principles of primacy and full effectiveness of EC law apply.[34] As a result of the TEC and TEU, MS no longer have sovereignty concerning EC matters. In many cases a majority decision of the Council binds all MS, institutional rules must be interpreted uniformly and MS must take all steps to ensure the fulfilment of Treaty obligations, including that national courts are required to apply EC law in the context of national decisions. In this regard, together with the other Treaty principles set out above, the principle of cooperation in good faith or loyal cooperation is considered of great importance to the ECJ. The jurisdiction of the ECJ is also compulsory and its decisions are not only binding but are supported by the imposition of sanctions. Lenaerts and van Nuffel (2005, p14) cite the landmark decision in *Costa v ENEL*[35] where the ECJ held that the MS themselves brought the EC legal order into being, limiting their sovereignty in so doing:

> *[b]y creating a Community of unlimited duration, having its own institutions, its own personality, its own legal capacity and capacity of representation on the international plane and, more particularly, real powers [as a result of the Member States' having limited their own powers or transferred them to the Communities].*

In *Van Gend & Loos*[36] it was held that the status of Community law in national legal systems is a matter of EC law itself, meaning that it is for the ECJ and not the MS to determine the nature and effect of EC law. National provisions must be interpreted in accordance with EC law as a result of the decision in *Marleasing*[37] and national provisions that conflict with EC law must not be applied, as a result of the decision in *Simmenthal.*[38] This duty, which is known as the doctrine of sympathetic interpretation or indirect effect, applies to not only national courts but also public bodies including those that exercise administrative functions; it also applies to agreements concluded between MS that conflict with EC law. Since the decision in *Francovich*, individuals may also claim damages from an MS whose breach of EC law causes them to suffer loss or damage, regardless of whether the breach is attributable to the executive, legislature or judiciary.[39] This is clearly distinct from the general focus of international law (with some exceptions in the human rights field), where the focus is solidly on the relationship between states. The reason the Court decided this was above all the fact that the treaties established institutions with powers to affect both MS and their citizens.

Principle of direct effect of EC law

Again in connection with the relationship between EC and national law, the principle of direct effect of EC law also has a significant role in ensuring that the obligations of EC law are fully applied.[40] The case of *Van Gend & Loos* also held for the first time that EC law not only imposes obligations on individuals but also confers rights on them at the same time. National courts are obliged to protect the legal rights of citizens that derive from the direct effect of EC law in accordance with the principle of cooperation set out in Article 10 of the TEC. The decisive test for deciding whether a provision has direct effect or not is its content, which must be 'clear and unconditional and not contingent on any discretionary implementing measure'.[41]

A provision therefore has direct effect where a court is able, without any further implementing measures, to reach an interpretation that can be applied to the case being considered, under which individuals can enforce rights deriving from it.

Both primary and secondary EC law is capable of having direct effect. A number of Treaty provisions have been held by the ECJ to have direct effect and others have not, which are included in a list compiled by Schermers and Waelbroeck (2001, pp183–185). Lenaerts and van Nuffel (2005, p702) emphasize that transposition of the treaties is not needed if they have direct effect,[42] distinguishing between horizontal and vertical direct effect (see also Mastroianni, 1999), which is also examined in Chapter 8 in relation to the environment, as follows:

> *Where a treaty provision is recognised as having direct effect, an individual may therefore rely upon it both against Community and national authorities (vertically) and against other individuals (horizontally). Such a provision has direct effect from the time when it enters into force or, as the case may be, from the end of the transitional period.*

With regard to secondary EC law, regulations are 'directly applicable' under Article 249 of the TEC and are therefore binding on national authorities without the need for transposition into the legal system of the MS. However, provided the same criteria for direct effect is satisfied, an individual can also rely on a provision in a regulation against another individual (for example, it can also have horizontal direct effect). This is not the same as a regulation being directly applicable and therefore providing a remedy to an individual against the national authorities,[43] which is achieved automatically as a result of its direct applicability and is thereby similar to vertical direct effect. There is no horizontal direct effect in the case of directives, which, if the requirements for direct effect are satisfied, can only provide remedies against the national authorities (for example, they can only have vertical direct effect). The case of *Marshall I* is authority for this proposition, the reasoning being that under Article 249 of the TEC a directive is only binding in relation to 'each Member State to which it is addressed'.[44] For directives to put individuals in the same position as regulations, it is therefore necessary for directives to be correctly transposed into the national law of an MS.[45] However, even where a directive has not been correctly transposed (if at all), national law must still be interpreted as far as possible in conformity with the requirements of the directive under Articles 10 and 249 of the TEC, with conflicting national law disallowed.

ENFORCEMENT OF EUROPEAN LAW

As Lenaerts and van Nuffel (2005, p443) comment:

> *The founding fathers of the Communities opted for a system under which enforcement of Community law was left in principle to the national courts. A dispute relating to Community law may be brought before the Court of Justice or the Court of First Instance (including the judicial panels) only if this is permitted in accordance with one of the procedures prescribed by the Treaties. Exceptionally, the Court of Justice has interpreted its own jurisdiction in a manner exceeding the literal scope of a given procedure, inter alia in order to fill a lacuna in the system of legal protection or to secure the coherence of the Community's legal order.*

To add to this is the role of the Commission as the 'guardian of the treaties', which brings with it a range of powers outlined below.

Commission

Informal and formal complaints (which may be from citizens of the EU) are submitted to it concerning non-compliance, to which the Commission is required to respond. If it finds that the Council or Parliament have breached EC law, it can bring action before the ECJ for annulment or a failure to act in accordance with Articles 230 and 232. If it is an MS that is at fault, the Commission will first give notice of this, provide an opportunity to respond and remedy matters and, if needed, give a reasoned opinion with which the MS is required to comply within a stated time. If this is not done, then under Article 226 of the TEC, the action may be brought before the ECJ. If the ECJ decides the MS has breached EC law it will make an order requiring compliance, failing which the Commission will ask the ECJ to order payment of a lump sum or penalty payments under Article 228. The supervision exercised by the Commission extends to making sure that MS also comply with binding international law, binding as a result of European ratification of international treaties or demonstration of sufficient levels of state practice.

ECJ

The powers of the ECJ are clearly delimited in the treaties, and concern four matters (see generally Koppen, 2005). First, the Court decides disputes between Community institutions and bodies, both directly following action for annulment or failure to act. Second, the Court decides disputes between the EC and the MS, which as shown below, may come as a result of an action by the Commission; they may also come as a result of action by an MS, which may include a failure to act by one of the institutions. In both the first and second cases, institutions and MS have the right to intervene and make submissions.[46] Third, the Court can hear and decide cases between the MS, under Articles 227 and 239 of the TEC. Fourth and finally, the Court provides protection to natural and legal persons where a national court makes reference to it for a preliminary ruling on interpretation of Treaty law or on the validity or interpretation of acts of the EC institutions.

National courts

The courts of each MS determine all disputes there in regard to the application of EC law. Despite the roles of the Commission and ECJ outlined above, each is considered a 'Community court' because of the overall decentralized enforcement of EC law. Where needed, national courts make references for preliminary rulings from the ECJ. If national law is applied contrary to EC law, the Commission can take action as outlined above for infringement of EC law, which may provide an entitlement in damages in order to repair the breach.

TOPICAL ISSUES: THE EU CONSTITUTION, THE 'DEMOCRATIC DEFICIT' AND THE REFORM TREATY

In Chapter 2 a number of topical issues were explored in relation to international law. These focused on whether international law has a constitutional basis and on the self-contained regimes in international law, such as the EU. The most significant topical issue in European law is also its constitutional basis, in the light of criticisms concerning a 'democratic deficit' in the EU, and the failure of the 2005 referenda in France and the Netherlands on whether or not those MS should ratify the European Constitution (Mathiesen, 2003, p38; Beck, 2005; Joerges, 2005; Rödl, 2005; Hurrelmann, 2007; Wagner, undated). The draft Treaty establishing a formal Constitution for Europe was adopted in 2004 in order to clarify the constitutionality of the supranational legal order and provide greater democratic legitimacy on the institutions; it was to do this by replacing the TEU and TEC.[47] All MS needed to approve the constitutional changes if they were to come into effect, some by referenda, and the failure of the electorates of France and the Netherlands to approve the Constitution resulted in the constitutional project being suspended.[48]

As indicated, the Reform Treaty/Treaty of Lisbon has filled the void left by the constitutional project, albeit with many differences to take into account the reluctance of many to see national sovereignty eroded. The Treaty is still designed to increase the efficiency and effectiveness of European decision making processes, improving democratic accountability and the rule of law.[49] However it no longer contains constitutional characteristics, with the use of the word 'constitution' being deleted, there being no 'Union Minister of Foreign Affairs' and no mention of symbols of the EU such as the flag, anthem or motto. The original intention to replace regulations and directives with 'laws' and 'framework laws' has also been curtailed. Yet the competences of the EU and MS have been clarified, the CFSP specified, the role of national parliaments enhanced, the Charter of Fundamental Rights formalized, and some moves made in the area of Police and Judicial Cooperation in Criminal Matters (PJCC).[50]

CONCLUSIONS

This chapter has explained the complexities of European law and its relationship with national and international law, as updated to take account of the Lisbon Treaty. It can safely be concluded that European law is a legal order distinct from any other, of independent operation and of unparalleled global significance as a result of its territorial reach and hence the number of states and individuals subject to it. Several matters are the subject of further explanation and analysis in Chapter 8, which examines European environmental law. The general Treaty principles are supplemented by principles that have been derived specifically in the environmental domain, and the legal bases for law making are examined with respect to specific legal acts, notably the EIA directive itself, which is analysed in Chapter 9. In that chapter, case law of the ECJ on the EIA directive, in particular concerned with MS non-compliance in transposition and implementation, is analysed, and examples are given of the role of the Commission in reporting generally are given, again in the context of the EIA Directive. Finally, the roles of the Council and Parliament in adopting the amended EIA directive are considered.

NOTES

1   Authors distinguish between primary and secondary EC law (see Dhondt, 2003, p35; Lenaerts and van Nuffel, 2005, p665); in this context, primary law refers to the Treaty law establishing the EC and EU and secondary law refers to the legislative acts of the institutions, typically regulations and directives. Chapter 1 explained that constitutional law is the highest form of law with which all other law must comply; this is also the case with the European treaties, as they comprise the 'constitutional law' with which regulations and directives must comply. Chapter 1 also distinguished primary and secondary legislation in a common law context as meaning statutes and delegated legislation (Acts of Parliament and regulations). In the

context of EC law it is important to be aware that directives are not 'Acts' of the European Parliament, and 'regulations' are not delegated legislation. Regulations in the EC law sense are binding on MS without the need for implementing measures so are the strongest form of law making aside from the constitutional law of treaties. Neither regulations nor directives are strictly speaking 'acts' of the European Parliament because the decision making processes in the EC are very different to those at a national level, where the legislature is always the law making body. While its influence on the law making process has increased in recent years as a result of Treaty amendments, the European Parliament does not dominate the process as in individual countries; the European Council has a primary role.

2   In the absence of a European Constitution, the treaties are effectively the constitutional law of the EC and EU, and the sources of law outlined in this chapter are therefore limited to them, the legislative acts of the institutions, the case law of the ECJ and international law applicable to the EC and EU. The ECJ described the treaties as 'the constitutive charter of a [Union] based on the rule of law', (see ECJ, Case 294/83 *Les Verts v European Parliament* [1986] ECR 1339, para 23; and Opinion 1/91 *Draft agreement between the Community, on the one hand, and the countries of the European Free Trade Association, on the other, relating to the creation of the European Economic Area* [1991] ECR I-6079, para 21).

3   There are numerous established texts on European law for legal practitioners and others. One of the more recent, co-authored by a judge of the ECJ and providing detailed information on the constitutional aspects of the law in particular, is Lenaerts and van Nuffel (2005), which is used and referenced for much of this chapter, and the help of which in writing this chapter (in updating the present author's own understanding in particular) is gratefully acknowledged. Others include Craig and de Búrca (2008), Hartley (2007), Arnull (2006), Arnull et al (2006), Chalmers et al (2006), Steniner et al (2006) and Weatherill (2006).

4   The ECSC Treaty 1951 established a common market in coal and steel, and the EAEC Treaty 1957 aimed to create a nuclear industry across Europe; the ECSC Treaty was for a fixed term of 50 years and came to an end in July 2002.

5   Unfortunately, because of its significance the Single European Act is frequently reduced to the acronym 'SEA' by European lawyers and European environmental lawyers. To avoid confusion with strategic environmental assessment here, the full title is used.

6   Article 8 of the TEU of 7 February 1992 amended the Treaty establishing the EEC to establish the EC. As explained in Chapter 8, Articles 130r–130t (now Articles 174–176) provided competence in the environmental sphere for the first time.

7   The EU is now regarded to comprise three pillars: the first is the Community pillar of the *acquis communautaire* (see note 26 below), the second and third are the cooperation between the MS over common foreign and security policy (CFSP), and police and judicial cooperation in criminal matters (PJCC). The use of the term 'EU law' is only strictly appropriate when referring to the legal rules under the second and third pillars. While plain English is the stated medium of this book wherever possible, the *acquis communautaire* is one term that is in common usage in the EC and is hence unavoidable.

8   Other than the TEU and the Lisbon Reform Treaty, all the other treaties that have amended the original EEC Treaty are collectively referred to as the EC treaties or simply the TEC. The Lisbon Reform Treaty contains two substantive clauses amending the TEU and TEC. The TEU will keep its name and the TEC will be called the Treaty on the Functioning of the European Union (TFEU), the Union thereafter having a single legal personality. See Presidency Conclusions, Brussels, 21/22 June 2007, p15, as discussed further at the end of this chapter.

9   Federalism was explicitly rejected by a number of MS, and the rejection of the European Constitution ensured that there were to be clear limits imposed on the powers of the EU for the time being. The Reform Treaty acknowledges the abandonment of the constitutional project, which would have repealed all existing treaties and replaced them with a single text

entitled Constitution; instead the existing treaties are retained, albeit amended as noted above. See Presidency Conclusions, 2007, p15.

10   The rules concerning treaty interpretation in the VCLT 1969, for example, have been replaced by rules set out in the TEC and TEU, as developed by the ECJ and other institutions. The application of international law within the Union beyond the TEC and TEU remains governed by the VCLT 1986; this is explained briefly here in the section on the relationship between international and European law, with further discussion in Chapter 12.

11   For examples of where the texts of the treaties have been referred to as the constitution of the EC, see the references cited in Lenaerts and van Nuffel (2005, note 49, p17).

12   The EU's external policy is based on the external powers of the EC and actions of the institutions and MS pursuant to the CFSP. Article 300 of the TEC lays down the procedure by which the EC concludes agreements with non-member countries or international organizations. The EC has legal personality by virtue of Article 281 of the TEC; Article 24 of the TEU gave power to the Council to conclude agreements with non-member countries and international organizations on behalf of the EU; if the EU is bound by these agreements is must be regarded as having legal personality under international law. See Lenaerts and van Nuffel, 2005, p817 specifically, and Chapters 19 and 20 generally, for more information that is beyond the scope of the present work. See also Macleod et al (1996).

13   See Article 54 of the 1969 VCLT. Article 48 of the TEU now contains a general amendment procedure that replaces the procedures in the earlier treaties. Provision is also made for altering specific provisions by means of a special procedure, which, unlike Article 48, does not require an intergovernmental conference. For details on both, including restrictions on the ability of MS to alter the Community legal order that distinguishes European law from international law, see Lenaerts and van Nuffel (2005, pp342–350). For details of procedures permitting MS to not comply in full with treaty obligations, which are similar to the reservations possible in international law, see the same authors, pp365–380. Some authors disagree with this synopsis of the relationship between international and European law, such as Klabbers (2002) and Koivurova (2007); this is a matter that is discussed in Chapter 12.

14   See Framework agreement on relations between the Parliament and the Commission of July 5, 2000, point 13.

15   This is considered further in Chapter 10. Briefly, the Commission IA process is not examined in detail in this book because it is not a form of SEA, including as it does reference to all types of effect. It is, however, illustrative of an increased focus on the impacts of policy and legislative proposals that are now considered in a number of countries as a means of producing 'better regulation' (for example, in the UK). Together with the few examples of EA applied to policies and legislation (for example, in the Netherlands and Finland), and as given added momentum by the focus on policy and legislative proposals in the SEA Protocol, they do, however, provide a wealth of evidence of the growing need for EA to be applied at the most strategic levels that (currently at least) the SEA Directive fails to address.

16   Complaints of maladministration can also be submitted to the European Ombudsman, which is closely connected to the Parliament, in accord with Article 195 of the TEC.

17   See note 6 above for the legal basis of environmental proposals.

18   ECJ, Case 138/79 *Roquette Frères* [1980] ECR 3333.

19   Protocol on the Statute of the Court of Justice, annexed by the Treaty of Nice to the TEU, the TEC and the EAEC Treaty [2001] OJ C/80/53.

20   These approaches were described in Chapters 1 and 2. See also Marsden (2006a, 2006b, 2008) for examples in a Hong Kong context.

21   As examples, the Benelux countries, Cyprus, the Baltic States and Poland are monist systems and give precedence to international laws over their national law; the UK, Ireland, Denmark, the Czech and Slovak Republics, Hungary and Malta are dualist systems and implementing

legislation was/is needed. For further information on all of the MS and literature on the relationship between each and the EC see Lenaerts and van Nuffel (2005, pp679–700).

22 See Protocol (No 9) to the EU Treaties and the Community Treaties on the role of national parliaments in the European Union, annexed by the Amsterdam Treaty to those Treaties [1997] OJ C340/113, point 1. As a result, Declaration (No 13) annexed to the TEU on the role of national parliaments in the EU is given binding force.

23 See *Van Gend & Loos* discussed below.

24 See Directive 2004/38/EC of the European Parliament and the Council of 29 April 2004 on the right of a citizen of the Union and their family members to move and reside freely within the territory of the Member States [2004] OJ L158/77.

25 As noted above, primary EC law is the law of European treaties; secondary EC law is the acts of the institutions, case law and international law adopted by the institutions.

26 One of the objectives of the EU as now set out in Article 2(5) of the TEU is 'to maintain in full the *acquis communautaire* and build on it'. This generally refers to existing substantive EC law as interpreted and applied by the ECJ.

27 For further information, see Lenaerts and van Nuffel (2005, pp711–738) who emphasize the fundamental rights.

28 For discussion of the subsidiarity principle generally in the literature, see Emiliou (1992) and Toth (1992); for discussion of the principle with respect to environmental policy, see Brinkhorst (1993), Lenaerts (1994) and Wils (1994).

29 In common parlance, one should not 'use a sledgehammer to crack a nut'. For discussion of the principle of proportionality, see de Búrca (1993) and Emiliou (1996); for discussion of the weighting of the interests of trade and environmental protection by the ECJ, see Notaro (2000).

30 See Protocol (No 30) [1997] OJ C340/105. For any Community legislation, the reasons on which it is based must be stated to justify compliance with the principles. The Parliament and Council have also to consider whether Commission proposals are compliant, and the Commission is to report annually on the application of Article 5.

31 The integration principle is of considerable significance to Part II of this book. It is the only principle in the TEC that deals specifically with environmental protection and it has an obvious relationship with the SEA Directive. The most detailed legal reference to the principle is Dhondt (2003).

32 For discussion see Temple Lang (2001).

33 They cite two cases on this point, indicating that the obligation to implement has been clarified in the case law principally regarding directives. See ECJ, Case C-162/99 *Commission v Italy* [2001] ECR I-541, para 22; and ECJ, Case C-313/99 *Mulligan* [2002] ECR I-5719, paras 46-54.

34 See generally Delicostopoulos (2003).

35 ECJ, Case 6/64 *Costa* [1964] ECR 585, at 593.

36 ECJ, Case 26/62 *Van Gend & Loos* [1963] ECR 1, at 10–12.

37 ECJ, Case C-106/98 *Marleasing* [1990] ECR I-4135, para 8. Betlem (2002) has indicated that interpreting national law in conformity with EC law has made the question of the direct effect of EC law unnecessary.

38 ECJ, Case 106/77 *Simmenthal* [1978] ECR 629, para 17. See also the decision in ECJ, Case C-213/89 *Factorame* [1990] ECR I-2433, paras 14–15.

39 ECJ, Case C-6 and 9/90 *Francovich and Bonifaci* [1991]. Three conditions must be met for this: first the rule of law infringed must be intended to confer rights on individuals, second the breach must be sufficiently serious, and third there must be a direct causal link between the breach of the obligation and the damage sustained. See Steiner (1993) and Craig (1993).

40 See generally, Prinssen and Schrauwen (2002) and Craig (1997).

41 ECJ, Case 44/84 *Hurd* [1986] ECR 29, para 47.

42 Transposition in this context means introducing national legislation to give effect to the treaty. This is not the same as a dualist legal system needing to obtain legislative approval to ratify the treaty in the first place, which will always be needed in dualist systems first, regardless of whether the treaty later has direct effect.

43 These include what have been termed 'emanations of the state', which in the UK context means the privatized utility companies. See ECJ, Case C-188/89 *Foster v British Gas* [1990] ECR I-3313.

44 ECJ, Case 152/84 *Marshall I* [1986] ECR 723, para 48. See also ECJ, Case C-91/92 *Faccini Dori* [1994] ECR I-3325, para 24, where the Court stated:

> *[t]he effect of extending that case law [on the direct effect of directives] to the sphere of relations between individuals would be to recognise a power in the Community to enact obligations for individuals with immediate effect, whereas it has competence to do so only where it is empowered to adopt regulations.*

45 For an example of the extensive commentary on this, see Betlem (1995).

46 Observations are often made in connection with requests for preliminary rulings on the interpretation of EC law, which may result in national law being in breach of EC law.

47 The Treaty is in three parts. Part I sets out the EU's objectives and values, Part II the Charter of Fundamental Rights, and Part III the EU's policies.

48 Several authors have discussed the adopted European Constitution (and constitutionalism) from other perspectives, notably judicial (Tridimas, 2004; Everson and Eisner, 2007) and environmental (Jans and Scott, 2003; Jans, 2003). The shelving of the constitutional project following the failed MS referenda renders much of this academic and irrelevant. Note, however, that under the Reform Treaty a Declaration has been made on the primacy of European law, and that environmental policy will now be supplemented by a reference to climate change.

49 Some of the other changes to be made by the Reform Treaty are that the co-decision procedure will be extended, qualified majority voting will be the general rule in the Council, the Commission President will be elected by the Parliament, the Union will have a single legal personality with the pillar structure removed, national parliaments will be able to control subsidiarity through a new mechanism, and the Charter of Fundamental Rights will be legally binding having the same legal rank as the treaties even though it is not contained within the Reform Treaty.

50 See Presidency Conclusions, Brussels, 21/22 June 2007, p16.

REFERENCES

Arnull, A. (2006) *The European Union and its Court of Justice*, 2nd Edition, Oxford University Press, Oxford

Arnull, A., Dashwood, A., Dougan, N., Ross, M., Spaventa, E. and Wyatt, D. (2006) *Wyatt and Dashwood's European Union Law*, 5th Edition, Sweet and Maxwell, London

Beck, G. (2005) 'The problem of kompetenz-kompetenz: A conflict between right and right in which there is no praetor', *European Law Review*, vol 30, no 1, pp42–67

Betlem, G. (1995) 'Medium hard law – still no horizontal direct effect of European Community directives after *Faccini Dori*', *Columbia Journal of European Law*, vol 1, no 3, pp469–496

Betlem, G. (2002) 'The doctrine of consistent interpretation – managing legal uncertainty', *Oxford Journal of Legal Studies*, vol 22, no 3, pp397–418

Brinkhorst, L. (1993) 'Subsidiarity and European Community environmental policy: A panacea or a pandora's box?', *European Environmental Law Review*, January, pp16–24

Chalmers, D., Hadjiemmanuil, C., Monti, G. and Tomkins, A. (2006) *European Union Law. Text and Materials*, Cambridge University Press, Cambridge

Craig, P. (1993) '*Francovich*, remedies and the scope of damages liability', *Law Quarterly Review*, vol 109, pp595–621

Craig, P. (1997) 'Directives: Direct effect, indirect effect and the construction of national legislation', *European Law Review*, vol 22, pp519–538

Craig, P. and de Búrca, G. (2008) *EU Law. Text, Cases and Materials*, 4th Edition, Oxford University Press, Oxford

Delicostopoulos, J. S. (2003) 'Towards European procedural primacy in national legal systems', *European Law Journal*, vol 9, no 5, pp599–613

De Búrca, G. (1993) 'The principle of proportionality and its application in EC law', *Yearbook of Environmental Law*, pp105–150

Dhondt, N. (2003) *Integration of Environmental Protection into other EC Policies: Legal Theory and Practice*, Europa Law Publishing, Groningen

Emiliou, N. (1992) 'Subsidiarity: An effective barrier against "the enterprises of ambition"?', *European Law Review*, vol 17, no 5, pp383–407

Emiliou, N. (1996) *The Principle of Proportionality in European Law – A Comparative Study*, Kluwer, London/The Hague

Everson, M. and Eisner, J. (2007) *The Making of a European Constitution: Judges and Law Beyond Constitutive Power*, Routledge-Cavendish, London

Hartley, T. C. (2007) *The Foundations of European Community Law*, 6th Edition, Oxford University Press, Oxford

Hurrelmann, A. (2007) 'European democracy, the 'permissive consensus' and the collapse of the EU constitution', *European Law Journal*, vol 13, no 3, pp343–359

Jans, J. (ed) (2003) *The European Convention and the Future of European Environmental Law*, Europa Law Publishing, Groningen

Jans, J. and Scott, J. (2003) 'The Convention on the future of Europe: An environmental perspective', *Journal of Environmental Law*, vol 15, no 3, pp323–339

Joerges, C. (2005) 'Rethinking European law's supremacy: A plea for a supranational conflict of laws' in Joerges, C. (ed) *Rethinking European Law's Supremacy*, EU Working Paper LAW No 2005/12, European University Institute Department of Law, Florence, pp5–27

Klabbers, J. (2002) *An Introduction to International Institutional Law*, Cambridge University Press, Cambridge

Koivurova, T. (2007) personal communication, December

Koppen, I. J. (2005) 'The role of the European Court of Justice' in A. Jordan (ed) (2005) *Environmental Policy in the European Union*, 2nd Edition, Earthscan, London, pp67–86

Lenearts, K. (1994) 'The principle of subsidiarity and the environment in the European Union: Keeping the balance of federalism' *Fordham International Law Journal*, vol 17, pp846–895

Lenaerts, K. and van Nuffel, P. (2005) *Constitutional Law of the European Union*, Thomson Sweet and Maxwell, London

Marsden, S. (2006a) 'Constitutional interpretation in Hong Kong: Do common law approaches apply when the National People's Congress Standing Committee interprets the Basic Law?', *LAWASIA Journal*, pp99–124

Marsden, S. (2006b) 'Regional autonomy, judicial criticism and the 2005 interpretation. Judicial independence in Hong Kong compromised again?', *Hong Kong Law Journal*, vol 36, no 1, pp117–142

Marsden, S. (2008) 'Conflicting approaches to interpretation of Hong Kong's Basic Law: Can an understanding of European law help?', under review

Mastroianni, R. (1999) 'On the distinction between vertical and horizontal direct effect of directives: What role for the principle of equality?, *European Public Law*, vol 5, p417

Mathieson, A. (2003) 'Public participation in decision making and access to justice in EC environmental law: The case of certain plans and programmes', *European Environmental Law Review*, vol 12, no 2, pp36–52

Macleod, I., Hendry, I. D. and Hyatt, S. (1996) *The External Relations of the European Communities*, Clarendon Press, Oxford

Notaro, N. (2000) 'The new generation case law on trade and the environment', *European Law Review*, vol 25, no 5, pp467–487

Obradovic, D. and Lavranos, N. (eds) (2007) *Interface between EU Law and National Law*, Europa Law Publishing, Groningen

Prinssen, J. and Schrauwen, A. (eds) (2002) *Direct Effect: Rethinking a Classic of EC Legal Doctrine*, Europa Law Publishing, Groningen

Rödl, F. (2005) '"There is no legitimacy beyond democracy" – and its consequences', in Joerges, C. (ed) *Rethinking European Law's Supremacy*, EU Working Paper LAW No 2005/12, European University Institute Department of Law, Florence, pp55–66

Schermers, H. G. and Waelbroeck, D. F. (2001) *Judicial Protection in the European Union*, Kluwer, The Hague

Steiner, J. (1993) 'From direct effects to Francovich: Shifting means of enforcement of Community law', *European Law Review*, vol 18, pp3–22

Steiner, J., Woods, L. and Twigg-Flesner, C. (2006) *EU Law*, Oxford University Press, Oxford

Temple Lang, J. (2001) 'The duties of co-operation of national authorities and courts under Article 10 EC: Two more reflections', *European Law Review*, vol 26, pp84–93

Toth, A. G. (1992) 'The principle of subsidiarity in the Maastricht Treaty' *Common Market Law Review*, vol 29, pp1079–1105

Tridimas, T. (1999) *The General Principles of EC Law*, Oxford University Press, Oxford

Tridimas, T. (2004) *The ECJ and the Draft Constitution: A Supreme Court for the Union?*, Federal Trust for Education and Research Online Paper 05/04 March 2004, www.fedtrust.co.uk/default.asp?groupid=0&search=takis%20tridimas

Wagner, M. (undated) 'National parliaments and democratic control in the EU', *Federal Trust Discussion Paper 3*, Federal Trust, London

Weatherill, S. (2006) *Cases and Materials on EU Law*, 7th Edition, Oxford University Press, Oxford

Wils, W. P. J. (1994) 'Subsidiarity and EC environmental policy: Taking people's concerns seriously', *Journal of Environmental Law*, vol 6, no 1, pp85–91

CHAPTER 8

European Environmental Law

CHAPTER OUTLINE

In common with the framework set out in the first part of this book, and following the overview of European law given in Chapter 7, this chapter examines the development and current status of European environmental law,[1] before the principal legal instruments of relevance to the SEA Directive (the EIA and related directives) are analysed in Chapter 9; these other procedural or 'horizontal' directives in turn provide more specific context to the evaluation of the SEA Directive in Chapter 10.[2] The chapter consists of three parts. Where possible, reference is made to the relevance of historical developments, such as the Environmental Action Programmes, treaty amendments, underlying principles and compliance and enforcement matters from the perspective of the EIA and SEA Directives.

The first part is a historical overview, with reference to the environmental law and policy of the EC/EU, the legal competence to legislate for environmental matters within and outside the EC/EU, and the institutions responsible. The second part discusses the underlying general and environmental principles and objectives, with a focus on those of particular relevance to EA at all levels, the precautionary, preventive and polluter pays principles, together with the principle of sustainable development.[3] This part includes reference to the incorporation of these principles into the legislation and case law of the EC. The final part examines compliance with EC environmental law, including implementation and enforcement issues such as the application of the doctrine of direct effect to environmental matters. Some conclusions of relevance concerning the application of European environmental law to SEA are then presented.

EUROPEAN ENVIRONMENTAL LAW

European environmental law, or EC environmental law, in common with international environmental law, is now a significant subdiscipline in its own right, with a huge body of primary and secondary materials and associated literature.[4] An explanation and analysis of European environmental law is just as important for environmental and legal practitioners to be able to understand the significance of SEA law at a European level as it is SEA law at an international level. This is because it consists of a distinct area of law with a need for legal competence(s) to be established and key underlying principles that must be taken into account in law making, implementation and interpretation. It is also an area of law that will draw on the procedures and techniques of the ECJ in other areas of EC law that already have an established or developing case law upon them. As such it is therefore important to remember that the future interpretation of the implementation of the SEA Directive will benefit from a mature jurisprudence and literature that includes consideration of the effects of EC environmental law on the MS.[5]

Historical development of EC environmental law and policy

The environmental law and policy of the EC has developed significantly in the relatively short time since the first policy proposals became legislative proposals and were subsequently adopted by the institutions of the EC (Kramer, 2002), largely through the framework of the Intergovernmental Conferences (IGCs) that led to the treaty amendments of the Single European Act, and the Maastricht, Amsterdam and Nice Treaties, and which will bring further changes as a result of the ratification of the Lisbon Reform Treaty. As seen in Chapter 7, the EC has a number of different institutions that take different positions on environmental matters. The Commission and ECJ have been relatively active in promoting environmental issues, the Commission as part of its remit as the body responsible for putting forward new proposals, and both as part of their roles in ensuring compliance with EC law. The importance of environmental issues was recognized in 1985, coincidentally the year in which the EIA Directive was adopted, when environmental protection was identified by the ECJ as one of the EC's 'essential objectives'.[6]

EC environmental policy emerged in the early 1970s and, according to Weale (2005, p127), initially 'led a tangible, if somewhat marginal, existence'. He points to the establishment of a Directorate General in the area and the Environment Council, representing the ministries of the national governments as examples of early initiatives. The meeting of the European Council in Paris in 1972, however, marked the 'beginnings of European environmental policy as a distinct sector of policy' (Weale, 2005, p127), and the Stockholm Conference in the same year (see Chapter 2) 'reflected the surge of public concern about environmental protection that had swept through the developed world in the late 1960s and early 1970s' (p127). The passage of NEPA in the US in 1969 and the beginnings of EA legislation were of course illustrative of these concerns at a national level.

The Environmental Action Programmes (EAPs) of the EC are a good example of how environmental policy is promoted and proposals derived, and illustrate the strategic approach of the EC to policy and law making in the area. Six EAPs have been prepared and adopted setting out the basis of EC policy and law for the coming period. Significant measures that will later become directives are often flagged and although the early EAPs had no mandatory status, the most recent has become legally binding,[7] as least in so far as the words used bring obligation to the measures contained within. Policy measures of significance that have featured in the EAPs include the environmental principles analysed below, such as the integration of environmental matters into all sectoral proposals (given a legal basis in the TEC, see below), and the importance of sustainable development to the EC. Kläne and Albrecht (2005, pp20–21) describe the provisions of the EAPs that are of relevance to EA. The first EAP of 1973 therefore laid emphasis on taking environmental impacts into account at an early stage, in particular sections 9, 10 and 11.[8] The third EAP is cited as the 'political impetus' for the EIA Directive in 1985 (p20).[9] The fifth EAP has the title 'towards sustainability' and therefore is 'regarding the SEA Directive – the most important' (p20).[10] Part 1, Section 7.3 also 'provided a rationale for the SEA Directive in explicit terms' (p21). The current EAP, the sixth, operates for the ten year period until 2012 and is based on the fundamental environmental principles of EC environmental law that are outlined and analysed below.[11]

The role of the ECJ is identified by many authors as being of great significance in fostering the growth of environmental law and policy in the EC (see Collins and Earnshaw, 1993; Somsen, 1996, 2003; Carnwath, 2004; McCown, 2005; Hedemann-Robinson, 2006; Jacobs, 2006). As was seen in the previous chapter and will be outlined further in this, the doctrine of direct effect and the primacy of EC law were developed early in its history and have been applied many times to environmental matters. As will also be seen below, the ECJ applied the law of the TEC that focused on market issues to environmental matters before specific environmental competence was included in the Treaty in 1986. Legislation was also passed and jurisprudence developed on a range of matters that 'go beyond any conceivable standards that would be strictly necessitated by a concern to ensure a single functioning market' (Weale, 2005, p128).

Increasing resources were devoted to environmental institutions in the EC, with DG XI, the Directorate General for the Environment, increasing its permanent staff considerably and with the establishment of the European Environment Agency.[12]

At the same time, there was greater emphasis placed on precaution and integration, together with other key principles (see below) in policy and law making. In the 1990s the use of voluntary agreements were added to the regulatory mix, which have been termed 'new environmental policy instruments' (NEPIs) and include eco-labels and eco-taxes (see Jordan et al, 2005).

The Amsterdam IGC that led to the ratification of the Amsterdam Treaty has been credited as strengthening the commitment to achieving sustainable development and environmental policy integration (Lenschow, 2001). Both are explored in detail below, and the relationship between them has recently been analysed in depth (Pallemaerts et al, 2007). The Nice IGC that resulted in the Nice Treaty was designed to address the three key issues of the size and composition of the Commission, the weighting of votes in the Council and the possible extension of qualified majority voting to new areas (Jordan and Fairbrass, 2005, p42).[13] Its impact on environmental law and policy development is therefore of less significance than the earlier IGCs that resulted in the Single European Act and the Maastricht and Amsterdam Treaties, and which have also been commented on extensively to date (Vandermeersch, 1987; Hession and Macrory, 1994; Macrory, 1999; Stetter, 2001; Wilkinson, 1992).

After the Nice Treaty, a 'Constitutional Treaty' was proposed. This has been examined extensively in regard to environmental matters (see, for example, Jans, 2003; Jans and Scott, 2003), although the failures of the French and Dutch referenda in 2005 brought the constitutional project to an end. More recently, the 2007 Lisbon IGC adopted a final text of the 'Reform Treaty', which has also to be approved before any changes come into effect; these will no doubt also be subject to extensive commentary in the future literature. The impact of the changes is considered to some extent in the sections below that concern competence for environmental matters and the principles that underscore law and policy making.

Treaty basis and responsible institutions

The first paragraph of Article 5 TEC states that '[t]he Community shall act within the limits of the powers conferred on it by this Treaty and the objectives assigned to it therein'. This means that unless the EC has a power to do something that is specified in the TEC, it lacks the ability to act. This section considers the power or competence to act in relation to environmental matters as found in the articles of the TEC, and the disputes that have arisen and may arise where more than one legal basis for action is available. Although the first few subsections focus on the internal competence to act (in relation to legislative acts originated by the institutions), the final subsection discusses the external power available to the EC institutions to act in relation to international treaties, which provides the link between international and European law. This is of clear relevance to the changes that have already been made to the EIA Directive (to comply with the Espoo and Aarhus Conventions) and that may be needed for the SEA Directive to comply with the SEA Protocol.

Initially the 1957 Treaty of Rome (the EEC Treaty, which was signed in March 1957 and came into force in January 1958) did not provide a specific power to legislate for environmental matters and general provisions in the Treaty had to be used. Peace and economic development through the establishment of the common market were the clear priorities of the original MS. In the period to 1972, only a small number of measures were passed with any environmental significance, such as directives concerned with vehicle emissions and packaging of dangerous substances,[14] and Articles 100 (now Article 94/95) and/or 235 (now Article 308) were used to justify the competence to act. The first (Article 100, now Article 94) was used on the basis that the measures were adopted with a view to approximate (or harmonize) the laws of each MS that affected the establishment of the common market, and the second (Article 235, now Article 308) where legislation was needed to attain one of the objectives of the EC but where the TEC has not provided the power to do so. As Davies (2004, p3) comments: 'This flexible application of the 1957 EEC Treaty ensured the early development of an environmental policy at the Community level'.

The ECJ accepted that environmental measures could be adopted under the original Article 100 (ex Article 100),[15] stating in *Commission v Italy* that 'provisions which are made necessary by considerations relating to the environment... may be a burden upon the undertakings to which they apply and if there is no harmonisation of national provisions on the matter, competition may be appreciably distorted'.[16] The original Waste Framework Directive is an example of a measure adopted under ex Article 100.[17] As to ex Article 235, as seen above, the ECJ affirmed in 1985 the need to protect the environment as one the 'essential objectives' of the EC. This was therefore used to good effect where environmental matters had no discernable effect on trade or industry and hence the functioning of the market. The Wild Birds Directive is an example of the use of ex Article 235 as its legal basis.[18] The objectives of the EC were of course helpfully laid out in the EAPs, enabling ex Article 235 to be effectively used in the absence of an enabling constitutional provision for the environment.[19] The position of objecting

MS could still be protected since both ex Articles 100 and 235 required unanimous decisions on legislative proposals to be reached in Council.

Changes made by the Single European Act

The Single European Act was signed in February 1986 and came into force in July 1987; since then the EC has had express powers to legislate for the environment, with the 'Environment Title' comprised of ex Articles 130r, 130s and 130t (now Articles 174, 175 and 176 TEC). Davies (2004, p6) comments that: 'The addition of the Environment Title to the Treaty represented an express acknowledgement of the existence and importance of the Community's environmental policy, as well as the opportunity to incorporate the objectives of that policy, and the principles upon which it is based, into the Treaty'. Ex Article 130r, now Article 174(1) states that the aim of the Community's policy is to preserve, protect and improve the environment, protect human health, ensure prudent and rational use of natural resources, and promote an international approach to regional or worldwide environmental problems. As will be discussed later, the policy aims at a high level of protection taking account of the diversity of situations in the EC regions. MS are to cooperate with third countries and competent international organizations.

It of course remained possible for more than one Treaty basis to be used to introduce legislative measures (Lenaerts and van Nuffel, 2005, pp86–100), and this was complicated as a result of the changes made by the Single European Act as it was decided that the cooperation procedure would not apply to legislation adopted under the Environment Title, and initially unanimity in Council was required for legislation adopted under ex Article 130s. The ECJ had to decide on the question of the correct legal basis for environmental matters in the *Titanium Dioxide* case of 1991, which had clear implications for the differing procedural bases for decision making.[20] Although the Court considered that the measure in question could have had a dual legal basis because of its aim and content, it was necessary to decide on the correct legal basis because different legislative procedures were applicable. If the internal market procedure of ex Article 100a were used (which was inserted by the Single European Act), a qualified majority vote in the Council was all that was needed (the 'cooperation procedure'); if ex Article 130s was used, unanimity was required and Parliament's role was marginalized. As a result of this the Court annulled the Directive under question and ruled that it should have been based on ex Article 100a.[21]

Changes made by the Maastricht, Amsterdam and Nice Treaties

The Maastricht and Amsterdam Treaties amended the legislative procedures for acts adopted under ex Article 100a and ex Article 130s, so that the Parliament and Council, in accordance with the co-decision procedure, were to decide what action is to be taken to achieve the objectives of the environment policy, with a few measures remaining subject to unanimity in Council.[22] In many areas therefore, the Parliament and Council had to adopt legislative acts (or EAPs) collaboratively, with the co-decision procedure providing Parliament with an effective veto over legislation adopted under ex Article 100a, the internal market provision. For matters falling within the Environment Title the cooperation procedure applied, which although it brought an end to the need for unanimity in Council, still provided less opportunities for Parliament to comment on legislative proposals of environmental significance.[23]

The Amsterdam Treaty made further changes so that the current position is that qualified majority voting under the co-decision procedure is standard for measures adopted under both Articles 95 (ex Article 100a) and 175 (ex Article 130s), with the Parliament now in a much stronger position to influence the outcome of environmental legislation.[24] Further, and in accordance with the principle of subsidiarity (see Chapter 7 and below), MS can always introduce more stringent measures (such as SEA laws) provided they are compatible with the TEC and have been notified to the Commission; however, this is an area where disputes are entirely possible.[25]

Legislation of relevance to environmental matters can still also be adopted under other provisions of the TEC, especially those that deal with the Common Agricultural Policy (CAP) and the Common Transport Policy (CTP). Davies (2004, pp11–12) discusses this and the procedural differences that underlie the different bases of action. A significant example is the application of Article 37 (ex Article 43) to implement measures for the CAP, which was used to amend measures to protect EC forests against air pollution and fire. Parliament successfully challenged the basis of the legislative action in the ECJ since at the time (before the Amsterdam Treaty) it only had to be consulted on such matters, with the Court concluding that measures that afforded protection to forests were judged to 'inherently form part of the environmental action for which the Community competence is founded on [ex] Article 130s of the Treaty'.[26] Davies (2004, pp12–13) indicates that despite a few minor changes being introduced by the Nice Treaty, the co-decision requirement was not applied to Article 37, with the result that, again, potential remains for future disputes over the correct legal basis for action with environmental consequences:

> *Accordingly, it remains the case that the European Parliament need only be consulted in relation to measures adopted under this provision. It would therefore be premature to assert that disputes as to the correctness of legal base will totally become a thing of the past when one recalls that adoption of legislation under an alternative Article 175 EC legal base will generally require the utilisation of the co-decision procedure.*

The Lisbon Reform Treaty has made further changes to decision making in the EU that will impact on environmental matters when ratified, notably the substantial extension of the co-decision procedure, that qualified majority voting will become the general rule in the Council, and the establishment of new legal bases including energy and the supplement to environmental policy of climate change.

External competence

One of the reasons why European directives are introduced or amended is to comply with international legal instruments that the EC is a party to.[27] Chapters 2 and 7 made reference to the special status of the EC as an autonomous regime in international law, without specifying the competence of the EC to act in relation to international treaties. Before the Single European Act was passed, the EC lacked specific Treaty power to act in such matters and the 'doctrine of parallelism' was developed as a means of legitimizing EC action externally. Essentially the doctrine was interpreted to mean that provided the EC had internal competence; it also had external competence.[28] Article 281 of the TEC gives the EC the legal personality needed to enter into international treaties, and in the *ERTA* case, the ECJ interpreted this to mean that: 'in its external relations the Community enjoys the capacity to establish contractual links with third countries over the whole field of objectives defined in Part One of the Treaty'.[29] In judgment, the ECJ therefore essentially approved of the doctrine in existence prior to the Treaty changes, allowing the EC to act externally when it had the power to do so internally and had in fact done so.[30]

Article 174(4) provided the EC with express competence to 'cooperate with third countries and with the competent international organisations', including the power to enter into 'agreements between the Community and the third parties concerned, which shall be negotiated and concluded in accordance with Article 300'. Environmental treaties that the EC has been a party to have typically been 'mixed' agreements, meaning that they must also be ratified by an MS. The ECJ has referred to this as a 'requirement of unity in the international representation of the Community'.[31] The second paragraph of Article 174(4) emphasizes the continued power of the MS to themselves conclude international treaties, and as such confusion remains as to the precise extent of the powers of each.[32]

What is beyond doubt, however, is that the EU is widely regarded as an environmental champion on the international scene, being a prime mover behind such developments at the Kyoto Protocol to the Climate Change Convention (see, for example, Vig and Axelrod, 1999; Delreux, 2006; Vogler and Stephan, 2007). While highlighting concerns about implementation, Andresen (2007), draws attention to its positive role in contrast to that of the US, which, in more recent times, has taken a more conservative international role. He states (para 2,2):

> The EU is an environmental pusher, not least due to the leadership vacuum created by the more reluctant US position. The EU considers the vision of sustainability and multilateralism as a part of its emerging identity. In a 2003 communication, the Commission implicitly attempted to establish a contrasting identity to that of the United States... Such language and aspirations may be dismissed as typical EU (Commission) rhetoric; indeed, the EU has often scored higher on ambitions and visions than on action and practical implementation.

Underlying objectives and principles

Chapter 7 discussed a number of general principles that underlie law making and implementation in the EC, several of which have been subject to interpretation by the ECJ. The subsidiarity, proportionality and integration principles are of the greatest general significance to EC environmental law. The Treaty also refers to specific environmental objectives and principles that must underlie policy and law making (Kramer, 1995). This section considers these in the context of guidance and ECJ jurisprudence.

General principles

EC competence in environmental matters is recognized as a shared responsibility with the MS, and in the exercise of their powers EC institutions must do so in accordance with the principle of subsidiarity, which has been subject to significant academic comment.[33] This helps explain the need for unanimity under Article 175 with respect to town and country planning, land use and water resources, which are traditionally areas over which the sovereignty of MS action has been jealously guarded, and which, in part, also explains why several MS have chosen to 'gold plate' the requirements of directives when they are already subject to, or are in line with, more stringent national provisions.[34]

Although not contained expressly in the Single European Act, it nonetheless introduced the subsidiarity principle as a condition for the legality of EC environmental action, ex Article 130r(4) stating that the Community 'shall take action relating to the environment to the extent to which the objectives... can be better attained at Community level than at the level of the individual Member States'. The Maastricht Treaty removed this provision and replaced it with a general provision in ex Article 3b (now Article 5 TEC), which applies the principle to all areas that do not fall within the EC's exclusive competence (for example, where the EC and MS both have the power to take action because the TEC does not remove the power from the MS, or where it is a shared responsibility, such as regards town and country planning, land use and water resources). Article 5 therefore states that the EC will take action 'only if and insofar as the objectives of the proposed action cannot be sufficiently achieved by the Member States and can therefore, by reason of the scale or effects of the proposed action, be better achieved by the Community'.

Because of concerns expressed about the effects of the subsidiarity principle, the Commission has supported combining it with the notion of 'shared responsibility', which also helps to avoid the perception that an either/or decision has to be made.[35] Davies (2004, p20) gives the example of the application of the Habitats Directive, which while an EC measure, nonetheless requires action at the MS level in deciding what national sites are in need of protection. The same indeed could be said of the SEA Directive, where the list of plans and programmes to be drawn up has been left largely to the MS, albeit with guidance from the Commission. As such, Davies concludes (2004, p20) that:

> *the vast majority of EC environmental measures can in fact be said to be in line with the principles of shared responsibility and subsidiarity as most measures take the form of directives which allow legally binding objectives to be established at the Community level while allowing the manner of practical application to be determined at national, regional or local levels.*[36]

The proportionality principle is applicable in all areas of EC competence, whether shared or not. Article 5, para 3 TEC states that: '[a]ny action by the Community shall not go beyond what is necessary to achieve the objectives of this Treaty'. Again, as much scope as possible is left to national governments, with an emphasis on framework directives, which are less likely to result in resistance from national governments (Jordan et al, 2005, p325). This avoids traditional 'command and control' methods with detailed binding restrictions, thereby permitting MS to take more stringent action should they so wish provided the basic requirements are met. This was discussed in the initial section of this chapter with respect to NEPIs, which have increasingly found favour.

The integration principle, while of specific relevance to environmental protection, is in fact a principle of general application (Wasmeier, 2001) and, although it was originally part of the Environment Title following the coming into force of the Single European Act,[37] is now found within Article 6 of the TEC, which states that 'environmental protection requirements must be integrated into the definition and implementation of Community policies and activities referred to in Article 3, in particular, with a view to promoting sustainable development'. The principle was first laid down in the Environment Title of the EC Treaty in 1987, with the stipulation that 'Environmental protection requirements shall be a component of the Community's other policies'. Later amendments by the Maastricht and Amsterdam Treaties refined this to 'Environmental protection requirements must be integrated into the definition and implementation of the Community policies and activities referred to in Article 3, in particular with a view to promoting sustainable development'.

There are, however, a number of questions concerning the legal meaning of the provision, which are explored in detail by Dhondt (2003). These include whether the principle is a substantive prohibition on environmental harm, and whether it provides the environment with priority over other concerns (p6). Grimeaud (2000, pp216–217) concurs with the doubts raised, which apply equally to the environmental protection and sustainable development requirements. The integration principle is closely related to the SEA Directive because of its application to specific sectors; it is also closely related to the Commission process for EA of its own policy and legislative proposals (see Chapter 10). Integration of course means a number of different things from an environmental perspective, additional to environmental policy integration and integrated approaches to impact assessment (Scrase and Sheate, 2002). The Commission reviewed the success of the integration principle in 2004, making recommendations to strengthen future application (Commission of the European Communities, 2004).

Environmental objectives

The promotion of sustainable development theoretically underlies all EC action, with Article 2 of the TEC initially emphasizing that Community activity would 'promote... sustainable and non-inflationary growth respecting the environment', the preamble to the TEU noting the determination of the MS to promote 'economic and social progress for their peoples, taking into account the principle of sustainable development' and Article 2 of the TEU referring to 'balanced and sustainable development' as an objective. Article 2 of the TEC was later amended to note the need for 'balanced and sustainable development of economic activities', together with 'a high level of protection and improvement of the quality of the environment'.[38] However, as with all statements of this type, the practical application of these aspirations is less easy to define and makes judicial interpretation challenging to say the least, even given the views set out by the Commission and the Council on the issue.[39] Recourse to the jurisprudence of international tribunals would no doubt be needed, with the acceptance that much of the relevant international law is largely of a soft law nature, with little consequent binding effect.[40] Despite this, it is true to say that the application of certain tools, such as EIA, SEA and access to information, participation and access to justice contribute to the overall aim (see, in part, Davies, 2004, p31).

Together with the general objective of sustainable development, as seen earlier, EC environmental policy is also guided by specific objectives found in Article 174(1) of the Environment Title, which 'provide assistance in defining the realm within which the Community can exercise its environmental competence' (Davies, 2004, p36) and which state that Community policy shall contribute to the following objectives:

- *preserving, protecting and improving the quality of the environment;*
- *protecting human health;*
- *prudent and rational utilisation of natural resources;*
- *promoting measures at international level to deal with regional or worldwide environmental problems.*

Despite problems of textual definition (what is meant by environment in the first objective?), broad interpretations of the first objective have typically been given by EC and MS institutions, to the extent that directives have been considered applicable to the full extent of the Exclusive Economic Zone of MS, in line with the approach adopted by international law and as related to the final objective in Article 174(1) above.[41] Protecting human health is a driver of many legislative acts, including the improvements to the quality of water brought about by the Water Framework Directive,[42] and is one of the greatest successes of EC environmental law given the reductions in emissions that have typically accompanied such measures. The objective of prudent and rational utilization of natural resources is closely related to international law expositions found in such documents as the Rio Declaration,[43] and is underlined as a priority area in the Sixth EAP as a condition of sustainable development.[44] Areas identified as a means to promote this objective are the EIA and Environmental Liability Directives (Davies, 2004, p40). The objective of promoting measures at the international level to deal with regional or worldwide environmental problems relates to the role of the EC as a party to international treaties; many have been adopted, including the Espoo and Aarhus Conventions at a regional level.[45]

Environmental principles

Article 174(2) TEC outlines the principles on which its environment policy is based, which are the precautionary principle, the principle that preventive action should be taken, that environmental damage should, as a priority, be rectified at source, and that the polluter should pay.[46] In the *Peralta* case, the ECJ ruled that the principles provide only guidance to the direction of the EC's environmental policy, which suggests that legal action against institutions of the EC for failing to take the principles into account may not succeed.[47]

The precautionary principle is one of the most important of the principles, despite it not being defined in the Treaty, and is generally interpreted in line with Principle 15 of the Rio Declaration.[48] In 2000, the Commission adopted guidance on the application of the precautionary principle, which illustrates its broad scope beyond the natural environment to health issues in relation to humans, flora and fauna.[49] The Communication indicates that the institutions have a broad discretion whether to apply the precautionary approach, including waiting for new scientific evidence, although the reversal of the burden of proof has been supported in some circumstances.[50] When action is taken, however, there is a need for it to accord with other principles so that measures must be proportionate, non-discriminatory and consistent. Costs and benefits must also be taken into account.[51] The principle has notably featured in a number of directives, adding to the weight to be attached to it despite continuing uncertainties of interpretation.[52]

The preventive principle is related to the precautionary principle and has been a focus of all the EAPs;[53] it is designed to ensure that environmental damage is avoided in the first place rather than rectified later. The EIA and Information Directives are good examples of the application of the preventive principle in action.[54]

Related in turn to the preventive principle is the principle that environmental damage should, as a priority, be rectified at source, so if it is not possible to prevent the harm that has occurred, it should at least be controlled at source. The ECJ has considered the application of this principle in regard to waste.[55]

The polluter pays principle is another significant principle and emphasizes that those who are responsible for environmental harm should bear the costs of dealing with it. However, as with the precautionary principle, and in line with the difficulties that have arisen in international liability regimes,[56] it has suffered from definitional problems that have hampered its application. Guidance has therefore been limited, and until the fifth EAP it was only referred to in a few EC acts, such as the waste directives.[57] Following the fifth EAP, the application of NEPIs such as eco-taxes has improved the implementation of the polluter pays principle, at least at the national level, and the sixth EAP reaffirmed the importance of the polluter pays principle in a number of ways, including the proposal for a directive on Environmental Liability, which is examined in the next chapter. As Davies comments (2004, p55), 'The adoption in the future of a directive based on this proposal would certainly amount to the most far-reaching application to date of the polluter pays principle at the Community level'.

Application of and compliance with EC environmental law

Chapter 7 outlined the differences between primary EC law (the Treaties) and secondary EC law (the legislative acts of the institutions), discussed the principles of primacy and full effectiveness of the law, including the specific doctrines of direct and indirect effect, and considered enforcement matters. This final section contextualizes these matters in relation to environmental protection, discussing and analysing specific cases with respect to action taken by the Commission and ECJ. It is in the environment field that the Commission has taken a leading role in Treaty supervision, 'with almost one quarter of the current infringement dossiers against Member States falling within the environmental sector' (Macrory, 2007, p1). Once notified of such infringements, litigious action may begin in the ECJ.

The MS have the primary responsibility for the implementation and enforcement of EC law, as set out in Article 10 TEC, being required to transpose legislation into national law, ensure its practical application including monitoring and enforcement where needed (see, generally, Collins and Earnshaw, 1993). In practice, monitoring and enforcement of environmental matters typically falls to NGOs who have more practical reasons to be concerned about compliance, but who may lack the means to do so.[58] As a result of a failure of the MS to effectively implement and enforce EC law, and of the Commission to do much about it, its role as the 'guardian of the treaties' came in for criticism by the Parliament in 1984,[59] and in 1990 the Council emphasized the need for renewed commitment to the implementation and enforcement of environmental legislation.[60]

A group of environmental protection authorities in the MS known as the EU Network for the Implementation and Enforcement of Environmental Law (IMPEL), was established in 1992 with implementation and enforcement of EC environmental law as a specific focus. After the Maastricht IGC, 'better law making' has been central to the EC and EU, and the importance of coordination through the 'regulatory chain' has been emphasized.[61] The stages of the regulatory chain are the formulation of legislation, the transposition of legislation into national legal orders, the practical application of EC obligations at a national level, enforcement and evaluation and review of legislation. The formulation of legislation is primarily a matter for the Commission as seen in Chapter 7, and, in recent years, more attention has been focused on how to improve consultation procedures in respect of environmental protection matters, including an enhanced role for the European Environment Agency in developing policy and greater involvement of environmental NGOs.[62]

Direct and indirect effect of EC environmental law

As noted in Chapter 7, provided the relevant conditions are met, EC law is both directly and indirectly effective, although there are differences between primary law (the Treaties) and secondary law (regulations, directives and other legislative acts). Indirect effect, or the doctrine of sympathetic interpretation, means that national provisions must be implemented in conformity with EC law, whether or not they transpose EC law. Regulations have both horizontal and vertical direct effect, so individuals can enforce them against both the MS and other individuals. In contrast, directives cannot be enforced by individuals against other individuals because they regulate the actions of the MS (there remains no 'horizontal direct effect' of directives, Betlem, 1995; Holder, 1996). Provided directives are unconditional, sufficiently precise, can be relied on by interested individuals and the time limit for transposition has passed, they can, however, be enforced by individuals against the MS (there is 'vertical direct effect' of directives), which includes 'emanations of the state' such as privatized utility companies. A number of environmental directives have been considered to meet these criteria, such as measures for drinking water.[63] Framework provisions such as those contained within the waste directive have been held not to be directly effective, especially where provisions are also vague and ambiguous.[64]

With regard to the indirect effect of EC measures, there are several examples in European environmental law, and which are of assistance when MS fail to implement directives correctly, because national courts must still ensure the purpose and wording of a directive is applied. Davies (2004, p107) gives the example of *R v Secretary of State for the Environment, ex parte Greenpeace*, where the High Court held that a minister had to interpret national legislation in conformity with the Euratom Directive 80/836 as amended.[65] The main limitation on the practical application of the doctrine of indirect effect is that national courts are only obliged 'as far as possible' to interpret national law in the light of the wording and purpose of EC law, so if the wording and purpose of national law conflicts with EC law, national courts can still give effect to national law. In this case, the only remedy for an individual may be an action in damages against the MS, under the principles set out in the case of *Francovich* (see Chapter 7).[66] One of the first national cases to consider the application of this in an environmental context was a case concerned with the application of Directive 79/923 concerning water quality (Davies, 2004, p110).

Implementation

Implementation of EC law is a matter of transposing directives into national law, ensuring that national laws are in conformity with EC law and applying the law (Hattan, 2003, p274).[67] Although there is often some flexibility in implementing EC environmental law (Farmer et al, 2006), Article 211 of the EC Treaty requires the Commission to ensure that the provisions of the Treaty and measures taken under it are applied, which includes monitoring and enforcement.[68] Implementation by the MS must therefore be on time, correct and met in practice, failing which the Commission may take infringement proceedings under Article 226 TEC; this procedure, however, takes on average four to five years (Kramer, 2006). The Commission has an unlimited discretion to do this, and case law has confirmed that private persons cannot challenge a Commission decision on pursuing, discontinuing or staying proceedings, despite there being no 'formal division between the Commission's political and enforcement duties', which can lead to concerns about political influence (Hattan, 2003, p275). Where the Commission becomes aware of a breach and the decision to initiate proceedings is taken, a letter of formal notice is first sent to the accused MS, followed by a reasoned opinion if a satisfactory response is not received. The Commission may then refer the matter to the ECJ, although less than 20 per cent of cases reach this stage. Article 228 now also allows the Court to fine an MS if it fails to comply with a Court judgment.

Directives have, in practice, caused difficulties for many MS, often because of ambiguity and vagueness in the wording used as much as the discretion available to the MS. This has led to inconsistencies between different MS (often leading to enforcement action), and is frequently due to the amendments made by the Council to secure agreement of the MS, rather than in the initial draft prepared by the Commission. Directives must be transposed within the time stated and the Commission notified thereafter of the measures taken. Although there is discretion as to the form of these measures, the ECJ has indicated that implementation by administrative practice or non-binding circulars is inadequate when measures create rights for individuals.[69] Over-reliance on existing national legislation has, in practice, made it difficult for many MS to correctly implement EC law, where, by contrast, introducing new law in the area may be relatively straightforward.[70] The implementation of the EIA Directive in the UK, for example, was carried out by over 40 separate sets of regulations. Implementation includes practical application of domestic law, which may be the responsibility of a number of authorities at MS level, many of whom are under resourced. The establishment of IMPEL (above) was designed to assist in enabling national regulators to learn from the experiences of one another, and guidelines have been prepared at the EC level that deal with monitoring.[71]

Hattan (2003) indicates that there is a grey line between whether a directive has been transposed, whether national law is in conformity with EC law and whether it has been applied in practice in the three main stages of the implementation process. She also refers to the EIA Directive, stating (p274):

> *For example, national measures implementing only some of the Annex I projects in the Environmental Impact Assessment Directive could be seen as a failure to transpose the Directive, or as a failure to ensure conformity of those national measures with the directive. Furthermore, it could also be seen as a non-application case if an environmental assessment is not carried out because the type of project has not been transposed into national legislation.[72]*

Enforcement

Where there are failings on the part of the MS[73] enforcement becomes a matter for the Commission in conjunction with the ECJ and national courts.[74] Giving an enforcement role to the European Environment Agency was explicitly rejected by the MS, despite criticism of the arguably incompatible roles of policy maker and enforcer given to the Commission.[75] The Agency does, however, have a monitoring role in respect of MS measures, including assessing their efficiency. As indicated, the Commission remains responsible for bringing proceedings against defaulting MS before the ECJ (under Article 226 TEC), although individuals can also bring actions to protect rights in national courts where MS fail to implement obligations.[76] In the first instance, the Commission is often alerted to infringements by individuals or environmental NGOs, by written complaints brought to it. The Parliament can also petition the Commission to take action. However, individuals and groups are also completely dependent on the discretion of the Commission as to whether action will be taken; inevitably the Commission is selective and focuses on matters of major concern (Commission of the European Communities, 1996a; Hattan, 2003, pp284–285). Despite many political constraints (Macrory, 2007), Hattan (2003, pp275–276) indicates that: 'Greater accountability of the Commission is beginning to develop through improved transparency of the decision-making process, through more defined procedural rights of complainants and through the increasing power and effectiveness of the Ombudsman'.[77]

If the ECJ finds the MS is at fault, it must take appropriate measures to comply with the judgment (Macrory and Purdy, 1997; Koppen, 2005). Since Article 228 now allows the ECJ to impose a lump sum penalty or fines against an MS, and the Commission has requested specified penalty rates for environmental law infractions, compliance with judgments has improved (see also Hedemann-Robinson, 2006; Kramer, 2006).[78] Problems with the use of the procedure in an environmental context, however, include its length, reactionary and political nature, and communication and information difficulties. The alternative of action at the national level may be denied as a result of standing and financial restrictions (Carnwath, 2004; Dette, 2004).[79] In *Stichting*

Greenpeace Council (Greenpeace International) and Others v Commission, a lack of standing at a national level was also apparent at the EC level.[80]

CONCLUSIONS

This chapter has demonstrated the significance of and contribution made by European environmental law to European law generally. European environmental law now has both a long history and considerable jurisprudence, of more than equal measure to IEL. Despite the complexities and difficulties of enforcement, it is reasonable to conclude that being part of an autonomous legal system with such a broad reach ensures that it is more effective than IEL, which is dependent to a far greater extent on the willingness of individual states to implement treaties and customary law. The remedies available to individuals are a particularly notable feature of European environmental law. Further detailed comparisons are made in Chapter 12.

Chapter 9 that follows examines the procedural measures under European environmental law that have been approved and must be applied under the above framework. These are often termed 'horizontal' measures because they cut across sectoral boundaries. The EIA Directive itself is the most important for the purpose of this book, as supplemented by the Information, Participation and Liability Directives. Each has contributed greatly to the development of European environmental law and each has a bearing on the SEA Directive that will be examined in Chapter 10.

NOTES

1   For examples of standard texts in the area, readers are referred to Scott (1998), Jans (2000), Kramer (2000, as updated), Macrory et al (2004), Davies (2004), Lee (2005) and Macrory (2005); the Davies text is referred to extensively here as one of the most up to date of the recent books, incorporating the changes made by the Maastricht, Amsterdam and Nice Treaties. Caution needs to be exercised when relying on older materials as a result of the changes made to the TEC and TEU, and the fact that the case law of the ECJ is constantly evolving. See also Sands and Galizzi (2006).
2   They are termed 'horizontal' directives because they contain cross-cutting provisions of relevance to all sectoral proposals.
3   The integration principle is of particular relevance to SEA and is therefore considered in more detail in Chapter 10.
4   The SEA Directive and the ELD, for example.
5   For examples of materials that consider the impact of EC environmental law on the MS, in the context of the UK see Holder (1997) generally, Bishop et al (2000) with regard to land use planning and Carnwath (2004) with respect to the role of the ECJ.
6   ECJ, Case 240/83 *ADBHU* [1985] ECR 531, para 13.
7   This is identified by Kramer (2002, p164), and Kläne and Albrecht (2005, p21, fn3), the latter of whom indicate that the Sixth EAP is now published in section 'L' (for legislation) and not in section 'C' (communication and information).
8   First Programme of Action of the European Communities on the Environment, OJ 1973 C112/1 (for the years 1973–1976).

9   Third Programme of Action of the European Communities on the Environment, OJ 1982 C46/1 (for the years 1982–1986).

10   Fifth Programme of Action of the European Communities on the Environment, OJ 1993 C138/1 (for the years 1993–2000). More recently, note Commission of the European Communities (2005).

11   Programme of Action of the European Communities on the Environment, OJ 2002 L242 (for the years 2002–2012).

12   Weale (2005, p129) emphasizes that although the formal remit of the Agency is the collection and standardization of data, there remains potential for its role to be expanded because of concerns expressed about countries collecting data on their own performance. This is unlikely to extend to it being an EPA for the EC/EU, however, which was resisted at the outset and in many ways is a role of the Commission.

13   Jordan and Fairbrass (2005, p45) comment that the Lisbon IGC was dubbed the 'competences conference' as one of the main aims was to clarify the respective powers of the EU and the MS. It also attempted to simplify the Treaties and improve the role of national parliaments.

14   See Directive 72/306 regulating the emission of pollutants from vehicles fitted with diesel engines, OJ 1972 L190/1; and Directive 67/548 concerning the classification, packaging and labelling of dangerous substances, OJ 1967 L196/1.

15   The legal citation used where an article that appeared in an earlier Treaty has been renumbered is 'ex', hence 'ex Article 100' is used to denote the original provision.

16   ECJ, Case 91/79 *Commission v Italy* [1980] ECR 1099, para 81.

17   Directive 75/442 on Waste OJ 1975 L78/32.

18   Council Directive 79/409/EEC on the conservation of wild birds OJ 1979 L103/1.

19   The absence of specific constitutional power to take action for the environment is not uncommon, especially where constitutions predate governmental concern for environmental issues, typically the 1970s. Australia's Commonwealth Constitution 1900 is illustrative, as this does not contain such powers and constitutional amendment is not easily attained. In the absence of such specific provisions, the national government in Australia (the Commonwealth) has traditionally used a range of powers to achieve its environmental objectives, including its ability to take action in the realm of foreign affairs or to regulate action by corporations. The *Tasmanian Dam* Case, which was concerned with the application of the World Heritage Convention, is an excellent example. See *Commonwealth of Australia and Another v The State of Tasmania and Others* (1983) 158 CLR 1.

20   ECJ, Case C-300/89 *Commission v Council* [1991] ECR I-2867. For a full discussion of the case, see Davies (2004, pp6–9).

21   Since the decision, it has been concluded that where it is not possible to decide on the relative significance of a measure's dual objectives (environmental protection vs competition distortion), then the ECJ would be likely to endorse the legal base that provides the Parliament with the greatest influence in the applicable legislative procedure. See Davies (2004, p9) citing Lenaerts (1994).

22   These include provisions affecting town and country planning, land use (excepting waste) and water resource management. See Article 175(2)(b) TEC. For discussion of the EU's limited competence on spatial planning matters, see Navajas (2006). The vagueness of these provisions has resulted in litigation, with the ECJ needing to interpret whether internal EC rules concerning the implementation of an international treaty should have been adopted on the basis of a qualified majority or unanimity. See ECJ, Case C 36/98 *Spain v Council* [2001] ECR I-779, and the discussion in Davies (2004, pp15–17), which includes commentary on the interpretative approach taken by the Court.

23   See Chapter 7 for more detail on the distinction between the two procedures.

24   Davies (2004, p11) gives the example of the changes made to Directive 2000/60 establishing a framework for Community action on water policy, OJ 2000 L327/1, adopted in late 2000 as an example of where the Parliament was able to strengthen the content of such legislation.

25 Without going into the technicalities, MS are able to apply stricter national laws after harmonization (transposition of EC law) of measures adopted under Article 175 (the Environment Title) than under Article 95, which means there remains potential for legal issues to arise about which is the appropriate legal basis to take action under the TEC in environmental matters, despite the co-decision procedure now being applicable for both. This is addressed by Macrory (1999, p178) as discussed in Davies (2004, p11), and means that the *Titanium Dioxide* litigation may be revisited in the future. Davies (2004, pp58–64) elaborates on the potential for MS to decide on higher national standards after harmonization, with reference to the so-called 'environmental guarantee' (which applies to internal market legislation) and is noted by Articles 95(4) and 95(5). The guarantee provides that MS may not necessarily reduce their existing national level of environmental protection following the adoption of a harmonizing EC measure, or that they may still introduce higher environmental standards after the introduction of harmonizing measures.

26 ECJ, Cases C-164/97 and C-165/97 *European Parliament v Council* [1999] ECR I-1139. See Davies (2004, p12, fn62) for discussion of related jurisprudence.

27 The Commission has stated that approximately a third of EC environmental policy aims to implement international treaty obligations; see Commission of the European Communities (2000b, p21); see also Delreux (2006) and Hey (1998).

28 See McGoldrick (1997), p48, Nollkaemper (1987) Thieme (2001) and Loibl (2002), the last of which discusses the powers of the EU in external relations.

29 ECJ, Case 22/70 *Commission v Council (ERTA)* [1971] ECR 263, para 14.

30 Two examples where the EC adopted international agreements where it had not concluded internal laws on related matters were with respect to the Convention for the Prevention of Marine Pollution from Land Based Sources (Paris) 13 ILM 352 (1974), 352, in force 6 May 1978; and also the Framework Convention on Climate Change, 31 ILM (1992), 851, in force 21 March 1994. See Davies (2004, p41, fn 89, citing Nollkaemper (1987, pp73–74) and Jans (2000, p81)).

31 See Opinion 1/94 (re the WTO agreement) [1994] ECR I-5267.

32 There is confusion because although in theory the EC has exclusive competence following the *ERTA* case, if legislative acts are adopted under Article 175 they amount to minimum standards only that the MS can expand on in their national laws (see Article 176). In these cases, the MS are able to exercise their sovereign right to conclude related treaties in conjunction with the EC. See Davies (2004, p42, fn94).

33 See, for example, Lenaerts (1994), Wils (1994) and Freestone and Somsen (1997).

34 As explained earlier in this book, 'gold plating' EC law means doing more than the law requires and is also discussed in note 25 above. One of the criticisms of subsidiarity (and proportionality) is that where MS laws are harmonized, they are sometimes reduced to the 'lowest common denominator' in order to ensure adoption. As such, gold plating provides an opportunity to do more where in line with the wishes of the electorate of the MS concerned. The Parliament has also expressed this concern; see Resolution A3-0380/92 on the application of the principle of subsidiarity to environment and consumer protection policy, OJ 1993 C42/40.

35 Fifth Environmental Action Programme, Chapter 8. See above note 10.

36 The TEC Protocol on the Application of the Principles of Subsidiarity and Proportionality, para 6 interestingly notes that to accord with the principle '[o]ther things being equal, directives should be preferred to regulations and framework directives to detailed measures'. This is a clear way of permitting more discretion to the MS over the choice of implementation. The substance of the guidance with respect to the environment is discussed by Davies (2004, pp20–23) for readers wishing more information. Of note is that environmental problems with transboundary impact, or where benefits would be produced 'by reason of scale or effects' are identified as matters of clear EC concern, although the ambiguous nature of the guidance suggests its practical help may be of limited use.

37 Ex Article 130r(2), which stated '[e]nvironmental protection requirements shall be a component of the Community's other policies'. The Maastricht Treaty, also ex Article 130r(2), changed the wording to '[e]nvironmental protection requirements must be integrated into the definition and implementation of other Community policies'.

38 Article 174(2) also notes that EC environmental policy 'shall aim at a high level of protection taking into account the diversity of situations in the various regions of the Community'. This therefore provides significant discretion as to not only the meaning of 'high level of protection', but also the ability to vary from it, which can be justified by the need to also take other considerations into account, including costs and benefits. The view of the ECJ is that the level of protection 'does not necessarily have to be the highest that is technically possible'; see Case C-284/95 *Safety Hi-Tech Srl v S & T Srl* [1998] ECR I-4301, para 49. The Lisbon Reform Treaty will amend the TEU by inserting a new Article 2(3) which states that:

> The Union shall establish an internal market. It shall work for the sustainable development of Europe based on balanced economic growth and price stability, a highly competitive social market economy, aiming at full employment and social progress, and a high level of protection and improvement of the quality of the environment. It shall promote scientific and technological advance.

39 See Commission of the European Communities (1992); Decision No 2179/98/EC of the European Parliament and of the Council of 24 September 1998 on the Review of the European Community Programme of Policy and Action in relation to the Environment and Sustainable Development, *Towards Sustainability*, [1998] OJ L275; Commission of the European Communities (2001); and Council Recommendation on the broad guidelines of the Economic Policies of the Member States and the Community, OJ 2001 L179/1, para 3.8

40 See Chapter 3 and note, in particular, the *Gabcíkovo-Nagymaros* case of 1997 and Principle 3 of the Rio Declaration that indicates that development 'must be fulfilled so as to equitably meet developmental needs of present and future generations'.

41 See *R v Secretary of State for Trade and Industry ex parte Greenpeace Ltd* [2000] Env LR 221 (considered in Chapter 12) and Article 2 of Directive 2001/81 on National Emissions for Certain Atmospheric Pollutants OJ 2001 L309/22.

42 Directive 2000/60 establishing a framework for Community action on water policy, OJ 2000 L327/1.

43 See Principle 8, Declaration of the United Nations Conference on Environment and Development, UN Doc. A/CONF.151/26/Rev.1, *Report of the UNCED*, vol 1 (New York); B&B Docs 9, 1992.

44 See Programme of Action of the European Communities on the Environment, OJ 2002 L242.

45 See Chapter 4.

46 For the principle that environmental damage should be rectified at source and the polluter pays principle, see ECJ, Case C-293/97 *Standley, Metson* [1999] ECR I-2603, paras 51–53 (testing EC law against these principles); ECJ, Joined Cases C-175/98 and C-177/98 *Lirussi and Bizarro* [1999] ECR I-6881, para 51; ECJ, Case C-318/98 *Fornasar* [2000] ECR I-4785, para 38 (interpretation of EC law in the light of those principles). For discussion of the polluter pays principle in the literature, see Vandekerckhove (1993).

47 ECJ, Case C-379/92 *Criminal proceedings against Matteo Peralta* [1994] ECR I-3453. See also discussion in Grimeaud (2000, pp216–217).

48 See Chapters 3 and 6 for more detail, and, in a European context, Hancher (1996) and Douma (2000).

49 Commission of the European Communities (2000a). See also the BSE cases concerning the link between the 'mad cow' disease and the dangers of its transmission to humans: ECJ, Case C-180/96 *UK v Commission* [1998] ECR I-2265; and ECJ, Case C-157/96 *R v MAFF, Commissions of Customs and Excise ex parte National Farmers Union et al* [1998] ECR I-2211.

50 See the proposal for the Sixth EAP, Commission of the European Communities (2001), para 8.3.

51 See Commission of the European Communities (2000a, pp18–21).

52 Aside from the SEA Directive itself, it also features prominently in Directive 96/61/EC on integrated pollution prevention and control OJ 1996 L257/26; Douma (2000, pp134–135) indicates that national legislation transposing this directive that fails to give the precautionary principle at least due consideration by authorities when deciding on the 'best available techniques' to use, could be subject to a court challenge.

53 See the first Programme of Action of the European Communities on the Environment, OJ 1973 C112/1 Title II, para 1.

54 For the Information Directive, see Directive 90/313 on access to environmental information, OJ 1990 L158/56, which has been repealed and replaced by Directive 2003/4/EC, OJ 2003 L41/26.

55 See ECJ, Case C-209/98 *Kobenhavns Kommune* [2000] ECR I-3743; and ECJ, Case 2/90 *Commission v Belgium* [1992] ECR I-4431 as just two examples.

56 See the discussion in Chapter 3 for example.

57 See Council Recommendation regarding Cost Allocation and Action by Public Authorities on Environmental Matters, OJ 1975 L194/1.

58 See *R v Secretary of State for the Environment, ex parte RSPB* [1997] Env LR 431, which illustrates the financial difficulties of such groups taking action.

59 Resolution on the treatment of waste in the EC, OJ 1984 C127/67.

60 European Council, *Declaration on the Environmental Imperative*, Dublin, Bull. EC 1990 Vol 23, No 6, p18.

61 Commission of the European Communities, *Implementing Community Environmental Law*, COM (96) 500 final, Annex 1. The Council adopted a Resolution on the drafting, implementation and enforcement of Community environmental law, OJ 1997 C321/1 in response to this.

62 See the discussion in Davies (2004, pp69–78) for further detail.

63 From 22 December 2007 the water framework directive will be the applicable provision (Directive 2000/60 establishing a framework for Community action in the field of water policy, OJ 2000 L327/1) for EC measures on drinking water.

64 See ECJ Case, C-236/92 *Comitato di Coordinamento per la Difesa della Cava v Regione Lombardia* [1994] ECR I-483.

65 *R v Secretary of State for the Environment, ex parte Greenpeace* [1994] Env LR 401.

66 This is also limited, however, because one of the conditions is that the measure in question must be capable of granting rights to individuals; directives such as the Habitats Directive may not provide this, although the Environmental Information Directive may (Davies, 2004, p109).

67 Chapter 7 examined the different types of EC secondary legislation (directives, regulations etc.). Regulations are often used to implement international law into EC law because it is advantageous that MS are bound by international law uniformly. This would not be the case if directives were used as they allow MS discretion as to the form and methods by which they are implemented.

68 Note that the Commission has produced annual reports on monitoring the application of EC law for some time (see, for example, 1996b, 1997, 1999a), and since then has carried out annual surveys on the implementation and enforcement of EC environmental law (see, for example, 1999b, 2003).

69 ECJ, Case C-131/88 *Commission v Germany* [1991] ECR I-825. See Jans (2000, pp135–159) for detailed requirements of transposition.

70 The challenge for accession MS of having to introduce completely new laws on areas where there were previously none is often highlighted. However, long standing MS may have the other problem of needing to make significant changes to national law to implement.

71 See Recommendation of the Parliament and Council providing for minimum criteria for environmental inspections in the Member States, 2001/331/EC, OJ [1991] L118, which is intended to check and promote compliance with EC law and act as a deterrent to environmental violations.

72 Hattan (2003) examines the prioritization given by the Commission to these three elements of enforcement, in accordance both with official Commission policy and unofficial practice. She concludes that while there was, in the recent past, a tendency to focus on transposition and conformity matters to the detriment of practical application, this trend has not been continued. The blurring of the distinction between the three and the emphasis given to certain sectoral matters (nature conservation, in particular), are two of the reasons given for this. See also Cashman (2006) who also examines the example of nature conservation in the Commission's enforcement of environmental law.

73 Note that there is a new proposal for a directive on the protection of the environment through criminal law, which is applicable to natural and legal persons in a national context. The proposal lays down a list of environmental offences that must be considered criminal by all MS, although it does not create any new illegal acts. Unless already provided for, MS, by transposing the directive, will therefore only have to attach to existing prohibitions some criminal sanctions. See Commission of the European Communities (2007) *Proposal for a directive of the European Parliament and of the Council on the protection of the environment through criminal law,* COM(2007) 51 final, Brussels, 9 February 2007.

74 The Commission Action Plan on Improving and Simplifying the Regulatory Environment, COM (2002) 278 final, p18 recommends closer coordination and exchange of information between the Commission and national authorities in order to improve the monitoring and application of EC law.

75 See Williams (1994) and Hattan (2003, note 8), which indicates that unlike other areas of EC law, such as competition, fisheries, nuclear, veterinary and customs, there is no environmental inspectorate to independently investigate potential breaches, a role that has been denied to the European Environment Agency.

76 As seen in Chapter 7, MS can also take action against other MS where there are alleged breaches, although for political reasons this route is rarely taken.

77 As an indication of this, note Regulation (EC) No 1367/2006 of 6 September 2006 of the European Parliament and of the Council on the application of the provisions of the Aarhus Convention on Access to Information, Public Participation in Decision Making and Access to Justice in Environmental Matters to EC institutions and bodies. Hattan also refers to the Communication from the Commission on Relations with the Complainant in Respect of Infringements of Community Law, COM (2002) 141 final.

78 Commission of the European Communities (1997), p50.

79 The problems of individual and group action were considered earlier in this book. Despite the ratification of the Aarhus Convention by MS and the EC, national procedures may still effectively deny the ability of some to take action if they lack a direct interest in the matter (such as a property right), and the cost of litigation is often prohibitive. Such matters must be rectified if an MS or an institution of the EC is not to be found in breach of the obligations of the Convention (see Chapters 4 and 9). See Rehbinder (1996)

80 ECJ Case C-321/95P *Stichting Greenpeace Council (Greenpeace International) and Others v Commission,* [1998] ECR I-1651. The Environmental Information, Public Participation and Environmental Liability Directives already contain some access to justice provisions, and the proposed Directive on Access to Justice is expected to ensure full implementation of the Aarhus Convention.

REFERENCES

Andresen, S. (2007) 'Key actors in UN environmental governance: Influence, reform and leadership', *International Environmental Agreements*, vol 7, no 4, pp457–468

Betlem, G. (1995) 'Medium hard law – still no horizontal direct effect of European Community directives after *Faccini Dori*', *Columbia Journal of European Law*, vol 1, no 3, pp469–496

Bishop, K., Tewdwr-Jones, M. and Wilkinson, D. (2000) 'From spatial to local: The impact of the European Union on local authority planning in the UK', *Journal of Environmental Planning and Management*, vol 43, no 3, pp309–334

Carnwath, R. (2004) 'Judicial protection of the environment: at home and abroad', *Journal of Environmental Law*, vol 16, no 3, pp315–327

Cashman, L. (2006) 'Commission compliance promotion and enforcement in the field of the environment', *Journal for European Environmental and Planning Law*, vol 5, pp385–400

Collins, K. and Earnshaw, D. (1993) 'The implementation and enforcement of EC environmental law' in Judge, D. (ed) *A Green Dimension for the EC*, Frank Cass, London, pp238–242

Commission of the European Communities (1992) Commission Communication of 27 March 1992, *Towards Sustainability: A European Community Programme of Policy and Action in relation to the Environment and Sustainable Development*, COM (92) final, Commission of the European Communities, Brussels

Commission of the European Communities (1996a) *Communication from the Commission on Implementing Community Environmental Law*, COM (96) 500 final, [1996] C4-0591/96, Commission of the European Communities, Brussels

Commission of the European Communities (1996b) *Fourteenth Annual Report on Monitoring the Application of Community Law*, COM 1997, OJ 1997 C332/1, Commission of the European Communities, Brussels

Commission of the European Communities (1997) *Fifteenth Annual Report on Monitoring the Application of Community Law*, OJ 1998 C250/1, Commission of the European Communities, Brussels

Commission of the European Communities (1999a) *Sixteenth Annual Report on Monitoring the Application of Community Law*, COM 1999 301, Commission of the European Communities, Brussels

Commission of the European Communities (1999b) *First Annual Survey on the Implementation and Enforcement of Community Environmental Law*, Office for Official Publications of the European Communities, Luxembourg, Commission of the European Communities, Brussels

Commission of the European Communities (2000a) *Communication from the Commission on the Precautionary Principle*, COM (2000) 1, Commission of the European Communities, Brussels

Commission of the European Communities (2000b) *Europe's Environment: What Directions for the Future?*, Commission of the European Communities, Brussels

Commission of the European Communities (2001) *A Sustainable Europe for a Better World: A European Union Strategy for Sustainable Development*, COM (2001) 264, Commission of the European Communities, Brussels

Commission of the European Communities (2003) *Fourth Annual Survey on the Implementation and Enforcement of Community Environmental Law*, SEC (2003) 804, Commission Staff Working Paper (7 July 2003), Commission of the European Communities, Brussels

Commission of the European Communities (2004) *Integrating Environmental Considerations into Other Policy Areas – A Stocktaking of the Cardiff Process*, Commission Working Document, COM(2004)394 final, Commission of the European Communities, Brussels

Commission of the European Communities (2005) *Communication from the Commission to the Council and the European Parliament: Draft Declaration on Guiding Principles for Sustainable Development*, COM (2005) 218 final, Commission of the European Communities, Brussels

Davies, P. (2004) *European Union Environmental Law*, Ashgate Publishing, Aldershot

Delreux, T. (2006) 'The European Union in international environmental negotiations: A legal perspective on the internal decision-making process', *International Environmental Agreements*, vol 6, pp231–248

Dette, B. (2004) 'Access to justice in environmental matters before the European Court of Justice – present situation and recent developments', *Environmental Law Network International*, vol 2, pp20–25

Dhondt, N. (2003) *Integration of Environmental Protection into other EC Policies: Legal Theory and Practice*, Europa Law Publishing, Groningen

Douma, W. (2000) 'The precautionary principle in the EU', *Review of European Community and International Environmental Law*, vol 9, no 2, pp132–143

Farmer, A., ten Brink, P. and Kettunen, M. (2006) 'Taking advantage of flexibility in implementing EU environmental law', *Journal for European Environmental and Planning Law*, vol 5, pp395–411

Freestone, D. and Somsen, H. (1997) 'The impact of subsidiarity' in J. Holder, *The Impact of EC Environmental Law in the United Kingdom*, John Wiley, Chichester, pp87–99

Grimeaud, D. (2000) 'The integration of environmental concerns into EC policies: A genuine policy development?', *European Environmental Law Review*, vol 9, no 7, pp207–218

Hancher, L. (1996) 'EC environmental policy – a pre-cautionary tale?', in D. Freestone and E. Hey (eds) *The Precautionary Principle and International Law: The Challenge of Implementation*, Kluwer Law International, London, pp194–223

Hattan, E. (2003) 'The implementation of EU environmental law', *Journal of Environmental Law*, vol 15, no 3, pp273–288

Hedemann-Robinson, M. (2006) 'Article 228(2) EC and the enforcement of EC environmental law: A case of justice delayed and denied? An analysis of recent legal developments', *European Environmental Law Review*, November, pp312–342

Hession, M. and Macrory, R. (1994) 'Maastricht and the environmental policy of the Community: Legal issues of a new environment policy', in D. O'Keefe and P. M. Twomey (eds) *Legal Issues of the Maastricht Treaty*, Chancery Law Publishing, London, pp151–170

Hey, E. (1998) 'The European Community's courts and international environmental agreements', *Review of European Community and International Environmental Law*, vol 7, pp4–10

Holder, J. (1996) 'A dead end for direct effect? Prospects for enforcement of European Community environmental law by individuals', *Journal of Environmental Law*, vol 8, no 2, pp313–335

Holder, J. (1997) *The Impact of EC Environmental Law in the United Kingdom*, Wiley, Chichester

Jacobs, F. (2006) 'The role of the European Court of Justice in the protection of the environment', *Journal of Environmental Law*, vol 18, no 2, pp185–205

Jans, J. (2000) *European Environmental Law*, Kluwer, London

Jans, J. (ed) (2003) *The European Convention and the Future of European Environmental Law*, Europa Law Publishing, Groningen

Jans, J. and Scott, J. (2003) 'The Convention on the future of Europe: An environmental perspective', *Journal of Environmental Law*, vol 15, no 3, pp323–339

Jordan, A. and Fairbrass, J. (2005) 'European Union environmental policy after the Nice Summit' in A. Jordan (ed) (2005) *Environmental Policy in the European Union*, (2nd Edition, Earthscan, London, pp42–46

Jordan, A., Wurzel, R., Zitto, A. R. and Brückner, L. (2005) 'European governance and the transfer of 'new' environmental policy instruments (NEPIs) in the European Union' in A. Jordan (ed) (2005) *Environmental Policy in the European Union*, (2nd Edition, Earthscan, London, pp917–335

Kläne, C. and Albrecht, E. (2005) 'Purpose and background of the European SEA Directive', in M. Schmidt, E. João and E. Albrecht (eds) *Implementing Strategic Environmental Assessment*, Springer-Verlag, Heidelberg, pp15–29

Koppen, I. J. (2005) 'The role of the European Court of Justice' in A. Jordan (ed) (2005) *Environmental Policy in the European Union*, (2nd Edition, Earthscan, London, pp67–86

Kramer, L. (1995) *EC Treaty and Environmental Law*, 2nd Edition, Sweet and Maxwell, London

Kramer, L. (2000) *EC Environmental Law*, 4th Edition. (now 6th Edition, 2006), Sweet and Maxwell, London

Kramer, L. (2002) 'Thirty years of EC environmental law: Perspectives and prospectives', *Yearbook of European Environmental Law*, vol 2, pp181–182

Kramer, L. (2006) 'Statistics on environmental judgments by the EC Court of Justice', *Journal of Environmental Law*, vol 18, number 3, pp407–421

Lee, M. (2005) *EU Environmental Law: Challenges, Change and Decision-Making*, Hart Publishing, Oxford

Lenearts, K. (1994) 'The principle of subsidiarity and the environment in the European Union: Keeping the balance of federalism' *Fordham International Law Journal*, vol 17, pp846–895

Lenaerts, K. and Van Nuffel, P. (2005) *Constitutional Law of the European Union*, Thomson Sweet and Maxwell Law Book Company, Sydney

Lenschow, A. (ed) (2001) *Environmental Policy Integration: Greening Sectoral Policies in Europe*, Earthscan, London

Loibl, G. (2002) 'The role of the EU in the formation of international environmental law' *Yearbook of European Environmental Law*, vol 2, pp223–240

Macrory, R. (1999) 'The Amsterdam Treaty: an environmental perspective' in D. O'Keefe and P. M. Twomey (eds) *Legal Issues of the Amsterdam Treaty*, Hart Publishing, Oxford, pp177–178

Macrory, R. (2005) *Reflections on 30 Years of EU Environmental Law: A High Level of Protection*, Europa Law Publishing, Groningen

Macrory, R. (2007) 'Supra-national enforcement of environmental law: Compliance mechanisms in the European Union', *ICLG to: Environment Law*, Global Legal Group, London, pp1–4

Macrory, R., Havercroft, I. and Purdy, R. (2004) *Principles of European Environmental Law*, Europa Law Publishing, Groningen

Macrory, R. and Purdy, R. (1997) 'The enforcement of EC environmental law against member states' in J. Holder (ed) *The Impact of EC Environmental Law in the United Kingdom*, John Wiley, Chichester, pp27–50

McCown, M. (2005) 'Judicial law-making and European integration: The European Court of Justice' in J. Richardson (ed) *European Union: Power and Policy-Making*, Routledge, London, pp171–178

McGoldrick, D. (1997) *International Relations Law of the European Union*, Longman, New York

Navajas, T. P. (2006) 'The new instruments to achieve sustainable territorial development in the EU', *Journal for European Environmental and Planning Law*, vol 4, pp340–351

Nollkaemper, A. (1987) 'The EC and international environmental cooperation – legal aspects of external Community powers', *Legal Issues in European Integration*, vol 2, pp55–91

Pallemaerts, M., Herodes, M. and Adelle, C. (2007) *Does the EU Sustainable Development Strategy Contribute to Environmental Policy Integration?*, draft, Institute for European Environmental Policy, Brussels

Rehbinder, E. (1996) 'Locus standi, community law and the case for harmonisation' in Somsen, H. (ed) (1996) *Protecting the European Environment: Enforcing EC Environmental Law*, Blackstone, London, pp151–166

Somsen, H. (2003) 'Discretion in European Community environmental law: An analysis of ECJ case law', *Common Market Law Review*, vol 40, pp1413–1453

Sands, P. and Galizzi, P. (2006) *Documents in European Community Environmental Law*, Cambridge University Press, Cambridge

Scott, J. (1998) *EC Environmental Law*, Addison Wesley Longman, Harlow

Scrase, J. I. and Sheate, W. R. (2002) 'Integration and integrated approaches to assessment: What do they mean for the environment?', *Journal of Environmental Policy and Planning*, vol 4, pp275–294

Somsen, H. (1996) *Protecting the European Environment: Enforcing EC Environmental Law*, Blackstone, London

Stetter, S. (2001) 'Maastricht, Amsterdam and Nice: the environmental lobby and greening the treaties', *European Environmental Law Review*, vol 10, no 5, pp150–159

Thieme, D. (2001) 'EC external relations in the field of the environment' 10:8/9 *European Environmental Law Review*, pp252–264

Vandekerckhove, K. (1993) 'The polluter pays principle in the European Community', *Yearbook of Environmental Law*, pp201–262

Vandermeersch, D. (1987) 'The Single European Act and the environmental policy of the European Community', *Environmental Law Review*, vol 12, pp407–429

Vig, N. J. and Axelrod, R. S. (1999) 'The European Union as an environmental governance system' in N. J. Vig and R. S. Axelrod (eds) (1999) *The Global Environment: Institutions, Law and Policy*, Earthscan, London, pp72–97

Vogler, J. and Stephan, H. R. (2007) 'The European Union in global environmental governance: leadership in the making?', *International Environmental Agreements*, vol 7, no 4, pp389–413

Wasmeier, M. (2001) 'The integration of environmental protection as a general rule for interpreting Community law', *Common Market Law Review*, vol 38, pp159–177

Weale, A. (2005) 'Environmental rules and rule-making in the European Union' in A. Jordan (ed) (2005) *Environmental Policy in the European Union*, 2nd Edition, Earthscan, London, pp125–140

Wilkinson, D. (1992) 'Maastricht and the environment', *Journal of Environmental Law*, vol 4, no 2, pp221–239

Williams, R. (1994) 'The European Commission and the enforcement of environmental law: an invidious position', *Yearbook of Environmental Law*, vol 14, pp351–400

Wils, W. P. J. (1994) 'Subsidiarity and EC environmental policy: Taking people's concerns seriously', *Journal of Environmental Law*, vol 6, no 1, pp85–91

CHAPTER 9

The EIA and other Horizontal Directives

CHAPTER OUTLINE

This chapter considers and evaluates the role of the EIA Directive as the precursor to the SEA Directive, including the amendments made to it to incorporate changes required by the EC ratification of the Espoo and Aarhus Conventions. Implementation challenges are outlined and structural similarities with the SEA Directive considered. Aside from the changes to the EIA and Environmental Information Directives, the Aarhus Convention has also been responsible for the development of two specific horizontal directives, the Public Participation and proposed Access to Justice Directives, and a Regulation applying its provisions to EC institutions and bodies, which are also discussed in this context.[1] In line with the structure set out in Chapter 3 (which examined the linked duties of harm prevention, cooperation and compensation for damage), links with the Environmental Liability Directive are also analysed.

THE ENVIRONMENTAL IMPACT ASSESSMENT DIRECTIVE

The EIA Directive has had a significant influence on the application of EIA systems in the MS, many of which had no such systems prior to its coming into force; for those MS with EIA systems already in place, revisions were generally needed to secure compliance, although some MS had systems in place that exceeded the requirements of the directive, notably the Netherlands. The EIA Directive has also had a fundamental role concerning the development of subsequent law, particularly the SEA Directive, and experience with it has been of great value in the development of the other horizontal directives outlined here. Finally, it has also been influential globally on approaches taken to developing new legislation for EA, especially in federal or regional contexts comparable to the EC, but also in individual countries keen to learn from the best European practice.

Historical overview

EC Directive 85/337 (the original EIA Directive)[2] was adopted in 1985 and entered into force on 3 July 1988. Largely because of its impact upon the planning systems of the MS and decision making and practice, it took many years to finally be adopted (Wathern, 1988, pp200–201; McHugh, 1994; Gilpin, 1995, p74; Wood, 1995, p32; Krämer, 2007, pp131–132;). It required a number of public and private projects to be assessed as to their significant direct and indirect effects on the environment prior to approval. A second group of projects had to undergo assessment if impacts were expected in view of the nature, size or location of them. The Directive laid down principles for assessment, consultation of the general public and participation of environmental administrations. Such requirements could be integrated into existing consent procedures, provided the provisions were fully included. Although it had some influence on administrative planning at local and regional levels, administrations often tried to circumvent its provisions by deciding on the location of a project before the assessment was carried out. In some instances also, the procedures were applied only in a planning context, which required revisions to other consent processes to ensure full compliance.

The original EIA Directive was revised in 1997 by Directive 97/11/EC (the amended EIA Directive)[3] in order to provide greater clarity and supplement and improve the rules on assessment procedure (see below). In the recitals, which are often referred to by the ECJ in interpreting individual provisions,[4] the amended Directive again affirmed that EIA is a fundamental instrument of EC environment policy that is based on the precautionary, preventative and polluter pays principles, as well as the requirement that environmental damage should be rectified at source (see Peters, 1996; Sifkakis, 1998). The drivers behind the amended Directive were the 1993 Commission implementation report (see below) and the need for EC law to reflect the obligations of the Espoo Convention. Yet the revised version has also attracted criticism because of its loose drafting and that consent may be granted even when serious negative effects are expected. Directive 2003/35/EC (the Public Participation Directive, see further below)[5] made further changes to the EIA Directive in order to ensure the implementation of the Aarhus Convention (Jendroska, 2006).

Procedural provisions

The original Directive's procedures were mandatory with respect to 9 broad classes of project listed in Annex I and discretionary with respect to 11 project categories listed in Annex II. The amended Directive significantly adds to the number of projects requiring EIA, with mandatory application to 21 broad categories listed in Annex I and discretionary application to 12 project categories listed in Annex II. The amended Directive provides for screening, clarifying the way in which an MS can determine whether Annex II projects require assessment (Sheate, 1997); Article 4 requires a formal procedure for the determination, publicly available, and Annex III stipulates a range of criteria that must be taken into account in setting thresholds or in a case by case examination.

Article 5 deals with scoping, setting out a procedure that can be followed by the responsible authority in relation to a developer. No formal requirement is made for a mandatory scoping procedure that could include a checklist of matters to be covered in the assessment.[6] A developer must, however, provide an outline of the main alternatives and reasons, which has been widely supported. Davies (2004, p164) comments:

The requirement that developers must provide an outline of the main alternatives studied was added by the amending directive. Prior to this change, Member States exercised discretion as to whether or not the developer should identify alternatives in this way. This particular amendment must be seen as a significant improvement in the EIA procedure particularly when one bears in mind that EIA reports often insufficiently covered alternatives.

Article 7 of the Directive contains a provision dealing with transboundary impacts, triggered when an MS is aware that the project is likely to have significant effects on the environment of another MS, or the latter requests its application. Documentation must be forwarded to the affected state, with the information contained within forming the basis for consultations 'necessary in the framework of the bilateral relations between the two states'. In referring to the two earlier reports, Woodliffe (2002, p144) states that 'there was scanty evidence on the use of Article 7', and that 'several states without a formal provision did in fact notify neighbouring states of projects'. The amended Directive delegates to the MS the 'detailed arrangements for implementing' all of the aspects of the transboundary consultation procedure that is provided for in Article 7. Transboundary procedure was also amended further under Directive 2003/35/EC (the Public Participation Directive).

Article 3 of Directive 2003/35/EC has made a number of additional significant amendments to the EIA Directive, many to comply with the Aarhus Convention (note generally Palerm, 2000; Jendroska, 2005b, 2006; Verschuuren, 2005).[7] Article 1(2) has inserted a definition of 'the public' and 'the public concerned', the latter of which includes not only the public affected or likely to be affected by the decision but also those having an interest in environmental decision making, such as NGOs who are explicitly referred to. Article 1(4) has removed the complete exemption from assessment of projects for national defence, and Article 2(3) requires that information produced on alternative assessment procedures be made public when an MS decides to exempt specific projects from the Directive.[8] Articles 6(2) and (3) contain detailed provisions on information to be made available and a requirement that it be released early in the process. Articles 6(4)–(6) require early and effective opportunities for public participation, with reasonable timeframes. Article 9(1) requires the public to be informed of the main reasons for the decision and of the consultation process.

Article 10a provides for access for the public concerned to the courts or other independent and impartial bodies to challenge 'the substantive or procedural legality' of decisions, acts or omissions (Article 10a[1]), which must be 'fair, equitable, timely and not prohibitively expensive' (Article 10a[5]); the public concerned must, however, have a 'sufficient interest' or 'maintain the impairment of a right' (Article 10a[1]). MS retain the power to decide in accordance with their national legal system at what stage decisions, acts or omissions may be challenged (Article 10a[2]), and what constitutes a sufficient interest or impairment of a right (Article 10a[3]); this limits the potential for challenges, although 'wide access to justice' is specified as an objective in determining what a 'sufficient interest' or 'impairment of a right' means (Article 10a[3]), which restricts MS discretion. MS must also provide the public with practical information on access to administrative and judicial review procedures (Article 10a[6]).

Ryall (2007c, pp195–202) analyses the meaning of Article 10a in some detail, including its specific application in an Irish context (pp202–218). With regard to access to courts or other independent and impartial bodies, she refers to the overarching principle of effective judicial protection developed by the ECJ in the case of *Unión de Pequeños Agricultores v Council* that requires that 'an individual who considers himself wronged by a measure which deprives him of a right or advantage under Community law must have access to a remedy against that measure and be able to obtain complete judicial protection'.[9] Ryall (2007c, pp197–198) comments that this principle: 'aims to give effect to the Rule of Law through access to judicial control. It is grounded in the constitutional traditions of the Member States and in Art 6 and 13 of the European Convention on Human Rights (ECHR)' (see also discussion on pp200–202).[10] She therefore concludes (p198):

> *It follows that where a Member State purports to comply with the requirements of Art10a[1] by putting in place a system of review before a body that is not a court, the principle of effective judicial protection demands that access to judicial control must also be available.*

Article 10a is likely to result in increased litigation, with the EIA Directive being interpreted by the ECJ in the light of Article 6 of the Aarhus Convention, (which concerns specific activities, see Ryall, 2007b, pp255–256),[11] the principle of effective judicial protection and also the principle of consistent application, or indirect effect (Drake, 2005; Ryall, 2007c, p215, and see Chapters 7 and 8). Ryall (2007c) also refers to several other interpretation issues, notably the reference to 'wide access' in respect of standing in conjunction with the ability of the MS to decide what constitutes a 'sufficient interest' or 'impairment of a right' in Article 10a[3]. She comments (p198): 'This inbuilt contradiction will lead to difficulties of interpretation in cases where a challenge is mounted to a restrictive national standing rule on the basis of alleged non-compliance with Art 10a[1] and [3]'. She also comments (p199) on the minimum standards set out in Article 10a[5], notably that the procedure must not be 'prohibitively expensive', which has been subject to litigation in the ECJ as discussed further below.

Implementation and enforcement

As seen in Chapters 7 and 8, implementation and enforcement are matters for the Commission and ECJ, together with the national courts. The Commission monitors transposition and compliance by the MS and reports periodically on such matters. If necessary, action is commenced before the ECJ in accordance with the procedure outlined in the previous two chapters.

Commission

Implementation failings with regard to the EIA Directive have been subject to studies carried out by the Commission in its role as 'guardian of the Treaties'. The Commission was first required to report on the application and effectiveness of the EIA Directive in July 1990, but the review was delayed until April 1993 as a result of insufficient information sent by MS; delays can be expected in reporting on the SEA Directive for much the same reason: a lack of experience in implementation. The EIA Directive report identified major failings and differences in the application and interpretation of the original Directive among MS.[12] The Commission did, however, conclude that the number of assessments undertaken was 'very impressive', and that consent decisions had been influenced by the assessments in a number of 'larger environmentally sensitive projects' (p52). The findings of the 1993 report were used in drafting the amended EIA Directive adopted in 1997.

The second review of the Directive was also in 1997 and highlighted the many different EIA systems that operated across the EU. The key findings of the 1997 review were: while EIA features regularly in consent processes, there is a wide variation between those processes in MS; there are a number of different interpretations and procedures for Annex II projects; quality control over the EIA process is deficient; MS do not give enough attention to the consideration of alternatives; improvements had been made concerning public participation and consultation; and that the ambiguity and lack of definition regarding key terms in the Directive remained a concern to the MS.

The Commission reported in January 2003 that infringement proceedings were being pursued against eight MS for non-compliance. In relation to one of these countries, Ireland, the Commission referred to the ECJ the fact that the decision in *Commission v Ireland* (see below) had not been complied with, and proposed that a daily fine be levied. The most recent five year review published in June 2003 revealed that implementation remained problematic with respect to a number of issues, such as screening, scoping, cumulative impacts, alternatives, the quality of the reports and failure to incorporate the results in consent decisions.[13] Several MS had not implemented its revised provisions and it was clear that together with nature conservation, waste and water matters, EIA continues to produce the majority of infringement proceedings requiring the involvement of the ECJ.

ECJ

The original and amended Directives have been considered several times by the ECJ, particularly in relation to thresholds and discretion.[14] In *Kraaijeveld BV v Gedeputeerde Staten van Zuid-Holland (Kraaijeveld)*,[15] the applicants sought to quash a decision to construct a dyke in the Netherlands. The case is significant because it considered the role of national courts in ensuring that MS do not exceed the limits of their discretion; in turn the national courts referred three questions to the ECJ for its consideration. The first was the purpose of the original Directive, with the ECJ agreeing with the Commission that the significance of the *environmental* effects of the works in question was paramount (as set out in the recitals) and therefore no distinction could be drawn between canalization and reinforcing dykes. The Dutch government had argued that the latter works were exempt from the Directive because they had overriding *social* objectives (the prevention of flooding and navigation).

The second question dealt with the matter of modification of the dyke, and the ECJ again took a broad, purposive approach to interpretation and concluded that modifications to existing dykes had to be assessed despite the absence of specific provision in Annex II of the original Directive (Collins, 2000, p7). As Tromans and Fuller (2003, p27) comment: 'This aspect of the decision brings home very forcefully the willingness of the ECJ to extend the scope of the EIA Directive beyond what its wording might immediately suggest, in order to safeguard or fulfil the Directive's objectives'. The third question, which has recurred in later cases, considered the effect of an MS laying down criteria that would exempt all projects of a certain type, which the ECJ held to be invalid.

Annex II was later considered by the ECJ in *World Wildlife Fund (WWF) v Autonome Provinz Bozen*,[16] under which an Italian authority had concluded that a project did not require EIA because it was an extension of an existing project and fell outside the relevant thresholds. Following *Kraaijeveld* and demonstrating the application of the principles derived there to later cases, the ECJ held that the discretion available to MS to exempt projects was limited as the Directive covered modifications to projects as well as new ones. The Court also held that alternative administrative procedures and projects approved by legislative procedures had still to satisfy the objectives and other requirements of the Directive. In the particular circumstances, the exception for projects concerned with national defence did not cover the restructuring of a military airport for commercial use. Shortly afterwards, the ECJ emphasized that national courts have an important role in reviewing whether national authorities have kept within the limit of their discretion, either in relation to the exemption of projects under Article 4(2) or to the provision of information under Article 5(1).[17]

In *Commission v Ireland*[18] the ECJ had to consider the matter of the transposition of Article 4(2) of the Directive in relation to the conversion of land, which was subject to Annex II. It held that Ireland was in breach not necessarily in relation to the implementation on the ground, but in regard to the wording used in its transposing legislation. As the Court stated: 'In order to prove that the transposition of a directive is insufficient or inadequate, it is not necessary to establish the actual effects of the legislation transposing it into national law: it is the wording of the legislation itself which harbours the insufficiencies or defects of transposition'.[19] In the case the Court also gave consideration to the matter of cumulative effects, stipulating that MS must not split a project into smaller components if the effect is to avoid the objective of the Directive.

In 1995 the ECJ considered the matter of 'projects in the pipeline', with the Court concluding in *Commission v Germany*[20] that the date on which a consent application is lodged is the basis for determining whether the EIA Directive applies. However, if consent for a project was granted before the date of the directive but no progress had been made with construction as required by national law, a fresh application in compliance with the EIA Directive would subsequently be necessary for construction to commence.[21] Another matter brought before the ECJ dealt with the obligations of MS regarding transboundary impacts. In *Commission v Belgium*[22] the Commission took infringement proceedings against Belgium, succeeding in an argument that the Flemish and Brussels regions had failed to comply with requirements relating to works with a transboundary impact.

In 2004 the ECJ interpreted the meaning of 'development consent' in the case of *R (Wells) v Secretary of State for Transport, Local Government and the Regions*.[23] Although the judgment considered the original EIA Directive, which was before the formal requirement for development consent was introduced, Harwood (2004, p271) comments that: 'it is implicit in the judgment that development consent is required to be in place'. The case held that a review of conditions was development consent, confirming an earlier House of Lords decision.[24] The ECJ emphasized that EIA should be carried out at the first stage in the process if possible, but that if effects were also likely at a later stage relating to implementation, then a subsequent assessment should also be carried out. The implications of the *Wells* decision have already been considered in a practical context. Černy and Jendroska (2007, p19 and n3, p21) discuss transport infrastructure cases in the Czech Republic, Poland, Slovakia and Estonia, and question whether the outcomes of established separate procedures may be considered 'development consents', or the 'principal decision' for which the consent should be sought. They also express concern that assessment should be carried out at a later stage of the process, should EIA become necessary then.

Two years later, the ECJ decided on the question of how much flexibility is available to an MS in deciding on the 'detailed arrangements' governing public participation in the EIA Directive, including the question of fees payable. In *Commission v Ireland*[25] the Court decided that the action of an MS must not undermine the effectiveness of a directive in practice, especially the role of the public, which was acknowledged in the earlier case of *Commission v Spain*.[26] However, the Court held that an MS is free to impose a participation fee provided it does not constitute an obstacle to the exercise of participation rights in the Directive. While expressing concern about the implications of the judgment, Ryall (2007b, pp251–252) highlights how analogies were drawn with other horizontal directives of relevance, notably the Environmental Information and Participation Directives (see below). She comments:

> *The Court drew on the Community rules governing the right of access to environmental information to bolster this point. It noted that Article 5 of Directive 90/313/EEC, and now Directive 2003/4/EC, provides that Member States may levy a reasonable charge for the supply of information. This provision demonstrated that the Community legislature did not believe that a reasonable fee was incompatible with the guarantee of access to information. It followed by analogy that an administrative fee was not, in principle, incompatible with the EIA Directive.*

The broader questions of the application of the doctrines of indirect effect (sympathetic interpretation) and direct effect (both vertical and horizontal) in EC law have been examined by Tromans and Fuller (2003, pp32–45) and Davies (2004, pp105–106 and 174-176), partly in relation to the EIA Directive as implemented by the UK.[27] As such, for the doctrine of indirect effect to be satisfied, there is a need for English law, for example, to be interpreted consistently with EC law wherever possible, which, in some instances, may require the strict wording of national legislation to be departed from, provided the related principle of legal certainty is not ignored completely. Some have argued that this may not be possible, and that rather than relying on the doctrine of sympathetic interpretation, the more important consideration is whether EC law has been correctly transposed.[28]

As to the direct effect of the EIA Directive, it is possible for some provisions of it to be (vertically) directly effective (by an individual against an MS) but not others, depending on whether the conditions for direct effect as originally laid down have been complied with or not. Although some of the case law in the national courts[29] initially suggested that because the third of these conditions could not be satisfied (that MS must not be left with any discretion concerning the implementation of an obligation), it was not possible for the EIA Directive (which allowed discretion) to be directly effective, other cases have suggested otherwise, particularly because there are limits to the discretion exercised. Tromans and Fuller (2003, pp36–39) indicate that the lack of clarity in ECJ rulings, despite reference to direct effect in each of the cases considered above, has been a major problem, with judgments failing to examine the matter with the precision needed. However, Harwood (2004, p275) highlights that the *Wells* decision of the ECJ allowed the individual (Mrs Wells) to require the UK to enforce the Directive and carry out an assessment. With regard to the potential horizontal direct effect of directives (by an individual against another individual/developer), the courts have, as in other areas of EC law, proven unwilling to see its expansion, regardless of the implications of those affected, who may be individuals challenging development by state authorities.[30]

Overall, however, and at a time before several of the above cases expanded individual remedies further, Collins (2000, p11) comments: 'Perhaps the most important consequence of the Court's case law for the operation of the EIA Directive has not been so much its interpretation of the Directive itself but rather the plenitude of remedies that it affords to those who seek to rely upon its provisions'. Given the additional rights provided by the adopted and proposed directives outlined below, the current restrictions on individual and NGO access to the ECJ and national courts may be relaxed further in the future, providing an even greater range of remedies to individuals to challenge decisions. Others remain more circumspect, however, with Krämer (2007, pp134–138) drawing attention to the difficulties in practice in enforcing quality control, despite opportunities for individuals and groups to voice their concerns.

OTHER RELATED HORIZONTAL DIRECTIVES

There are three other horizontal directives that relate closely to the SEA Directive: the Environmental Information, Public Participation and Environmental Liability Directives. The first was adopted in 1990 and replaced by an updated directive in 2003, the second was also adopted in 2003 and the third in 2004. Another directive, dealing with Access to Justice is currently being considered, which, with the Environmental Information and Public Participation Directives is designed to ensure the full implementation of the Aarhus Convention in the EU. The Environmental Liability Directive is particularly interesting because of how it completes the picture of harm prevention, cooperation in transboundary situations and compensation for environmental damage, which are arguably the three most important duties of any international or regionally based environmental law system, of which EA is an important part.

Environmental Information Directive

Directive 90/313/EEC of 7 June 1990 on the freedom of access to information on the environment[31] initiated, in the words of recital (2) to Directive 2003/4/EC of 28 January 2003,[32] 'a process of change in the manner in which public authorities approach the issue of openness and transparency, establishing measures for the exercise of the right of public access to environmental information which should be developed and continued'. Following a review of the original Directive by the Commission and the signature by the EC of the Aarhus Convention, it was decided to replace the original

Directive with a new legislative text.[33] Other developments, such as the increased use of information technology, had an impact upon the content and procedural provisions of the new Directive.

Revisions to the original Directive include an amended definition of environmental information and public authorities and tighter restrictions on any exceptions that can prevent the release of the information. Article 1 sets out the two objectives of the new Information Directive as:

> *(a) to guarantee the right of access to environmental information held by or for public authorities and to set out the basic terms and conditions of, and practical arrangements for, its exercise; and (b) to ensure that, as a matter of course, environmental information is progressively made available and disseminated to the public in order to achieve the widest possible systematic availability and dissemination to the public of environmental information.*

Although traditional exceptions to disclosure remain in Article 4, including 'material in the course of completion or unfinished documents or data', 'internal communications', or if the disclosure of the information would affect 'the confidentiality of proceedings of public authorities, where such confidentiality is provided for by law', the grounds for refusal 'shall be interpreted in a restrictive way, taking into account for the particular case the public interest served by disclosure'. Any refusal is required to be in writing within specified time limits if so requested, and reasons with details of the review procedure are to be provided. Article 6 contains provisions for access to justice for applicants whose requests have been ignored, wrongfully refused, inadequately answered or otherwise not dealt with in accordance with the Directive. The provisions refer to administrative review 'by an independent and impartial body established by law', with such procedure to be 'expeditious and either free of charge or inexpensive'. They also provide for 'access to a review procedure before a court of law, in which the acts or omissions of the public authority concerned can be reviewed and whose decisions may become final' and 'shall be binding on the public authority'.

All of the above suggest a changed culture of access to environmental information, with a focus on information availability as a norm rather than an exception. The underlying weight of the obligations in the Aarhus Convention has permeated EC law to such an extent as to prevent MS exercising too great a discretion, or at least to ensure that such discretion is limited and reviewable. It is also a clear demonstration of how international law can apparently have a greater binding effect when also implemented by EC law because of the legal effect of EC law in the MS and the much greater problems inherent in changing EC law. If international law is only binding in a state as a result of introducing national legislation and/or state practice, it is always possible for a state to change that law/practice in accordance with government policy, or indeed withdraw from an international treaty. The limitations on enforcing obligations in international law are significant; in contrast, the Commission and ECJ are readily able to enforce obligations in EC law. Changing EC law is subject to the agreement of the other MS depending on the procedures used, a far greater task, lending much greater weight to a Directive's obligations. Withdrawal from the EU is unprecedented, has significant difficulties and is extremely unlikely given that the benefits of membership outweigh the costs.

The changed culture of access to environmental information clearly has benefits for those sympathetic to a future revision of the SEA Directive (see Chapter 10) that may entail assessment of policies and legislation, both areas where traditionally a culture of secrecy has prevailed. It also benefits the application of the SEA Directive currently to plans and programmes, which have also been traditionally considered the preserve of government, the development of which has limited the access of publicly available information. Experience with the SEA Directive in its current form (and indeed the Information and Participation Directives) may well overcome some of these longstanding concerns, producing a government audience that is more receptive to suggestions of greater openness, especially if some MS also provide information on the assessment of policy and legislative proposals (as indeed some do on an individual basis currently) but as also advocated by the SEA Protocol.

Public Participation Directive

As seen above, Directive 2003/35/EC, the Public Participation Directive, which was adopted on 26 May 2003,[34] has made a number of changes to the EIA Directive to ensure compliance with the Aarhus Convention. However, the Public Participation Directive has also specific reference to public participation in respect of certain plans and programmes, which ensures a close relationship with the SEA Directive. Recital (10) of the Public Participation Directive indicates that 'certain Directives in the environmental area which require Member States to produce plans and programmes relating to the environment ... do not contain sufficient provisions on public participation', which is now a requirement of Article 7 of the Aarhus Convention. This reference is not to the SEA Directive, which, because it was adopted after the Aarhus Convention was ratified by the EC, supposedly contains such provisions already,[35] but to Directives such as the IPPC Directive, which is specified.[36] Recital (10) obliquely refers to this also by stating that 'other relevant Community legislation already provides for public participation in the preparation of plans and programmes'. Article 1 of the Public Participation Directive contains these objectives.

Article 2 of the Directive defines the public and indicates the extent of the public participation obligations with reference to Annex I, which includes application to Directives on waste, hazardous waste, packaging waste, nitrates and ambient air quality.[37] Article 2.5 states that the Article shall not apply to plans and programmes set out in Annex I of the SEA Directive (see Chapter 10) or under the Water Framework Directive (see Chapter 11), which contain separate procedures for public participation and are discussed later. Article 3 deals with amendment of the EIA Directive (see above) and Article 4 with amendment of the IPPC Directive. Article 5 requires the Commission to report on the application and effectiveness of the Public Participation Directive by mid-2009, including proposals for amendment that may include extending the scope to other plans and programmes relating to the environment.

Article 2 defines the public to mean one or more natural or legal persons, associations, organizations or groups, ensuring a broad interpretation that will permit individuals and environmental groups to fully participate. The main restriction on this is that the identification of the public is for the MS to decide. Early and effective opportunities for participation, in the modification or review of plans or programmes specified in Annex I must be given, with information made available to the public who must be able to comment on it, 'when all options are open before decisions on the plans and programmes are made'. Plans and programmes designed for the 'sole purpose' of serving national defence or taken in case of civil emergencies are excluded.[38] Decision makers must take 'due account' of the results of public participation, and the public must be informed of subsequent decisions and the reasons on which they are based.

Proposed Access to Justice Directive

As indicated above, currently individuals and NGOs have limited access rights to both national and European courts, although in some instances provisions have been interpreted liberally to allow local residents or groups to challenge decisions (Ziehm, 2005). In England and Wales, for example, the right to challenge decisions of the Secretary of State on their merits applies to any 'person aggrieved'; the right to challenge the way in which decisions have been reached (a 'judicial review') requires a claimant to demonstrate a 'sufficient interest' in the matter to which the claim relates (Tromans and Fuller, 2003, pp214–216). The former challenge is one based on its facts, the latter concerns procedural matters.

A proposal for a Directive of the European Parliament and of the Council on access to justice in environmental matters was made in 2003,[39] which, if adopted by the MS, would require changes to be made to MS law over and above those introduced to the EIA Directive and IPPC Directive as a result of the Public Participation Directive discussed above. The proposal is designed to implement Article 9 of the Aarhus Convention in the MS, which is a provision for the enforcement of environmental law in general (Ebbesson, 2002). Dette (2004) outlines the background to the provision, its substantive obligations and anticipated difficulties in gaining approval by the MS. However, notwithstanding its lack of popularity by many governments, who are concerned at the implications, the significance of Article 9(3) in particular is clear (Dette, 2004, p21):

> *The great importance of Art. 9(3) is that it enables members of the public, including individuals and environmental organisations, to invoke the power of law when environmental law has been violated. By that it aims to overcome the fact that the environment has no legal interest defender.*

Articles 9(4) and 9(5) of the Aarhus Convention will also be implemented by the proposed directive in the MS. The first states that 'review procedures shall provide adequate and effective remedies, including injunctive relief as appropriate, and be fair, equitable, timely and not prohibitively expensive'. The second requires the parties 'to ensure, that information is provided to the public on access to administrative and judicial review procedures and to consider the establishment of appropriate assistance mechanisms to remove or reduce financial and other barriers to access to justice'.[40]

In Europe, the TEC currently provides that any natural or legal person can only institute proceedings directly against an EC institution if the person is the 'addressee of the institutions decision or if the decision is of direct and individual concern to the person'. Dette (2004, pp22–23) indicates that this provision (found in Article 230(4) of the EC Treaty) has severely limited the ability of challenges:

> *In a series of decisions the ECJ has held that persons are to be considered 'individually concerned' by a decision if it 'affects them by reason of certain attributes which are peculiar to them or by reason of circumstances in which they are differentiated from all other persons and by virtue of these factors distinguishes them individually just as in the case of the person addressed'.*

This ECJ adjudication has been criticized because it requires the identification of a 'closed class' of affected individuals in order to invoke the criterion of 'direct and individual concern' and allow access to the ECJ.

Dette (2004, p22) comments that the provision was set out in the 1960s before environmental matters became a concern in the EU with a view to individual interests of producers, but that it is entirely inappropriate in relation to environmental matters to continue to apply this provision. As it currently stands, it is also not compliant with Article 9(3) of the Aarhus Convention. She refers to recent case law in the CFI, which indicates some apparent shift in judicial opinion, however, the CFI decision was later overruled by the ECJ, returning to the status quo.

Regulation implementing the Aarhus Convention with respect to the EC institutions

In order to ensure that EC law is made fully compliant with the Aarhus Convention, a Regulation was adopted in 2006 that should ensure that individuals and groups are in future able to challenge decisions of EC institutions and bodies.[41] Standing under the Regulation is limited to 'recognised qualified entities', which means environmental NGOs acting at the EC level with an organizational and institutional structure. Although limited, this is considered by Dette (2004, p24) to be 'in line with Article 9(3), as this provision gives the Parties the possibility to lay down criteria for members of the public to be granted legal standing'. The definitions of 'Community acts and omissions' and 'environmental law' are broad, which should ensure that most relevant decisions and fields of law are covered. The weakness of the Regulation is, however, that the definition of 'Community institutions and bodies' does not include bodies acting in a judicial or legislative capacity and that the Regulation must be read in conjunction with Article 230(1) of the TEC, which still limits access to justice to the ECJ. Krämer (2007, p142) also questions whether the political will is present to ensure the Regulation is implemented in practice, especially in conjunction with assessments under other requirements:

> *The internal EC administrative resistance against environmental impact assessments for plans and programmes is considerable. In particular, it is feared such assessments would lead to slowing down the envisaged measures and would unduly delay the adoption and implementation of EC plans. Though the same argument also applies to national plans and programmes, it is better heard at EC level, because there is no public opinion which would counterbalance the administration's greed for acceleration. Considerations have gone so far as to reflect whether transboundary networks could not be declared to be of 'European interest' and thereby be exempted from the requirements of environmental impact assessments under existing EC directives.[42]*

The Regulation does, however, provide a definition of plans and programmes to which it applies, in recital 9 and Article 2(e), which also contains similar components to the definition in the SEA Directive and Protocol. Article 2(1)(e)(iii) states that:

> *'plans and programmes relating to the environment' means plans and programmes which contribute to, or are likely to have significant effects on, the achievement of the objectives of Community environmental policy, such as laid down in the Sixth Community Environment Action Programme or in any subsequent general environmental action programme.*

Linking the definition of plans and programmes (and the assessment therefore) to objectives, however imprecise, at least goes someway to addressing criticisms of EA as lacking a substantive focus (see Chapters 3 and 11 in particular), as if they fail to comply with these objectives they should not be approved. The reality, however, is likely to accord more with the comments made by Krämer (2007) above.

Environmental Liability Directive

Directive 2004/35/CE on environmental liability[43] (the Environmental Liability Directive, ELD) has been much discussed during the course of its legislative history, including over three decades of discussion on provisions for compensation for environment or environment related damage (Krämer, 2006, p29).[44] Through a public law system, the Directive is designed to implement the polluter pays principle (Article 1)[45] and links site contamination with biodiversity loss. As such, it focuses on environmental damage (which should be concrete and quantifiable) to protected species and natural habitats, water and land (Article 2, 3 and Annex III) (see Brans, 2006; Fehr et al, 2007). Damage to protected species and natural habitats is defined in accordance with the Habitats and Wild Birds Directives,[46] and water damage is defined in accordance with the Water Framework Directive (see Chapter 11). Land damage is contamination of soil that creates a significant risk of human health being adversely affected. Traditional damage to individuals, including economic loss, is therefore outside of the limits of the Directive (Article 3.3) unlike many other national regimes for site contamination and the common law of many jurisdictions that provides for such remedies.[47] The Directive is also not retrospective (Article 17).

Recital 2 sets out the 'fundamental principle' of the Directive, which is that operators, defined as either private or public bodies (Article 2.6), who have caused the damage or imminent threat of it, are to be held financially liable (Article 8), 'in order to induce operators to adopt measures and develop practices to minimise the risks of environmental damage so that their exposure to financial liabilities is reduced'.[48] Causation between the damage and the polluter(s) must be demonstrated before an operator can be made to bear the costs of preventive and remedial measures (including the assessment of damage and costs incurred in administering the scheme). Operators may be exempt where their activities have obtained prior approval by a regulator (Article 8.4(a)), or where the emission or activity was not considered by an MS authority to cause environmental damage according to current best practice (the 'state of the art' defence).

Establishing an environmental management system that includes voluntary as well as mandatory EA procedures can assist in providing a state of the art defence. Such procedures may be required where projects fall under the EIA Directive or plans and programmes under the SEA Directive, and as an operator can be either a private or public body, the provisions of either or both may be relevant in any given situation. However, applying EA to activities on a voluntary basis is also a wise precaution in any due diligence strategy and may provide a suitable defence under Article 8.4(b). It is also very much in line with the application of the precautionary principle, which should arguably underlie the ELD as much as the polluter pays principle. De Sadeleer (2006) comments that even though the Directive may not mention the precautionary principle, the ELD must still be consistently interpreted in accordance with it following Article 174(2) of the TEC. His view (p99) is that the state of the art defence in Article 8.4(b), which relates closely to the duty of care, is generally not compliant with the precautionary principle:

> *Precaution... echoes doubt: uncertainty replaces knowledge, and anticipation takes the place of foreseeability. The duty of care must therefore be rethought in the light of this new principle. In this context, it is not merely the person who has failed to take all preventive measures against a well-understood or foreseeable risk who should be considered at fault, but also the person who, in a situation of uncertainty or doubt, has failed to adopt a precautionary approach in order to avert a still uncertain risk.*

Arguably, the conduct of an effective EA at strategic and project levels may provide greater adherence with the precautionary principle than the measures perhaps contemplated by De Sadeleer (2006). De Mulder (2006, p279) discusses the relationship between the EIA and SEA Directives and the ELD. Further to the discussion of the relationship between EIA and compensation for environmental damage in an international law context (see Chapter 3), he believes the ELD can be 'regarded as a tool for an improved application of the EU Assessment Directives as Article 8 of the ELD indicates more clearly what the impact of a legally required ex ante assessment could be'. He concludes (p279) as follows, emphasizing that assessment at both the strategic and project levels can assist with establishing a state of the art defence:

> *[Article 8.4] makes clear that the absence of an impact assessment, when legally required, or the use of a poor quality report that is not in accordance with the state of the art, might have serious consequences. Given the structural links between the environmental assessment requirements and decision-making procedures, both at the project and planning levels, the environmental liability issue cannot be confined to the project level.*

Where persons are affected or likely to be adversely affected by environmental damage, they should have the opportunity to ask an authority to take action (Article 12); as mentioned, Article 3.3, however, explicitly excludes the right of a private party to claim compensation. NGOs with an environmental protection role should 'be given the opportunity to properly contribute to the effective implementation of this Directive' (recital 25). Such persons should also have access to procedures to review the authority's decisions (Article 13), which links closely with the measures proposed in the Access to

Justice Directive. On whether or not these measures are compliant with the Aarhus Convention,[49] Krämer (2006, p46) comments: 'the watchdog role of environmental organisations, foreseen in Articles 12 and 13 of the Directive, is of considerable value, as this is capable of ensuring transparency in the bargaining process'.

CONCLUSIONS

The success of the EIA Directive and other horizontal measures for environmental protection and public participation must ultimately be examined in the broader context of whether such measures work in practice. Undoubtedly the influence of the Aarhus Convention on the horizontal directives has been considerable, with the *Commission v Ireland* ECJ decision in the area of public participation under the EIA Directive drawing on the rules related to access to information. The *Wells* decision has since been highlighted as indicative of the (vertical) direct effect of the EIA Directive, and it can only be a matter of time before the other horizontal directives are considered by the ECJ.

Despite many acknowledged advances, De Boer (2005, p86) considers that it is vital to ask broader questions of the relevance of EIA in Europe today. In following a theme picked up early in this book and highlighted throughout, he contrasts the substantive obligations of the Habitats Directive (see Chapter 11) with the procedural requirements of EIA Directive, to emphasize the structural shortcomings of EIA, concluding that: 'The success of the Habitats Directive, based on a clear goal of protecting certain species, provides a lesson. The EIA Directive does not come close to this success because it requires only that environmental impacts (and alternatives) be taken into account'. The same criticism can arguably be made of the procedural focus of the SEA Directive, which is examined in Chapter 10.

NOTES

1 The EIA, Environmental Information, Public Participation, (proposed) Access to Justice and Environmental Liability Directives may be termed 'horizontal directives' since they apply to a number of crosscutting matters. See Macrory (2007, p2). Each is referenced below.
2 Directive 85/337 on the assessment of the effects of certain public and private projects on the environment; OJ No L175/40.
3 Directive 97/11; OJ No L073/5.
4 Tromans considers this matter at length, see Tromans and Fuller (2003, pp20–23).
5 Directive 2003/35/EC of the European Parliament and of the Council of 26 May 2003 providing for public participation in respect of certain plans and programmes relating to the environment and amending with regard to public participation and access to justice Council Directives 85/337/EEC and 96/61/EC. OJ L 156, 25 June 2003. Directive 96/61/EC is the Directive on integrated pollution prevention and control (IPPC).
6 See the discussion in Davies (2004, pp162–164), in which the benefits of the Dutch approach are advocated.

7   On the implications of the Aarhus Convention for EC law, see: Ebbesson (2002); Davies (2002); Zschiesche (2002); Lee and Abbott (2003); Mathieson (2003); Getliffe (2004); Dette (2004); Carnwath (2004, p318); Jendroska (2005a); and Scott (2002, pp999–1002).

8   The Commission has produced guidance on the specific application of Article 2(3) of the EIA Directive to clarify what 'exceptional cases' means in connection with the ability to apply an alternative assessment process. See Commission of the European Communities (2006). As with all guidance of this kind, the Commission states: 'This document represents only the views of the Commission services and is not of a binding nature... It must be emphasised that, in the last resort, it rests with the European Court of Justice (ECJ) to interpret a Directive' (p3).

9   ECJ Case C-50/00P *Unión de Pequeños Agricultores v Council* [2002] ECR I-6677, at 39. See also Dougan (2004, Chapter 1) and Prechal (2005, pp134–145) referred to by Ryall (2007c).

10 The rule of law was discussed in Chapter 1. For earlier reference to the ECHR, see Chapter 7, where it was referred to in relation to the section on the European Constitution. The ECHR is of course an international treaty operating in the European context in the same way that (in large part at least, if Canada and the US are excluded), the Espoo and Aarhus Conventions do.

11 This is of course also true of the other directives that implement its provisions, including the SEA Directive, which is arguably not compliant with Article 7 of the Convention, which concerns plans, programmes and policies (Mathiesen, 2003; see Chapter 10).

12 COM (93), 28 Final. Vol 12. This report has been updated a number of times since, including 1998.

13 See Commission of the European Communities (2003).

14 For further commentary on the cases that follow, please refer to Tromans and Fuller (2003, pp25–32), from which much of the text that follows is derived. The English Court of Appeal summarised the European case law in *Berkeley v Secretary of State for the Environment, Transport and the Regions ('Berkeley 2')*, which is considered at length on p31 and pp75–78. See also Ladeur and Prelle (2001).

15 ECJ, Case C-72/95 *Kraaijeveld BV v Gedeputeerde Staten van Zuid-Holland* [1996] ECR I-5403.

16 ECJ, Case C-435/97 *World Wildlife Fund (WWF) v Autonome Provinz Bozen* [1999] ECR I-5613.

17 See ECJ, Case C-287/98 *Luxembourg v Linster* [2000] ECR I-6917.

18 ECJ, Case C-392/96 *Commission v Ireland* [1999] ECR I-5901.

19 Above, para 60; see also Collins (2000) and Ryall (2007a) for a full account of Ireland's experience with the EIA Directive.

20 ECJ, Case C-431/92 *Commission v Germany* [1995] ECR I-2189.

21 See the discussion in Davies (2004, pp 171–173), and note Kunzlik (1995) in relation to the British cases.

22 ECJ, Case 133/94 *Commission v Belgium* [1996] ECR I-2323.

23 ECJ, Case C-201/02 *R (Wells) v Secretary of State for Transport, Local Government and the Regions* [2004] ECR 000.

24 Much has been written on the EIA Directive in the UK. In additional to the references already cited, see also: Alder (1993); Ward (1993); Elvin and Robinson (2000); Weston (2002); Pugh-Smith and Harwood (2003); Stallworthy (2004); Macrory (1991, 2004); Holder (2004) and Holder and McGillivray (2007).

25 ECJ, Case C-216/05 *Commission v Ireland* [2006] ECR I-000.

26 ECJ, Case C-332/04 *Commission v Spain* [2006] ECR I-000.

27 The doctrines were comprehensively considered in Chapters 8 and 9 in relation to EC law generally and EC environmental law in particular, to which readers are referred.

28 See Jans (2000, p205) as cited in Tromans and Fuller (2003, p34).

29 Note the Scottish, English, Irish and Dutch cases referenced by Tromans and Fuller (2003, p36). Davies (2004, p105) also refers to *Twyford Parish Council v Secretary of State for the*

Environment and Secretary of State for Transport [1993] Env LR 37, at 46, where, however, the comments of McCullough, J. (that the rights of the individual needing protection by the national court were above all the right to be consulted) were *obiter dicta*, meaning that they were not binding upon future cases. In *Wychavon DC v Secretary of State for the Environment and Velcourt Ltd* [1994] Env LR 239, Turner, J. held that none of the provisions of the EIA Directive would be capable for direct effect, although the Court of Appeal later concluded that the directive was capable of having direct effect. As seen, ECJ decisions including *Kraaijeveld* took a more positive approach to the direct effect of the EIA Directive

30   Tromans and Fuller (2003) examine this on pp39–44, together with the matter of liability where a state has failed to implement a directive (under the principles in *Francovich*, see Chapter 7), which he concludes would not allow an individual a right to damages against the state where no direct or indirect effect is possible, primarily because the provisions of the EIA Directive are procedural in nature and do not intend to confer substantive rights on individuals that can be linked to any damage suffered.

31   Council Directive 90/313/EEC of 7 June 1990 on the freedom of access to information on the environment, OJ 1990 L158/56.

32   Directive 2003/4/EC of the European Parliament and of the Council of 28 January 2003 on public access to environmental information and repealing Council Directive 90/313/EEC, OJ 2003 L41/26.

33   For a commentary on the original Information Directive, see Hallo (1996), Kimber (1998) and Janssen (1998).

34   Directive 2003/35/EC of the European Parliament and of the Council of 26 May 2003 providing for public participation in respect of certain plans and programmes relating to the environment and amending with regard to public participation and access to justice Council Directives 85/337/EEC and 96/61/EC. OJ L156, 25 June 2003.

35   Note the comments of Mathiesen (2003), discussed in relation to the SEA Directive in Chapter 11, which indicate the SEA Directive is non-compliant with Article 7 of the Aarhus Convention.

36   The Public Participation Directive introduced a new Article 15a to the IPPC Directive, entitled 'Access to Justice' (Directive 96/61/EC on integrated pollution prevention and control OJ 1996 L257/26), which is in similar terms to Article 10a that was introduced to the EIA Directive discussed above.

37   Council Directive 75/442/EEC of 15 July 1975 on waste, Article 7(1); Council Directive 91/689/EEC of 12 December 1991 on hazardous waste, Article 6(1); Directive 94/62/EC of the European Parliament and of the Council of 20 December 1994 on packaging and packaging waste, Article 14; Council Directive 91/676/EEC of 12 December 1991 concerning the protection of waters against pollution caused by nitrates from agricultural sources, Article 5(1); Council Directive 96/62/EC of 27 September 1996 on ambient air quality assessment and management, Article 8(3).

38   See *Bozen*, discussed above in note 16, where the ECJ decided that projects involving national defence had to be construed narrowly.

39   Proposal for a directive of the European Parliament and of the Council on access to justice in environmental matters, COM(2003) 624 final.

40   Dette (2004, pp21–25) discusses current access to justice provisions in the EC in her article, specifically with regard to current standing rights before the ECJ, including outlining a proposal for a regulation implementing the Aarhus Convention with respect to the EC institutions themselves. See Proposal for a Regulation of the European Parliament and of the Council on the application of the provisions of the Aarhus Convention on Access to Information, Public Participation in Decision Making and Access to Justice in Environmental Matters to EC institutions and Bodies, COM (2003) 622 final.

41   Regulation (EC) No 1367/2006 of 6 September 2006 of the European Parliament and of the Council on the application of the provisions of the Aarhus Convention on Access to Information, Public Participation in Decision Making and Access to Justice in Environmental Matters to EC institutions and bodies.

42   Krämer (2007, pp142–147) also considers the internal provision for the assessment of EC legislative proposals (see Peters, 2004). As indicated earlier, this is not examined in this book because it is more closely connected with a desire to reduce the regulatory burden rather than positively improve such proposals. Krämer (2007, p146) concludes scathingly: 'The "impact assessment" approach by the Commission cannot, therefore, be considered a serious contribution to assess the environmental effects of proposed legislation and policy orientation'.

43   Directive 2004/35/CE of the European Parliament and of the Council, 21 April 2004, on environmental liability with regard to the prevention and remedying of environmental damage.

44   See Betlem and Brans (2006), Fogleman (2006) and Anstee-Wedderburn (2007) generally.

45   Some have doubted that the ELD has done enough to ensure implementation of the polluter pays principle, see Coroner (2007).

46   The Directive also allows an MS to define protected species and natural habitats in accordance with national legislation, see recital 6. Operators should also be made liable for activities that pose an actual or potential risk for human health and the environment, regardless of whether a species or habitat is protected, see recital 10, although in these cases fault or negligence (failure to exercise a duty of care) must be shown.

47   Traditional damage is assessed under international regimes and the law of an MS; in a common law system, this is typically through the private law of tort (civil wrongs); see Wilde (2002) and Bates et al (2004) for further explanation.

48   For a detailed discussion of the position of an operator, especially in a transnational context, see Betlem (2006). Note that a compulsory insurance scheme is not included at present, see Faure (2003).

49   For a commentary on the role of individuals and public interest groups under the scheme of the ELD, see Brans (2006, pp199–200), who notes the failure of the ELD to comply with Article 9.3 of the Aarhus Convention, which allows private individuals and groups the opportunity to participate in the enforcement process. Under the ELD there is no such right, merely the opportunity to request that public authorities take action.

REFERENCES

Alder, J. (1993) 'Environmental impact assessment – the inadequacies of English law' *Journal of Environmental Law*, vol 5, no 2, pp203–220

Anstee-Wedderburn, J. (2007) 'A consideration of the implementation of the Environmental Liability Directive to date', *Journal for European Environmental and Planning Law*, vol 3, pp221–226

Bates, J., Birtles, W. and Pugh, C. (2004) *Liability for Environmental Harm*, Reed Elsevier, London

Betlem, G. (2006) 'Transnational operator liability' in Betlem, G. and Brans, E. (eds) (2006) *Environmental Liability in the EU: The 2004 Directive Compared with US and Member State Law*, Cameron May, London, 2006, pp149–188

Betlem, G. and Brans, E. (eds) (2006) *Environmental Liability in the EU: The 2004 Directive Compared with US and Member State Law*, Cameron May, London, 2006

Brans, E. (2006) 'Liability for damage to public natural resources under the 2004 EC Environmental Liability Directive – standing and assessment of damages' in Betlem, G. and Brans, E. (eds)

(2006) *Environmental Liability in the EU: The 2004 Directive Compared with US and Member State Law*, Cameron May, London, 2006, pp189–215

Carnwath, R. (2004) 'Judicial protection of the environment: At home and abroad', *Journal of Environmental Law*, vol 16, no 3, pp315–327

Černy, P. and Jendroska, J. (2007) 'Transposition and implementation of EIA Directive in some EU member states (with special emphasis on transport infrastructure cases)', *Environmental Law Network International*, vol 1, pp18–24

Collins, A. (2000) 'The Environmental Impact Assessment Directive as interpreted by the Court of Justice', paper delivered to the Irish Centre for European Law Conference on Environmental Impact Assessments and Planning, Belfast, 11 May 2000

Commission of the European Communities (1993) *Report on the Implementation of Directive 85/337/EEC on the assessment of the effects of certain public and private projects on the environment*, COM(93)28 final, Commission of the European Communities, Brussels

Commission of the European Communities (1998) *Evaluation of the Performance of the EIA Process*, Final Report, vol 1, Commission of the European Communities, Brussels

Commission of the European Communities (2003) *Report from the Commission to the European Parliament and Council on the Application and Effectiveness of the EIA Directive (Directive 85/337/EEC as amended by Directive 97/11/EC) – How Successful are the Member States in Implementing the EIA Directive*, COM (2003) 0334 final, Commission of the European Communities, Brussels

Commission of the European Communities (2006) *Directive 85/337/EEC on the assessment of the effects of certain public and private projects on the environment (EIA Directive), as amended: Clarification of the application of Article 2(3) of the Directive*, Office for Official Publications of the European Communities, Luxembourg

Coroner, F. (2007) 'Member states missing the opportunity to implement "polluter pays" principle', *Environmental Law Network Review*, vol 1, pp30–31

Davies, P. (2002) 'Public participation, the Aarhus convention, and the European Community' in D. N. Zillman, A. R. Lucas and G. Pring (eds) *Human Rights in Natural Resource Development: Public Participation in the Sustainable Development of Mining and Energy Resources*, Oxford University Press, New York, pp155–185

Davies, P. (2004) *European Union Environmental Law*, Ashgate Publishing Ltd, Aldershot

Dette, B. (2004) 'Access to justice in environmental matters before the European Court of Justice – present situation and recent developments', *Environmental Law Network International*, vol 2, pp20–25

De Boer, J. J. (2005) 'Editorial: Impact of the European EIA Directive', *Impact Assessment and Project Appraisal*, vol 23, no 2, p86

De Mulder, J. (2006) 'The expansion of environmental assessment in international law: The Protocol on Strategic Environmental Assessment to the Espoo Convention', *Environmental Law and Management*, vol 18, pp269–281

De Sadeleer, N. (2006) 'Polluter pays, precautionary principles and liability' in Betlem, G. and Brans, E. (ed) (2006) *Environmental Liability in the EU: The 2004 Directive Compared with US and Member State Law*, Cameron May, London, 2006, pp89–101

Dougan, M. (2004) *National Remedies before the Court of Justice: Issues of Harmonisation and Differentiation*, Hart Publishing, Oxford

Drake, S. (2005) 'Twenty years after Von Colson: The impact of "indirect effect" on the protection of the individual's Community rights', *European Law Review*, vol 30, p329

Ebbesson, J. (ed) (2002) *Access to Justice in Environmental Matters in the EU*, Kluwer Law International, The Hague

Elvin, D. and Robinson, J. (2000) 'Environmental impact assessment', *Journal of Planning and Environmental Law*, September, pp881–882

Faure, M. (ed) (2003) *Deterrence, Insurability and Compensation in Environmental Liability: Future Developments in the European Union*, Springer, Vienna/New York

Fehr, K. H., Friedrich, B. and Scheil, S. (2007) 'Liability Directive – a useful tool for nature protection?', *Journal for European Environmental and Planning Law*, vol 2, pp110–128

Fogleman, V. (2006) 'Enforcing the Environmental Liability Directive: Duties, powers and self-executing provisions', *Environmental Liability*, vol 4, pp127–146

Getliffe, K. (2004) 'Proceduralisation and the Aarhus Convention: Does increased participation in the decision-making process lead to more effective EU environmental law?', *Environmental Law Review*, vol 4, p107

Gilpin, A. (1995) *Environmental Impact Assessment: Cutting Edge for the Twenty-First Century*, Cambridge University Press, Cambridge

Hallo, R. (ed) (1996) *Access to Environmental Information in Europe: The Implementation and Implications of Directive 90/313/EEC*, Kluwer Law International

Harwood, R. (2004) 'EIA, development consent and duties on the member state', *Journal of Environmental Law*, vol 16, no 2, pp261–278

Holder, J. (2004) *Environmental Assessment: The Regulation of Decision Making*, Oxford University Press, Oxford

Holder, J. and McGillivray, D. (eds) (2007) *Taking Stock of Environmental Assessment: Law, Policy and Practice*, Routledge-Cavendish, Abingdon

Jans, J. (2000) *European Environmental Law*, Kluwer, London

Janssen, J. (1998) 'Access to environmental information: recent developments on access to environmental information: Transparency in decision making', *European Environmental Law Review*, October, p268

Jendroska, J. (2005a) 'Aarhus Convention and Community Law: The interplay', *Journal for European Environmental and Planning Law*, vol 2, no 1, pp12–21

Jendroska, J. (2005b) 'Public information and participation in EC environmental law: Origins, milestones and trends' in R. Macrory (ed) *Reflections on 30 Years of EU Environmental Law: A High Level of Protection*, Europa Law Publishing, Groningen, pp62–86

Jendroska, J. (2006) 'Public participation in environmental decision making: implementation of the Aarhus Convention requirements in EC law' in T. Ormond, M. Führ and R. Barth (eds) *Environmental Law and Policy at the Turn of the 21st Century*, Lexxion, Berlin, pp37–50

Kimber, C. (1998) 'Understanding access to environmental information: The European experience' in T. Jewell and J. Steele (eds) *Law in Environmental Decision Making*, Clarendon, Oxford

Krämer, L. (2006) 'Directive 2004/35/EC on environmental liability' in Betlem, G. and Brans, E. (ed) (2006) *Environmental Liability in the EU: The 2004 Directive Compared with US and Member State Law*, Cameron May, London, 2006, pp29–47

Krämer, L. (2007) 'The development of environmental assessments at the level of the European Union' in Holder, J. and McGillivray, D. (eds) (2007) *Taking Stock of Environmental Assessment: Law, Policy and Practice*, Routledge-Cavendish, Abingdon, pp131–148

Kunzlik, R. (1995) 'Environmental impact assessment: The British cases', *European Environmental Law Review*, vol 4, pp336–344

Ladeur, K. H. and Prelle, R. (2001) 'Environmental assessment and judicial approaches to procedural errors – a European and comparative law analysis', *Journal of Environmental Law*, vol 3, no 2, pp185–198

Lee, M. and Abbot, C. (2003) 'The usual suspects? Public participation under the Aarhus Convention', *Modern Law Review*, vol 66, no 1, pp80–108

Macrory, R. (1991) 'Environmental assessment: Critical legal issues on implementation' in D. Vaughan (ed) *EC Environment and Planning Law*, Butterworth, London

Macrory, R. (2004) 'Principles of judicial review on environmental assessment', *Journal of Environmental Law*, vol 16, no 2, pp279–288

Macrory, R. (2007) 'Supra-national enforcement of environmental law: Compliance mechanisms in the European Union', *ICLG to: Environment Law*, Global Legal Group Ltd, 2007, pp1–4

Mathieson, A. (2003) 'Public participation in decision making and access to justice in EC environmental law: The case of certain plans and programmes', *European Environmental Law Review*, vol 12, no 2, pp36–52

McHugh, P. (1994) 'The European Community Directive – an alternative environmental impact assessment procedure?', *Natural Resources Journal*, vol 34, pp 589–600

Palerm, J. (2000) 'An empirical – theoretical analysis framework for public participation in environmental impact assessment', *Journal of Environmental Planning and Management*, vol 43, no 5, pp581–600

Peters, E. (2004) 'The European Commission's sustainability impact assessment project: experience and current challenges' paper presented to the Annual Conference of the International Association for Impact Assessment, Vancouver, 24–30 April

Peters, H. J. (1996) 'The significance of environmental precaution in the Environmental Impact Assessment Directive', vol 5, *European Environmental Law Review*, p210

Pugh-Smith, J. and Harwood, R. (2003) 'EIAs – Mantraps and Tiger pits', mimeo, 39 Essex Street, London

Prechal, S. (2005) *Directives in EC Law*, 2nd Edition, Oxford University Press, Oxford

Ryall, A. (2004) 'Implementation of the Aarhus Convention through Community environmental law', *Environmental Law Review*, vol 6, p274

Ryall, A. (2007a) *Effective Judicial Protection and the Environmental Impact Assessment Directive in Ireland*, Hart Publishing, Oxford

Ryall, A. (2007b) 'EIA and public participation: Determining the limits of member state discretion', *Journal of Environmental Law*, vol 19, no 2, pp247–257

Ryall, A. (2007c) 'Access to justice and the EIA directive: The implications of the Aarhus Convention' in Holder, J. and McGillivray, D. (eds) (2007) *Taking Stock of Environmental Assessment: Law, Policy and Practice*, Routledge-Cavendish, Abingdon, pp191–218

Scott, J. (2002) 'Law and environmental governance in the EU', *International and Comparative Law Quarterly*, vol 51, no 4, pp996–1005

Sheate, W. R. (1997) 'The EIA amendment directive 97/11/EC – a small step forward?', *European Environmental Law Review*, vol 6, no 8/9, pp235–243

Sifakis, A. (1998) 'Precaution, prevention and the Environmental Impact Assessment Directive', *European Environmental Law Review*, vol 7, p349

Stallworthy, M. (2004) 'Once more unto the breach: English law rationales and environmental assessment', *Journal of Planning Law*, p1472–1490

Tromans, S. and Fuller, K. (2003) *Environmental Impact Assessment - Law and Practice*, Reed Elsevier, London

Verschuuren, J. (2005) 'Public participation regarding the elaboration and approval of projects in the EU after the Aarhus Convention', *Yearbook of European Environmental Law*, vol 4, p29

Ward, A. (1993) 'The right to effective remedy in EC law and environmental protection: A case study of UK judicial decisions concerning the environmental assessment directive', *Journal of Environmental Law*, vol 5, no 2, pp222-244

Wathern, P. (1988) 'The EIA Directive of the European Community' in Wathern, P. (ed) (1988) *Environmental Impact Assessment: Theory and Practice*, Unwin Hyman, London, pp192–209

Weston, J. (2002) 'From Poole to Fulham: A changing culture in UK environmental impact assessment decision-making?', *Journal of Environmental Planning and Management*, vol 45, no 3, pp425–443

Wilde, M. (2002) *Civil Liability for Environmental Damage: A Comparative Analysis of Law and Policy in Europe and the United States*, Kluwer Law International, The Hague

Wood, C. (1995) *Environmental Impact Assessment: A Comparative Review*, Longman, London

Woodliffe, J. (2002) 'Environmental damage and environmental impact assessment' in M. Bowman and A. Boyle (2002) *Environmental Damage in International and Comparative Law: Problems of Definition and Valuation*, Oxford University Press, Oxford, pp133–147

Ziehm, C. (2005) 'Legal standing for NGOs in environmental matters under the Aarhus Convention and under Community and national law', *Journal of European Environmental and Planning Law*, vol 4, pp287–300

Zschiesche, M. (2002) 'The Aarhus convention – more citizens' participation by setting out environmental standards?', *Environmental Law Network International*, vol 1, pp21–29

The SEA Directive

CHAPTER OUTLINE

This chapter analyses the historical background, legal basis and effect, objectives, procedures, transposition, implications and experience to date of the SEA Directive. As the most detailed widely applicable and legally binding of the SEA laws considered, it has inevitably been subject to extensive commentary and detailed guidance, and, as such, Chapter 10 is undoubtedly the most significant of all the chapters in this book. It builds on the previous chapter as the SEA Directive has very close procedural links with the EIA Directive and other horizontal directives.[1] It also relates very closely to the next chapter, which examines related EC laws. Both Chapter 9 and Chapter 11 must therefore be closely considered when reading Chapter 10.

SEA is a means of integrating environmental protection into all EC policies, especially when applied beyond plan and programme levels of decision making. When the EC, or a majority of the MS, ratifies the SEA Protocol there are likely to be moves to ensure the application of the SEA Directive to policy and legislative proposals, as the Commission IA process[2] does currently with EC proposals.[3] The analysis of the SEA Directive's procedural provisions considers similarities and differences with the SEA Protocol and the potential legal implications of particular provisions; links with the Aarhus Convention and the directives outlined in Chapter 9 are also examined. As stated, Chapter 11 examines the other EC laws that relate to the SEA Directive or include elements of SEA, notably the Habitats and Wild Birds Directives, the Water Framework Directive and the Structural Funds Regulations. For structural and practical reasons, other than in passing, the current chapter does not consider these links here in detail.

Historical overview

Council Directive 2001/42/EC on the assessment of the effects of certain plans and programmes on the environment (SEA Directive) was adopted on 27 June 2001.[4] The SEA Directive contains 20 recitals, 15 articles and 2 annexes. It has many similarities with the process stages of the EIA Directive discussed in Chapter 9, notably screening, scoping, reporting, consultation and participation, decision making and monitoring. It has generated significant interest in the literature in advance and since its adoption, in particular, since its transposition date of 21 July 2004, by which time all MS were expected to have introduced implementing legislation. This interest is ongoing as practical implementation continues, the anticipated SEA Directive review is prepared by the Commission,[5] and further ratifications of the SEA Protocol are made.

The SEA Directive has its origins in consideration given to assessment of strategic proposals in the discussion of the original EIA Directive. In reporting to the Commission on EIA in the 1970s, consultants Lee and Wood (1976) felt that project EIA should be the 'first stage of a European EIA system which would eventually encompass policies and plans, once more than rudimentary experience of this type of assessment had been gained' (Wood, 1995, p33). Wathern (1988, p201) comments on the failure of the Commission to give effect to the recommendations of Lee and Wood, the limited focus on project EIA at the time of the adoption of the EIA Directive and the prospects for EIA if restrained in this way:

> *It is unlikely that they envisaged this first meagre step taking a decade. With publication of the final directive [in 1985] it is clear that the attempt to commit the member states to further directives containing provisions for EIA in plan making and policy formulation have failed. It is clear that a Community preventive environmental policy will not be achieved using this device.*[6]

Dalal-Clayton and Sadler (2005, p54) date the initial commitment to preparing the SEA Directive to 1987, with the first stated intention to also include the assessment of policy proposals. Feldmann et al (2001, p205) refer to the first report on the application and effectiveness of project EIA by the Commission (1993) as an important trigger, which demonstrated that assessment of projects was simply too late if effects and alternatives were not to be pre-empted by earlier decisions. The Fifth Environmental Action Programme, 'Towards Sustainability' (Commission of the European Communities, 1992), is cited by Sheate (2003a, p331) and Kläne and Albrecht (2005, pp20–21) as providing a rationale for the SEA proposal, as this stated unequivocally that: 'Given the role of achieving sustainable development, it seems logical, if not essential, to apply an assessment of the environmental implications of all relevant polices, plans and programmes'.[7]

However, opposition from many MS ensured that a proposal for a directive was still some way off. Sheate (2003a, p333) emphasizes that (despite the failings of the EIA Directive identified) any SEA proposal was to remain separate from the amendments made to the EIA Directive. He refers to two drafts in the early 1990s that were abandoned at the Edinburgh Heads of Government Summit in 1992 as a result of the UK veto (see Černy and Sheate, 1992). By the time a draft was publicly consulted on in 1995, all reference to policies had been removed. An agreed draft directive was therefore not finalized until the end of 1996 (Commission of the European Communities, 1996; von Seht and Wood, 1998; Feldmann, 2001), a decade after the initial commitment was made. This was in part as a result of positive experiences of several MS with SEA at a national level[8], together with support from the Parliament and NGOs (Feldmann et al, 2001 p205). As with discussions on the EIA Directive, there remained considerable opposition from many MS, including the UK, which attempted to limit plans and programmes to be assessed to town and country plans and programmes.[9]

In October 1998 an amended proposal was put before the Parliament and significant revisions were made resulting in an amended version of the draft directive being released (Commission of the European Communities, 1998). Importantly, amendments were made that resulted in town and country planning plans and programmes being only one category rather than the defining criteria as to which plans and programmes would be affected.[10] Discussion on the proposed SEA Directive benefited from the context of other SEA activity across the EC, in particular, provisions in the Habitats Directive, Structural Funds Regulations and the transEuropean networks,[11] the first two considered in Chapter 11 (Feldmann et al, 2001, p204; Kläne and Albrecht, 2005, p23).

Kläne and Albrecht (2005) conclude that between 1989 and 1996 about six different alternative proposals for the SEA Directive were considered, leading up to the adoption of the 'common position' by the Environment Ministers of the MS in December 1999.[12] Despite efforts of the Parliament to apply the Directive to as broad a range of plans and programmes as possible, they describe the 1999 common position reached as the 'lowest common denominator', with the exclusion of many plans and programmes in the 'trimmed version', which was unanimously agreed and formally adopted by the MS on 30 March 2000 (p24). However, the Parliament only approved this on 6 September 2000 subject to amendment, on which the Commission gave its opinion on 16 October 2000. In the conciliation process that began on 27 February 2001 most of the Council's positions were carried. Yet inclusion of a monitoring provision, found in Article 10 of the Directive, appears to have been the most significant of the Parliament's required changes, made possible by the changes to decision making as a result of the Amsterdam Treaty. Kläne and Albrecht (2005, p24) comment:

> the delegation of the European Parliament succeeded in some point[s]... in particular the idea of monitoring (Art. 10 SEA Directive), which was proposed by the European Parliament with the argument, that conservation of the environment is often agreed upon, but the realisation is rarely controlled. This success is owed [to] the entry into force of the Amsterdam Treaty which strengthened the position of the European Parliament in co-decision procedures.

On 31 May 2001, the Parliament adopted the Directive and on 5 June 2001, the Council adopted the Directive. It was published in the Official Journal on 21 July 2001, from when it entered into force, with MS having until 21 July 2004 to transpose the Directive into their national legislation and give effect to it.

Legal basis and effect

The legal basis of the SEA Directive is set out in the first recital to the Preamble as being both Article 174 (environmental protection) and Article 6 (environmental integration and sustainable development) of the TEC. As seen in Chapter 8, Article 175(1) enables the Council and Parliament to take action to achieve the objectives established by Article 174, in accordance with the co-decision procedure with qualified majority voting. The only exceptions are the derogations under Article 175(2), which include provisions of a fiscal nature and measures concerning town and country planning, land use (excepting waste management and general measures) and water management, in which case the cooperation procedure with unanimity is required. Although there was some debate over the application of Article 175(2) to the SEA Directive proposal, since Article 175(2) had not come into force at the time of the enactment of the SEA Directive, it was not possible to base the SEA Directive upon it (Kläne and Albrecht, 2005, n1, p18). Nevertheless, as the SEA Directive concerned additional matters to the measures included in Article 175(2), several MS concluded that Article 175(1) was in any event more appropriate, which ensured potentially easier approval for the SEA Directive than if Article 175(2) had been required, although, in the circumstances, it made little difference.[13]

The adoption of future measures under Article 175(2) TEC still requires unanimity however, and despite the legal basis for the adoption of the SEA Directive being Article 175(1), it is entirely possible that future amendments to it or consolidation with the EIA Directive, following ratification of the SEA Protocol and/or reviews undertaken by the Commission may be under Article 175(2), will need a unanimous vote. This will undoubtedly make it more difficult to achieve future changes to the SEA Directive, although if amendments are needed because of the ratification by the EU of the SEA Protocol, they may be harder politically, if not legally, to resist.[14]

The argument that unanimity in accordance with Article 175(2) may be needed for future amendment of the SEA Directive or consolidation with the EIA Directive is given added weight following the decision of the ECJ in *Spain v Council*.[15] In that case, the Court took the view that future EC measures that sought to introduce regional or urban management plans that regulated an MS territory, land or water resources would need unanimity in Council, as indeed would major infrastructure projects of relevance such as motorways, dams and reservoirs. This was because they would affect the use of a limited resource (as a quantitative measure), of which it was decided that MS should be able to retain a veto over. If quality were the issue, then a qualified majority was all that was needed, as in the case of the adoption of the Water Framework Directive. In this particular context, with regard to the EIA and SEA Directives, Davies (2004, pp17–18) therefore emphasizes:

> *It might now be argued that any further measures of this nature or amendments to the Environmental Impact Assessment Directive or Strategic Environmental Assessment Directive will henceforth require the unanimous support of the Member States in so far as they affect management plans or strategic projects concerning the infrastructure of a Member State.*[16]

With regard to the potential direct and indirect effect of the SEA Directive, Chapters 7 and 8 contain discussion generally, and Chapter 9 provides analysis specifically with regard to the EIA Directive, much of which is relevant here. Without commenting on specific provisions of the SEA Directive at this point (which are outlined below), it can be concluded that there will be no horizontal direct effect of the SEA Directive so that individuals will not be able to rely on provisions against other individuals for the underlying reason that a directive is addressed to an MS. However, provided provisions of the SEA Directive are unconditional, sufficiently precise, can be relied on by interested individuals and the time limit for transposition has passed, it is quite possible that they can have vertical direct effect, allowing individuals to require an MS, or an 'emanation of a state', such as a privatized utility company, to enforce them.

The *Kraaijeveld* and *Wells* decisions by the ECJ (see Chapter 9) provide authority for this proposition in connection with procedural provisions of the EIA Directive. Until the SEA Directive is itself tested in the courts, these decisions should have persuasive influence on the MS, and once the SEA Directive is considered by the courts they are likely to be applied. Sheate et al (2005, pp17–18) highlight the relevance of the EIA case law to the SEA Directive. Particular cases are referred to below in discussing specific procedural provisions.

With regard to the indirect effect of the SEA Directive, or 'sympathetic interpretation', national provisions must be interpreted in accordance with EC law and national provisions that conflict with EC law must not be applied, which would mean that failings in transposition must, 'as far as possible', be rectified by national courts and other public bodies that exercise administrative functions. Given the possibility that non-compliant national law could still prevail if the national body considered the MS was substantially compliant, in this case it may be necessary for an individual who has suffered loss or damage as a result of the breach of the MS to attempt to seek a remedy in damages against the MS under the authority of *Francovich* (see Chapter 7). As seen in Chapter 9, Tromans and Fuller (2003, pp39–44) consider that a court would not allow an individual to claim damages in cases dealing with the EIA Directive because its provisions are procedural in nature and do not intend to confer substantive rights on individuals that can be linked to any damage suffered. However, the *Wells* decision (and changes to the EIA Directive as a result of the Participation Directive) may have changed this conclusion, which would also have implications for the similar procedural provisions of the SEA Directive.

Objectives

The objective of the SEA Directive, as set out in Article 1, 'is to provide for a high level of protection of the environment and to contribute to the integration of environmental considerations into the preparation and adoption of plans and programmes with a view to promoting sustainable development'. Environmental protection, integration and sustainable development are all key policies of the EC, as explained in Chapter 8 in connection with general principles (integration) and environmental objectives (those forming part of sustainable development, including environmental protection). Environmental principles are also discussed in Chapter 8, including the precautionary, preventive and polluter pays principles. Kläne and Albrecht (2005, pp18–21) discuss these in relation to the SEA Directive, as well as the principle of public participation that now features strongly following implementation of the Aarhus Convention (discussed below in relation to specific procedural provisions). As will be seen, the emphasis on, and relationship between, environmental protection, integration and sustainable development has changed over time largely as a result of outcomes agreed at the European Council.[17]

As outlined in Chapter 1 and elsewhere, and as in other areas of environmental law it is also important to be aware of the words used in specific legal provisions for SEA such as the SEA Directive, including both the objectives and the context. Some provisions may create powers rather than duties, which are discretionary rather than mandatory, and to which a legal challenge in administrative law (typically judicial review in common law jurisdictions) will prove difficult provided a decision maker has exercised that discretion appropriately. The use of the word 'promote' in Article 1, for example, provides significant discretion especially when linked to a principle such as sustainable development, which, as seen in Chapter 3, is vague and subject to differences of opinion, even given policy guidance as to its meaning. The meaning of 'high level of protection' has been considered by the ECJ to not have to be the highest technically possible, especially as Article 174(2) permits taking costs and benefits into account.[18]

Environmental protection

As stated, Recital 1 of the Directive refers to Article 174 of the TEC, which provides that EC policy on the environment is to contribute to the preservation, protection and improvement of the quality of the environment, the protection of human health and the prudent and rational utilization of natural resources and that it is based on the precautionary principle. The legal meaning of this was considered in Chapter 8, entailing significant discretion as to how that contribution is made and how environmental preservation, protection and enhancement is balanced alongside human health and utilization of natural resources. While the precautionary principle is the basis of such a determination, the position of this in international law, especially since the *Gabčíkovo-Nagymaros* case (see Chapter 3), remains uncertain; in European law, the *Peralta* decision (see Chapter 8) held that principles such as the precautionary principle provide only guidance on the direction of EC environmental policy, suggesting legal action for failing to take it into account may not succeed.

Annex I(e) of the Directive also refers to the international legal context, stating that the environmental report that is required under Article 5 must outline 'the environmental protection objectives established at international, Community or Member State level, which are relevant to the plan or programme and the way those objectives and any environmental considerations have been taken into account during its preparation'. As Marsden and De Mulder (2005, p53) comment: 'This is significant because it highlights that Community environmental policy cannot be viewed in a vacuum; rather it is subject to international law and policy, where relevant'.[19] This is also seen in Recitals 3 and 7 of the Directive, which recognize the role of SEA in international law. Recital 7 refers to the Espoo Convention, which was discussed in Chapter 4, and Recital 3 refers to the CBD (discussed in Chapter 6), which requires parties to integrate as far as possible and appropriate the conservation and sustainable use of biological diversity into relevant sectoral and cross-sectoral plans and programmes. As seen above and discussed further below, environmental policy integration has a key role to play in the promotion of both environmental protection and sustainable development.

Environmental policy integration

The integration principle outlined in Chapter 8 is of clear relevance to EIA and SEA and both are tools of environmental policy integration (EPI). SEA especially, with its focus on evaluating the environmental consequences of strategic proposals aims to contribute to the decision making process information that can enable environmental protection to be integrated into strategic proposals, with the stated overall objective of also contributing to sustainable development. The relationship between EPI and the SEA Directive has been considered in detail by Feldmann et al (2001), Sheate (2003a, 2003b, 2004) and Sheate et al (2003). Kläne and Albrecht (2005, p21) comment on the relationship as set out in the current Sixth EAP:

> *One of the mentioned political focal points of the Sixth Environmental Action Programme is the integration of environmental policy into other political fields (section 7.1). Therefore the SEA Directive, though enacted before the enforcement of the Sixth Environmental Action Programme, fits perfect[ly] to this subject, and it can be assumed that further political fields will be provided with different assessment methods.*

Recital 1 of the Directive also refers to Article 6 of the TEC, which, as seen in Chapter 8, provides that environmental protection requirements are to be integrated into the definition of EC policies and activities with a view to promoting sustainable development. Recital 1 therefore provides the policy framework for SEA to play a role towards sustainability. In basing itself firmly on the precautionary principle, the EC policy on the environment also recognizes that uncertainty characterizes any policy and planning decision.

The Charter of Fundamental Rights of the EU was proclaimed by the Council, Commission and European Parliament in December 2000 and is designed to strengthen the protection of fundamental rights. It is addressed to the institutions and bodies of the EC and the MS when implementing EC law. Article 37 of the Charter states that a 'high level of environmental protection and the improvement in the quality of the environment must be integrated into the policies of the Union and ensured in accordance with the principle of sustainable development'. Davies (2004) discusses the possible legal effect of this if the provisions of the Charter are integrated into the TEU in the future. He comments (pp57–58):

> *Let us assume for the sake of argument that Article 37 is indeed attributed legally binding status. The provision could be said to add much needed definition to the integration principle in the sense that not only must environmental protection requirements be integrated into the definition and interpretation of all Community policies in accordance with Article 6 EC, but the level of integration must additionally afford a high level of environmental protection. It might also be said to place an onus on the ECJ to assess whether relevant policies afford this level of protection. However, it would still be highly unlikely that a policy approach could be made the subject of a successful judicial review on the basis it fails to provide a high level of protection when one bears in mind the broad discretion of Community institutions in adopting policy, and the ambiguous nature of the concept of a high level of protection.*

The Charter of Fundamental Rights will be legally binding when the MS have ratified the Lisbon Reform Treaty. A new Article 6 of the TEU states that it will have the same status as the Treaties, although it will not extend the competences of the EU in any way and its text will not appear in the TEU. The Charter was formally proclaimed on 12 December 2007, and a Protocol introduces specific measures for the UK and Poland, establishing exceptions regarding the jurisdiction of the ECJ and national courts for the protection of rights recognized by the Charter.

Article 4(2) of the Directive stipulates that: 'The requirements of this Directive shall either be integrated into existing procedures in Member States for the adoption of plans and programmes or incorporated in procedures established to comply with this Directive'. From a formal perspective and based on efficiency considerations it is clear that the 'integration track' in Article 4(2) offers advantages. De Mulder (2001, p19) states that: 'the SEA Directive is 'an important step towards the realisation of a concrete integration approach'. He draws attention to the integration of environmental concerns in planning processes that the SEA Directive will contribute towards and states that 'a more integrated system of planning means that environmental criteria are incorporated throughout the planning process, which could help to implement the concept of sustainable development' (pp14–15). The question remains to what extent the opportunity has been used by the MS in transposing and applying the SEA Directive, which the report may demonstrate, albeit as limited by the short period of application. Marsden and De Mulder (2005, p54) comment:

> [T]his approach does not guarantee an effective outcome with respect to the integration of environmental considerations. Communications between experts at EU-level meetings indicate that the ongoing discussions on preparing draft SEA legislation in the Member States are very much about the tension between the environment administration and the other policy fields regarding the assurance of an effective SEA process within the existing planning procedures.

Sustainable development

Recital 2 of the Directive refers to the Commission Communication (1992) known as the Fifth Environment Action Programme: *Towards Sustainability – a European Community Programme of Policy and Action in Relation to the Environment and Sustainable Development*, as supplemented by the Council decision on its review[20] which, as cited above, affirmed the importance of SEA. The Sixth EAP also considers SEA (and EIA)[21] requiring the full and effective use and implementation of EIA and SEA as one of the further efforts for the integration of environmental protection requirements into the preparation, definition and implementation of EC policies and activities (Article 3, paragraph 3). Article 1 of the SEA Directive, in setting out its objectives, recognizes the importance of the sustainable development context provided by Articles 174 and 6 of the TEC, as cited in the recitals. Sustainability is also incorporated into Article 2 of the TEC and Article 2 of the TEU.

The EU Sustainable Development Strategy is also an important part of EU environmental policy, adopted since the SEA Directive (OPOCE, 2002). Under this sustainable development is defined as the method to meet the needs of the present generation without compromising those of future generations (p9). Economic development, environment protection and social justice are linked, with a focus on long term issues, connections between different policy areas and complexity. As sustainable development means improving the quality of policy making, it is closely linked to existing EU procedures for EA, Better Regulation and Governance (Kläne and Albrecht, 2005, pp19 and 27–28).

Procedural provisions

The SEA Directive contains provisions that are mainly of a procedural nature. These are in many instances similar and/or related to the EIA Directive, with requirements for screening, scoping, consultation, monitoring and decision making.[22] Article 2(b) defines EA as 'the preparation of an environmental report, the carrying out of consultations, the taking into account of the environmental report and the results of the consultations in decision-making and the provision of information on the decision in accordance with Articles 4 to 9'. Sheate (2003a, p335) comments on this as follows: 'Other than not relating to policies [or legislation], this definition in conjunction with Arts 4 to 9, would appear to compare quite favourably with a comprehensive definition of SEA that combines the essential parts of two well-known definitions'. The only provisions that contain substantive legal rights in the Directive, which can potentially be enforced by those concerned, are those that deal with public participation. The relationship between the ELD (considered in Chapter 9) and the SEA Directive may potentially also invoke the issue of liability for breach of the SEA Directive, as this is also a substantive legal provision.

The jurisprudence of the ECJ on the EIA Directive and related provisions is extensive, and much of this is directly relevant to the SEA Directive given the close relationship between the laws. The meaning of 'authority', 'project', 'plan', 'development consent', 'significant environmental effects', 'environmental effects', 'cumulative effects' and 'likely to have' have all been subject to interpretation. The implications of exceeding or preventing the exercise of discretion or failing to comply with requirements for transboundary impacts, and the flexibility available to decide on detailed public participation requirements and access to information have also all been considered by the ECJ. The text that follows considers many of these matters with reference to previous and forthcoming chapters to avoid unnecessary duplication where possible.

Screening

The mandatory application of the Directive is limited, but is closely related to the EIA Directive, as explained in the official SEA Directive Guidance (Reps of the MS/CEC, 2003).[23] Until the ECJ considers the SEA Directive explicitly, this guidance document is the most authoritative statement available to the MS about implementation.[24] Not only are policy and legislative proposals excluded (Sheate, 2003a, p342; Jendroska and Stec, 2003, p108; Albrecht, 2005, p40; Marsden and De Mulder, 2005, p53),[25] but there are strict criteria established in Articles 2 and 3 that emphasize that plans and programmes must be formally required and be prepared for listed sectors (which must, in turn, set the framework for the future development consent of projects under the EIA Directive), or must be plans that are required to be assessed under the Habitats Directive (in an English context, see, for example, Tromans and Machart, 2001; Robinson and Elvin, 2004).

In total, 66 paragraphs of the Guidance (Reps of the MS/CEC, 2003, pp5–20) are concerned with the application, or 'scope', of the SEA Directive, explaining the detailed extent of these vital provisions that indicate whether an assessment is mandatory or not. As para 3.1 outlines:

Article 2 sets out certain characteristics which plans and programmes must possess for the Directive to apply to them. Article 3 then sets out rules for determining which of those plans and programmes are likely to have significant effects on the environment and must therefore be subject to environmental assessment.

Without dwelling too greatly on what may quite accurately be termed the 'legal plumbing' of the SEA Directive, some detailed comment is inevitably needed.[26] To assist

This diagram is intended as a guide to the criteria for application of the Directive to plans and programmes (PPs). It has no legal status.

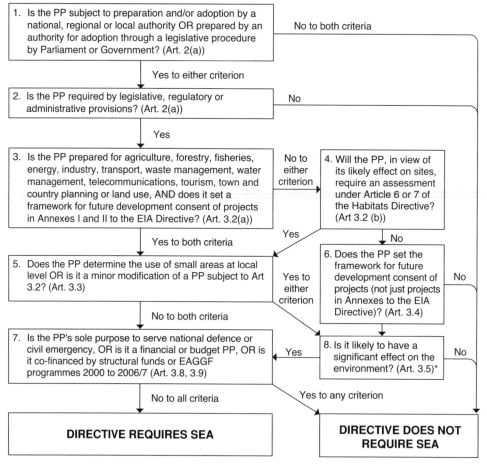

*The Directive requires Member States to determine whether plans or programmes in this category are likely to have significant environmental effects. These determinations may be made on a case by case basis and/or by specifying types of plan or programme.

Source: ODPM, 2005, p13

Figure 10.1 *Criteria for application to plans and programmes*

with this, a flowchart has been reproduced as Figure 10.1, setting out the screening criteria. The text that follows relates to but does not duplicate the flowchart precisely as other detailed matters must necessarily be discussed.

First, plans and programmes must be prepared and/or adopted by a public body *and* must be required by a legislative, regulatory or administrative provision. Other than privatized authorities (see *Foster v British Gas*),[27] the Directive generally places no obligations on private bodies (Reps of MS/CEC, 2003, para 3.13) and is therefore distinct from the EIA Directive, which has always applied to both public and private project proponents.[28] Albrecht (2005, p42) nonetheless raises some concerns in the German context regarding plans prepared by private parties and adopted by public bodies, giving the examples of land use plans under the German Federal Building Law and the Remediation Plan prepared under the German Federal Soil Protection Act. It is likely that if these plans are prepared in the context of a legislative requirement imposed on a public authority, and the involvement of the private body is merely on a consultancy basis, then the Directive would apply. If, alternatively, the plans are prepared pursuant to legislative requirements imposed on private proponents, then it is unlikely that they would be subject to the SEA Directive because the definition of an authority would not have been satisfied. The other possibility is if the authority is nonetheless required to adopt the private plan, in which case the SEA Directive could still apply.

Formality is always a clear requirement of the preparation/adoption and the provision mandating the proposals; as such plans and programmes prepared voluntarily are not subject to the SEA Directive, although MS always have the choice whether to apply its provisions more extensively if they wish. A legislative power such as '*may* prepare a plan or programme', must therefore be clearly distinguished from a legislative duty such as '*must* prepare a plan or programme', or indeed a decision to prepare a plan or programme where no power or duty exists (para 3.15).

While administrative provisions may, in some instances, not be legally binding, if a plan or programme is required by them, then they may also be subject to the SEA Directive (para 3.16) if they also set the framework for development consent. Provisions can therefore be required by either the legislative or executive branch of government, at national, regional or local levels (para 3.14), which brings considerable flexibility and also comprehensive application, at least to the provision in question. *Kraaijeveld* (see Chapter 9) is cited as authority for the proposition that a directive should be given a wide scope and broad purpose, the guidance suggesting that 'Member States are advised to adopt a similar approach in considering whether an act is considered a plan or programme falling within the scope of Directive 2001/42/EC' (para 3.4).

Albrecht (2005) gives examples of German plans to emphasize that the decision as to whether a plan or programme is formally required is not an easy one. Plans for federal highways are based on the German Federal Highways Act, and although they are not directly required by that law, the existence of the plan is the condition for further development plans and measures. She therefore concludes (pp39–40) that such plans and programmes should be assessed 'because otherwise the basic primary plan is not subject to SEA but the later (and depending on the primary) plan has to be assessed'. She also concludes that: 'Member States should draw a wide circle of plans and programmes which have to be assessed, to avoid a violation against the SEA Directive by not including all relevant plans and programmes to the transposition acts'.

Second, plans and programmes themselves are not defined any further than this, meaning that what is defined as a plan or programme for the purposes of Articles 2 and 3 depends on what Articles 2 and 3 say and not what a plan or programme may be called.[29] In some jurisdictions therefore, what may be termed a plan may in another jurisdiction be thought of as a programme and vice versa; a 'strategy' or 'guideline' may also be a plan or programme if it meets the requirements of the Directive. Albrecht, (2005, p40) and Sheate, (2004, p120) refer to 'strategies' in Scotland as being beyond the obligations of the SEA Directive as they encompass policy matters. This is considered in the implementation section at the end of this chapter.[30] Albrecht (2005, p39) also refers to German law where the terms 'plans and programmes' are not used in a standardized way, despite the tendency for plans to be more detailed than programmes. However, if there is any doubt as to whether to assess them or not, the *Kraaijeveld* decision on what amounts to a *project* should be specifically applied to the word project where it appears in the SEA Directive (Reps of the MS/CEC, 2003, paras 3.29 and 3.30), and the wide scope/broad purpose approach to what amounts to a plan or programme should therefore be applied to avoid being in breach of the application of the Directive. Sheate (2003a, p345) further cites the *Bund Naturshutz* decision in this respect, in which the ECJ commented:

> *the purpose of the directive should not be lost by the projects which should be subject to an environmental impact assessment being given a form which renders an environmental impact assessment meaningless. The Member States must ensure that the obligation to carry out an environmental impact assessment is not circumvented by a definition that is over-strict or otherwise inappropriate, in the light of the purpose of the directive.*[31]

Third, plans and programmes include modifications to them, so that amendments to land use plans, for example, are to be treated in the same way under the SEA Directives as if a new plan were to be prepared. Modifications to *projects* prepared *under* the plan or programme would be subject to the requirements of the EIA Directive or related provision (such as the Habitats Directive) rather than the SEA Directive. The definition of plans and programmes also includes those that are co-financed by the EC (such as those undertaken in the transport, regional, economic and social development sectors). In some of these cases, other legislative requirements (such as the Structural Funds Regulations)[32] must also be complied with (Reps of the MS/CEC, 2003, para 3.8). The relationship between the SEA Directive and these other EC laws is examined in Chapter 11.

Fourth, an environmental assessment must be carried out for plans and programmes that are likely to have significant environmental effects *and* the plan or programme must also set the framework for future development consent of projects under the EIA Directive, either automatically because they are listed sectors (Article 3(2)(a)), or because an MS has decided to assess them regardless (Article 3(4)).[33] The sectors listed are: agriculture, forestry, fisheries, energy, industry, transport, waste management, water management, telecommunications, tourism, town and country planning or land use.[34] Article 3(2)(b) further states that an EA must also be carried out for all plans and programmes that require an assessment in accordance with the Habitats Directive (see Chapter 11).

The meaning of '*likely to have significant environmental effects*' is an important consideration throughout the SEA Directive. Para 3.50 of the SEA Directive Guidance (Reps of MS/CEC, 2003) states that: 'the use of the word "likely" suggests that the environmental effects to be considered are those which can be expected with a reasonable degree of probability'. In *Commission v Ireland* (see Chapter 9) the ECJ stated that 'a project is likely to have significant effects where by reason of its nature, there is a risk that it will cause a substantial or irreversible change in those environmental factors, irrespective of its size'.[35] The meaning of significant environmental effects was also considered in *Commission v Ireland* where the Court stated that: 'Even a small-scale project can have significant effects on the environment if it is in a location where the environmental factors set out in Article 3 of the [EIA] Directive, such as fauna and flora, soil, water, climate or cultural heritage, are sensitive to the slightest alteration' (see para 3.60).[36] Unlike the EIA Directive, the SEA Directive makes no reference to direct and indirect effects, which, while it has caused concern (Sheate, 2003a, p344), does not mean that indirect effects will necessarily not be required to be assessed in all instances, given the test of significance.

Annex II of the Directive outlines the criteria for determining significant effects, where SEA under the Directive is discretionary under Article 3(4). Sheate (2003a, pp336 and 343) contrasts this 'catch-all category' with the EIA Directive, which has resulted in several development proposals not requiring EIA because they are not within one of the Annex lists in the Directive. This is where the plan or programme is not within a listed sector but still sets the framework for development consent of projects; alternatively it is within a listed sector but is not listed in one of the Annexes of the EIA Directive (Reps of MS/CEC, 2003, para 3.37). In both cases, to comply with Article 3(5), the MS must decide if significant effects are likely in accordance with *all* of the criteria set out (para 3.45), although they may also consider additional criteria if they wish (para 3.49). Specified criteria include 'the relevance of the plan or programme for the integration of environmental considerations in particular with a view to promoting sustainable development' and 'the relevance of the plan or programme for the implementation of Community legislation on the environment' (for example, plans and programmes linked to waste management and water protection).

The criteria can either be applied on a case by case basis or by specifying types of plans or programmes, or by a combination of both approaches (see paras 3.40–3.42). The SEA Directive Guidance emphasizes that the power in Article 3(5) to specify types of plans and programmes must not be used to exempt entire classes of plans and programmes from assessment. There remains a need to exercise discretion in these cases to avoid an administrative law challenge. *Kraaijeveld* is again cited in this regard, as is the case of *WWF v Bozen*, also considered in Chapter 9. Para 3.43 comments:

> *exclusion from environmental assessment may not be justified in many cases. It might well be that at the outset not enough information is available at the plan or programme level to be sure that none of the plans or programmes in the proposed class will have significant environmental effects. Furthermore, care would be needed to avoid pre-empting decisions on the application of the Directive to future plans and programmes which might not share all the characteristics of the class in question. For example, changes in the law might create new plans and programmes which would need consideration in order to determine whether the Directive applied to them.*

The meaning of '*set the framework* for future development consent' is not defined in the Directive, but is also an important provision needing interpretation. Sheate (2003a, p342) gives a UK example of the type of plan or programme that may be considered to set the framework for future development consent as the national and regional water resource strategies produced by the Environment Agency of England and Wales, 'which set the policy context in which future project decisions will be taken, e.g. new reservoirs, water abstraction, and water transfer schemes, all of which will be subject to the EIA Directive'. In some instances, however, plans and programmes may set the framework for future development consent indirectly, which has been acknowledged by the Commission (Sheate, 2003a, note 55).[37] The SEA Directive Guidance (Reps of the MS/CEC, 2003, para 3.23) interprets the expression generally as follows:

> *The words would normally mean that the plan or programme contains criteria or conditions which guide the way the consenting authority decides an application for development consent. Such criteria could place limits on the type of activity or development which is permitted in a given area; or they could contain conditions which must be met by the applicant if permission is to be granted; or they could be designed to preserve certain characteristics of the area concerned (such as the mixture of land uses which promotes the economic vitality of the area).*

The meaning of '*development consent*' was interpreted in the *Wells* decision (see Chapter 9) in relation to the EIA Directive. Of particular relevance to the SEA Directive is the emphasis by the ECJ on assessment being carried out at the first stage in the process if possible, suggesting that where plans or programmes are located in a tiered hierarchy, assessment of the highest level proposal should always take place first, consistent with SEA theory and good practice (see Sheate et al, 2005, p18). Paras 3.24–3.28 of the SEA Directive Guidance (Reps of the MS/CEC, 2003) cite the examples set out in Annex II of the SEA Directive. Land use plans are a particularly clear example that contain criteria for determining what kind of specific development can take place. Others may be far less clear, and in such instances there will be a need to consider carefully (on a case by case basis) whether the framework for development consent is set. Some examples also pertain only to certain MS and not others, so generalization must be avoided while comparisons will inevitably be made. Para 3.27, for example, refers to the plans and programmes that in some MS establish legally binding conditions with which future development consent must conform, and para 3.31 refers to town and country planning plans and land use plans, which have different meanings in the MS. Above all, what should be recognized is that development consent is not limited to a grant of planning permission, but can encompass many different types of licenses, permissions and permits.

Fifth, plans and programmes that determine the use of small areas at local level and minor modifications to plans and programmes as in Article 3(2) also require environmental assessment if an MS determines they are likely to have significant environmental effects. The meaning of *small areas, local level* and *minor modifications* is not defined in the SEA Directive. In relation to size, the SEA Directive Guidance suggests that differences between the MS mean that interpretation must be on a case by case basis (Reps of the MS/CEC, 2003, para 3.33). 'Local level' produces similar issues albeit that it suggests there is a contrast between national and regional levels. Although the Guidance expresses concern that since in some MS local authority areas can be very large 'and an exemption for the whole of such an area would be a major loophole in the scope of application', the jurisprudence of the ECJ in relation to the exercise of discretion and giving effect broadly to EA provisions would indicate such an approach would be unlikely to succeed. The SEA Directive Guidance suggests that a general definition of 'minor modifications' would be unlikely to serve any useful purpose and that rather, it should be 'considered in the context of the plan or programme which is being modified' (para 3.36). The important factor is the likelihood of significant environmental effects, not the size of the modification, as even small modifications may produce significant effects in some cases.

Sixth, certain plans and programmes are excluded from the SEA Directive, in accordance with Article 3(8). These are specified to be plans and programmes of which the *sole purpose* is to serve national defence or civil emergency, and financial or budget plans or programmes. The first exemption is indicated by the SEA Directive Guidance to be a stricter test than the EIA Directive, which, under Article 1(4), does not apply to 'projects serving national defence purposes'. However in *WWF v Bozen* that was concerned with restructuring of a military airport to allow for its commercial use, the ECJ held that the exemption under Article 1(4) was to be construed narrowly, no doubt influencing the drafting of Article 3(8) of the SEA Directive. In applying the SEA Directive exemption, it is therefore the purpose of the plan or programme that must be considered, not its effects. As to civil emergencies, the Guidance draws a distinction between plans or programmes to prevent emergencies and those to deal with emergencies. In the former case, assessments would likely be needed. Little guidance is provided on financial or budget plans or programmes, other than to say that they would include annual budgets of authorities at national, regional and local level (para 3.63). Financial plans and programmes could also include those that describe how a project is to be financed or how grants and subsidies are to be distributed (para 3.63).

Seventh, the timing of the EA is subject to Articles 4(1) and 13(3). Article 4(1) emphasizes that the assessment must be carried out during the preparation of the plan or programme and before its adoption or submission to the legislative procedure. The assessment must not be carried out after the plan or programme is finalized therefore. Article 13(3) applies the requirements to those plans and programmes formally begun after the entry into force of the Directive, regardless of whether they were required at that time by national law or not, unless they were begun earlier but not adopted or submitted to the legislative procedure until over two years later, in which case an MS can decide and must inform the public of this.[38] However, the SEA Directive Guidance suggests that in the latter case where only minor work was begun on the plan or programme before the date of the entry into force of the Directive, an assessment would still be appropriate. Sheate (2003a, p339) correctly identifies these transitional arrangements as a way of attempting to avoid the implementation problems that beset the introduction of the EIA Directive, and known as 'projects in the pipeline' (see Chapter 9).

Scoping

Article 5(1) outlines the terms of reference for the report, which must identify, describe and evaluate matters including the 'reasonable alternatives' to the likely significant effects on the environment of 'implementing' the plan or programme, 'taking into account the objectives and the geographical scope of the plan or programme'. The terms of reference or scope of the report are to be determined in conjunction with the authorities designated by the MS as consultees under Article 6(3); the public have no role in this process. While the Directive does not specify who is responsible for preparing the report, the SEA Directive Guidance indicates that it would likely be the proponent (Reps of the MS/CEC, 2003, para 5.8). The meaning of *implementation* of the plan or programme is not indicated in the Directive, and the Guidance states that it depends to a large extent on the 'character of the plan or programme' (para 5.9). While not entirely helpful, it goes on to emphasize (para 5.10) that 'an assessment has to focus on the part of implementation that is likely to have significant environmental effects'. This would seem to be an area for potential legal challenges, especially where implementation of a plan or programme cannot be reduced to the implementation of specific single projects (para 5.9), and unless all parts of implementation are studied, potentially significant effects may be ignored (para 5.10).

Annex I provides more detail on what the environmental report must contain (Reps of the MS/CEC, 2003, paras 5.19–5.30). Annex I(h) includes a requirement to provide an 'outline of the reasons for selecting the alternatives dealt with, and a description of how the assessment was undertaken including any difficulties (such as technical deficiencies or lack of know-how) encountered in compiling the required information'. Article 5(3) suggests that relevant information available on the environmental effects of the plans and programmes obtained at other levels of decision making or through other EC legislation (see Chapter 11) may be used for providing this information.

The Directive does not specify whether the report is a separate document to the plan or programme or not, although it must be a more comprehensive provision of information than under the EIA Directive (Sheate, 2003a, p335; Albrecht, 2005, pp46–47). Article 2(c) merely defines the report as a part of the plan or programme documentation with a specified content. The SEA Directive Guidance does, however, suggest that if it is integrated into the plan or programme documentation (in accordance with Article 4(2)), then 'it should be clearly distinguishable as a separate part'. Another more controversial possibility is that the report could be part of a sustainability assessment, outlining environmental, social and economic effects. Para 5.5 of the SEA Directive Guidance suggests this, 'provided it fully met the requirements of the Directive'. The suggestion is controversial because it cuts through the heart of what many believe SEA should be concerned with, which is a proactive tool for environmental protection, rather than a means of balancing environmental, social and economic concerns. Arguably, it may not be possible to 'fully me[e]t the requirements of the Directive' if the objective of a 'high level of protection' for the environment is compromised through such a process of dilution (see Chapter 1).

The Directive does not specify what is meant by a *reasonable alternative* to a plan or programme. The objectives and geographical scope of the plan or programme must clearly be considered, and it is likely that different alternatives within the plan or programme will be assessed as a means of fulfilling the stated objectives. As the SEA Directive Guidance states: 'Ideally, though the Directive does not require that, the final draft plan or programme would be the one which best contributes to the objectives set out in Article 1' (para 5.14). What must not be done is to select inappropriate alternatives that serve the proponent's case in gaining approval, which means also that they must be alternatives that fall within the competence of the authority concerned (para 5.14).

Article 12(2) states that: 'Member States shall ensure that environmental reports are of a sufficient quality to meet the requirements of this Directive', which, in practice, will fall to the proponent authority, having regard to the provisions of Article 5 and Annex I, together with the results of consultation with other authorities and the public. If the procedural and substantive requirements of the Directive are followed, the SEA Directive Guidance concludes that a 'minimum standard' will at least have been attained (para 6.5).

Consultation, participation and information provision

Article 6 of the Directive is concerned with consultation and participation and is intended to implement Article 7 of the Aarhus Convention, which has been a significant influence on the SEA Directive.[39] Its provisions are incorporated into the SEA Directive insofar as they apply to plans and programmes covered by the Directive.[40] As seen, the definition of EA in Article 2(b) includes consultation and taking account of the results of consultation in decision making, emphasizing its importance in the overall scheme of the SEA Directive. This has largely been as a result of the driver of the Aarhus Convention, however, although as seen some commentators rightly question whether Article 7 of the Convention has been adequately transposed into Article 6 of the Directive (see Mathiesen, 2003, p46; De Mulder, 2006, p274), which would leave open the possibility of legal challenge where MS fail to transpose Article 7 correctly into their national legal systems.[41]

The Directive requires that authorities designated by MS on the basis of their specific environmental responsibilities[42] must be consulted in determining whether certain plans or programmes are to be assessed (Article 3(6)), in determining the scope and level of information to be contained within the environmental report (Article 5(4)), and on the draft plan or programme and environmental report (Article 6(2)). Article 6(3) is directed at authorities that comprise formal governmental and public authorities in an organizational capacity, rather than individual experts (Reps of the MS/CEC, 2003, para 7.11, and note 17). Mandatory involvement of these designated authorities in deciding on the terms of reference of the environmental report (Article 5(4)) is a matter not included under the EIA Directive and is therefore designed to improve on current practice.[43]

The public must also be consulted on the draft plan or programme and the environmental report (Article 6(2)), if the public is 'affected or likely to be affected by, or having an interest in, the decision-making' (Article 6(4)). The public is also defined broadly in Article 2(d) as any natural or legal person, including their associations, organizations or groups. The SEA Directive Guidance suggests that groups of individuals will be included whether they are natural or legal persons (para 7.6), meaning regardless of whether they have a separate legal identity.[44] Clearly the relevant public in each case will be different, depending on whether the decision making affects or interests the public concerned, which will have to be considered in each instance (paras 7.16–7.17). Heiland (2005, p423) indicates that it is the role of the MS to determine this, which will entail a complex assessment of who is affected or not, and who has an interest in the matter. Current national legislation in some instances does not make such distinctions, Heiland citing the example of Germany under the Federal Building Code and Spatial Planning Act (2005, p423).

Information must also be made available to the public at various stages in the process to enable the public to participate if appropriate. First, Article 3(7) provides that information on whether the plan or programme requires an SEA must be made available, including the reasons for not requiring an EA if applicable. Second, Article 6(1) provides that the environmental report and draft plan or programme must be made available. Third, once the plan or programme has been adopted, the adopted plan or programme must be made available, including measures that deal with monitoring in accordance with Article 9(1)(c). This information must also be provided to the designated authorities. Article 9 is considered in more detail later.

Article 6(5) leaves the matter of the detailed arrangements for the information to be provided and manner of consultation of the authorities and public to the MS, with no detail as to the means of information provision or consultation, which, in contrast, is included in the procedures for the EIA Directive (Reps of the MS/CEC, 2003, para 7.19) and also the SEA Protocol, which requires making information publicly available 'by public notice or other appropriate means, such as electronic media' (Jendroska and Stec, 2003, p109).[45] However, the MS are not entirely free to determine these matters. Article 6(2) requires that the authorities and the public must be given an 'early and effective opportunity within appropriate time frames to express their opinion', which needs to be specified in legislation and sufficient 'for opinions to be properly developed and formulated on lengthy, complex, contentious or far-reaching plans or programmes' (Reps of the MS/CEC, 2003, para 7.10). An MS must also ensure that whatever arrangements are put in place ensure the effectiveness of the Directive in practice (especially regarding the rights of the public), which may also entail a consideration of other related EC provisions. This was the matter for the ECJ to consider in *Commission v Ireland* (see Chapter 9), which was concerned with the comparable provision under the EIA Directive. The SEA Directive Guidance emphasizes the importance of appropriate information provision, para 7.8 commenting as follows:

> *Appropriate publicity arrangements will be needed, and the information will need to be readily accessible. Also, interpretation in the light of Article 7 in conjunction with Article 6(3) of the Aarhus Convention[46] would suggest effective dissemination either by public notice or individually as appropriate. This is true too for the information to be made available under Articles 3(7) and 9(1). In addition it might be appropriate for members of the public who have objected to a proposal to be informed individually about the decision.*

Transboundary consultations may be relevant in some cases and are dealt with in Article 7 of the SEA Directive, which contains similar provisions to the EIA Directive in accordance with the Espoo Convention, which uses the terminology 'state of origin' and 'affected state' (see Chapter 4).[47] Under Article 7(1) if a plan or programme is likely to have significant environmental effects on another MS, or the other MS so requests, the draft plan or programme and environmental report must be forwarded to the other MS before the plan or programme is adopted or submitted to the legislative procedure. Under Article 7(2), if the other MS wishes, consultations must be begun to attempt to reduce or eliminate such effects. Detailed arrangements must be agreed on consultation and information matters to ensure the affected MS has an opportunity to provide its opinion within a reasonable time frame (Article 7(3)). The SEA Directive Guidance (Reps of the MS/CEC, 2003, para 7.26) comments that existing bilateral arrangements under the Espoo Convention may be utilized for this purpose, or multilateral arrangements may be set up where needed.

Decision making

Under Article 8, the environmental report, the results of the consultation of the public and authorities (including any transboundary consultation) must be taken account of in the final preparation of the plan or programme and before its adoption or submission to the legislative procedure. This again is reflective of the Aarhus Convention requirement for due account to be taken of the outcome of the public participation. Sheate (2003a, p338) refers to the significance of taking the information into account at this time because it occurs before the decision making process, hence providing for an 'earlier public influence on the planning process than in the EIA Directive'.

Article 9(1) requires MS to make available a range of material to designated authorities, the public or another MS (where transboundary consultations have occurred). These include the adopted plan or programme; a statement summarizing how environmental considerations have been integrated into the plan or programme, the environmental report and opinions expressed have been taken account of; the reasons for choosing the adopted plan or programme, in the light of the other reasonable alternatives dealt with; and the monitoring measures decided upon. Article 9(2) provides discretion to the MS as to how the information in Article 9(1) is to be provided, although notification is expected to be similar to the EIA Directive. Unlike the EIA Directive, however, there are no provisions for confidentiality regarding the plan or programme or environmental report, presumably in part reflecting the fact that the SEA Directive is concerned with public proposals, whereas the EIA Directive is concerned with public and private proposals, the latter of which may be commercially sensitive. Taken together, Articles 8 and 9 are significant provisions directed at transparent and accountable decision making.

Monitoring

Article 10 of the Directive provides for significant environmental effects of the implementation of plans and programmes to be monitored in order that unforeseen adverse effects can be identified at an early time and to carry out remedial action where needed. As such, the SEA Directive Guidance comments that 'Article 10 extends Member States' duties beyond the planning phase to the implementation phase' (Reps of the MS/ CEC, 2003, para 8.1). As seen above, Article 9(1)(c) requires that monitoring measures be provided as part of the information provision; Annex I(i) further requires that monitoring measures must be described as part of the environmental report.

The Directive does not define what monitoring means, which authority or body is responsible, the time or frequency of monitoring, methodology or consequences; Article 10 therefore avoids laying down detailed legal provisions (Barth and Fuder,

2002, p10). Annex I(g) does, however, require the report to outline 'the measures envisaged to prevent, reduce and as fully as possible offset any significant adverse effects'. It also does not establish what technical methods should be deployed, although indicators to determine the likely significance of effects can be used that are based on the criteria that the Directive sets out. The criteria are set out in Annex II and are of two types: characteristics of the plans and programmes, and characteristics of the effects and the area likely to be affected. Paras 8.4–8.14 of the SEA Directive Guidance contain useful suggestions as to how to best put in place effective measures. These include monitoring the cumulative effects of different plans and programmes (para 8.11).[48] Appendix I of the SEA Directive Guidance is also of assistance, entitled 'Practical guidance on monitoring'.[49] Monitoring includes the follow-up of significant transboundary effects.[50]

Importantly, the SEA Directive does not require an MS to modify a plan or programme as a result of monitoring. The SEA Directive Guidance comments (para 8.13): 'This is consistent with the general approach of environmental assessment, which facilitates an informed decision, but does not create substantive environmental standards for plans or programmes'. Whether or not this is good enough is perhaps a controversial yet needed question, which raises similar questions about the lack of substantive obligations in EIA and SEA. Many commentators today recognize follow-up in EA as being the weakest link in the entire process, and this is an area that the EC could and should address as a result of the review of the SEA Directive, perhaps in conjunction with changes also to the EIA Directive.[51]

If the plan or programme is modified as a result of monitoring, it is important to recognize that this may again require an EA in accordance with Article 2(a), unless it is of a minor nature and an MS decides that significant environmental effects are not likely. Since the modifications are likely to offset or mitigate adverse environmental effects the need for assessment may appear unlikely, however, it remains possible that unexpected effects may occur elsewhere as a result of action taken, so consideration must always be given. Article 10(2) allows existing monitoring arrangements to be used to avoid establishing new processes where not needed. Para 8.16 of the SEA Directive Guidance suggests that data collected under other EC legislation, such as the Water Framework Directive or IPPC Directive (see Chapter 11), may be used for monitoring in accordance with Article 10, 'provided that they are relevant for the respective plan or programme and its environmental effects'.[52]

Overall, the IMPEL Project highlights the flexibility of approaches that may be utilized in complying with Article 10 of the SEA Directive (Barth and Fuder, 2002, p6):

> *One of the main conclusions drawn by the working group is that scope, depth and way of monitoring depend very much on the characteristics of each type of plan or programme. Art. 10 of the SEA Directive refrains from laying down detailed requirements and leaves thus enough flexibility to develop flexible and individual solutions adapted to the respective type of plan and programme.*

Transposition and implementation

To coordinate the transposition of the SEA Directive a European Group of Experts on EIA and SEA was established, meeting twice a year. At the meeting in Vaxholm in 2001 it was decided to set up a Drafting Group led by Finland and the UK to create the SEA Directive Guidance document, which was intended to provide assistance to the MS in implementation. The draft was discussed in the expert meetings and finalized by the Representatives of the Member States and the Environment Directorate General of the European Commission in 2003. As stated, the guidance has no legal status, as only the ECJ can decide on the legal meaning of directives and other EC law. However, it does provide an official commentary on the Directive and, if followed, will improve harmonization throughout the EU (Kläne and Albrecht, 2005, p25).

Legal requirements and the 'margin of discretion'

Article 14 of the SEA Directive indicates that its requirements came into force on 21 July 2001, and in accordance with Article 13 transposition of the Directive into the national law of each MS was to have occurred by 21 July 2004. Late or incorrect transposition of directives is not uncommon, however, given the difficulties in harmonizing existing procedural requirements that in the MS vary widely in form and content. Transposition of the amended EIA Directive is instructive; four years after the deadline for transposition of this had passed, only one country had *not* been subject to infringement proceedings or action before the ECJ. Taking 'into account its unclear terminology and other legal deficiencies' it will probably be 'more difficult to introduce the SEA Directive to national legal systems', especially into the Accession States that in many instances have no current related legal requirements (Sommer, 2005, pp70–73).[53] Article 249 of the TEC contains the obligation to transpose directives into national law, which contrasts with the more general obligation to take necessary measures to fulfil Treaty obligations found in Article 10 of the TEC. This is the conclusion reached by Knopp and Albrecht (2005, p58) in analysing this particular aspect of legal compliance.[54]

Article 4(2) of the SEA Directive states that the requirements of the Directive are to be integrated into existing procedures in the MS for the adoption of plans and programmes, or incorporated in procedures established to comply with the Directive. Knopp and Albrecht (2005, pp63–66) consider the range of means by which directives can be transposed in order to comply with EC law. Paras 4.3–4.4 of the SEA Directive Guidance indicate how the preparation process for the plan or programme may need 'to be adjusted to agree with the demands of the Directive'. This is an excellent example of legal provisions resulting in changes to existing procedures, a matter that remains highly contested in relation to the assessment of policy and legislative proposals, where the majority view in the SEA literature maintains that SEA processes must adapt to policy and legislative procedures rather than that they should change to take account of them. EC law takes priority over the national law of an MS, so there is no choice but to make changes to ensure compliance. Article 4(3) suggests tiering as a means of avoiding duplication of assessment. The rationale and approach to take to this is explained further in paragraphs 4.5–4.7 of the Guidance.

Risse et al (2003) examine what they describe as the MS 'margin of discretion' in implementing the SEA Directive. They describe this as follows (p455):

> *While some aspects of the SEA process are compulsory and well defined in Directive 2001/42/EC, Member States have some latitude in implementing other aspects of the SEA process. This discretionary margin can be the result of imprecisions in the Directive's stipulations or from issues not explicitly addressed by the Directive, but that can nevertheless be taken into consideration by the Member States in implementing their SEA process.*

The authors analyse each of the procedural provisions of the Directive, indicating the discretionary margin available to the MS. For example, in considering screening, should the Directive also be applied to policies and legislation? In relation to the timing, should SEA be integrated into the preparation of strategic proposals? In relation to public participation, what format should be used? In relation to decision making, should environmental impacts be weighted differently to social and economic impacts? In relation to monitoring, should the public be involved? Although certain matters may be interpreted by the ECJ based on past experience with other directives and the interpretation of EC law generally, overall, they conclude (p467) that 'the general requirements prescribed by the Directive are not restrictive and leave ample room for creativity, flexibility and adaptability to suit each Member State's context'.

Although emphasizing that there may be some opportunities to challenge MS decision making where is unduly restricts public participation, Krämer (2007, p141) concludes somewhat pessimistically on the legal remedies available where implementation of the SEA Directive is challenged as incorrect:

> *[I]t has to be underlined that no judicial remedy is foreseen when the environmental report is bad, the consulted public was unduly restricted, a consultation did not take place at all or the results of a consultation are not taken into consideration in the final plan. I am of the opinion that, at least in cases where it is obvious which public is likely to be affected by the plan, that public has the possibility of judicial review should it not be consulted. In these cases, its right to be heard is infringed.*[55]

Reported experience to date

At the time of writing (December 2007) three years have passed since the transposition date of the SEA Directive and six years since it came into force. As such, experience in transposition and implementation is growing, as reported in the academic literature. In 2004 a special issue (vol 14) of the journal *European Environment* reported on progress towards meeting the requirements of the SEA Directive, discussing practice in Austria, the UK, Germany, Italy, Sweden and Slovenia. Most of the papers dealt with land use or transport planning, the two areas of the most advanced practice. Other papers considered energy and water sectors.[56] Conclusions reached overall include the need for policies to also be assessed, the importance of vertical and horizontal integration of SEA in plan making, the significance of guidelines and the definition of sustainability objectives and targets, the role of tiering, and the need for checks and balances where planning processes are highly politicized.[57]

In 2005, Sheate et al reported to the Commission on the relationship between the EIA and SEA Directives (see further Chapter 11), including case studies of seven EU MS undertaken between July 2004 and March 2005 concerning potential overlaps between the two Directives (pp25–57). In 2007, the transposition status in each of the 25 EU MS was summarized by Fischer (see Chapter 5 of his book), outlining the legislation transposing the SEA Directive, the guidance released to support authorities conducting SEA and the extent of SEA application. This followed publication evaluating transposition and current practice of the SEA Directive by Zagorianakos in the legal literature (2006), and transposition in relation to biodiversity (European Environmental Bureau, 2005). Thérivel and Walsh (2006, p664) indicate that only nine MS transposed the Directive on time, with another six fully or mostly transposing it by July 2005. By mid-2006, Fischer (2007, p91) indicates that only three states were yet to transpose, although the federal state of Germany and Italy, with strong regional powers, had yet to implement fully.

Experience in the UK has been particularly well documented, (see generally Thérivel and Walsh, 2006), in part because of the high level of existing English experience with sustainability appraisal (Smith and Sheate, 2001) and major changes to land use planning; devolution, which has resulted in different implementation experiences, some of which go beyond the requirements of the Directive (for example, Brooke et al, 2004; Jackson and Illsley, 2006, 2007); and the detailed guidance that has been prepared by government (ODPM, 2005).

Thérivel and Walsh (2006) report on a questionnaire survey undertaken in July 2005 of all local planning authorities in England and Wales; these plans account for around 70 per cent of SEAs carried out in England and Wales, and include land use plans, transport plans and those relating to waste and minerals. The information obtained indicates that about 80 per cent of SEAs were being carried out as an integral part of plan making, an important requirement of the SEA Directive if the consideration of alternatives is to be effectively carried out. Sheate et al (2004) draw out wider implications from the UK approach for implementation across the EU as a whole, in particular in relation to transposition, screening and support, and in regard to the water and energy sectors as well as land use planning. They conclude, highlighting the potential future application to policies (p90):

> *The potential breath of application of the SEA Directive – if interpreted as having a wide scope and broad purpose – could have significant implications in terms of changes to practice and need for allocation of resources, and also by having a very real impact in improving the integration of the environment into strategic decision making. However the application of SEA to plans and programmes will inevitably expose the lack of SEA at the policy level, just as the EIA Directive exposed the lack of SEA at programme and plan levels.*

Scotland's devolved administration, the Scottish Executive, decided to apply the SEA Directive to all public sector policies, plans and programmes subject to Scotland's jurisdiction, and is therefore a good example of gold plating the Directive's requirements (Jackson and Dixon, 2006).[58] Under the Environmental Assessment (Scotland) Act 2005 policies (termed 'strategies') that are likely to have significant environmental effects are assessed, regardless of whether they set the framework for development consent of projects, or whether they are required by legislative, regulatory or administrative measures. Scotland decided to abandon attempts at integrated/sustainability appraisal (Esson et al, 2004; Jackson and Illsley, 2007), preferring to use SEA 'simply to identify the environmental implications of PPPs'; this included 'tighter requirements' on regulatory authorities and statutory consultees 'in respect of screening, scoping and public consultation' (Jackson and Illsley, 2006, pp370–371).

CONCLUSIONS

This chapter has analysed the legal provisions of the SEA Directive in detail and related them to its context in European environmental law. It has highlighted areas of uncertainty or ambiguity and discussed relevant case law and guidance that may indicate how the ECJ would interpret such uncertainty or ambiguity if called on. Examples from a few MS have been provided to indicate how legal traditions affect the transposition and implementation of the Directive, and some of the challenges that may lie ahead, especially so in the light of experience with the EIA Directive. Changes will undoubtedly be needed to fully implement the Aarhus Convention, and potentially also the SEA Protocol, if and when it is finally ratified as required.

Although the Commission was required by Article 12(3) of the SEA Directive to send a first report on the application and effectiveness of the SEA Directive to the European Parliament and Council before 21 July 2006, this has apparently not yet happened, and is unlikely until the Commission has received adequate information from the MS. The review of the SEA Directive permits the opportunity to consider consolidation with the EIA Directive, as advocated by Sheate (2003a, p347) and others.[59] It also permits the opportunity to extend application to policy and legislative proposals, driven by the SEA Protocol and legislated experience in a few of the MS or devolved administrations within. The relationship between the SEA Directive and the other related European Law discussed in Chapter 11 suggests further consolidation of European EA requirements may also be needed.

NOTES

1 See generally Sheate et al (2005).
2 See Commission of the European Communities (2002).
3 While the Commission IA process considers all types of impacts and therefore cannot be described as SEA, it does at least demonstrate that the EC itself has shown that assessment of the highest levels of strategic proposals are potentially suitable for assessment. The process has been subject to commentary by a number of authors, including Peters (2004), Lee and Kirkpatrick (2004), Wilkinson et al (2004) and Adelle et al (2006).
4 Council Directive 2001/42/EC of 7 June 2001 on the assessment of the effects of certain plans or programmes on the environment, [2001] OJ L197.
5 The report from the Commission to the Council and Parliament was due 21 July 2006, but it is unlikely until sufficient experience with implementation is gained.

6 Sheate (2003a, p331) emphasizes that the intent of the Commission at the time of the original EIA Directive was to establish a firm legal foothold for project assessment, and attempt to avoid the litigation that had accompanied the introduction of EIA in the US under the National Environmental Policy Act 1969. He goes on to state that although there were also concerns raised at the time about the lack of methodology for assessing strategic proposals, to an extent this was also true of project level assessment, and comments 'it is often legislation that leads to the development of appropriate methodologies rather than the other way round'. Comparisons between EIA and SEA in the EC and US have been subject to much interest. See, for example, Underwood and Alton (2003).

7 See Part I-Section 7.3.

8 The Netherlands introduced legislative provisions for SEA in 1987 and Denmark in 1993.

9 For more detail on the 1996 (COM (96) 511 final) proposal, see Sheate (2003a, p333).

10 'Town and country', urban and regional, land use or spatial plans are the most common category of strategic proposals assessed. As such they have probably received the most commentary in the literature; see, for example, Jones et al (2005) and Fischer (2002).

11 See Decision No 1692/96/EC of the European Parliament and of the Council of 23 July 1996 on Community guidelines for the development of the trans-European transport network, [1996] OJ L 228.

12 Feldmann et al (2001, p206) state that ten rounds in the Environment Working Group of the Council were needed to reach a compromise text to which the Environment Ministers could politically agree in December 1999. They give credit to the Germany Presidency of the Council for starting the discussion of the SEA proposal in 1999 and for the Finnish Presidency for concluding the negotiations later that year (pp205–206). There appears little doubt that the ability of an MS holding the Presidency to set the agenda for the Council (with a proactive position on environmental matters) went a long way to moving the situation forwards.

13 The SEA Directive was unanimously approved, indicating that it made little difference to the basis of competence at the time. Albrecht (2005, pp32–33) explores in more detail the application of Article 175 and other possible bases on which the SEA Directive could have been adopted. She also emphasizes that as the SEA Directive contains some very specific provisions, it leaves little scope for transposition that is at variance with the Directive. This could be significant where, for example, the doctrine of indirect effect is deployed (see in discussion section below).

14 As seen in Chapter 7, the EC is a monist legal system, and, in theory, there is therefore strictly no need to transpose international legal obligations into EC law. If the EC enters into international agreements under Article 300 of the TEC they are binding on the EC institutions and MS and form part of the EC legal order from when they enter into force. They also take precedence over EC law, which must be interpreted in conformity with such international norms. Yet arguably the need for unanimity in ratifying international law such as the SEA Protocol remains under Article 300, which, in practice, means that this is little different from the need for unanimity under Article 175(2). See, however, note 15 below.

15 The vagueness of these provisions has resulted in litigation, with the ECJ needing to interpret whether internal EC rules concerning the implementation of an international treaty should have been adopted on the basis of a qualified majority or unanimity. See ECJ, Case C-36/98 *Spain v Council* [2001] ECR I-779, and the discussion in Davies (2004, pp15–17), which includes commentary on the interpretative approach taken by the Court.

16 There of course remain limitations on the ability of the Council or individual MS to refuse to take measures where they are obligations that have already been accepted by the EC or individual MS in ratifying international instruments such as the SEA Protocol.

17 At the Cardiff Summit of June 1998, for example, the Heads of Government committed the EU to the integration of the environment in all EU policies, the 'Cardiff process'. At the

Lisbon Summit in 2000, the aim for the EU was 'to become the most competitive and dynamic knowledge-based economy in the world, capable of sustainable growth and more and better jobs and greater social cohesion' (European Council, Lisbon Presidency Conclusions 23 and 24 March 2000).

18 See Chapter 8 note 40.

19 Chapter 12 focuses on the relationship between international and European law. Feldmann et al (2001, p207), De Mulder (2001, p15), Sheate (2003a, p334), Marsden (2004), Marsden and De Mulder (2005, pp 53–55), Kläne and Albrecht (2005, pp19–20), Albrecht (2005, pp33–34), De Mulder (2006) and many others also recognize the role of international law, primarily the Aarhus Convention, as underlying aspects of the Directive.

20 Decision No 2179/98/EC of the European Parliament and of the Council of 24 September 1998 on the Review of the European Community Programme of Policy and Action in relation to the Environment and Sustainable Development, *Towards Sustainability*, [1998] OJ L275.

21 See Commission of the European Communities (2001).

22 The words screening and scoping are not used in the SEA Directive, although somewhat confusingly Article 3, which deals with screening, is entitled 'scope', setting out the application of the Directive (Reps of the MS/ CEC, 2003, note 6 on p5). Also confusingly, the word screening is used in para 3.40 of this Guidance to denote case by case examination, specifying types of proposals or combining approaches. The words screening and scoping are used below in common with EIA provisions worldwide: screening therefore generally means what to assess (whether an evaluation is required for this purpose or not) and scoping means deciding on the terms of reference for a report.

23 Representatives of the Member States and the Environment Directorate General of the European Commission (2003), abbreviated in this book to Reps of the MS/EC, 2003. As commented elsewhere, the document has no binding status. See para 1.5, p3, which states: 'The document represents only the views of the Commission and is not of a binding nature...It must be emphasised that, in the last resort, it rests with the European Court of Justice (ECJ) to interpret a Directive'. The document draws on the jurisprudence of the ECJ, especially decisions relating to the EIA Directive. As always in transposing EC law, it is open to an MS to go further than EC law if it wishes and introduce more extensive measures than a directive requires. This is discussed in the section on transposition at the end of this chapter, with regard to the experience of Scotland.

24 The guidance will be considered throughout this section and also in relation to transposition in the MS towards the end (see Gao, 2006). It is supplemented by guidance released in the MS themselves; see, for example, ODPM (2005).

25 See Reps of the MS/CEC (2003, note 4, p3), which contrasts the SEA Protocol.

26 Thanks are due to one of the reviewers of the book proposal for raising this concern and urging a certain restraint; inevitably the diverse target audience suggests what may be too detailed for one part of the audience may be insufficient for the other.

27 ECJ, Case C-188/89 *Foster v British Gas* [1990] ECR I-3313. This was discussed in an earlier chapter in relation to the meaning of an authority, which the ECJ has held includes privatized utility companies. See Reps of the MS/CEC (2003, para 3.12).

28 Some private bodies have nonetheless decided to apply SEA to their own strategic proposals, as described in the literature. See Jay (2007, and extensive references therein) and Münchenberg (2002).

29 The meaning of a plan was considered by the ECJ in Case C-387/97 *Commission v Greece* [1997] in relation to Article 6 of the Waste Framework Directive 75/442, or Article 12 of Directive 78/319. It stated that 'legislation or specific measures amounting only to a series of ad hoc normative interventions that are incapable of constituting an organised and coordinated system for the disposal of waste and toxic and dangerous waste cannot be regarded as [such] plans'. See paragraph 3.5 and footnote 7, SEA Directive Guidance. The application of the SEA Directive to waste management plans is considered in Chapter 11.

30   Note also that the Habitats Directive refers to plans and projects rather than plans and programmes (see Chapter 11).

31   ECJ, Case C-392/92 *Bund Naturshutz and Others v Bavarian Higher Regional Court* [1994] ECR I-3717, paragraph 70. Despite this apparent assurance from the ECJ, there would appear to be several instances where the inability to determine the precise nature of a development proposal may result in the proposal not being assessed adequately. Sheate (2003a, p345; 2004, p122) draws attention to the situation of 'salami slicing' that continues to beset power and road schemes in particular, whereby an uncoordinated series of projects is typically undertaken over a period of time with little strategic framework set in advance. He comments (2003a, p345) 'If the SEA Directive cannot address this problem it will be a continuing loophole between EIA and SEA'.

32   Note, however, that plans and programmes co-financed under the current respective programming periods of Regulations 1260/1999/EC and 1257/1999/EC are exempt from the scope of the SEA Directive (see Chapter 11).

33   If they are plans and programmes relating to one of the listed sectors and set the framework for the development consent of projects they are deemed to be likely to have significant environmental effects and must be assessed. If they are not and set the framework for the development consent of a project that is not listed, an MS can decide if they have significant environmental effects in accordance with criteria set out.

34   These sectors are subject to review, together with the types of plans and programmes, as Article 12(3) of the Directive contains a provision that is designed to further improve integration which states:

> With a view further to integrating environmental protection requirements, in accordance with Article 6 of the Treaty, and taking into account the experience acquired in the application of this Directive in the Member States... a report [on the application and effectiveness of this Directive will be provided before 21 July 2006, and] will be accompanied by proposals for amendment of this Directive, if appropriate. In particular, the Commission will consider the possibility of extending the scope of this Directive to other areas/sectors and other types of plans and programmes.

35   This confirms Australian jurisprudence in relation to the *Environment Protection and Biodiversity Conservation Act 1999* (EPBC Act) that is considered by McGrath (2005, p31), notably the application of the *Tillman's Butcheries* case that stated that 'likely to have' means there is a real chance or possibility regardless of whether or not it is more than 50 per cent. This is significant because usually to satisfy a civil court of the evidence presented to it, it must be more probable than not (over 50 per cent) or what is called 'the balance of probabilities'. In a criminal court, because of the possibility of a custodial sentence being handed down, the evidence must be even more convincing (75 per cent) or 'beyond reasonable doubt'.

36   Again the Australian jurisprudence demonstrates similar conclusions. In *Booth v Bosworth* (2001) the Federal Court defined 'significant impact' under the EPBC Act as an impact that is 'important, notable or of consequence having regard to its context or intensity'. See Bates (2006, pp324–325) where a related definition of 'all adverse impacts' was widely interpreted in the *Nathan Dam* case to include indirect as well as direct impacts.

37   Examples of plans and programmes to which SEA is likely to apply in England and Wales are set out by Sheate (2004, p121), and for land use and transport include Regional Spatial Strategies, Local Development Frameworks, Regional Economic Strategies, Waste Plans, Minerals Plans, Regional Transport Strategies and Local Transport Plans.

38   The entry into force of the Directive was on 21 July 2004, which means that the later date would be after 21 July 2006.

39 The meaning, advantages and disadvantages and practicalities of public participation in relation to the SEA Directive are examined by Heiland (2005). He discusses case studies to date to illustrate.

40 Directive 2003/35/EC applies the Aarhus Convention to certain plans and programmes that are not subject to the SEA Directive (see Chapter 9). Some authors have also considered the rights of the public in relation to policies and legislation, which may also be included in the future scope of the SEA Directive. See Kravchenko (2002) and Jendroska and Stec (2003, pp108–109).

41 Mathiesen (2003) provides a detailed analysis of public participation in EC environmental law, including a close analysis of the relationship between the SEA Directive and Aarhus Convention provisions on participation. The relationship between the SEA and other related Directives is also analysed (pp45–46), which is the subject of the next chapter.

42 Although the SEA Directive allows MS to decide how this is achieved, designating authorities will often be done by legislation, hence the expression 'statutory consultees'.

43 Notably the public are not involved in this stage under either the EIA or SEA Directives despite advocates suggesting that 'public scoping' as it is known would improve the process considerably. Practicality and confidentiality issues continue to exclude the public from this important stage in the process, which effectively limits the consideration of alternatives thereafter.

44 A separate legal identity provides protection to the shareholders of a company or the managers of an association, or makes it easier for the company or association to do particular tasks (such as enter into contracts or take part in litigation) as a result of legislation or court rules. Scott (2002, pp999–1002) examines the notion of individual and collective interests and the judicial protection that may be afforded to them in relation to the SEA Directive and Aarhus Convention requirements. Carnwath (2004, pp318–319) provides examples of broad and limited approaches to standing (access to the courts), referring to Hungary, Spain and the UK.

45 Jendroska and Stec (2003, p109) also contrast the SEA Directive with the SEA Protocol in relation to the requirement under the former to consider the public interest when deciding on what to include in the environmental report, which is not a requirement under the latter.

46 The SEA Directive Guidance has confusingly mixed up the references to the SEA Directive and the Aarhus Convention here. Article 7 refers to the Aarhus Convention and Article 6(3) refers to the SEA Directive, not the other way round as is suggested.

47 Meyer-Steinbrenner (2005) examines public participation for SEA in a transboundary context, considering methodological aspects and discussing a pilot project affecting Germany, Poland and the Czech Republic, which may provide assistance with future application of the Directive's provisions in this regard.

48 The relationship between the assessment of cumulative effects and the SEA Directive was analysed in James et al (2003). Barth and Fuder (2002, p12) indicate that Article 10 does not specify whether the environmental effects of each plan or programme must be monitored individually or not, but that if they are monitored together, 'it may help to better identify cumulative effects'.

49 The IMPEL report on Article 10 defines monitoring 'as an activity of following the development of the parameters of concern in magnitude, time and space'. The report distinguishes the following tasks that comprise this: 'the collection/gathering of environmental information, the processing of the information and the interpretation or evaluation of the information'. See Barth and Fuder (2002, p6).

50 Although Article 7 of the Espoo Convention has resulted in bilateral agreements between states as to significant effects, Barth and Fuder (2002, p27) emphasize that in the context of European law, 'the provisions on "significant environmental effects" need to be interpreted

by the European courts and applied by the Member States as uniformly as possible. So far, there is no room for bilateral agreements'.

51 See generally Morrison-Saunders and Arts (2004).

52 See also Barth and Fuder (2002, pp14–15). Although Article 5(1) and Article 9(1) of the SEA Directive do not require that detailed arrangements for monitoring are made publicly available, the authors emphasize the importance of Directive 90/313/EEC (as now repealed and replaced by Directive 2003/4/EC, OJ 2003 L41/26) in relation to environmental information.

53 Accession States are those that are in the process of joining the EC and contrast with existing MS. Sommer (2005) considers the example of Poland, which at the end of 2001 enacted 271 Acts of Parliament aimed at harmonization with EC law.

54 Subject to the arguable autonomy of European law, the international law of treaties (found largely in the Vienna Convention, see Chapter 2), may apply principles to the interpretation of the TEC and TEU. One of these is that a special provision takes precedence over a general provision, in Latin '*lex specialis derogat lex generalis*'. Feldmann et al (2001, p213) also consider the application of this principle when analysing the relationship between the SEA Directive and other relevant directives such as the Habitats Directive (see Chapter 11).

55 Note, however, Krämer's reference (2007, p135) to the decision in ECJ, Case C-239/04 *Commission v Portugal* [2006], where he comments (with my emphasis):

> At the end of 2006... the Court of Justice gave a very remarkable judgment. In Case C-239/04, it was decided that an administration which had made an impact assessment, but had not examined a reasonable alternative to the project in question – a motorway – did not make an impact assessment. Though the judgment concerned an impact assessment under Art 6 of Directive 92/43 (the Habitats Directive), it may also have a considerable effect on the interpretation of Directive 85/337.

Similar implications may also be expected regarding the SEA Directive, especially given the stronger emphasis placed on alternatives.

56 With respect to the energy sector and the application of the SEA Directive Guidance, see Gao (2006). Gao questions the utility of the Guidance, which, in his view, fails to provide the clarity needed to apply the SEA Directive. The application of the SEA Directive to the fisheries sector has also been examined in a paper prepared for an environmental NGO (Brown and Hjerp, 2006), which also examines overlap with the Habitats Directive (p14).

57 See Fischer (2004a; 2004b).

58 Several of the Nordic countries have also gold plated the provisions of the Directive, notably Denmark and Finland, which had legal provisions in force some time before the SEA Directive came into force. For explanation, see Hilding-Rydevik (2003) and Lerstang and Tesli (2004). The Netherlands is another country whose SEA provisions predate those of the SEA Directive.

59 Sheate et al (2005, pix) suggest several other matters that could be considered as part of the review process, including the definitions of project, programme and plan.

REFERENCES

Adelle, C., Hertin, J. and Jordan, A. (2006) 'Sustainable development "outside" the European Union: What role for impact assessment?', *European Environment*, vol 16, pp57–72

Albrecht, E. (2005) 'Legal context of the SEA Directive – links with other legislation and key procedures' in M. Schmidt, E. João and E. Albrecht (eds) *Implementing Strategic Environmental Assessment*, Springer-Verlag, Heidelberg, pp31–56

Barth, R. and Fuder, A. (2002) *IMPEL Project: Implementing Article 10 of the SEA Directive 2001/42/ EC: Final Report*, Öko-Institut e.V, Darmstadt

Bates, G. (2006) *Environmental Law in Australia*, LexisNexis Butterworths, Sydney

Brooke, C., James, E., Jones, R. and Thérivel, R (2004) 'Implementing the strategic environmental assessment (SEA) directive in the south west of England', *European Environment*, vol 14, pp138–152

Brown, J. and Hjerp, P. (2006) *The Application of Strategic Environmental Assessment in the UK Fisheries Sector*, WWF/IEEP, London

Carnwath, R. (2004) 'Judicial protection of the environment: At home and abroad', *Journal of Environmental Law*, vol 16, no 3, pp315–327

Černy, R. J. and Sheate, W. R (1992) 'Strategic environmental assessment: Amending the EA directive', *Environmental Policy and Law*, vol 22, no 3, pp154–159

Commission of the European Communities (1992) *Towards Sustainability: A European Community Programme of Policy and Action in relation to the Environment and Sustainable Development*, Commission Communication of 27 March 1992, COM (92) final, Commission of the European Communities, Brussels

Commission of the European Communities (1993) *Report on the Implementation of Directive 85/337/ EEC on the assessment of the effects of certain public and private projects on the environment*, COM (93) 28 final, Commission of the European Communities, Brussels

Commission of the European Communities (1996) *Proposal for a Council Directive on the assessment of the effects of certain plans and programmes on the environment*, COM (96) 511 final, 4 December 1996, Commission of the European Communities, Brussels

Commission of the European Communities (1998) *Amended Proposal for a Council Directive on the assessment of the effects of certain plans and programmes on the environment*, COM (99) 73 final, December 1998, Commission of the European Communities, Brussels

Commission of the European Communities (2001) *Environment 2010: Our Future, Our Choice, the Sixth Environment Action Programme 2001-2010*, Commission Communication of 2001, COM (2001) 31 final, Commission of the European Communities, Brussels

Commission of the European Communities (2002) *Communication from the Commission on Impact Assessment*, COM (2002) 276 final, Commission of the European Communities, Brussels

Commission of the European Communities (2004) *Integrating Environmental Considerations into Other Policy Areas – A Stocktaking of the Cardiff Process*, Commission Working Document, COM (2004) 394 final, Commission of the European Communities, Brussels

Dalal-Clayton, B. and Sadler, B. (2005) *Strategic Environmental Assessment: A Sourcebook and Reference Guide to International Experience*, Earthscan, London

Davies, P. (2004) *European Union Environmental Law*, Ashgate Publishing Ltd, Aldershot

De Mulder, J. (2001) 'The new directive on strategic environmental assessment', *Environmental Law Network International Review*, vol 1, pp14–20

De Mulder, J. (2006) 'The expansion of environmental assessment in international law: The Protocol on Strategic Environmental Assessment to the Espoo Convention', *Environmental Law and Management*, vol 18, pp269–281

Esson, G., Reekie, B. and Jackson, T. (2004) '"Objective-led" SEA in a Scottish local authority', *European Environment*, vol 14, pp153–164

European Environmental Bureau (2005) *Biodiversity in Strategic Environmental Assessment: Quality of National Transposition and Application of the Strategic Environmental Assessment Directive*, European Environmental Bureau, Brussels

Feldmann, L. (2001) 'The proposal for a directive on strategic environmental assessment for certain plans and programmes' in Kleinschmidt, V. and Wagner, D. (eds) *Strategic Environmental Assessment in Europe – 4th European Workshop on EIA*, Kluwer, Dortrecht, pp20–40

Feldmann, L., Vanderhaegen, M. and Pirotte, C. (2001) 'The EU's SEA directive: Status and links to integration and sustainable development', *Environmental Impact Assessment Review*, vol 21, no 3, pp203–222

Fischer, T. B. (2002) *Strategic Environmental Assessment in Transport and Land Use Planning*, Earthscan, London

Fischer, T. B. (2004a) 'Editorial – Progress towards meeting the requirements of the European SEA Directive', *European Environment*, vol 14, pp55–57

Fischer, T. B. (2004b) 'Editorial – Progress towards meeting the requirements of the European SEA Directive - II', *European Environment*, vol 14, pp135–137

Fischer, T. B. (2007) *Theory and Practice of Strategic Environmental Assessment*, Earthscan, London

Gao, A. (2006) 'SEA guidance: A reinterpretation of the SEA directive and its application to the energy sector', *European Environmental Law Review*, May, pp129–148

Heiland, S. (2005) 'Requirements and methods for public participation in SEA' in M. Schmidt, E. João and E. Albrecht (eds) *Implementing Strategic Environmental Assessment*, Springer-Verlag, Heidelberg, pp421–432

Hilding-Rydevik, T. (ed) (2003) *Environmental Assessment of Plans and Programs: Nordic Experiences in Relation to the Implementation of the EU directive 2001/42/EC*, Nordregio, Stockholm, Sweden

Jackson, T. and Dixon, J. (2006) 'Applying strategic environmental assessment to land-use and resource management plans in Scotland and New Zealand: A comparison', *Impact Assessment and Project Appraisal*, vol 24, no 2, pp89–101

Jackson, T. and Illsley, B. (2006) 'Strategic environmental assessment as a tool of environmental governance: Scotland's extension of the European Union SEA directive', *Journal of Environmental Planning and Management*, vol 49, no 3, pp361–383

Jackson, T. and Illsley, B. (2007) 'An analysis of the theoretical rationale for using strategic environmental assessment to deliver environmental justice in the light of the Scottish Environmental Assessment Act', *Environmental Impact Assessment Review*, vol 27, pp607–623

James, E., Tomlinson, P., McColl, V. and Fry, C. (2003) *Final Report – Literature Review / Scoping Study on Cumulative Effects Assessment and the Strategic Environmental Assessment Directive*, Unpublished project report prepared for Centre for Risk and Forecasting, Environment Agency of England and Wales, Wokingham, UK

Jay, S. (2007) 'Customers as decision-makers: Strategic environmental assessment in the private sector', *Impact Assessment and Project Appraisal*, vol 25, no 2, pp75–84

Jendroska, J. and Stec, S. (2003) 'The Kyiv Protocol on strategic environmental assessment', *Environmental Policy and Law*, vol 33, no 3/4, pp105–110

Jones, C., Baker, M., Carter, J., Jay, S., Short, M. and Wood, C. (eds) (2005) *Strategic Environmental Assessment and Land Use Planning: An International Evaluation*, Earthscan, London

Kläne, C. and Albrecht, E. (2005) 'Purpose and background of the European SEA Directive', in M. Schmidt, E. João and E. Albrecht (eds) *Implementing Strategic Environmental Assessment*, Springer-Verlag, Heidelberg, pp15–29

Knopp, L. and Albrecht, E. (2005) 'Transposition of the SEA directive into national law – challenges and possibilities' in M. Schmidt, E. João and E. Albrecht (eds) *Implementing Strategic Environmental Assessment*, Springer-Verlag, Heidelberg, pp57-67

Krämer, L. (2007) 'The development of environmental assessments at the level of the European Union' in Holder, J. and McGillivray, D. (eds) (2007) *Taking Stock of Environmental Assessment: Law, Policy and Practice*, Routledge-Cavendish, Abingdon, pp131–148

Kravchenko, S. (2002) 'Effective public participation in the preparation of policies and legislation', *Environmental Policy and Law*, vol 32, no 5, pp204–208

Lee, N. and Kirkpatrick, C. (2004) *A Pilot Study of the Quality of European Commission Extended Impact Assessments*, Working Paper Series No 8, Impact Assessment Research Centre, Institute for Development Policy and Management, University of Manchester, Manchester

Lee, N. and Wood, C. (1976) *The Introduction of Environmental Impact Statements in the European Community*, ENV/197/76, Commission of the European Communities, Brussels

Lerstang, T. and Tesli, A. (2004) 'Experiences from Norwegian and Nordic case studies on SEA', paper presented at IAIA 2004 Vancouver, Canada 24th Annual Meeting, 26–29 April

Marsden, S. (2004) 'Legal basis of SEA development: Case study on the SEA directive', *World Bank SEA Training Project for China*, World Bank, Washington DC, www.worldbank.org/wbi/sdenveconomics/sea/materials.html

Marsden, S. and De Mulder, J. (2005) 'Strategic environmental assessment and sustainability in Europe: How bright is the future?', *Review of European Community and International Environmental Law*, vol 14, no 1, pp50–62

Mathieson, A. (2003) 'Public participation in decision making and access to justice in EC environmental law: The case of certain plans and programmes', *European Environmental Law Review*, vol 12, no 2, pp36–52

McGrath, C. (2005) 'Key concepts of the Environment Protection and Biodiversity Conservation Act 1999', *Environmental and Planning Law Journal*, vol 22, pp20–39

Meyer-Steinbrenner, H. (2005) 'Public participation for SEA in a transboundary context' in M. Schmidt, E. João and E. Albrecht (eds) *Implementing Strategic Environmental Assessment*, Springer-Verlag, Heidelberg, pp433–442

Morrison-Saunders, A. and Arts, J. (eds) (2004) *Assessing Impact: Handbook of EIA and SEA Follow-up*, Earthscan, London

Münchenberg, S. (2002) 'Strategic environmental assessment: A business perspective' in S. Marsden and S. Dovers (eds) *Strategic Environmental Assessment in Australasia*, The Federation Press, Annandale, NSW, pp182–194

ODPM (Office of the Deputy Prime Minister) (2005) *A Practical Guide to the Strategic Environmental Assessment Directive*, ODPM, London

OPOCE (2002) *A European Union Strategy for Sustainable Development*, Luxembourg

Peters, E. (2004) 'The European Commission's sustainability impact assessment project: Experience and current challenges' paper presented to the Annual Conference of the International Association for Impact Assessment, Vancouver

Reps of the MS/CEC (Representatives of the Member States and the Environment Directorate General of the European Commission) (2003) *Implementation of Directive 2001/42/EC on the assessment of the effects of certain plans and programmes on the environment*, 23 September 2003, Commission of the European Communities, Brussels

Risse, N., Crowley, M., Vincke, P. and Waaub, J. P. (2003) 'Implementing the European SEA directive: The member states' margin of discretion', *Environmental Impact Assessment Review*, vol 23, pp453–470

Robinson, J. and Elvin, D. (2004) 'The environmental assessment of plans and programmes', *Journal of Planning and Environmental Law*, pp1028–1048

Scott, J. (2002) 'Law and environmental governance in the EU', *International and Comparative Law Quarterly*, vol 51, no 4, pp996–1005

Sheate, W. R. (2003a) 'The EC directive on strategic environmental assessment: A much needed boost for environmental integration', *European Environmental Law Review*, vol 12, no 12, pp331–347

Sheate, W. R. (2003b) 'Environmental integration and sustainable development in the EU: Changing conceptions and potential for conflict in environmental assessment', *Environmental Policy and Law*, vol 33, no 5, pp222–233

Sheate, W. R. (2004) 'The SEA directive 2001/42/EC: Reinvigorating environmental integration', *Environmental Law and Management*, vol 16, no 3, pp119–124

Sheate, W. R., Dagg, S., Richardson, J., Aschemann, R., Palerm, J. and Steen, U. (2003) 'Integrating the environment into strategic decision-making. Conceptualising policy 3EA', *European Environment*, vol 13, pp1–18

Sheate, W. R., Byron, H. and Smith, S. (2004) 'Implementing the SEA directive: Sectoral challenges and opportunities for the UK and EU', *European Environment*, vol 14, no 2, pp73–93

Sheate, W. R., Byron, H., Dagg, S. and Cooper, L. (2005) *The Relationship between the EIA and SEA Directives: Final Report to the European Commission*, Contract number: ENV.G.4./ETU/2004/0020r, Imperial College Consultants, London

Smith, S. and Sheate, W. R. (2001) 'Sustainability appraisal of English regional plans: incorporating the requirements of the EU strategic environmental assessment directive', *Impact Assessment and Project Appraisal*, vol 19, no 4, pp263–276

Sommer, J. (2005) 'Some legal problems of implementing the SEA directive into member states' legal systems' in M. Schmidt, E. João and E. Albrecht (eds) *Implementing Strategic Environmental Assessment*, Springer-Verlag, Heidelberg, pp69–79

Thérivel, R. and Walsh, F. (2006) 'The strategic environmental assessment directive in the UK: 1 year onwards', *Environmental Impact Assessment Review*, vol 26, pp663–675

Tromans, S. and Fuller, K. (2003) *Environmental Impact Assessment: Law and Practice*, Reed Elsevier, London

Tromans, S. and Machart, C. (2001) 'Strategic environmental assessment: Early evaluation equals efficiency?', *Journal of Planning and Environmental Law*, pp993–996

Underwood, P. and Alton, C. (2003) 'Could the SEA-directive succeed within the United States?', *Environmental Impact Assessment Review*, vol 23, pp259–261

Von Seht, H. and Wood, C. (1998) 'The proposed European Directive on environmental assessment: Evolution and evaluation', *Environmental Policy and Law*, vol 28, no 5, pp242–250

Wathern, P. (ed) (1988) *Environmental Impact Assessment: Theory and Practice*, Unwin Hyman, London

Wilkinson, D., Fergusson, M., Bowyer, C., Brown, J., Ladefoged, A., Monkhouse, C. and Zdanowicz, A. (2004) *Sustainable Development in the European Commission's Integrated Impact Assessments for 2003: Final Report*, Institute for European Environmental Policy, London

Wood, C. (1995) *Environmental Impact Assessment: A Comparative Review*, Longman, London

Wood, C. and Djeddour, M. (1992) 'Strategic environmental assessment: EA of policies, plans and programmes, *Impact Assessment Bulletin*, vol 10, no 1, pp3–22

Zagorianakos, E. (2006) 'A qualitative evaluation of current transposition and implementation practice of the SEA Directive in EU Member States', *Journal of European Environmental and Planning Law*, vol 6, pp535–548

CHAPTER 11

Relationship between the SEA, EIA and other Related Directives

CHAPTER OVERVIEW

The SEA Directive was considered in the previous chapter and in Chapter 9 the EIA and other horizontal directives were outlined because of the historical and structural relationship they have to the SEA Directive. This chapter primarily considers the relationship between the SEA Directive and other EC laws that require plans and programmes, and in some cases also strategic assessment, looking at the Habitats[1] and Water Framework[2] Directives in particular. It begins by analysing the content of Article 11 of the SEA Directive, which states that the provisions of all relevant directives must also be applied, in some cases by way of coordinated or joint procedures. The relationship between the SEA Directive and the EIA Directive is then analysed in more detail to summarize and build on the previous two chapters. The relationship between the SEA Directive and the Habitats (including discussion of the allied Wild Birds Directive[3]) and Water Framework Directives is next evaluated, together with the Nitrates,[4] Waste[5] and Air Quality Framework[6] Directives, which also contain provisions for plans and programmes. The main procedural provisions of each of these laws is outlined with reference to the guidance produced and, where relevant, case law of the ECJ to illustrate the relationship to the SEA Directive. Before concluding, the chapter examines the relationship between the SEA Directive and the Structural Funds regulations,[7] which also contain provisions for SEA.

Article 11 of the SEA Directive

Article 11 of the SEA Directive concerns overlaps between the SEA Directive and other EC law, including the EIA Directive. Although the SEA Directive states that EA is required in certain circumstances under its own provisions, some plans and programmes are also required under other directives, which themselves may also mandate EA. Article 11 is therefore an important provision that establishes the relationship between each. Article 11(1) states clearly that an EA carried out under the SEA Directive, 'shall be without prejudice to' the requirements of the EIA Directive and other EC law. This means that unless there are indications to the contrary, all other laws continue to apply, and the failure to consider the provisions of each in every instance may result in legal action being taken for infringement.

The relationship between the EIA Directive and the SEA Directive is fairly straightforward, at least superficially, the former applying to projects, and the latter to plans and programmes. Plans and programmes must generally also set the framework for the future development consent of projects listed in the EIA Directive. However, as an indication of some of the complexities of the relationship between the two Directives, in some instances a plan or programme may set the framework for more than one project, in which case, as para 9.4 of the SEA Directive Guidance (Reps of the MS/CEC, 2003) indicates, 'application would be cumulative', meaning that assessment must be applied in each case. The same is also true of the application of other EC laws, such as the Habitats Directive, although the SEA Directive itself also contains specific requirements on this (note Article 3.2(b)).

Provided the requirements of each of the relevant EC laws are satisfied, Article 11(2) provides discretion for an MS to provide for coordinated or joint procedures, where there is an obligation to carry out an EA of the effects of plans and programmes under different directives. The aim is to avoid duplication of assessment, an important underlying rationale of SEA in its relationship to EIA. Sheate et al (2005, p11) outline the potential for joint/coordinated procedures between the EIA and SEA Directives, and also consider the potential to establish parallel procedures for EIA and SEA (pp75–76), where the SEA 'should address the wider strategic implications of the scheme (beyond the normal immediate geographical and temporal scope of an EIA), while the EIA can be more focused on the location-specific aspects' (p76). However, tiering, as explained further below, should remain the norm.

Relationship between the SEA and EIA Directives

The most detailed analysis of the relationship between the SEA and EIA Directives was the report prepared for the Commission in 2005 by Sheate et al, which includes a comparative textual analysis of the provisions of both. Despite acknowledged limitations in the timing of the research leading up to the report,[8] it nonetheless provides an excellent evaluation of the potential overlaps between the Directives, with recommendations for the MS and the Commission for the short, medium and long term.[9] The main areas of overlap are where large projects (such as those dealing with urban development, and transport and electricity infrastructure) are made up of several smaller projects,[10] or have more than local significance, and which therefore have potential to be defined either as projects, plans or programmes or all of these, for example, where projects require the amendment of land use plans (which themselves require SEA), before a developer can apply for development consent and carry out EIA; or where plans and programmes set binding criteria for the subsequent consent for projects; and in relation to tiering generally (Sheate et al, 2005, pp72–74). The authors comment in the Executive Summary (pv):

> *Such overlaps can create confusion as to the definition of the action concerned, and therefore whether it meets the criteria for requiring the application of either or both of the EIA and SEA Directives. Approaches adopted by Member States in trying to resolve the potential for overlap were seen to relate particularly to where EIA had previously been applied to certain PPs or where certain projects might now be subject to SEA as well as EIA.*

Taking one example, in some cases it may be that the plan or programme, rather than the project, comprises the development consent for a proposal, in which case expected tiering of a later project level assessment may not occur. This may result in some MS because of existing national or regional procedures, and in this case there will be a need for coordination additional to the existing structural links between the SEA and EIA Directives. Albrecht (2005, p36) cites Article 2a of the German Federal Building Code in conjunction with Article 17 of the German EIA Act, which requires an EIA for the resolution of certain Legally Binding Land-Use Plans. Because these are typical, she indicates that 'there could be an overlap of SEA and EIA'. The problem is ultimately one of definition, and the Commission (in the promulgation of guidance and legislative review) and ECJ (in interpreting the law), will, in time, need to address this carefully. As Sheate et al (2005, p 71) comment:

> *The potential for overlaps exists where the 'object' being assessed falls both within the definition of a 'project' set out in the EIA Directive and the definition of 'plans and programmes' under the SEA Directive. From this research it is this issue of 'project' and 'plan/programme' definition that represents the single largest area of potential complexity and confusion.*[11]

Para 9.15 of the SEA Directive Guidance (Reps of the MS/CEC, 2003) emphasizes the differences between the SEA and EIA Directives that will need to be taken into account in such cases. 'Compared to the SEA Directive, the EIA Directive does not require consultation of other authorities when there is a case by case examination (Article 4(2)), has different requirements about notification of decisions on screenings, and has no requirements on quality or monitoring'.[12] Additionally, the SEA Directive places more emphasis on alternatives (including the 'do nothing' alternative), and the information produced in the assessment should be taken account of at an earlier stage than in the EIA process. Overall, whatever overlaps may be present in the application of the SEA and EIA Directives (including the potential for proposals to fall between the two, and therefore demonstrate that there may be gaps/loopholes as well as overlaps),[13] the requirements of each law must always be complied with in order to prevent legal challenges. Figure 11.1 is a flowchart that sets out the relationship between the EIA and SEA Directives, indicating which assessment procedures apply.

Aside from the relationship with the EIA Directive, the directives with the closest relationship with the SEA Directive are the Habitats, Wild Birds and Nitrates Directives, and the Water, Waste and Air Quality Framework Directives, which are considered in the next section. The first two are linked through the Natura 2000 Network of protected sites and because the provisions for 'appropriate assessment' of plans and projects (see below, in Article 6(3) of the Habitats Directive) apply to both Directives in accordance with Article 7 they are therefore outlined together. The other Directives also have requirements for plans or programmes to be prepared or adopted by an authority, Parliament or government, and, in some cases, they set the framework for the development consent of projects. Provided they are likely to have environmentally significant effects, Articles 2, 3 and 4 of the SEA Directive require an assessment during the preparation of the plan or programme and before its adoption or submission to the legislative procedure, either through integration into existing procedures or by incorporation into new procedures.

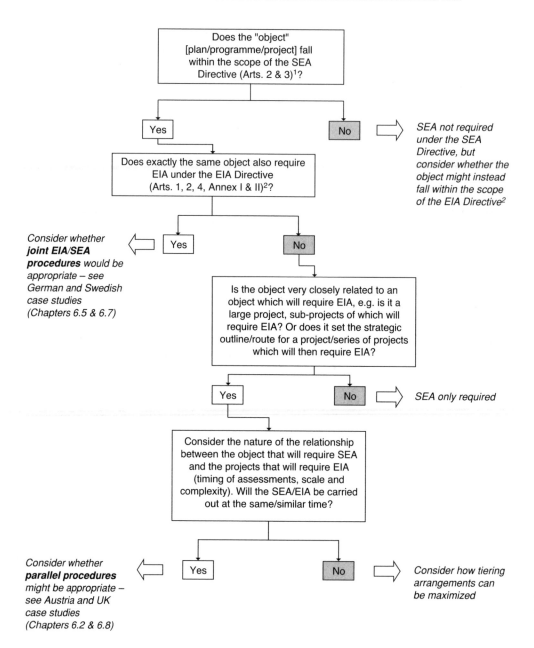

Notes:
[1]Or within the scope of MS legislation on SEA if this is broader than the SEA Directive.
[2]Or within the scope of MS legislation on EIA if this is broader than the EIA Directive.

Source: Sheate *et al*, 2005, pviii

Figure 11.1 *The relationship between the EIA and SEA Directives – which assessment procedures apply?*

Habitats and Wild Birds Directives

The 1992 Habitats Directive attempts to provide comprehensive protection of certain habitats, largely because the Berne Convention did not achieve satisfactory results (see Chapter 3). In particular, it did not stop the slow but progressive disappearance of natural habitats in Western Europe; this is continuing at a rapid pace and must today be examined in the context of biodiversity protection[14] and sustainability.[15] The protection system includes designation and protection measures for habitats ('special areas of conservation', 'SACs' or 'SCAs') (see Ball, 1997; Harte, 1997; Nollkaemper, 1997; Reid, 1997; Jans, 2000). The 1979 Wild Birds Directive attempts to provide comprehensive protection to birds and their habitats ('special protection areas', 'SPAs') (see Baldock, 1992; Wils, 1994; Freestone, 1996; Owen, 2001). The overall intention of both has been to establish 'a coherent European ecological network', known as Natura 2000, which was put in place by the Commission Decision of 18 December 1996, concerning a site information format for proposed Natura 2000 sites and requiring MS to have designated areas by 2004 at the latest.[16]

Full application of both has proved difficult to date, with frequent legal action against MS in breach[17] and criticism that neither has been as comprehensive as suggested (De Sadeleer, 2007, p176; Krämer, 2007, p139). Other criticism has been directed towards the emphasis given to procedural aspects of the law, with inadequate focus on implementation in practice (Beunen, 2006). This is the age old concern that has featured prominently in the EA literature, with substantive effectiveness being subordinated to procedural effectiveness (Marsden, 1998); the Review of the Habitats Directive also draws attention to this problem (Commission of the European Communities, 2003a, p18). Other implementation concerns relate to failures in governance and injustice, resulting in conflict (Paavola, 2003/2004). This section analyses legal aspects of the Directive's relevance to SEA, and necessarily involves detailed consideration of provisions under the Habitats Directive, in particular, Articles 6(3) and 6(4), which are essential to understanding how SEA is considered in the Directive. These provisions for appropriate assessments and their relationship to biodiversity conservation are discussed generally by Montini (2001), without the benefit of the ECJ jurisprudence outlined below.

Until 2005, ECJ jurisprudence on both Directives was largely limited to consideration of compliance with provisions for designation of sites.[18] With regard to the Wild Birds Directive, for example, the ECJ held that the Spanish government was in breach (*Santona Marshes*)[19] and that Germany had also failed to fulfil its obligations (*Leybucht Dykes*).[20] With regard to the Habitats Directive, in a series of British cases in national and European courts, application to the interim protection of sites was considered,[21] application to territorial waters examined (*Greenpeace*),[22] and the ECJ later concluded that an MS cannot take account of economic, social or cultural requirements or regional and local characteristics when designating SACs (*First Corporate Shipping*);[23] it had earlier drawn the same conclusions with regard to SPAs (*Lappel Bank*)[24] and SACs (indirectly) (*Cairngorm*).[25] The SEA Directive Guidance (Reps of the MS/CEC, 2003, p49) emphasizes that proposals designating candidate sites would not trigger the SEA Directive because in itself it would not normally result in a planning or programming decision.

In addition to designation responsibilities, obligations are placed on MS under Article 6 of the Habitats Directive to establish necessary conservation measures involving specific management plans or integrated into other development plans (Article 6(1)), take appropriate steps to avoid deterioration of natural habitats and species and disturbance of species (Article 6(2)), and ensure that 'appropriate assessments' are carried out of plans or projects that are likely to have a significant effect upon European sites, and which are not directly connected with or necessary to the management of such sites (Article 6(3)).[26] Commission guidance on the interpretation of Article 6 has been produced (Commission of the European Communities, 2000) and updated with respect to Article 6(4) (Commission of the European Communities, 2007); the guidance includes applicable methodology (Commission of the European Communities, 2001b). Article 6(4) contains exemptions, where an MS can implement a plan or project despite a negative assessment. Article 7 applies Article 6(2), 6(3) and 6(4) to the Wild Birds Directive from the implementation date of the Habitats Directive or date of classification or recognition by the MS under the Wild Birds Directive, whichever is the latest.[27]

Article 6(3) relates closely to the SEA Directive, as Article 3(2)(b) of the SEA Directive states that 'an environmental assessment shall be carried out for all plans and programmes... which, in view of the likely effect on sites, have been determined to require an assessment pursuant to Article 6 or 7 of Directive 92/43/EEC.[28] As such, there will be many instances where the SEA and Habitats Directives apply cumulatively if there are effects from plans on sites pursuant to Article 6 or 7 of the Habitats Directive. In these cases, the SEA Directive guidance recommends a combined procedure that fulfils the requirements of both Directives, which would therefore need to be in accordance with the procedural provisions of the SEA Directive (containing, for example, detailed requirements for consideration of reasonable alternatives, consultation, public participation and monitoring) and the Habitats Directive, fulfilling the requirements of Articles 6(3) and 6(4) (which include an opinion from the Commission, and little discretion to give priority to non-environmental interests). These provisions in the Habitats Directive are outlined in detail below (for comparisons, see Mathiesen, 2003, p45; Albrecht, 2005, p38).

While it is clear from guidance produced on Article 6 of the Habitats Directive (Commission of the European Communities, 2000) that an appropriate assessment is not exactly the same as an EA that may be required under the EIA Directive (the former being narrower in scope (para 4.5.2)), the guidance indicates that information provided in the EIA process may be used to inform the appropriate assessment under Article 6(3) (paras 4.5.1–4.5.2). The integration of assessment processes may therefore have significant benefits for reducing potential impacts upon habitats. This has already been seen with regard to the role of SEA (and EA in general) in biodiversity conservation, which was the subject of Chapter 6.

As stated, it was only in 2005 that the ECJ had an opportunity to consider Article 6(3) of the Habitats Directive in detail and clarify the meaning and relationship between some of the terms. These had not previously been legally considered and therefore remained open to interpretation, whatever the Commission Guidance indicated. In the *Waddenzee* case,[29] a Dutch national court requested the ECJ to answer five questions related to the interpretation of Article 6,[30] which has provided an important judicial analysis of the requirements that will most likely be binding upon future interpretations. Verschuuren (2005, p276) comments on the significance of the case:

For two reasons this is an important judgment. The first is because the Court goes into great detail explaining the meaning of Article 6(3) and 6(4) of the Habitats Directive, and the relationship of these provisions to Article 6(2). This explanation was long overdue, since the provisions of Article 6(3) and 6(4), for many years now, have been at the centre of fierce discussions on major projects in many – if not all – member states ... There were earlier decisions in which Article 6 played a role, but in none of these did the Court go into much detail. It is beyond doubt that the current decision will be influential on much of the decision-making under the Birds and Habitats Directives throughout the EU in the coming years.

Second, the Court goes into the question of direct effect in a clear way without much reservation. In my view, the Court goes beyond its more careful considerations in the Wells case.[31]

The first question asked required the Court to consider the meaning of 'plan or project' in Article 6(3). It did this by comparing the definition of project in the EIA Directive, concluding that mechanical cockle fishing is within the concept of project, given that both Directives seek to prevent activities proceeding unless they have been assessed. This confirmed the earlier Commission guidance on the matter (Commission of the European Communities, 2000, p31). The ECJ also concluded that the fact that the activity had been carried on for many years did not mean that each application should not be assessed, which it clearly did. Unfortunately for purposes of interpretation of the SEA Directive, the Court did not consider the meaning of 'plan' as distinct from 'project' in the Directive.[32] The Commission Guidance (Commission of the European Communities, 2000, p31) considers 'plan' to have a very broad meaning, in accordance with an opinion expressed by the Advocate General on the matter.[33]

The second question asked of the ECJ was the relationship between Article 6(2) and 6(3). 6(2) (in conjunction with Article 7, which applies the provision to the SPAs designated by the Wild Birds Directive) requires MS to take steps to avoid deterioration of habitats and significant disturbance of species within. Article 6(3) requires an appropriate assessment of plans or projects not directly connected with the management of the site. The Court concluded that if it is decided following the application of Article 6(3) that there will be no adverse effect, then there will generally be no deterioration or disturbance in accordance with Article 6(2); however, if the plan or project subsequently gives rise to deterioration or disturbance, then Article 6(2) can be used to remedy the situation.

The third question asked the Court to decide in what circumstances an appropriate assessment was necessary. The ECJ decided that this is needed 'if it cannot be excluded, on the basis of objective information, that it will have a significant effect on that site, either individually or in combination with other plans or projects' (para 45 of judgment). In doing so, the ECJ recognized the importance of cumulative effects and applied the precautionary principle to its determination (para 44).[34] In addition to deciding that the 'mere probability' of effects was all that was needed (para 41), and that Article 6(3) was analogous to Article 2(1) of the EIA Directive in that the concern was to assess projects that are 'likely to have significant effects' (para 42), the Court held that 'It follows that the first sentence of Article 6(3) of the Habitats Directive subordinates the requirement for an appropriate assessment of the implications of a plan or project to the condition that there be a *probability or a risk* that the latter will have significant effects on the site concerned' (para 43, my emphasis).[35] The relationship between the site's conservation objectives and significant effect was also considered, with the Court concluding that if it is likely that the objectives will not be undermined, then there are not likely to be any significant effects.

The fourth question required the ECJ to decide whether an appropriate assessment had to take any particular form. The Court concluded that while the answer to this was negative, it must take into account cumulative effects,[36] precede its approval and take full account of the precautionary principle to the effect that an authorization must only be granted if the authority is convinced the plan or project will not adversely affect the integrity of the site. Only if the exemptions in Article 6(4) were applicable could the situation be different (see below). The Court defined an appropriate assessment as follows (para 60):

> *[A]n appropriate assessment of the implications for the site concerned of the plan or project implies that, prior to its approval, all the aspects of the plan or project which can, by themselves or in combination with other plans or projects, affect the site's conservation objectives must be identified in the light of the best scientific knowledge in the field. The competent national authorities, taking account of the appropriate assessment. . .for the site concerned in the light of the site's conservation objectives, are to authorise such an activity only if they have made certain that it will not adversely affect the integrity of the site. That is the case where no reasonable scientific doubt remains as to the absence of such effects.*

The fifth question asked the ECJ whether, when a national court is called on to consider the lawfulness of an authorization for a plan or project, it can also consider the available limits of discretion of the national authority, even where EC law has not been appropriately transposed. The Court held that incorrect transposition did not avoid the binding effects of the law, given the obligations imposed by Article 249 of the TEC (see Chapters 7 and 8) and by the Directive itself. The *Kraaijeveld* decision (see Chapters 8 and 9) further held that the duty to take all appropriate measures to apply EC law binds all MS authorities, including the courts. The ECJ also examined the vertical direct effect of the Habitats Directive and held (Judgment, para 66) that:

> *As regards the right of an individual to rely on a directive and of the national court to take it into consideration, it would be incompatible with the binding effect attributed to a directive by Article 249 EC to exclude, in principle, the possibility that the obligation which it imposes may be relied on by those concerned.*

One matter not examined by the ECJ and that relates to both the fourth and fifth questions is that of public participation, which is discretionary in accordance with Article 6(3), which states that the national authorities shall agree to the plan or project only after having ascertained that it will not adversely affect the integrity of the site concerned 'and, if appropriate, after having obtained the opinion of the general public'. Palerm (2006, p136) discusses pubic participation in the context of the Rotterdam Mainport development project, which benefited from the Article 6(4) exemption. Where the plan or project is not subject to other EC law (in particular, the SEA or EIA Directives, where public participation is a requirement), 'where appropriate' would need to be considered in the light of the Aarhus Convention, which is binding in EC law regardless of whether individual directives have incorporated its requirements or not. In advocating that public participation is a success factor in effective decision making and illustrating this with reference to the Rotterdam case, Palerm (2006, p136) comments:

> [I]n the light of the spirit of the Aarhus Convention and the Habitats Directive, public participation should always be 'appropriate' for decisions made in the context of Article 6(3) of the Habitats Directive. The EC would do well in promoting an amendment to the Habitats Directive so this ambiguity is eliminated, and public participation compliant with Article 6 of the Aarhus Convention is required for all assessments under Article 6(3) of the Habitats Directive.[37]

There have been numerous cases of incorrect transposition of the Directive. In *Commission v Germany*[38] the Court held that German implementation of the Habitats Directive was non-compliant because, 'In the ECJ's opinion, it did not appear that the criteria excluding the duty to carry out an assessment were capable of ensuring that those projects were never likely to have a significant effect on the protected sites' (Ureta, 2007, p90). The ECJ also held that the refusal to grant permission for installations causing emissions 'only where it was foreseeable that they directly affected a SCA' (Ureta, 2007, p91) was also in breach. Ureta (2007, p91) concludes with a comment of general application to MS failings in implementing EC law:

> In fact, as the ECJ rightly observed, the German authorities had tried to justify the legality of the Federal law on nature protection by relying on technical rules and administrative practices. However, as was clearly stated in consistent case-law, such practices are not sufficient to transpose the requirements set out in environmental directives.

In accordance with Article 6(4), if despite a negative assessment and the absence of alternatives a plan or project must nevertheless be carried out for 'imperative reasons of overriding public interest', compensatory measures must be taken (Holder, 2004). However, if the site hosts a priority natural habitat and/or a priority species, the only considerations that may be raised relate to public health or public safety, to 'beneficial consequences of primary importance for the environment', or after the Commission has commented thereon, to other 'imperative reasons of overriding public interest'. Unnerstall (2006) emphasizes the balancing of environmental and economic factors that is inherent in Article 6(4) and indicates the need for it to be interpreted in accordance with the EU definition of sustainable development, which is true of all directives including the SEA Directive.[39] Krämer (2007, pp139–140) is critical of the consultation role of the Commission and the guidance produced, commenting: 'Not one single project is known to have been given up or significantly amended following the Commission's consultation, in order to preserve the natural habitat from the planned economic development. And Commission guidance on the interpretation of Art 6 has not had a measurable effect'.

Ureta's article (2007, pp91–96) considers in detail the application of the Commission guidance to the exemption provisions in Article 6(4).[40] As he indicates, there are no detailed ECJ rulings on the interpretation of this, so the Commission guidance is generally all that is available to assist those in implementing the requirements. Since it deals with the ability of MS to approve plans or projects despite negative assessments, Article 6(4) is of significant legal interest, and it is therefore extremely surprising that it has yet to be judicially considered in depth. Judicial definition of '*imperative reasons*' and '*overriding public interest*' are particularly needed.

The guidance makes clear that the exemption provisions must be applied in a specific order to meet the requirements of Article 6(4) (2007, p4). First, the alternative put forward for approval must be the least damaging for habitats, for species and for the integrity of the Natura 2000 site, regardless of economic considerations, and no other feasible alternative must exist that would not affect the integrity of the site. Second, there must be imperative reasons of overriding public interest (see below). Third, all compensatory measures that are needed to ensure the protection of the overall coherence of the Natura 2000 network have to be taken; such measures should only be considered when mitigation measures have first been applied and they must be communicated to the Commission. The burden of proof in showing that Article 6(4) is applicable falls on the person seeking to utilize it, as the updated guidance (Commission of the European Communities, 2007, p4) indicates:

> *Being an exception to Article 6(3), this provision can only be applied to circumstances where all the conditions required by the Directive are fully satisfied. In this regard, it falls on whoever wants to make use of this exception to prove, as a prerequisite, that the aforementioned conditions do indeed exist in each particular case.*

Alternatives include the zero option if significant negative effects on the integrity of the site have been identified.[41] In another infraction case involving Germany, the Commission argued that the search for alternative sites for industrial and commercial development was not limited by the municipal boundary, and that disadvantages connected with an alternative was no ground for failing to consider it (Ureta, 2007, p95). The relationship between the consideration of alternatives and overriding public interest has been expressed in a judicial opinion as follows:

> *among the alternatives short-listed the choice does not inevitably have to be determined by which alternative least adversely affects the site concerned. Instead, the choice requires a balance to be struck between the adverse effect on the integrity of the SPA and the relevant reasons of overriding public interest.*[42]

With regard to the question of overriding public interest specifically, because the Habitats Directive does not provide a definition, other EC law that uses similar words can be examined for assistance in interpretation (Commission of the European Communities, 2007, pp7–8). Although the Commission has indicated that for a public interest to be overriding it must be a long term interest (p8), where the Commission has been required to give its opinion on the application of this under the section, its opinions have apparently not been consistent. Ureta (2007, p92) gives examples of projects having been approved as part of the Trans-European Networks as justification for such an interest, but argues that the mere fact of this should not prevail over the Directive's requirements, illustrating the point with reference to where the ECJ has ruled on the incompatibility of nature conservation and other EC polices in the past.[43] Socio-economic aspects have been put forward in many instances as imperative reasons of overriding public interest, with opinions being given supporting projects in regions affected by exceptionally high unemployment, and where high levels of dependence on maritime transport are affected.[44]

With regard to compensatory measures, the updated guidance examines this matter in great detail (Commission of the European Communities, 2007, pp10–21). Despite definition in the Directive, the Commission concludes that they must be distinguished from mitigation measures (which must first be considered); these are specific to the plan or project and aim to offset negative impacts by providing compensation relating precisely to the negative effects on the habitat or species. They constitute the last resort and must only be used when other safeguards are ineffectual.[45] In *Commission v Austria*,[46] the ECJ held that the compensatory measures adopted following a negative assessment were inappropriate for avoiding the negative effects with a margin of safety (Ureta, 2007, pp89-90). Ureta criticizes the Commission in its opinion concerning the project for the construction of the Airbus aeroplane (see note below), because as Germany had failed to propose a sufficient number of sites to comply with Article 4 of the Habitats Directive, the Commission acknowledged that 'it was not in a position to fully assess whether the compensatory measures and their timing were going [to] ensure the overall coherence of the Natura 2000 network' (p95).[47]

Compensation raises a number of interesting legal issues in relation to the Habitats Directive that are explored by the Commission (Commission of the European Communities, 2007, pp19–20). First, it is important to ensure temporary protection is made available for candidate sites, which should ideally have a legal basis in national law. Second, enforcement tools at the national level are needed to ensure 'full implementation and effectiveness' (p19) of compensation. These can be linked to liability regimes that have a basis in EC law such as under the ELD and EIA Directive (see Chapter 9).[48] Third, compulsory acquisition of property may be necessary in some cases to ensure protection, and legal regimes for this must be effective. Fourth, the cost of compensation must be borne by the promoter of the plan or project, in line with the polluter pays principle.

The final legal matters for consideration under Article 6(4) are that of the opinion needed from the Commission in the event that the site hosts a priority natural habitat or species. First, it is important to recognize that where the plan or project is likely to affect a priority natural habitat or species, 'special treatment' is needed (Commission of the European Communities, 2007, p21). In these circumstances the imperative reasons of overriding public interest must relate to human health and public safety or overriding beneficial consequences for the environment if damage to the site is to be allowed. None of these matters are defined by the Directive, and once more, they are generally interpreted with reference to other EC law (Commission of the European Communities, 2007, pp22–23). An example was in the *Leybucht Dykes* case (see note 20) where, while it preceded adoption of the Habitats Directive, the Court's approach influenced the drafting of Article 6. In the case, in the Commission's summary (p23), the Court confirmed that the danger of flooding and the protection of the coast 'constituted sufficiently serious reasons to justify the dyke works and the strengthening of coastal structures as long as those measures [were] confined to a strict minimum'.

With regard to the need for an opinion from the Commission if the exemption is to be allowed, the ECJ has confirmed that the Commission will only give an opinion when sites have been placed on the list of sites, not for candidate sites (Commission of the European Communities, 2007, p23). There is no procedure specified for obtaining or giving the opinion or its contents,[49] and while it must be given it does not, in itself, have any binding effect as the MS can decide to implement the plan or project even if the opinion is negative. If the MS decides to proceed despite a negative opinion, the Commission's only remedy is to challenge the MS if there is some breach of the Directive or EC law generally.

Water Framework Directive

The Water Framework Directive was adopted on 23 October 2000 with the intention of ending the fragmented approach to water policy in the EU, with a large number of related measures providing for quality standards, action plans, reporting and monitoring provisions in relation to different aspects of water.[50] The Directive takes a broad view of water management and has as its key objectives the prevention of any further deterioration of water bodies, and the protection and enhancement of the status of aquatic ecosystems and associated wetlands. It aims to promote sustainable water consumption and will contribute to mitigating the effects of floods and droughts.[51] Integration with other sectoral policies is seen as particularly important, for example, there is specific mention of the impact that inland surface water may have on the coastal zone, although it will above all have primary effects on land use planning in MS (White and Howe, 2003; Howarth, 2007, p166).

Chave (2001, pix) states that the Water Framework Directive 'is probably the most significant legislative instrument in the water field to be introduced on an international basis for many years'.[52] The 2000 Directive therefore aims at a holistic and integrative approach to achieve 'good ecological status' for all water bodies,[53] which, according to Grimeaud (2004, p29), requires:

> '[T]he designation of river basin districts as hydrological integrated water units, the synchronization of surface and groundwater and connected territorial ecosystems, the simultaneous use of emission limit values and environmental quality standards, and the elaboration of river basin management plans [RBMPs] and programmes of measures [PoMs] in which all relevant national measures are to be notified and implemented in a coordinated fashion.'

The Water Framework Directive is a good example of the need to integrate related directives under the umbrella of an overarching regulatory framework, of which the Waste Framework Directive is perhaps the most significant effort to date.[54] Discussion in the previous section of the absence of a framework directive for biodiversity (which could serve to better integrate and expand on the current Wild Birds and Habitats Directive requirements with other provisions), and the ongoing consideration to a closer relationship between the EIA and SEA Directives, perhaps consolidated, perhaps under the framework of a horizontal requirement dealing with access to information, public participation, access to justice and environmental liability is something that may be considered in the future.[55]

The relationship between the Water Framework Directive and the SEA Directive has been examined by several authors given the requirement in the former for environmental impacts of human activity to be reviewed (together with an economic analysis) (Article 5(1)) in mandatory RBMPs and PoMs (Article 4(1)). Article 13 (RBMPs) and Article 11 (PoMs) contain the detailed provisions (see Chave, 2001, pp34–36, 98–121; Grimeaud, 2004, pp35–36).[56] If either the RBMPs or PoMs set the framework for the future development consent of projects (for examples of these, see Howarth, 2007, p169), the trigger in Article 3(2)(a) of the SEA Directive therefore also mandates assessment under the SEA Directive since they are prepared for a listed sector (water management).[57] In turn, the SEA Directive provision for coordinated or joint procedures (Article 11(2)) is likely to be utilized, rather than each Directive carrying out a separate assessment of environmental impacts, at least where RBMPs and PoMs are concerned. The important matter is to ensure that in all cases the requirements of both Directives (and any other relevant EC law) is fully implemented, although in making determinations on this it is important to be aware that courts are likely to take a purposive approach to interpretation, in accordance with that applied to date regarding the EIA Directive (Howarth, 2007, pp165 and 169).

Gullón (2005, pp517–521), Carter and Howe (2006, pp290–296) and Howarth (2007) examine the procedural linkages between the two Directives, Gullón in detailed tabular form including a thorough comparison of the respective objectives, general procedural provisions and specific public participation requirements (pp517–520). Carter and Howe comment on p292 on the potential for coordinated or joint procedures: 'The work programme [for the implementation of the Water Framework Directive], prepared with meeting the requirements of the SEA Directive in mind, would ideally identify the key stages of RBMP development at which assessment procedures should be integrated'. Carter and Howe (2006, p292) identify six procedures that they believe are requirements of both of the Directives and that could therefore be dealt with in a coordinated or joint manner. These are the collection of baseline data, the assessment of alternatives and options, the assessment of policies, the suggestion of mitigation measures, the development of monitoring procedures and the development of consultation and public participation procedures.

The collection of baseline data is required under Article 5(1) and Annex II, V and VII of the Water Framework Directive, which mandates characterization of the river basin and groundwater bodies, and is used to formulate the PoMs and assess the impact of any pressures identified together with future monitoring procedures. Carter and Howe (2006) highlight that baseline data is also central to the preparation of environmental reports (under Article 5 (1) and Annex I of the SEA Directive), as SEA Directive reports must describe the environmental characteristics of the areas likely to be affected by the plan or programme assessed and any environmental problems in the area. They comment on the benefits of these approaches as follows (pp292–293):

Information collected during the river basin characterisation process will provide a wealth of data on water resources to inform this stage of SEA report preparation. Similarly, any baseline data obtained during previous SEAs, for example land use plan SEAs relating to the area covered by the RBD [river basin district], could be used to inform river basin characterisation procedures. Baseline data gathered could subsequently be used to help predict impacts on the water environment during RBMP

> *SEAs, assessments of water quality required by the WFD [Water Framework Directive] and during SEAs of other relevant PPPs such as land use or transport plans.*

The assessment of alternatives and options is addressed by both Directives, with the SEA Directive's explicit focus in Article 5(1) on reasonable alternatives and the reasons for selecting the chosen alternative in Article 9(1)(b), and the Water Framework Directive's implicit provision for 'option screening', which Carter and Howe believe 'must be undertaken during the early stages of RBMP preparation' (2006, p293) to identify the options best able to assist in the achievement of key objectives. Certain proposals are, however, exempt under both directives, with Article 3(8) of the SEA Directive avoiding the need to assess plans or programmes that have the sole purpose of serving a civil emergency, and (for example) Article 4(6) providing for 'temporary deterioration' in the status of water bodies as a result of extreme floods and prolonged droughts, both of which may result in a civil emergency. The danger here for environmental protection is that while the SEA Directive's strict provisions for the consideration of alternatives would need to be taken into account in the assessment of the environmental effects of RBMPs, there are many circumstances in which it can be envisaged that the exemptions will be deployed for reasons of 'overriding public interest',[58] which may result in compromise to the spirit of both Directives, even while it is compliant on paper and consistent with the practice of sustainable development and the focus of EA on procedural rather than substantive dimensions. As Carter and Howe comment (2006, p293):

> *Although SEA procedures provide the opportunity to strengthen RBMPs through identifying sustainable options, political and economic priorities many [sic] nevertheless constrain the achievement of good water status through requiring actions, for example the straightening and channelisation of rivers, that compromise the achievement of the WFD's [Water Framework Directive's] goals. Although SEAs can help to identify sustainable options, they cannot ensure their selection.*

Howarth (2007, p151) argues persuasively that a key contrast between the Water Framework and SEA Directives is that only one of them focuses on the substantive dimension of harm prevention: 'The former is based upon explicit and reasonably precise environmental objectives and standards, against which assessments are to be made, whereas the latter is not'. He therefore emphasizes that the SEA Directive (in common with the EIA Directive) fails to relate significance criteria 'to objective and precise standards of what is environmentally acceptable, [and] serves to install the same quality of aimlessness in the SEA process as has been noted in respect of EIA'. While a harsh and exaggerated criticism, which if taken in isolation ignores the value of information generated and participation provided in the decision making process (which Howarth recognizes on pp152 and 159–160, albeit with continuing and justifiable reservations), it is of course fundamentally correct and in accordance with the criticisms levelled at EA from an international law perspective (see Chapter 9). Until there is a clear link between EA and harm prevention (which may of course never come, especially in the light of the difficulties in establishing liability regimes at international and European level), such criticisms will continue to be voiced and the utility of EA will remain limited by unclear lines of discretionary decision making, heavily weighted in favour of economic interests.[59]

One of the key benefits of assessing RBMPs would appear to be that there is scope to evaluate the detailed policies contained within them. This was one of the key conclusions of Chapter 10, as identified by Sheate et al in their report to the Commission (2005, p16). While the SEA Directive does not explicitly apply to the assessment of policies therefore in the design of coordinated or joint procedures applicable to RBMPs, consideration may need to be given to the policies established by the MS to deliver good water status in the river basin district. Unfortunately, Carter and Howe (2006, p 294) fail to provide more information on this 'procedure', which they argue is relevant to both Directives, but the content of the supplementary PoMs, in particular, provides room for policies to be assessed as part of the overall evaluation. Annex VI of the Directive indicates that the supplementary measures include a wide range of regulatory tools, both legal, policy and economic.

Mitigation is a key part of the procedural provisions of the SEA and Water Framework Directives, although it is mostly implicit in both. In carrying out the EA during the preparation of the plan or programme in accordance with Article 4(1) of the SEA Directive, and in taking the results of the report into account at this time (under Article 8) the aim is to mitigate effects at the outset. Article 9(1)(b) further provides for the MS to ensure that when a plan or programme is adopted, a statement is made available summarizing how environmental considerations have been integrated into the plan or programme. Annex I(g) is the most explicit provision, as the information that must be provided for the environmental report includes 'the measures envisaged to prevent, reduce and as fully as possible offset any significant adverse effects on the environment of implementing the plan or programme'. Under the Water Framework Directive, it is necessary to consider changing the content of the RBMP to address impacts identified in the assessment, which include problems that exist that could limit the achievement of good status of waters. The PoMs subsequently developed and included within RBMPs are largely designed to provide the mitigation needed. Article 11 therefore provides that the PoMs must take 'account of the results of the analyses required under Article 5, in order to achieve the objectives established under Article 4'. Furthermore, detailed provisions that are part of Article 11 include 'measures to prevent or control the input of pollutants' (Article 11(3)(h) for diffuse sources liable to cause pollution) and 'measures to eliminate pollution of surface waters' (Article 11(3)(k)). Annex II point 1.5 of the Directive also refers to the requirement to evaluate impacts in order to 'optimise the design' of PoMs, which presumably includes the need for mitigation. Point 2.2 adds to this.

Monitoring is explicit to both Directives and is an important advance on earlier laws that failed to incorporate provisions for follow-up. Article 10(1) of the SEA Directive requires that significant effects of the implementation of plans and programmes are monitored to identify unforeseen adverse effects and take remedial action, and Article 10(2) permits the use of existing monitoring arrangements where appropriate. Article 8 of the Water Framework Directive provides more detailed arrangements that relate to surface water status, groundwater status and protected areas. These include the need in Article 8(1) 'to establish a coherent and comprehensive overview of water status in each river basin district'. Timelines are indicated, and technical specifications described in Annex V, which differentiates between surveillance, operational and investigative monitoring. Because of the far more detailed nature of the provisions in the Water Framework Directive, and Article 10(2) of the SEA Directive, Carter and Howe (2006, p295) state: 'It is likely [that]... the development of monitoring procedures to meet the WFD's [Water Framework Directive's] requirements will drive the monitoring of water resource issues during SEAs' (see also Howarth, 2007, pp185–186).

The final procedure which the SEA and Water Framework Directives have in common, albeit subject to differences, is the requirement for consultation and public participation, which in general has been motivated by the provisions of both the Aarhus and Espoo Conventions (see Chapter 4), the latter given the significance of the transbounday element in both Directives. Articles 6 and 7 of the SEA Directive (considered in detail in Chapter 10) are directed in large part to the preparation of the environmental report, with some differences in the consultation/participation of authorities and the public. Article 14 of the Water Framework Directive focuses on the preparation of the RBMP and is designed to 'encourage the active involvement of all interested parties... in particular in the production, review and updating of the river basin management plans'. Detailed timelines are specified for compliance. Carter and Howe (2006, pp295–296) again stress the potential for coordinated and joint procedures in respect of consultation and participation on water management plans such as the RBMPs. Gullón (2005, p520) and Howarth (2007, p181) highlight that in most areas the Water Framework Directive requirements exceed those of the SEA Directive, the former drawing attention to a specific guidance document on public participation that has been made available to support the Directive. As such, these are again likely to be applied to coordinated or joint assessments of impacts of RBMPs or PoMs (see Howarth, 2007, p183).

Aside from the strategic assessment of RBMPs and PoMs, other plans and programmes assessed by the SEA Directive may influence water management in relation to the Water Framework Directive, and vice versa. Carter and Howe (2006, pp296–297) refer to land use plans in particular given that land and water use planning are designed to support one another and that the regulation of water is often 'inseparable from land use planning activities' (p296). There are a number of dimensions to this, which are examined by White and Howe (2003, pp623–629) in looking generally at the relationship between planning and the Water Framework Directive in England and Wales.[60] These include changed planning responsibilities, reinforcing the environmental agenda in relation to the water resource, strengthening the regional focus of planning, clarifying the role of planning practice and planning policy, increasing the importance of stakeholders, and potentially revising the notion of a European spatial planning policy.[61] In relation to SEA specifically, another dimension is clearly that land use plan SEAs may need to be 'adapted to look specifically at ground and surface water, and chemical and ecological status, as required by the WFD [Water Framework Directive]' (Carter and Howe, 2006, p296). Planning policy guidance may also need to be changed to ensure future plans and their amendments take account of the Water Framework Directive.

As Howarth (2007, p166) indicates, 'the additional status of RBMPs in guiding decisions about land use must also be considered'. Howarth therefore discusses (pp166–169) whether RBMPs can be regarded as a land use plan as well as a water management plan or programme, which would trigger the SEA Directive in respect of their setting the framework for additional/related development consents. He summarizes the recent changes in land use planning in England and their relationship to water management and concludes (pp168–169):

In a system that is plan-led, such as in England, there is good reason to suppose that WFD plans act as a 'guide' to future development. Therefore, even if, read in isolation, WFD plans did not 'set the framework' for future development – which is disputed – their status in planning determinations means that they are capable of having this role within the land use planning system.

Finally, the relationship between the Water Framework Directive and the Habitats Directive should also be explained. Howarth (2007, pp169–172) examines this, as assessment of RBMPs and PoMs may 'arise independently of whether or not the plan or programme sets the framework for future development consent of a listed project'. The original Habitats Directive Guidance produced by the Commission (Commission of the European Communities, 2000, para 4.3.2) suggests that water management plans are included in the definition of 'plan or project' under the Habitats Directive, and that plans or projects 'not directly concerned with or necessary to the management of the site' should not be interpreted too strictly so as to exclude proposals, as some may have mixed objectives (para 4.3.3). In these cases, the guidance suggests that it may be possible to separate the different objectives of a mixed plan, so that, for example, those that are not directly connected to the management of a site undergo assessment, while those that are do not. A commercial timber harvesting plan is the example given (para 4.3.3). Despite ambiguity in the SEA Directive Guidance (Reps of the MS/CEC, 2003, p55) that suggests that either a RBMP is excluded from an appropriate assessment because it is directly relevant to the management of the site or because it would be unlikely to have significant effects on a site, Howarth (2007) concludes that as RBMPs will also include water utility functions they have many of the characteristics of a mixed plan and therefore that: 'Similar considerations might arise in relation to a RBMP under the WFD' (p171).

Nitrates, Waste Framework and Air Quality Framework Directives

A few other directives have been identified as relevant to the SEA Directive,[62] although none of them have an explicit requirement for assessment of these plans or programmes that is comparable to Article 6(3) of the Habitats Directive[63] or Article 5(1) of the Water Framework Directive. However, in the same way that RBMPs (and possibly PoMs) have to be assessed under Article 3(2)(a) of the SEA Directive if they are prepared for a listed sector and set the framework for future development consent of listed projects, so too may other plans and programmes provided they are subject to preparation by an authority and are required by a formal provision in accordance with Article 2(a) of the SEA Directive.

The Nitrates Directive is the first example, and attempts to address the fact that the main cause of diffuse pollution of waters is nitrates from agricultural sources. Although the use of nitrogen-containing fertilizers and manures is regarded as necessary for European agriculture under the CAP, it poses an environmental risk when used excessively or is not controlled adequately. The objective of the Directive is therefore to reduce water pollution caused or induced by nitrates from agricultural sources and to prevent such pollution.

Article 5(1) of the Directive requires action programmes to be established by MS for designated vulnerable zones. Although the SEA Directive Guidance (Reps of the

MS/CEC, 2003, p48) indicates that 'these action programmes are mainly directed towards certain agricultural practices rather than projects', they 'could be considered as "programmes" within the meaning of the SEA Directive and would therefore require environmental assessment'. This would be the case because they are to be prepared by an authority and are required by a formal provision; they are also prepared for a listed sector (agriculture) and may potentially set the framework for the future development consent of a listed project (such as intensive livestock units).

The Waste Framework Directive, codified in 2006, is the second example. It is designed to protect human health and the environment against harmful effects caused by the collection, transport, treatment, storage and tipping of waste. Article 1(1)(a) states that waste 'shall mean any substance or object in the categories set out in Annex I which the holder discards or intends or is required to discard'. Since the original Directive in 1975, 'waste' has been subject to frequent interpretation by the ECJ; the 2006 Directive incorporates these interpretations as at its adoption. Other key definitions, including 'disposal' and 'recovery' are also defined in Annex IIA and B.

Article 7(1) requires the competent authority to prepare waste management plans relating to the type, quantity and origin of waste to be recovered or disposed of; general technical requirements; any special arrangements for particular wastes; and suitable disposal sites or installations. Clearly, plans prepared for the last of these categories (Article 7(1)(d)) may set the framework for the development consent of a listed project, as also identified by the SEA Directive Guidance, which refers to Annex I(9) and (10) and Annex II(11)(b) of the EIA Directive (2003, p48). Article 9(1) of the Waste Framework Directive reinforces this, as it states that for the purposes of implementing Article 7, 'any establishment or undertaking which carries out the operations specified in Annex IIA (disposal operations) shall obtain a permit from the competent authority'. Given that the plans are prepared by an authority for a listed sector (waste management) and are formally required, the Guidance therefore concludes:

> *Such waste management plans would normally be covered by the SEA Directive and assessment would automatically be required, following Article 3(2)(a), provided all the other conditions of application are fulfilled. Furthermore, there may be plans which do not directly identify suitable disposal sites or installations but set the criteria for them and/or delegate this task to lower tier plans (e.g. regional or provincial plans). These plans also seem to set the overall framework for subsequent development consents and should therefore also be covered by the SEA Directive.*

The Air Quality Framework Directive is the third example. This Directive is focused upon avoiding, preventing or reducing harmful air pollutants. In part, this requires defining and establishing objectives and setting limit values and alert thresholds. Thereafter, an assessment of ambient air quality in accordance with Articles 5 and 6 of the Directive is needed, and where pollutants are higher than limit values, under Article 8(3) plans or programmes must be prepared or implemented to attain the limit value within specified time limits.

There are various requirements for air quality plans and programmes, as set out in Article 8 generally, and Annex IV, which sets out the content needs of local, regional or national programmes. Integrated plans may be prepared for all pollutants (Article 8(4)) and the public must be informed (Article 8(3)). The SEA Directive Guidance (Reps of the MS/CEC, 2003, p49) indicates that while the Air Quality Framework Directive contains a requirement for plans and programmes to be prepared by an authority, they are unlikely to be prepared for a listed sector. However, it is quite possible for them to set the framework for development consent of an unlisted project, and in many cases they are likely to have significant environmental effects. As such, they would have to be assessed under Article 3(4) of the SEA Directive.

Structural Funds Regulations

The structural funds are an aid package aimed at the EU's disadvantaged regions. The regulations implementing them specify that environmental factors must be incorporated into regional development programmes (Environmental Resources Management, 1998), but there was little evidence of this in the first programming periods from 1989 to 1993 (Clement and Bachtler, 1997). Thereafter, environmental appraisal was made a mandatory obligation, with Sheate (2003, p343, note 58) referring to key case law in the early 1990s that ensured that the European Commission could no longer ignore the potential for EC funds to result in environmentally damaging schemes.[64] Despite this, the incorporation of the environment still remained limited (Clement and Bachtler, 1997; Keller, 1997; Bradley, 1999), although it later took on an improved role (Roberts, 2001), assisted by efforts of individual MS (Balfors and Schmidtbauer, 2002). Certain aspects have, however, remained weak, especially as related to SEA best practice (Fischer, 2003) or sustainable development more generally (see Macleod, 2005).

The structural funds provide for several types of plans and programmes, with the Community Support Framework, Operational Programmes and Single Programming Documents assessed for the 'expected impact' on the environment. As such, in common with the Habitats and Water Framework Directives, they contain separate requirements not only for plans and programmes to be produced, but also for them to be assessed. Article 41(2)(b) of the Structural Funds Regulation in particular requires:

> [A]n ex-ante evaluation of the environmental situation of the region concerned, in particular of those sectors which will presumably be considered affected by the assistance. . . The ex ante evaluation shall give a description, quantified as far as possible, of the existing environmental situation and an estimate of the expected environmental impact of the strategy and assistance on the environmental situation.[65]

Article 3(9) of the SEA Directive states that it does not apply to plans and programmes co-financed under the current programming periods of the Structural Funds. As Albrecht points out (2005, p39): 'The reason is, that the Directive is addressed only to the Member States and does not apply to the institutions of the Community'. Article 12(4), however, states that the Commission shall report on the relationship between the SEA Directive and the Structural Funds Regulations with a view to ensuring a coherent approach between the SEA Directive and the Regulations. As such, while the SEA Directive does not appear currently to be applicable to the structural funds regulations, the situation will change in the future.[66] This is recognized in guidance produced for the new programming period, which runs from 2007–2013 (Greening Regional Development Programmes Network, 2006). In a foreword by the Commission, the guidance states (p1):

The new round of the Structural and Cohesion Fund Operational Programmes will run from 2007–13. Many of these Operational Programmes may require assessment under the SEA Directive, particularly if they include projects covered by the Environmental Impact Assessment (EIA) Directive. Moreover, Member States may find it useful to apply SEAs to the National Strategic Reference Frameworks.

CONCLUSIONS

This chapter has shown that the SEA Directive has close procedural links to the EIA Directive, especially as EA for listed sectors under the latter must set the framework for projects listed under the former. The interpretation of many of the terms in the SEA Directive (such as 'project') draws on the experience with interpretation of terms in the EIA Directive, at least in the official guidance currently. The SEA Directive also has close procedural links with the Habitats Directive, which is explicitly mentioned in the SEA Directive. The chapter has discussed the relevant legislation and applicable case law on this, which has recently served to clarify several provisions of the Habitats Directive to assist in coordinating this relationship. The Water Framework Directive also has close procedural links with the SEA Directive and, in common with the Habitats Directive, contains its own requirements not just for the production of plans (and programmes) but also assessment, triggering the need for coordination of procedures between the different laws.

Finally, the chapter has explored the other EC laws of relevance to the SEA Directive, notably the Nitrates, Waste and Air Quality Framework Directives, which contain requirements for plans and programmes of listed sectors to be produced by government, and that may set the framework for the development consent of projects, or have significant environmental effects requiring assessment regardless. The Structural Funds Regulations have also briefly been summarized because they are referred to in the SEA Directive, and will henceforth need to be assessed in accordance with their own provisions; they therefore have their own requirements for plans and programmes to be produced and assessed, which are analogous to the provisions in the SEA Directive.

This is the final chapter in the European law section of the book, and as such it is appropriate to emphasize the procedural basis of much of the EC environmental law discussed, particularly the EA provisions of the EIA, SEA and Habitats Directives that fail to explicitly limit harm to the environment. Howarth (2007, p189) contrasts the role of the Water Framework Directive from such provisions, commenting that 'the WFD procedures go beyond informing decision-makers of the existence of environmental factors which need to be "taken into account". They instruct decision-makers as to the weight to be attached to those factors'. Howarth sees no reason why such factors should not also be included in the EA directives, which will be discussed further in the next chapter. Chapter 12 therefore compares and contrasts European law with international law outlined in the first section, generally and specifically with respect to regulating SEA. As such, it enables closer comparisons to be made between the foregoing sections (including the procedural and substantive dimensions of EA), before final conclusions are presented.

NOTES

1   Council Directive 92/43/EEC on the conservation of natural habitats and of wild fauna and flora OJ 1992 L206/7, as amended by Council Directive 97/62 adapting the Directive to technical progress OJ 1997 L305/42.
2   Directive 2000/60 establishing a framework for Community action on water policy, OJ 2000 L327/1.
3   Council Directive 79/409/EEC on the conservation of wild birds OJ 1979 L103/1, as amended by Commission Directive 85/411 OJ 1985 L233/33, Council Directive 81/854 OJ 1981 L319/3, Commission Directive 91/244 OJ 1991 L115/41, Council Directive 94/24 OJ 1994 L164/9, and Commission Directive 97/49 OJ 1997 L223/9.
4   Council Directive 91/676/EEC of 12 December 1991 concerning the protection of waters against pollution caused by nitrates from agricultural sources, OJ L375, 31/12/1991 P.0001-0008.
5   Directive 2006/12/EC of the European Parliament and of the Council of 5 April 2006 on waste, OJ L114.
6   Council Directive 96/62/EC of 27 September 1996 on ambient air quality assessment and management, OJ L296, 21/11/1996 P. 0055-0063.
7   Council Regulation (EC) No 1260/1999 of 21 June 1999 laying down general provisions on the structural funds. Council Regulation (EC) No 1257/1999 of 17 May 1999 on support for rural development from the European Agricultural Guidance and Guarantee Fund (EAGGF) and amending and repealing certain Regulations.
8   The timing of the study (which began in mid-July 2004) was too late to provide guidance to the MS on implementation, but too early to describe the experience with problems that were emerging.
9   Readers are referred to the report for further information on the detailed overlaps between the EIA and SEA Directives, which is only summarized in the text here.
10 In Case C-227/01 *Commission v Spain* [2002], the ECJ held that the fact that an EIA had been carried out for the railway reservation general plan in 1993 did not mean that a subsequent EIA should not be undertaken for each detailed section. By contrast, the problem of what has been termed 'salami slicing' (whereby division of a large project into small projects has often resulted in negative strategic and cumulative effects not being assessed) has been common to date.
11 The ECJ has already considered the definitions of 'plan or project' in connection with the Habitats Directive (see below), which added to its consideration of the meaning of 'project' under the EIA Directive (see Chapter 9) will no doubt influence its future findings.
12 Some of the differences relating to public participation are explained by the fact that the SEA Directive was adopted after the Aarhus Convention came into force. The EIA Directive has since been amended by the Public Participation Directive (see Chapter 9, and Sheate et al, 2005, p8).
13 Compliance with the letter of the Directives may not comply with the spirit, and, as such, MS should remember the broad approach taken by the ECJ in this regard (see Chapters 8 and 9). Many significant effects may be cumulative, for example, which are often overlooked. Another example, provided by Sheate et al (2005, pix, and 67) is where certain plans set the framework for development consent of projects, yet the plans themselves are not formally required and therefore do not need to be assessed under the SEA Directive. Approaches adopted by the MS to address overlaps are examined in Sheate et al (2005, pp74–78).
14 In the Review of the Habitats Directive by the Commission (Commission of the European Communities, 2003a), the framework of biodiversity conservation policy in the EU is outlined (pp2–3), including the biodiversity strategy. The Review highlights (p3) that effective

implementation of the Habitats and Wild Birds Directives and the establishment of the Natura 2000 network 'are critical to meeting the EU and global 2010 targets'. The Commission guidance (Commission of the European Communities, 2000, p9) indicates that Article 6 is important in helping to achieve the aims of the Berne and Biodiversity Conventions. See also De Sadeleer (2007, p179), who, in comparing international and European law highlights that the absence of a framework directive for biodiversity has resulted in significant overlaps in the application of EC law, in particular, with respect to EA. Birnie (1996) addresses related matters. Also important to note is that since the Habitats and Wild Birds Directives fail to provide comprehensive protection of biodiversity; broader application of SEA (including outside the SEA Directive) is advocated in a European context, especially through spatial planning. This draws on advocacy and practice at the international level. In Dutch, Swedish and German contexts respectively see Kolhoff and Slootweg (2005), Balfors et al (2005) and Bröring and Wiegleb (2005) and Wiegleb and Bröring (2005).

15 See, for example, Unnerstall (2006) and Palerm (2006), who make significant contributions to the discussion concerning the application of Article 6(4) of the Habitats Directive in particular.

16 SACs and SPAs are collectively known as Sites of Community Importance (SCI). Note that for proposed SCI (candidate SACs and SPAs), although Articles 6(2), 6(3) and 6(4) do not apply, the ECJ has held that MS had still to provide protection as soon as they were proposed. See ECJ, Case C-117/03 *Dragaggi* [2005] Judgment of the Court, 13 January 2005, and ECJ, Case C-244/05 *Bund Naturschutz Bayern E.V.* [2006]. This latter case is commented on by Hamer (2007). See the discussion in Ureta (2007, p85) and note 1 of the updated Commission Guidance (Commission of the European Communities, 2007, p3).

17 There have been many examples of MS failing to draw up complete lists, or otherwise failing to comply with the requirements, as indicated in the Commission Review of the Habitats Directive (Commission of the European Communities, 2003a, pp6–7). The main problems are common internationally and emphasize the need for the environment to be integrated into all policy areas; the impact upon habitat from agriculture and tourism, and the failure of MS to adopt suitable measures for their protection. The relationship with the EIA Directive has been considered in a number of cases. See Marsden (2002, pp35–39).

18 In ECJ, Case 262/85 *Commission v Italy* [1987] ECR 3073, it was held that Italy had failed to comply by not bringing into force effective national legislation to comply with the Directive within two years.

19 In *Santona Marshes* (see ECJ, Case C-355/90 *Commission v Spain* [1993] ECR I-4221) the ECJ also held that it had not taken the appropriate measures to prevent the deterioration of the habitats in the area contrary to the Article 4 provisions. The case established that an MS was effectively under a duty to designate an area as an SPA and to protect it if it satisfied the ornithological criteria set out in the Directive. The Court also stated specifically that it would not be possible to achieve the Directive's objectives if MS obligations under Article 4(4) to avoid pollution or deterioration of habitats or any other disturbances affecting the birds arose once designation of an SPA had occurred. See Commission guidance (Commission of the European Communities, 2000, p11)

20 See ECJ, Case C-57/89 *Commission v Germany* [1991] ECR I-883. The *Leybucht Dykes* formed part of Ostfriesische Wattenmeer, also a listed site under the Ramsar Convention. The German government had favoured altering the line of the dyke to benefit the Leybucht harbour, and the Court had to decide whether and if so under what conditions an MS was entitled to reduce the size of an SPA. The Court held that the reinforcement of the dyke proposed was necessary to protect human life, but that the works should be kept to a minimum and should involve only the smallest reduction in the area of the SPA. The issue of site size and extent was also considered in the case of *WWF-UK and Another v Secretary of State for Scotland (Cairngorm)*, see below.

21   *R v Secretary of State for Transport and Secretary of State for the Environment, ex p. Berkshire, Buckinghamshire and Oxfordshire Naturalists' Trust Limited and Others* [1997] Env LR 80. In the application for judicial review, it was argued that the decision to proceed with the bypass by the Secretary of State necessarily frustrated any future decision to submit the site as a candidate SAC. This was despite the presence of snails on the site, which should arguably have been given protection regardless of the absence of a national listing on the site, and not have been subject to attempts to relocate them. Despite this, where the minister failed to provide this protection, the court held that there was no abuse of power.

22   In *R v Secretary of State for Trade and Industry and Others, ex p. Greenpeace* [2000] Env LR 221, Greenpeace successfully contended that the Habitats Directive may well apply beyond the 12 mile limit of the UK's territorial waters, despite the restriction of the implementing regulations to this limit. It was held that since some habitats and species were sea-based, the Directive could only achieve its aims if it extended beyond the 12 mile limit. Application to the Wild Birds Directive has now also been considered; see Owen (2001).

23   ECJ, Case C-371/89 *R v Secretary of State for the Environment, Transport and the Regions, ex p. First Corporate Shipping Ltd* [2001] Env LR 34.

24   ECJ, Case C-44/95 *R v Secretary of State for the Environment, ex p. RSPB* [1996] ECR I-3805 / [1997] QB 206 (*Lappel Bank*). In *Lappel Bank*, the Royal Society for the Protection of Birds (RSPB) challenged the decision of the Minister to designate the Medway Estuary and Marshes as an SPA, but to exclude from it an area of intertidal mudflat known as Lappel Bank. The basis of the decision was the expansion of the port of Sheerness, having regard to its economic significance at national and local level. The port was at the time a significant employer in an area with high unemployment. It was accepted that exclusion of the area from designation would 'probably result in a reduction of the wader and wildfowl populations of the Medway Estuary and Marshes'. While the Court confirmed that economic considerations have no role to play in designating such areas, it did not deal with the important issue of the size of the site. The Court also failed to provide interim relief to prevent the development, which in the meantime had destroyed the habitat.

25   *World Wildlife Fund-UK and Royal Society for the Protection of Birds v Secretary of State for Scotland and Others* [1999] Env LR 632, (*Cairngorm*). In *Cairngorm*, WWF and RSPB sought judicial review of decisions connected with the exclusion of areas from a candidate SAC. The Scottish court held that there was room for discretion in drawing up the boundaries, as long as they were made on ornithological grounds. Because the Court refused to rule on this in the absence of irrationality, economic factors would appear to have indirectly been attached a more significant role than conservation. Later, in *RSPB v Secretary of State for Scotland*, [2000] The Times Law Report, 12 September, it was further held necessary to consider the effect of proposed measures not only in relation to a species overall, but also in respect of the populations of the species in SPAs.

26   This means, for example, that assessment is not needed for management plans that are specifically prepared for the site in accordance with Article 6(1) of the Habitats Directive, the rationale presumably being that such plans already protect and conserve the features of the site. This is arguably contrary to best practice in other jurisdictions where management plans prepared for national parks and conservation areas are often assessed. The reason is that the assessment process is often more rigorous, inviting public participation, and reflecting the view that management plans may have negative as well as positive environmental effects. Given the requirement of the SEA Directive to report on positive as well as negative effects, and the fact that effects may be positive or negative depending on the target/receptor, this is not without merit. For examples in the US, see Dalal-Clayton and Sadler (2005, p107), and for further examples in Canada and the UK and comment on failings in Australia, see Marsden (2008).

27   Ureta (2007, p86) distinguishes between SPAs designated by June 1994 and those that comply with the criteria in Article 4(1) and 4(2) of the Wild Birds Directive but lack a formal designation. He concludes that it is only when sites have been designated that is it possible to utilize the exemptions available in Article 6(4) of the Habitats Directive, where a plan or project can proceed regardless of a negative assessment.

28   If the application for authorization of the plan or project was formally lodged before the expiry of the time limit for transposition of the Habitats Directive or before the MS joined the EU, the project is not subject to the requirements in Articles 6(3) or 6(4).

29   ECJ, Case C-127/02 *Landelijke Vereniging tot Behoud van de Waddenzee and Nederlandse Vereniging tot Bescherming van Vogels v Staatssecretaris van Landbouw, Natuurbeheer en Visserij*, Grand Chamber [2005] Env LR 14. The case concerned the issuance of licenses to the Netherlands cockle fishery for the mechanical fishing of cockles in the SPA of the Waddenzee. Two conservation organizations challenged a government decision to issue licenses, claiming that cockle fishing causes permanent damage to the geomorphology, flora and fauna of the Waddenzee's seabed, which reduces the food stocks of birds that feed on shellfish, leading to population decline. The organizations claimed this was contrary to the Habitats and Wild Birds Directives, in particular, Articles 6(2), (3) and (4). Notably, the minister claimed there was no need for an appropriate assessment to be undertaken because the activity had been undertaken for many years without intensification, and that only Article 6(2) applied.

30   The reference to the ECJ by the national court was by what is termed a 'preliminary ruling', which typically occurs in national court proceedings when a matter of EC law has not been determined previously. National proceedings are delayed while the ECJ provides the ruling that is then applied by the national court.

31   The direct effect of particular provisions of the Wild Birds Directive has also been approved in several instances by the ECJ. See De Sadeleer (2007, p177).

32   While approving the approach of the ECJ in relation to the definition of project, Verschuuren (2005, p279) highlights the fact that there remain many similar words used in related directives, such as 'installation' in the IPPC Directive, 'establishment' and a different 'installation' in the Seveso Directive, and 'organization' in the EMAS Regulation. Note that the *Kraaijeveld* decision also considered what amounts to a project (see Chapters 9 and 10).

33   See ECJ, Case C-256/98, *Commission v France* [1999], opinion of Advocate General Fennelly delivered on 16 September 1999.

34   The application of the precautionary principle in the judgment is discussed at length in the literature (see also Stokes, 2005). Verschuuren (2005, p281) believes that although the Court failed to take the opportunity to opine on the meaning of 'significant effect', applying the precautionary principle in the way it has effectively made this unnecessary. The application of the precautionary principle in Article 6(3) is believed to be very strict, which 'is a consequence of the way Article 6(3) has been formulated. In this provision, the EC legislature opted for a strict implementation of the precautionary *principle* into a legal *rule*. The Court rather tightly holds on to the literal text of Article 6(3)' (Verschuuren, pp281–282, and see Chapters 3 and 8). See also Ureta (2007, pp86–88), who comments (p87):

> *The reference to the precautionary principle was not superfluous. Quite the contrary, it was consistent with the wording of Article 6(3) and pursues a far reaching objective, namely, to limit national authorities' discretion when assessing whether a plan or project may embrace those adverse effects for SPAs and SCAs since the mere possibility of having significant effects on those areas makes it compulsory for the national authorities to carry out an assessment.*

Ureta (2007, p88, note 28) gives a striking Spanish example of where to date the Directive has certainly not been applied in this way. The Commission (Commission of the European

Communities, 2007) has now updated its Habitats Directive guidance to emphasize that 'in cases of doubt, or negative conclusions, the precautionary and preventive principles should be applied' (p3).

35 The updated Commission Guidance (Commission of the European Communities, 2007, p4) indicates that this decision was confirmed in ECJ, Case C-6/04 *Commission v UK* [2005], judgment of the Court 20 October 2005, para 54. See also ECJ, Case C-239/04 *Commission v Portugal* [2006], judgment of the Court 26 October 2006, para 24. In the latter case, Krämer (2007) comments on the implications for the EIA Directive (and possibly also the SEA Directive) of failing to consider reasonable alternatives. He states (p135, with my emphasis):

> At the end of 2006... the Court of Justice gave a very remarkable judgment. In Case C-239/04, it was decided that an administration which had made an impact assessment, but had not examined a reasonable alternative to the project in question – a motorway – did not make an impact assessment. Though the judgment concerned an impact assessment under Art 6 of Directive 92/43 (the Habitats Directive), it may also have a considerable effect on the interpretation of Directive 85/337.

36 Verschuuren (2005) believes that the failure of the Court to elaborate on the meaning of cumulative effects is more important. He comments (p281:

> the Court does not fully clear up this point. Do only cumulative effects of future projects have to be taken into account?, or the effects of existing projects as well (i.e. projects that were carried out in the past, such as an existing motorway)? And what about effects of autonomous developments, like the effects of climate change or invasive species?

37 Palerm (2006, p137) refers to a case in Finland where Article 6(4) was also applied, and comments that 'in this case a deliberative public participation process would have ensured transparency in the planning process and helped find an alternative solution not affecting the integrity of the Natura 2000 network'. The case, also involving a seaport (at Vuosaari Harbour) is analysed in detail by Nordberg (2007).

38 ECJ, Case C-98/03 *Commission v Germany* [2006] ECR I-53. The case concerned incompatibility of several domestic provisions with EC law.

39 This includes the principle of common but differentiated responsibility, which he argues must also be applied. As such, in considering the ability to proceed with plans or projects with negative effects under Article 6(4) he argues that proposals serving regional economic development may constitute an overriding public interest if the area concerned lags significantly behind the Community level, for example, in many of the Accession States.

40 In January 2007, the Commission updated its guidance on the application of Article 6(4). Many of the examples given by Ureta (2007) in his article are included in the updated guidance as indicated.

41 See Commission Guidance (Commission of the European Communities, 2007, p6).

42 See Opinion of the Advocate General in ECJ Case C-239/04, as discussed in Commission Guidance (Commission of the European Communities, 2007, p6).

43 In *Santona Marshes*, for example, (see above) the fact that the aquaculture infrastructure proposed had been financed by the EC was held not to deny the application of the Directive. In another case, the French argument that a reduction in wetlands was allowable due to the Common Agricultural Policy was also contested. See ECJ, Case 96/98 *Commission v France* [1999] ECR I-8531.

44 Examples given by Ureta (2007, pp93–95) include the construction of the A-20 motorway in Germany, implementation of a master plan extending underground coal mining (also in

Germany), extension of an existing plant to complete the production of an Airbus aeroplane (again in Germany), and the construction of a new port in Tenerife. See also Commission Guidance (Commission of the European Communities, 2007, pp8–9) for these and other examples.

45 Offsetting impacts is a well established technique in providing compensation. For recent examples in the literature, see Hayes and Morrison-Saunders (2007).

46 ECJ, Case C-209/02 *Commission v Austria* [2004] ECR I-1211. The case concerned a proposed extension of a golf course despite a negative assessment of the implications for the habitat of the bird species the corncrake in the SPA, the only population in the Central Alps that was likely to reproduce.

47 Again because of a lack of definition in the Directive 'overall coherence' has been considered in the updated guidance with respect to where it appears in other provisions (Commission of the European Communities, 2007, p11–13).

48 Since the ELD has been adopted there has been significant interest in the literature in how it can be utilized in nature protection, specifically because environmental damage is one of the concerns. See, for example, Brans (2006), Klaphake (2005), Kokott et al (2005) and Fehr et al (2007).

49 The Commission Guidance (Commission of the European Communities, 2007, p23) does however comment:

> *One must therefore refer once again to the economy and to the aims pursued by the provision in question. The opinion has to cover the assessment of the ecological values which are likely to be affected by the plan or project, the relevance of the invoked imperative reasons and the balance of these two opposed interests, as well as an evaluation of the compensation measures.*

50 See generally Commission of the European Communities (2001c). In accordance with Article 22(1) and 22(2) most of the existing EC water laws will be repealed and replaced by the new water regime. These include Council Directive 75/440/EEC of 16 June concerning the quality required for surface water intended for the abstraction of drinking water in the Member States, [1975] OJ L194/26 (the Surface Water Directive) (in 2007), Council Directive 78/659/EEC of 18 July 1978 on the quality of freshwaters needing protection or improvement in order to support fish life, [1978] OJ L222/1 (the Fish Life Directive) (in 2013), Council Directive 79/923/EEC of 30 October 1979 on the quality required of shellfish waters, [1979] OJ L281/47 (the Shellfish Directive) (also in 2013), Council Directive 76/464/EEC of 4 May 1976 on pollution caused by certain dangerous substances discharged into the aquatic environment of the Community, [1976] OJ L129/23 (the Dangerous Substances Directive) (in 2013), and Council Directive 80/68/EEC of 17 December 1979 on the protection of groundwater against pollution caused by certain dangerous substances, [1980] OJ L20/43 (the Groundwater Directive) (in 2013).

51 Note that Directive 2007/60/EC of the European Parliament and of the Council on the assessment and management of flood risks entered into force on 26 November 2007. This provides for assessment of the risk of flooding in river basins, the mapping of flood risks in all regions where there is a serious risk of flooding and the drawing up of flood risk management plans. The SEA Directive may apply to these plans if they set the framework for development consent, unless one of the exemptions applies.

52 Chave's 2001 book on the Water Framework Directive contains a summary of its provisions, including matters of transposition and planning; see also Howarth and McGillivray (2001). For a clear explanation of the effect of its legal provisions, Grimeaud (2004) is recommended, which includes a number of matters dealing with interpretation. Other articles of relevance include Matthews (1997); Howarth (1999); Farmer (2001); Kallis and Butler (2001); and

Grimeaud (2001a, 2001b and 2001c). The relationship between the Water Framework and SEA Directives is explored by Carter and Howe (2006) and Gullón (2005). Gullón discusses generally the advantages and disadvantages of applying SEA to the water sector (pp514–517). One of the strengths is that many water related projects have been poorly assessed to date because they lack a strategic dimension, which would include proposals for new dams, canals, desalination plants and the like. Cumulative and indirect impacts have also traditionally been ignored. The major difficulty of applying SEA she believes is the complexity of the hydrological planning process.

53   A range of exemptions are available to MS not to achieve good status in certain circumstances, as explained by Grimeaud (2004, pp31–33). One of these, as set out in Article 4(7) provides that an MS may be granted permission (b) to lower the status of a surface water from 'high' to 'good' following the undertaking of 'new sustainable human development activities'. Grimeaud (p32, note 31) relates this to the notion of 'overriding public interest' under the Habitats Directive (see above). Overriding public interest is also used explicitly in the Water Framework Directive as a means of avoidance of the Directive's provisions as part of the undertaking of 'new sustainable human development activities' (see Article 4(7)(c)). The relationship between the Water Framework Directive and the Wild Birds and Habitats Directives is discussed further by Grimeaud on pp33–34, which is relevant because the requirements of the former are more stringent in relation to the EC protected areas of SPAs and SACs. Chave (2001, pp148–157) also discusses the implications of the Water Framework Directive for protected areas (see Article 6 and Annex IV of the Directive). Finally, the relationship between the Water Framework Directive and the ELD is discussed by Grimeaud (2004) on p39 (in note 70), as water damage is also included.

54   Directive 2006/12/EC of the European Parliament and of the Council of 5 April 2006. See Davies (2004, Chapter 7). Note that since the Waste Framework Directive is commonly abbreviated in the literature as the 'WFD', the temptation to do so with respect to the Water Framework Directive has been avoided.

55   In 2001 and 2002 the Commission issued communications on the simplification and improvement of the Community regulatory environment, calling for a recasting of part of the *acquis communautaire*, 'which implies the withdrawal and replacement by single legal acts of many existing directives and regulations, including in the environmental field' (Grimeaud, 2004, p29). See Commission of the European Communities (2001a) and (2002). This includes the options of consolidation, codification, recasting and simplification; see explanation in Grimeaud (2004, note 15).

56   The Annexes to the Water Framework Directive provide further detail on what information is required; for example, Annex II, point 1.4 requires the identification of adverse anthropogenic pressures in terms of, for example, point and diffuse sources of pollution and significant water abstractions. RBMPs must also contain the information set out in Annex VII, which includes a summary of the significant pressures and impact of human activity, the PoMs, a list of exemptions relied on, a mapping of the relevant protected areas and of monitoring programmes. The PoMs may be either general (applying to the whole territory of the MS) or specific to each river basin district. Article 11(3) provides a list of compulsory (termed 'basic') measures that are the minimum requirement of the PoMs; these include details of other relevant EC laws.

57   Gullón (2005, p517) refers to the SEA Directive Guidance (Reps of the MS/CEC, 2003, p48) which states that 'it is not possible to state categorically whether or not the River Basin Management Plan and the Program of Measures are within the scope of the SEA Directive'. Howarth (2007, pp163–172) discusses whether preparation of RBMPs and PoMs trigger the requirements of the SEA Directive, and concludes (p172): 'there are sound reasons why adoption of RBMPs and PoMs under the WFD should require SEA in accordance with the criteria under the SEAD… there are strong, if not always compelling, reasons why WFD

planning should fall within the scope of the SEAD'. The greatest uncertainty is the meaning of 'set the framework' for the development consent of projects (p166) because it depends on the contents of the plan, and what is a 'measure' under the Water Framework Directive is not entirely clear. However, Howarth concludes (p166):

> *Notwithstanding this ambiguity, either the adoption of regulatory regimes or the application of those regimes in individual circumstances for the purpose of achieving the environmental objectives of the Directive, must surely 'guide', if not determine, the manner in which an authorisation for a particular project is formulated.*

58   See note 53 above.

59   Krämer, reflecting his extensive experience of the negotiation and enforcement of EC environmental law, (2007, pp135–136) expresses similar scepticism of the influence of EIA on decision making, commenting: 'As a general rule, one can state that the bigger a specific infrastructure or other project is, the earlier there is a political and financial decision on its realisation'. In these cases, perhaps not surprisingly, EIA is therefore limited by an inability to consider alternatives and limited to mitigating impacts rather than preventing them. Krämer goes on (p147):

> *There does not appear to be much evidence that environmental impact assessments have stopped environmentally harmful projects or have led to significant changes. On this, much depends on the responsible administration's determination to properly protect the environment. Environmental impact assessments allow the protection of the environment, but the provisions are so flexible that they hardly impose such a protection on the administration. This observation seems to apply to practically all Member States of EU-27.*

See further the discussion in Howarth (2007, pp152–153), and note that while both Krämer (p141) and Howarth (p154) welcome the SEA Directive, they maintain similar reservations about its ability to go beyond the procedural dimension. Howarth (p154) is, however, more positive about the potential for SEA of policy and legislative proposals, 'a fair amount of headway has been made in relation to the application of EA methodology in relation to policy and legislative proposals', than Krämer (p148) who states 'Experience to date seems to show that environmental impact assessments for legislation and political strategies do not work'.

60   For a (now somewhat dated) general consideration of the impact of EU law on planning in the UK, see Bishop et al (2000), which includes consideration of the EIA and Habitats Directives.

61   This latter dimension is unlikely given the derogations available under Article 175(2) TEC, which include measures concerning town and country planning and land use. Many MS would object to the EU having a wider role in these matters, which they see as falling within the national preserve.

62   In addition to the Nitrates, Waste and Air Quality Framework Directives, Mathiesen (2003, pp 45–46) also refers to the Seveso II Directive, which is concerned with the prevention or limitation of detrimental effects of major accidents at establishments where dangerous substances are present, and the IPPC Directive, which is designed to prevent emissions into air, water or soil by applying an integrated approach to permitting. While Article 12 of the Seveso II Directive provides that MS shall take into account the prevention of major accidents and limit their consequences in land use policies and other relevant policies through controls on the siting of new establishments etc., there are no requirements for plans and programmes to be produced that would trigger the SEA Directive. As such, as Mathiesen indicates (p46), the provisions of Seveso II would more likely serve to influence the content

of plans and programmes prepared in accordance with these policies. As regards the IPPC Directive, Mathiesen (2003, p46) suggests that modifications to large installations under the IPPC Directive (which contains detailed permit procedures including evaluation) 'may in some circumstances present an environmental issue of PorP-dimension' ('PorP' refers to a plan or programme). However, again there will be no formal trigger of the SEA Directive, but large project proposals may be analogous in some circumstances to a programme.

63 As seen above this mandates assessment under Article 3(2)(b) of the SEA Directive.
64 CFI, Case T-461/93 *An Taisce and World Wide Fund for Nature v Commission of the European Communities* [1994] 23 September. CFI, Case T-585/93 *Stichting Greenpeace Council (Greenpeace International) and Others v Commission of the European Communities* [1995] 9 August, (First Chamber).
65 'ex ante' means before, 'ex post' means after.
66 See Stöglehner (2002), who discusses whether the SEA Directive applies to the current round of structural funds in some detail, which may be of help to those considering future application of the SEA Directive to it.

REFERENCES

Albrecht, E. (2005) 'Legal context of the SEA Directive – links with other legislation and key procedures' in M. Schmidt, E. João and E. Albrecht (eds) *Implementing Strategic Environmental Assessment*, Springer-Verlag, Heidelberg, pp31–56

Baldock, D. (1992) 'The status of special protection areas for the protection of wild birds: Commission of the European Communities v Federal Republic of Germany, supported by the United Kingdom', *Journal of Environmental Law*, vol 4, no 1, pp139–144

Balfors, B. and Schmidtbauer, J. (2002) 'Swedish guidelines for strategic environmental assessment for EU structural funds', *European Environment*, vol 12, pp35–48

Balfors, B., Mortberg, U. and Gontier, M. (2005) 'Impacts of region-wide urban development on biodiversity in strategic environmental assessment', *Journal of Environmental Assessment Policy and Management*, vol 7, no 2, pp 229-246

Ball, S. (1997) 'Has the UK government implemented the habitats directive properly?' in J. Holder (ed) *The Impact of EC Environmental Law in the United Kingdom*, John Wiley, Chichester, pp215–227

Beunen, R. (2006) 'European nature conservation legislation and spatial planning: for better or worse?', *Journal of Environmental Planning and Management*, vol 49, no 4, pp605–619

Birnie, P. (1996) 'The European Community and preservation of biological diversity' in M. J. Bowman and C. Redgwell (eds) *International Law and the Conservation of Biological Diversity*, Kluwer Law International, The Hague, pp211–234

Bishop, K., Tewdwr-Jones, M. and Wilkinson, D. (2000) 'From spatial to local: The impact of the European Union on local authority planning in the UK', *Journal of Environmental Planning and Management*, vol 43, no 3, pp309–334

Bradley, K. (1999) 'Environmental appraisal of regional development plans in the context of the structural funds', *Environmental Impact Assessment Review*, vol 19, pp245–257

Brans, E. (2006) 'Liability for damage to public natural resources under the 2004 EC Environmental Liability Directive – standing and assessment of damages' in Betlem, G. and Brans, E. (eds) (2006) *Environmental Liability in the EU: The 2004 Directive Compared with US and Member State Law*, Cameron May, London, 2006, pp189–215

Bröring, U. and Wiegleb, G. (2005) 'Assessing biodiversity in SEA' in M. Schmidt, E. João and E. Albrecht (eds) *Implementing Strategic Environmental Assessment*, Springer-Verlag, Heidelberg, pp523–538

Carter, J. and Howe, J. (2006) 'The water framework directive and the strategic environmental assessment directive: Exploring the linkages', *Environmental Impact Assessment Review*, vol 26, pp287–300

Chave, P. A. (2001) *The EU Water Framework Directive: An Introduction*, IWA Publishing, Padstow

Clement, K. (2001) 'Strategic environmental awakening: European progress in regional environmental integration', *European Environment*, vol 11, pp75–88

Clement, K. and Bachtler, J. (1997) 'Regional development and environmental gain: Strategic assessment in the EU structural funds', *European Environment*, vol 7, pp7–15

Commission of the European Communities (2000) *Managing NATURA 2000 Sites: the Provisions of Article 6 of the Habitats Directive, 92/43/CEE*, Office for Official Publications of the European Communities, Luxembourg

Commission of the European Communities (2001a) *Commission Communication of 5 December 2001 on Simplifying and Improving the Regulatory Environment*, COM (2001) 726, Commission of the European Communities, Brussels

Commission of the European Communities (2001b) *Assessment of Plans and Projects Significantly Affecting Natura 2000 Sites – Methodological Guidance on the Provisions of Article 6(3) and (4) of the Habitats Directive 92/43/EEC*, November 2001, Commission of the European Communities, Brussels

Commission of the European Communities (2001c) *The Common Strategy of the Implementation of the Water Framework Directive*, Commission of the European Communities, Brussels

Commission of the European Communities (2002) *Commission Communication of 5 June 2002 on Action Plan – Simplifying and Improving the Regulatory Environment*, COM (2002) 278, Commission of the European Communities, Brussels

Commission of the European Communities (2003a) *Report from the Commission on the implementation of the Directive 92/43/EEC on the conservation of natural habitats and of wild fauna and flora* [SEC(2003)1478], COM/2003/0845 final, Commission of the European Communities, Brussels

Commission of the European Communities (2003b) *Fourth Annual Survey on the Implementation and Enforcement of Community Environmental Law*, SEC (2003) 804, Commission Staff Working Paper (7 July 2003), Commission of the European Communities, Brussels

Commission of the European Communities (2006) *Proposal for a directive of the European Parliament and of the Council on the assessment and management of floods*, 18 January 2006, Commission of the European Communities, Brussels

Commission of the European Communities (2007) *Guidance document on Article 6(4) of the 'Habitats Directive' 92/43/EEC – Clarification of the concepts of: alternative solutions, imperative reasons of overriding public interest, compensatory measures, overall coherence, opinion of the Commission*, Commission of the European Communities, Brussels

Dalal-Clayton, B. and Sadler, B. (2005) *Strategic Environmental Assessment: A Sourcebook and Reference Guide to International Experience*, Earthscan, London

Davies, P. (2004) *European Union Environmental Law*, Ashgate Publishing, Aldershot

De Sadeleer, N. (2007) 'EC law and biodiversity: How to save Noah's Ark', *Journal for European Environmental and Planning Law*, vol 3, pp168–180

Environmental Resources Management (1998) *A Handbook on Environmental Assessment of Regional Development Plans and EU Structural Funds Programmes*, European Commission, DGXI, Environment, Nuclear Safety and Civil Protection, London

Farmer, A. (2001) 'The EC Water Framework Directive', *Water Law*, vol 3, p40

Fehr, K. H., Friedrich, B. and Scheil, S. (2007) 'Liability Directive – a useful tool for nature protection?', *Journal for European Environmental and Planning Law*, vol 2, pp182–200

Fischer, T. B. (2003) 'Environmental assessment of the EU structural funds: The German objective 1 regional development plan and Berlin operational programme', *European Environment*, vol 13, pp245–257

Freestone, D. (1996) 'The enforcement of the wild birds directive: A case study' in H. Somsen (ed) *Protecting the European Environment: Enforcing EC Environmental Law*, Blackstone Press, London, pp229–250

Greening Regional Development Programmes Network (2006) *Handbook on SEA for Cohesion Policy 2007–2013*, Greening Regional Development Programmes Network/North East South West Interreg IIIC, Brussels

Grimeaud, D. J. E. (2001a) 'Reforming EU water law: Towards sustainability? (Part I)', *European Environmental Law Review*, vol 10, pp41–51

Grimeaud, D. J. E. (2001b) 'Reforming EU water law: Towards sustainability? (Part II)', *European Environmental Law Review*, vol 10, pp88–97

Grimeaud, D. J. E. (2001c) 'Reforming EU water law: towards sustainability?', *European Environmental Law Review*, Part III, vol 10, pp125–135

Grimeaud, D. J. E. (2004) 'The EC Water Framework Directive – An instrument for integrating water policy', *Review of European Community and International Environmental Law*, vol 13, no 1, pp27–39

Gullón, N. (2005) 'Links between the water framework directive and SEA' in M. Schmidt, E. João and E. Albrecht (eds) *Implementing Strategic Environmental Assessment*, Springer-Verlag, Heidelberg, pp513–522

Hamer, J. (2007) 'Judgment of the ECJ 14 September 2006, Case C-244/05, Bund Naturschutz Bayern E.V.', *Review of European Community and International Environmental Law*, vol 16, no 1, pp104–107

Harte, J. (1997) 'Nature conservation: The rule of law in European Community environmental protection', *Journal of Environmental Law*, vol 9, no 1, pp139–180

Hayes, N. and Morrison-Saunders, A. (2007) 'Effectiveness of environmental offsets in environmental impact assessment: Practitioner perspectives from Western Australia', *Impact Assessment and Project Appraisal*, vol 15, no 3, pp209–218

Holder, J. (2004) 'Overriding public interest in planning and conservation law', *Journal of Environmental Law*, vol 16, pp377–407

Howarth, W. (1999) 'Accommodation without resolution? Emission controls and environmental quality objectives in the proposed EC Water Framework Directive', *Environmental Law Review*, vol 1, p6

Howarth, W. (2007) 'Substance and procedure under the strategic environmental assessment directive and the water framework directive' in Holder, J. and McGillivray, D. (eds) (2007) *Taking Stock of Environmental Assessment: Law, Policy and Practice*, Routledge-Cavendish, Abingdon, pp149–190

Howarth, W. and McGillivray, D. (2001) *Water Pollution and Water Quality Law*, Shaw and Sons, Crayford

Howe, J. and White, I. (2002) 'The potential implications of the European Union Water Framework Directive on domestic planning systems: A UK study', *European Planning Studies*, vol 10, pp1027–1038

Jans, J. (2000) 'The Habitats Directive', *Journal of Environmental Law*, vol 12, pp385–390

Kallis, G. and Butler, D. (2001) 'The EU Water Framework Directive: Measures and implications', *Water Policy*, vol 3, no 2, pp125–142

Keller, A. (1997) 'Strategic environmental assessment of the European structural fund objective one programme for the Highlands and Islands of Scotland', *European Environment*, vol 7, pp63–68

Klaphake, A. (2005) 'The assessment and restoration of biodiversity damages', *Journal for European Environmental and Planning Law*, vol 4, pp268–276

Kokott, J., Klaphake, A. and Marr, S. (2005) 'Key elements of a liability regime taking into account ecological damages', *Journal for European Environmental and Planning Law*, vol 4, pp269–286

Kolhoff, A. and Slootweg, R. (2005) 'Biodiversity in SEA for spatial plans – experiences from the Netherlands', *Journal of Environmental Assessment Policy and Management*, vol 7, no 2, pp267–286

Krämer, L. (2007) 'The development of environmental assessments at the level of the European Union' in Holder, J. and McGillivray, D. (eds) (2007) *Taking Stock of Environmental Assessment: Law, Policy and Practice*, Routledge-Cavendish, Abingdon, pp131–148

Macleod, C. (2005) 'Integrating sustainable development into structural funds programmes: An evaluation of the Scottish experience', *European Environment*, vol 15, pp313–331

Marsden, S. (1998) 'Importance of context in measuring the effectiveness of strategic environmental assessment', *Impact Assessment and Project Appraisal*, vol 16, no 4, pp 255–266

Marsden, S. (2002) 'Protecting archaeological heritage in wetlands: The muddied waters of international, European, English and Australian law', *Environmental Law Review*, vol 4, no 1, pp26–50

Marsden, S. (2008) 'Environmental planning and management at Heard Island and McDonald Islands: Should strategic environmental assessment be applied more comprehensively?', under review

Mathieson, A. (2003) 'Public participation in decision making and access to justice in EC environmental law: The case of certain plans and programmes', *European Environmental Law Review*, vol 12, no 2, pp36–52

Matthews, D. (1997) 'The Framework Directive on Community water policy: A new approach for EC environmental law', *Yearbook of European Law*, p191

Montini, M. (2001) 'Habitats impact assessment: An effective instrument for biodiversity conservation?', *Environmental Liability*, vol 9, pp182–187

Nollkaemper, A. (1997) 'Habitat protection in European Community law: Evolving conceptions of a balance of interests', *Journal of Environmental Law*, vol 9, no 2, pp271–286

Nordberg, L. (2007) 'The Vuosaari harbour case: Implementation of the Habitats and Birds Directives in the Vuosaari harbour project', *Review of European Community and International Environmental Law*, vol 16, no 1, pp87–103

Owen, D. (2001) 'The application of the wild birds directive beyond the territorial sea of European Community member states', *Journal of Environmental Law*, vol 13, no 1, pp39–78

Paavola, J. (2003/2004) 'Protected areas governance and justice: Theory and the European Union's habitats directive', *Environmental Sciences*, vol 1, no 1, pp59–77

Palerm, J. (2006) 'The Habitats Directive as an instrument to achieve sustainability? An analysis through the case of the Rotterdam Mainport development project', *European Environment*, vol 16, pp127–138

Reid, C. T. (1997) 'Nature conservation law' in J. Holder (ed) *The Impact of EC Environmental Law in the United Kingdom*, John Wiley, Chichester, pp199–214

Reps of the MS/CEC (Representatives of the Member States and the Environment Directorate General of the European Commission) (2003) *Implementation of Directive 2001/42/EC on the assessment of the effects of certain plans and programmes on the environment*, 23 September 2003, Commission of the European Communities, Brussels

Roberts, P. (2001) 'Incorporating the environment into structural funds regional programmes: Evolution, current developments and future prospects', *European Environment*, vol 11, pp64–74

Sheate, W. R. (2003) 'The EC directive on strategic environmental assessment: A much needed boost for environmental integration', *European Environmental Law Review*, December, pp331–347

Sheate, W., Byron, H., Dagg, S. and Cooper, L. (2005) *The Relationship between the EIA and SEA Directives: Final Report to the European Commission*, Contract number: ENV.G.4./ETU/2004/0020r, Imperial College Consultants, London

Stöglehner, G. (2002) 'The EU-directive on strategic environmental assessment and its impact on structural funds', paper, Interdisciplinary Centre for Comparative Research in the Social Sciences, Vienna, available at www.iccr-international.org/regionet/docs/ws1-stoeglehner.pdf

Stokes, E. R. (2005) 'Liberalising the threshold of precaution – cockle fishing, the Habitats Directive, and evidence of a new understanding of "scientific uncertainty"', *Environmental Law Review*, vol 7, pp206–214

Unnerstall, H. (2006) '"Sustainable development" as a criterion for the interpretation of Article 6 of the Habitats Directive', *European Environment*, vol 16, pp73–88

Ureta, A. G. (2007) 'Habitats Directive and environmental assessment of plans and projects', *Journal for European Environmental and Planning Law*, vol 2, pp84–96

Verschuuren, J. (2005) 'Shellfish for fishermen or for birds? – Article 6 Habitats Directive and the precautionary principle', *Journal of Environmental Law*, vol 17, no 2, pp265–283

Wiegleb, G. and Bröring, U. (2005) 'Biodiversity programmes on global, European and national levels related to SEA' in M. Schmidt, E. João and E. Albrecht (eds) *Implementing Strategic Environmental Assessment*, Springer-Verlag, Heidelberg, pp539–554.

White, I. and Howe, J. (2003) 'Planning and the European Union water framework directive', *Journal of Environmental Planning and Management*, vol 46, no 4, pp621–631

Wils, W. P. J. (1994) 'The birds directive 15 years later: A survey of the case law and a comparison with the habitats directive', *Journal of Environmental Law*, vol 6, no 2, pp219–242

CHAPTER 12

Comparisons and Conclusions

CHAPTER OUTLINE

This final chapter examines the similarities and differences between international and European law generally, and in requiring SEA. It builds upon the earlier chapters and the conclusions of each, presenting a comparative analysis of how effective international and European law is as a means of regulation, especially in relation to the national legal traditions in Europe and worldwide that serve to implement that law. In the first section the relationship between international, European and national law is considered, with further explanation of the principles of direct and indirect effect as applied to both international and European law and the role of the EC/EU in international law (with examination of the changing treaty basis of the EU); some examples of the complexities of international and European law when jointly applied in a national context are also given. This first section is a highly technical area of the law, concerning as it does matters that in some instances are subject to debate between international and European lawyers.[1] In the second section the relationship between international and European law in regulating SEA is examined. This includes comparisons between international and European environmental law and the SEA Protocol and Directive; the relevance of SEA to conservation is also discussed with reference to the conservation conventions and other relevant directives.

RELATIONSHIP BETWEEN INTERNATIONAL, EUROPEAN AND NATIONAL LAW

There are many aspects to the relationship between international, European and national law as explored in the earlier chapters. The internal status of international law in European and national law depends on the constitutional situation in the state, whether monist or dualist.[2] Betlem and Nollkaemper (2003, p573) discuss the need for states to have accepted the validity of international law if it is to be binding on their national legal systems, which is the matter of self-executing and non-self executing treaties, or the 'Charming Betsy' Rule as so labelled in the US (see Chapter 2). While the treaty basis of the EC/EU suggests similarities with international law, as seen and as further explored below, many aspects of European law demonstrate an autonomous system operating within its own decision making and judicial structures, to the (almost complete) exclusion of international law. European law, rather than national law, determines the effect on the national legal order, so it is up to the ECJ not national courts to decide on this. The ratification of mixed agreements (where both the EC/EU and MS are generally a party to an international treaty) is one of the ways in which European and national law collectively bind themselves to international law. Yet overlapping jurisdictions have remained a problem, and environmental law examples of where conflicts have resulted from this are outlined.

Status of international law in European and MS law

The EC is a monist jurisdiction, and international law of all types, treaty or customary law, applies directly. Conway (2002, p683) cites authority that the test for the direct effect of international agreements appears to be identical to that of provisions of internal EC law – that it be clear, precise and unconditional if it is to afford individual rights.[3] In a footnote citing authorities, he comments that among the rules of international law that the ECJ has applied, or accepted the status of, are treaties to which it is not a party, including rules of treaty interpretation, the 1969 VCLT and treaty suspension.[4] In the MS or jurisdictions outside the EU, international law applies directly (or indirectly) depending on the constitutional situation in each, whether monist or dualist; where agreements are mixed (see below) the MS will also be bound independently of the ratification of the treaty by the EC because the national government will itself have ratified the treaty subject to, in dualist states, the approval of the legislature. However, for jurisdictions within the EU, if the EC/EU is bound then the MS will also be bound, regardless of whether the MS is a dualist jurisdiction or has independently ratified the treaty; this is because the MS is constitutionally bound by European law, which itself incorporates international law when a treaty has been ratified by the EC. The MS retains its autonomy in its ability through the Council of Ministers to fail to give its assent to the international treaty in question, which may prevent ratification. For customary international law, sufficient state practice may bind an MS.

Betlem and Nollkaemper (2003) examine the practice of indirect effect (also called consistent interpretation) in detail. As seen, this concerns the requirement that national courts should give effect to international (and European) law through a national law provision where the treaty or customary rule has not been incorporated into national law. They argue (p574) that unlike European law (where the ECJ has so ruled), although there is no 'comparative authoritative formulation of the principle' in international law, 'State practice allows one to infer an international duty of courts to interpret, within their constitutional mandates, national law in the light of international law'. Although the application of direct effect depends on whether a state is monist or dualist, indirect effect therefore does not. They indicate (p572) that, in practice, courts first attempt to interpret a rule of international law via a national rule (indirect effect); if this is not possible, they will then see if international law has to be applied whether or not it has been transposed into national law (direct effect). They conclude that there is therefore no fundamental difference in the application of international and European law in accordance with indirect effect.

The enforceability of international law will be greater when incorporated into European law because of the broader range of methods available to the European institutions, other MS and individuals concerned. Denza (1999) highlights the primacy of EC law and the role of direct effect (especially with regard to the implications for individuals) as significant distinguishing attributes. The supervisory role of the Commission and compulsory jurisdiction of the ECJ (especially its ability to apply sanctions) also deserve particular mention, as examined in Chapters 7 and 8 and further below. In contrast, as seen in Chapters 2 and 3, enforceability of international law is often problematic when states are found in breach of treaty commitments, especially where treaty regimes do not establish designated mechanisms to attribute responsibility and allow compensation, in particular, of non-state parties. Boyle (2005, p26) concludes on the ILC draft articles (that summarize the international position on state responsibility) that: 'The most obvious weakness of the present draft is the failure to require states as a matter of legal obligation to make provision for adequate redress in the event of transboundary damage'. Rest (2004, pp5–6) also points to the particular problem of transboundary or transnational effects, which he indicates fails to be adequately regulated in either international or national law as far as the rights of individuals are concerned, because of the general absence of compliance procedures or enforceable compliance procedures.

Status of European law in international and MS law

As seen in Chapter 7, the EC is to a large extent an 'autonomous regime', with its own political and judicial system, and European lawyers at least believe that international courts should defer to it. The treaty basis of the EC/EU, while in some respects analogous to other international treaties operating on a regional level, may generally exclude the application of VCLT, and interpretation of primary law is therefore a matter for the ECJ with reference to the TEC and TEU. In ratifying these Treaties, MS have therefore agreed to be bound by European law, as administered by the European institutions, in the same way that in ratifying another international treaty it is possible for state parties to determine the dispute settlement mechanisms that any breach will be subject to. The WTO regime has its own Dispute Settlement Understanding (DSU), for example, and as will be seen below other international agreements also provide for their own methods of resolving differences, which in some cases may arguably exclude general methods on the basis of special rules applying. Simma and Pulkowski (2006, pp485–490) explore this in detail in relation to the law of state responsibility, and indicate that despite the almost complete autonomous nature of the European legal system, the international law on state responsibility can still be resorted to as European law is silent in some areas. When the 'special' mechanisms under the European Treaties are exhausted therefore, it is open to an aggrieved state to utilize the procedures of international law. The main example given is the failure of a defaulting MS to comply with an ECJ ruling despite the application of Articles 227 and 228(2) TEC and Article 7 TEU.

     Conway (2002, pp685–691) explores Simma's original 1985 thesis as to the autonomous nature of the EC regime, which as seen above he argues still holds true.[5] In general the concept of autonomous regimes established by Conway (p685–686) is that 'first, the greater the exclusion of the general public international law rules, the greater the legal complexity within the regime; and secondly, the more such regimes, the greater the risk of conflicts between them'. In analysing whether the rules of international law are excluded regarding the EC/EU, Conway examines Article 292 of the TEC (which is concerned with dispute settlement), concluding that the law of international responsibility may still apply to MS even though recourse to the ICJ and other institutional methods may be denied by the Article. He goes on to examine the elements of European law that suggest an autonomous system (see note 1) but believes that despite these, if an MS refuses to provide a remedy/pay a lump sum when in breach of Treaty law, and continues to breach its obligations despite suspension of an MS rights under Article 309(1) TEC, there is little that can be done to enforce obligations unless international law is resorted to.[6] Simma and Pulkowski (2006, p519) conclude:

> To sum up: it is reasonable to conclude that EC law operates as a closed system of secondary rules for most practical purposes. Conceptually, however, it is not a self-contained regime since there remain scenarios in which a fallback on state responsibility remains feasible and necessary, and since such a fallback is not precluded by peculiar characteristics of the Community order. Only after the European Union has attained such a degree of integration that recourse to general international law is not conceivable without putting into question the whole raison d'être of the treaty framework might the conclusion of self-containment be justified. But this, it is submitted, is not (yet) the state of European integration.

Role of EC/EU and MS in external relations

Subject to international law, the European Treaties and MS law, both the European institutions (Commission and Council) and MS have the ability to be involved in international affairs.[7] Although international law is traditionally the domain of states, IGOs may also have power to act (see Chapter 2). Delreux (2006, p232) points to three conditions that are needed for the EC/EU to act in multilateral environmental negotiations and to become a party to MEAs. The first is that it must have legal personality,[8] the second is that it must be recognized by the negotiating parties and the third is that it must possess the competence to make binding commitments.[9] The EC currently has competence to conclude treaties through its institutions; the EU does not but informally operates in the same way, with some arguing that the power to conclude agreements concerning the second and third pillar issues provides this power (p233). This will change when the 2007 Lisbon Treaty is ratified by the MS, because the EU will replace the EC in its entirety and have a single legal personality within the framework of the TEU and the TFEU (the latter that will replace the TEC). New institutions within the EU will also have a role to play in external relations, notably the High Representative of the Union for Foreign Affairs and Security Policy.[10]

The matter of shared competences and mixed agreements between the EC/EU and the MS is also discussed by Delreux (2006, pp235–237).[11] As mentioned, the EC/EU must have power to act in any particular area, which is a matter set out in the Treaties, or else it may be implied as a result of interpretations by the ECJ. Competences may be either exclusive to the EC, or non-exclusive, meaning they are shared with the MS. Environmental policy is traditionally an area of shared competence, so either or both the EC/EU or the MS can take action, subject to the principle of subsidiarity. As seen in Chapter 8, Articles 174, 175 and 176 provide for MS competence to act in environmental policy matters, Article 176 allowing MS to 'gold plate' EC law by taking more stringent national measures. When both the EC/EU and one or more of the MS ratify an international treaty, the agreement is said to be a mixed one; this is also the case when both have competence but only the EC/EU or one or more MS are a party to it (Delreux, 2006, p237).[12] When MS are party to a mixed agreement there are some limits placed on their ability to act as a result of their membership of the TEC and TEU. As Delreux (2006, p242) indicates, Article 10 TEC stipulates the principles of Community loyalty and the duty of cooperation, 'meaning that the member states and the EC institutions are committed to cooperate and to do everything necessary to fulfil the obligations, principles and objectives of the Treaties'. Usually this takes the form of dual representation by the Commission and the MS, with both also having the right of initiative. The Council and the MS will be responsible for ratification of mixed agreements.

Problems of overlapping jurisdiction

In part because of the increased use of mixed agreements, problems have arisen where it is not clear whether international or European law is appropriate to regulate disputes between MS. In a handful of recent cases the complexities of overlapping international, European and national jurisdictions have been highlighted. This is a problem because it puts at risk the coherence of European law, fragments further international law and potentially invites states to 'forum shop' allowing them to choose a legal system that provides the best chance of a remedy in their favour. The *MOX plant* case between the UK and Ireland is an excellent example, as analysed by Churchill and Scott (2004), Lavranos (2005a, 2005b) and Cardwell and French (2007); others include the *Ijzerin Rijn* case between the Netherlands and Belgium as considered by Lavranos (2005a, 2005b) and Cardwell and French (2007, p127–28); the examples of transboundary EIA examined in the case of *Vuotos* and in the *North Calotte Region* as explored by Koivurova (2004, 2006) are also of relevance. Notably, problems of overlapping jurisdiction have also been highlighted with regard to SEA (De Mulder, 2006, p281).

In the *MOX plant* case, Ireland instituted proceedings against the UK first under the OSPAR Convention,[13] and second under UNCLOS. Very briefly, the OSPAR proceedings requested the UK to supply information Ireland claimed should have been made available during the consultation process on authorization of the plant, and in the UNCLOS proceedings Ireland claimed the authorization and operation of the plant breached or would breach provisions concerned with prevention of marine pollution, cooperation in the protection of the marine environment and EIA (see Chapter 3).[14] Despite the fact that both parties were MS, that the EC had also ratified the OSPAR Convention,[15] and that the matter of the dispute was also dealt with by substantive European law (the Information Directive), the OSPAR tribunal decided it had jurisdiction in the case. It therefore denied the jurisdiction of the ECJ and after considering only the law of the OSPAR Convention, ruled that there was no breach by the UK. In the second proceedings, the UNCLOS tribunal took a very different approach, staying the proceedings and requesting the parties to find out whether the ECJ had jurisdiction in relation to the matters in question.[16] The ECJ handed down its judgment in the case on 30 May 2006,[17] concluding that Ireland had breached its obligations under Articles 292 and 10 of the TEC.[18] In the *Ijzerin Rijn* or *Iron Rhine Railway* case, another tribunal took a third approach; the case concerned a dispute between the Netherlands and Belgium relating to which state was responsible for the costs needed to revitalize an international railway that had been disused for some time. Although both states recognized the potential application of EC law (which was relevant as a result of the line crossing an area protected by the Habitats Directive, and because of regulations concerning the Trans-European Networks) and in communication with the Commission committed themselves to comply with Article 292 TEC, nonetheless the tribunal itself refused to stay the proceedings and seek a ruling from the ECJ on the application of European law. Rather, somewhat bizarrely in finding in favour of Belgium, the tribunal took upon itself the task of examining matters of European law and then concluding they were not relevant (Lavranos, 2005b, p242). As Cardwell and French comment (2007, p127): 'Its reasoning is, at best, imaginative and would surely certainly raise metaphorical eye-brows within the ECJ itself'. Again the proper course for the tribunal to take would have been to stay the proceedings and request a ruling from the ECJ on whether the subject matter fell within its jurisdiction, which, as a result of the matters under consideration, it clearly did.

The *Vuotos* case was also concerned with the Habitats Directive, in particular whether Finland should have designated an area as an SAC, and whether a neighbouring state, Sweden, should have been consulted under the Nordic Environment Protection Convention[19] and also the Espoo Convention (which was invoked voluntarily by the Finnish authorities as it had yet to enter into force). The case concerned the construction of a dam, and proceedings were commenced under both Finnish and EC law for different purposes. Although the case was not concerned with the same matters of jurisdiction that underlay the rulings discussed above, it is illustrative of the complex relationships between international, European and national law that in some instances bring challenges to jurisdiction.[20] Koivurova (2004, p60) summarizes the complex nature of these relationships as seen in the *Vuotos* case as follows:

> *The Vuotos Case shows quite well the effects of the complex regulatory environment that exists today, especially for EU Member States. Almost all aspects of environmental protection are covered by international law, European Community law, as well as each Member State's own legal system. International law outlines the basic universal principles and regulates transboundary and global environmental problems; Community law focuses on the minimum standards for harmonization of Member States' environmental protection systems; and national laws stipulate the details of required behaviour and provide the institutional machinery to monitor and enforce the applicable norms. Even though in some cases the division of labour among the three systems works well, it is still often the case that the three overlap.*

Given the problems of overlapping jurisdiction and competence, it is appropriate to consider briefly what may be done to avoid them. With regard to overlaps that involve European law, it is first necessary to consider whether the EC/EU has competence for the matter under question, and, if so, for any international tribunal involved to refer the matter to the ECJ. With regard to matters for which the EC/EU does not have competence, various solutions have been put forward in the literature. Lavrarnos (2005b) examines the benefits of extending the jurisdiction of the ICJ, perhaps by making it a court of appeal in relation to other international courts and tribunals, creating a preliminary ruling system, extending the advisory jurisdiction of the Court or creating a new international environmental court, the last of these advocated by several authors.[21]

GENERAL COMPARISONS AND CONCLUSIONS BETWEEN INTERNATIONAL AND EUROPEAN ENVIRONMENTAL LAW OF RELEVANCE TO EIA AND SEA

Chapters 3 and 8 indicated similarities between international and European environmental law, and highlighted a variety of drivers for the development of the law at these two levels. In some instances international law has had a potent influence upon the development of European law, and also vice versa, with a healthy cross fertilization of principles and concepts. More broadly, the contribution of sustainable development to both legal systems has of course been recognized. With EIA as the organizing theme, underlying principles of both, notably the precautionary and cooperation/ participatory principles are of significant relevance to each system, with EIA or EA more generally used as a major tool in the application of the principles. The principles are recognized to some extent in customary and treaty law at the international level, and in the primary and secondary law of the EC; EC law arguably requires greater weight to be attached to consideration of such principles, however, as a result of their incorporation into the TEC and TEU; this includes the polluter pays principle that has minimal acceptance at the international level.[22] Enforcement at the EC level is also more straightforward than in international law, with the supervisory role of the Commission and compulsory jurisdiction of the ECJ. In relation to the enforcement of IEL, compliance is generally dependent on the individual treaty regime, which may include dispute settlement mechanisms that have been accepted by the state parties and subsequent implementation of their decisions.[23]

With regard to timing at both the international and European law levels, EA was first considered by the UNECE in 1975, with reports (1991 and 1992) including reference to PPPs. In preparing the Espoo Convention (adopted in 1991), it drew on the soft law of Principle 21 of the Stockholm Declaration 1972 and earlier UNEP work (1987); however, it is unquestionable that the national promulgation of NEPA 1969 in the US was the primary influence upon it and the original EIA Directive (adopted in 1985), with the political environment identified as conducive to the introduction of such provisions. The subsequent amendment of the EIA Directive (adopted in 1997) was in part necessary to reflect the obligations of the Espoo Convention, which had been ratified by the EC (and MS), and therefore illustrates the close relationship between international and European law. In turn the SEA Protocol and SEA Directive underscore the national role for SEA, albeit with some transboundary dimensions. Both legal instruments have been significantly affected by the Aarhus and Espoo Conventions, although as seen the procedural guarantees of the former in relation to strategic proposals are notably stronger regarding plans and programmes than policies and legislation; this is without doubt as a result of the less favourable political environment for extension of EA to these levels over more recent times.

While NEPA was also a significant early driver behind the information and participatory elements of EA, and EC law had preceded it to some extent (such as the 1990 Information Directive), the Aarhus Convention (adopted in 1998) has played a primary role in the recent development of international and European environmental law for both EIA and SEA. At the international level, its influence is seen in a number of other regimes, and at the European law level several directives, notably the (revised) Information, Participation and (proposed) Access to Justice Directives have their origins there, and others have also been revised as a result. The adoption of these Directives is also an excellent illustration of the close relationship between international and European environmental law, as each of these horizontal laws has been required as a result of the EC (and where relevant, MS) ratification of the Aarhus Convention. Chapters 9 and 10 should be read in connection with Chapter 4 of the book for instances of where provisions of the Aarhus Convention have yet to be fully transposed into European law, notably in the definition of the 'public concerned' and the requirement for access to justice provisions, which should be brought into effect without further delay.

Comparisons between the SEA Protocol and SEA Directive and the role of SEA in conservation

The SEA Protocol and SEA Directive are the two primary legal instruments at the international and European law levels responsible for regulating SEA and they have a close relationship with each other and related requirements in international and European law. Despite the notably far weaker context of sustainable development to the SEA Protocol compared to the SEA Directive, as a result of its long history and the timing of its adoption, the SEA Directive has played a primary role in the development of the SEA Protocol, hence the similarities in procedural provision. Yet there are a number of differences that can be highlighted in these conclusions in both the application and procedural provisions of the two legal instruments, which include matters such as public participation and enforcement.

Key differences in application identified include the following. First, subject to the possibility of an MS applying the SEA Directive beyond its current limitations to plans and programmes, the SEA Protocol specifies voluntary application also to policy and legislative proposals; while practically this may make little difference as MS are free to extend application should they wish, symbolically it makes a huge one as it suggests, quite rightly, that higher levels of decision making may be more appropriate targets for SEA. Second, while the SEA Protocol fails to refer to the assessment of cumulative effects, it does include specific reference to health effects thereby including health authorities as consultees; once matters of definition are resolved, this may expand the scope of its provisions considerably. Third, while there are no links with nature conservation treaties comparable to the links established between the SEA Directive and Habitats and Wild Birds Directives, screening for the SEA Protocol does include the additional sectors of mining (as part of the industry sector) and regional development.

Key differences in the procedural provisions include first, the lack of a specific reference to tiering in the SEA Protocol unlike the SEA Directive; this is accounted for by the particularly close relationship between the SEA and EIA Directives. The SEA Protocol has, however, followed much of the structure of this relationship with its reference to its own Annexes of projects for which the framework for future development consent is required. The use of similar wording in the SEA Protocol and Directive suggests that once the SEA Protocol is in force, there will be ready cross referencing between the two legal instruments when it comes to interpretation of many of the terms that are unclear at the present time, such as 'set the framework for future development consent of projects'. Second, parties should attempt to provide opportunities for public participation at the screening and scoping stages under the SEA Protocol; the SEA Directive only requires that the public be informed about the screening and scoping results, although information on the final decision is also specified unlike in the SEA Protocol. Third, the interests of the public and the information needs of the decision making body must be taken into account in the environmental report, which is not specified under the SEA Directive. Fourth, transboundary consultations are more detailed under the SEA Protocol than the SEA Directive, reflecting the close link with the Espoo Convention. Fifth, 'due account' must be taken of the results of the SEA in the decision making process, with emphasis placed on the need to prevent, reduce or mitigate the adverse effects. Sixth, the environmental and health authorities and the public must be informed of the monitoring undertaken, unlike the SEA Directive. Seventh, with regard to enforcement of each instrument, the SEA Directive benefits from being part of the European law system with the role of the Commission and ECJ in ensuring compliance; enforcement of the SEA Protocol is likely to be linked with the Espoo dispute settlement procedure, which may not be as effective. Further, links between the SEA, Habitats and Environmental Liability Directives *may* provide greater opportunities to address matters of liability and provide for compensation where a failure to carry out an SEA leads to environmental harm (De Mulder, 2006, pp278–281); liability for harm in IEL is also an emerging area of regulation, with many more uncertainties.

With respect to similarities between the two legal instruments, only two key aspects will be emphasized here, which focus on current problems and future changes. General procedural similarities have been outlined extensively in the previous chapters. First, as mentioned, both the SEA Directive and SEA Protocol have yet to fully implement the Aarhus Convention. The definition of 'the public concerned' requires transposition in part (Protocol) or full (Directive) and there is no access to justice provision in either legal instrument. These procedural provisions are particularly important in a legal context because they are capable of providing substantive legal remedies in both international and European law where they are not fully implemented. While it is unlikely that EA procedure will ever change as some have advocated to include a substantive prohibition on environmental harm (which would need to be linked to quantifiable objectives so that any breach were capable of legal remedy), substantive remedies for breach of the three pillars of the Aarhus Convention are likely to be far more common and available in the future. Second, and related, each legal instrument includes a review procedure that can be utilized to ensure such changes are included in the future. Other changes already flagged as worthy of consideration include the extension of the SEA Directive to policy and legislative proposals, the potential consolidation of the EA directives to simplify application and enforcement, a link between the SEA Protocol and the nature conservation treaties,[24] and a much stronger monitoring provision. Above all, however, it is recommended that the SEA Protocol is ratified as soon as possible in order to provide the momentum needed for future change.

NOTES

1   As such, while explanation is simplified as much as possible, the first part of this chapter is more likely to be of interest to environmental lawyers than non-lawyers.

2   The internal status of international law in a nation state is in one sense the same as the internal status of European law in an MS; that is, regardless of whether the nation state has more than one jurisdiction within and regardless of whether those jurisdictions have legislative powers as well as judicial ones, it is a matter for the state government to ensure the application and implementation of international and European law throughout. Devolved administrations in individual jurisdictions can always choose to gold plate requirements by doing more than a treaty or directive requires, subject to the constitutional provisions under which they were created. The role of Scotland within the UK and its implementation of the SEA Directive is an example.

3   Betlem and Nollkaemper (2003, p577) point out that since many courts consider international law to be directed to states they often refuse to grant direct effect, which would provide private parties with a remedy. As such, one of the key distinguishing features of European law over international law is the ability of the former to more easily provide remedies to individuals. As seen, however, such remedies are more usually attained against public authorities (vertical direct effect) than other individuals (horizontal direct effect) because while the European Treaties and regulations may have both vertical and horizontal direct effect, directives (which are addressed to the MS) can only have vertical direct effect.

4   See Churchill and Scott (2004, p683), which includes reference to both ECJ case law and additional academic secondary source materials. Note also Higgins (2003, pp6–10).

5   The four features of the EC legal order originally listed by Simma (1985) were: (1) proceedings before the ECJ; (2) deliberation before the Council; (3) secondary legislation dealing with a breach of Treaty obligations and consequences; and (4) direct effect of EC law before national courts. Conway (2002) adds the following: (5) *Frankovich* liability; (6) Article 228 TEC concerning fines for MS; and (7) Article 7 TEU, suspension of an MS' rights under Article 309(1).

6   The Lisbon Reform Treaty will introduce a new Article 49A to the TEC allowing for withdrawal from the EU, but this will be only at the request of the MS. Withdrawal from the Treaties is a matter discussed by Conway (2002, pp691–693), which was never contemplated by the original Treaties, with previous case law declaring the transfer of sovereignty by the MS to the EC to be 'permanent'. Conway emphasizes that the political developments at the EU level resulted in changes to this permanence, which Article 49A will formalize.

7   For examples and further information on the role of the European institutions and MEAs, see http://ec.europa.eu/environment/international_issues/agreements_en.htm

8   As explained in Chapter 1, individuals and companies have legal personality, and as discussed in Chapter 2, international institutions may also have. A legal personality is needed to enter into agreements of all types, whether simple contracts or international treaties. A new Article 46A to be inserted into the TEU by the Lisbon Treaty states that the Union shall have legal personality.

9   Having the necessary competence means that the institution has been given the power to take action in the relevant area. As seen in Chapters 7 and 8, in a European law context

competence may be shared between the EC and MS, giving each the power to take action in the environmental sector; a new Article 3b of the TEU to be inserted as a result of the Lisbon Treaty states that the 'limits of Union competences are governed by the principle of conferral', meaning that the MS has to give the EU the power to take action. As also seen, this is subject to the principle of subsidiarity, which has also been refined by the Treaty of Lisbon's Protocol on Subsidiarity. Categories and areas of EU competence are set out in new Articles 2A to 2E to be inserted into the TFEU, which will replace the TEC once the Reform Treaty has been ratified.

10   See Article 9E to be inserted into the TEU by the Lisbon Reform Treaty.

11   Article 300 TEC (see Delreux, 2006, pp238-241) currently regulates the procedure for EC decision making in external first pillar issues that include environmental policy, as supplemented by the substantive competence provided by Articles 174–176.

12   Citing other authorities, Delreux (2006, p237) gives five other reasons why agreements may be mixed: (1) when the competences are exclusively attributed to the EC, but when the agreement has budgetary consequences for the MS; (2) when the negotiating parties insist on both MS and EC participation, even within a field of exclusive EC competence; (3) when MS strive to become a party in an attempt to retain a position on the international scene; (4) when both are parties because the EC is keen to avoid international law violating EC law and an MS implementing international law differently; and (5) by using mixed agreements, difficult questions of the precise division of competences are avoided.

13   Convention for the Protection of the Marine Environment of the North East Atlantic, 1992 (1993) 32 ILM 1069.

14   Churchill and Scott (2004, p651) discuss the matter of the likely seriousness of any pollution arising from the operation of the plant in conjunction with the precautionary principle. Although they indicate that both the OSPAR Convention and UNCLOS rules of procedure may have prevented the reversal of the burden of proof that fell on Ireland to show significant damage, they comment: 'Had both Tribunals applied the precautionary principle, which is explicitly incorporated in Article 2(2)(a) of the OSPAR Convention, they might have reached a different view as to the burden of proof'.

15   The respective competences of the MS, European institutions and international tribunals are discussed in detail by Cardwell and French (2007, pp123–124), Churchill and Scott (2004, pp657–666, 670–672) and Lavranos (2005a, pp217–221).

16   Churchill and Scott (2004, pp653–655) highlight the fact that there have been two other cases brought before the UNCLOS dispute settlement procedures where the issue of the possible jurisdiction of a competing tribunal or dispute settlement system has arisen. The first concerned the *Southern Bluefin Tuna* cases, which related to proceedings under UNCLOS and the Convention for the Conservation of Southern Bluefin Tuna (1819 UNTS 359); the second concerned litigation between Chile and the EC over swordfishing, which involved UNCLOS and the WTO. Other cases of overlapping tribunals are examined by Higgins (2003, pp5–10).

17   ECJ, Case C-459/03, *Commission v Ireland*, 30 May 2006.

18   Article 292 concerns the undertaking of all MS not to submit a dispute relating to the interpretation or application of the Treaty to a method of settlement other than those provided for in the Treaty, and is identified as the main legal issue underlying the decisions by Lavranos (2005b, p240). As seen above, Article 10 concerns the duty of cooperation that the MS owe to the European institutions, which is highlighted by Cardwell and French (2007, pp124–125) as an important separate source of obligations on the MS.

19   Stockholm, 19 February 1974), 13 ILM (1974), 352.

20   For a detailed explanation of overlapping procedures concerning transboundary EIA in Northern Europe in particular, see Koivurova (2006), and in relation to SEA, Söderman (2006).

21 Note the references in Lavranos (2005b, note 37), and see Rest (2004), who also recommends the use of the PCA.

22 At both international and European law levels, national solutions to liability are clearly preferred despite indications that national jurisdictions are inadequate to deal with transboundary matters (see Rest, 2004, p5). Note the discussion of liability for environmental harm in Chapter 3, and the minimalist role of the ELD in Chapter 9.

23 States can always choose to gold-plate such provisions also should they wish, and many European MS have much stronger national laws that reflect this.

24 The link between SEA and conservation has been given appropriate recognition in the literature as discussed in Chapter 6 in particular. Chapter 11 also highlighted the important relationship between SEA and the Habitats and Wild Birds Directives, where a framework biodiversity directive was mentioned as a useful way of further organizing nature conservation law within a European law context; the CBD is already playing a partial role in this respect at the level of IEL, as supplemented by the links between the other conservation conventions largely at the level of EA. Impacts upon biodiversity, either negative or positive, must be emphasized in any EA procedure, and highlight the clear relationship between EA and the underlying precautionary principle. Note that the Habitats Directive is also not Aarhus compliant and appropriate amendment is needed.

REFERENCES

Betlem, G. and Nollkaemper, A. (2003) 'Giving effect to public international law and European Community law before domestic courts. A comparative analysis of the practice of consistent interpretation', *European Journal of International Law*, vol 14, no 3, pp569–589

Boyle, A. E. (2005) 'Globalising environmental liability: The interplay of national and international law', *Journal of Environmental Law*, vol 17, no 1, pp3–26

Cardwell, P. J. and French, D. (2007) 'Who decides? The ECJ's judgment on jurisdiction in the MOX Plant dispute', *Journal of Environmental Law*, vol 19, no 1, pp121–129

Churchill, R. and Scott, J. (2004) 'The MOX plant litigation: The first half-life', *International and Comparative Law Quarterly*, vol 53, pp643–676

Conway, G. (2002) 'Breaches of EC law and the international responsibility of member states', *European Journal of International Law*, vol 13, no 3, pp679–695

De Mulder, J. (2006) 'The expansion of environmental assessment in international law: The Protocol on Strategic Environmental Assessment to the Espoo Convention', *Environmental Law and Management*, vol 18, pp269–281

Delreux, T. (2006) 'The European Union in international environmental negotiations: A legal perspective on the internal decision-making process', *International Environmental Agreements*, vol 6, pp231–248

Denza, E. (1999) 'Two legal orders: divergent or convergent?', *International and Comparative Law Quarterly*, vol 48, pp257–284

Higgins, R. (2003) 'The ICJ, ECJ and the integrity of international law', *International and Comparative Law Quarterly*, vol 52, pp1–20

Koivurova, T. (2004) 'The case of Vuotos: Interplay between international, Community and national environmental law', *Review of European Community and International Environmental Law*, vol 13, no 1, pp47–60

Koivurova, T. (2006) 'Transboundary EIA in the North Calotte region from the perspectives of international and European Union Law' in The North Calotte Council, *EIA in the North Calotte Transboundary Areas*, North Calotte Publications, Report No 69, Tornio, pp40–50

Lavranos, N. (2005a) 'Concurrence of jurisdiction between the ECJ and other international courts and tribunals', *European Environmental Law Review*, August/September, pp213–225

Lavranos, N. (2005b) 'Concurrence of jurisdiction between the ECJ and other international courts and tribunals', *European Environmental Law Review*, October, pp240–249

Rest, A. (2004) 'Enhanced implementation of international environmental treaties by judiciary – access to justice in international environmental law for individuals and NGOs: Efficacious enforcement by the Permanent Court of Arbitration', *Macquarie Journal of International and Comparative Environmental Law*, vol 1, pp1–28

Simma, B. and Pulkowski, D. (2006) 'Of planets and the universe: Self-contained regimes in international law', *European Journal of International Law*, vol 17, no 3, pp483–529

Söderman, T. (2006) 'Assessment of the impacts of plans, programmes and policies in transboundary areas' in The North Calotte Council, *EIA in the North Calotte Transboundary Areas*, North Calotte Publications, Report No 69, Tornio, pp55–57

UNECE (1991) *Policies and Systems of Environmental Impact Assessment*, United Nations, New York

UNECE (1992) *Application of Environmental Impact Assessment Principles to Policies, Plans and Programmes*, ECE/ENVWA/27, United Nations, New York

UNEP (1987) *Goals and Principles of Environmental Impact Assessment*, United Nations, New York

PROTOCOL ON STRATEGIC ENVIRONMENTAL ASSESSMENT TO THE CONVENTION ON ENVIRONMENTAL IMPACT ASSESSMENT IN A TRANSBOUNDARY CONTEXT

The Parties to this Protocol,

Recognizing the importance of integrating environmental, including health, considerations into the preparation and adoption of plans and programmes and, to the extent appropriate, policies and legislation,

Committing themselves to promoting sustainable development and therefore basing themselves on the conclusions of the United Nations Conference on Environment and Development (Rio de Janeiro, Brazil, 1992), in particular principles 4 and 10 of the Rio Declaration on Environment and Development and Agenda 21, as well as the outcome of the third Ministerial Conference on Environment and Health (London, 1999) and the World Summit on Sustainable Development (Johannesburg, South Africa, 2002),

Bearing in mind the Convention on Environmental Impact Assessment in a Transboundary Context, done at Espoo, Finland, on 25 February 1991, and decision II/9 of its Parties at Sofia on 26 and 27 February 2001, in which it was decided to prepare a legally binding protocol on strategic environmental assessment,

Recognizing that strategic environmental assessment should have an important role in the preparation and adoption of plans, programmes, and, to the extent appropriate, policies and legislation, and that the wider application of the principles of environmental impact assessment to plans, programmes, policies and legislation will further strengthen the systematic analysis of their significant environmental effects,

Acknowledging the Convention on Access to Information, Public Participation in Decision-making and Access to Justice in Environmental Matters, done at Aarhus, Denmark, on 25 June 1998, and taking note of the relevant paragraphs of the Lucca Declaration, adopted at the first meeting of its Parties,

Conscious, therefore, of the importance of providing for public participation in strategic environmental assessment,

Acknowledging the benefits to the health and well-being of present and future generations that will follow if the need to protect and improve people's health is taken into account as an integral part of strategic environmental assessment, and recognizing the work led by the World Health Organization in this respect,

Mindful of the need for and importance of enhancing international cooperation in assessing the transboundary environmental, including health, effects of proposed plans and programmes, and, to the extent appropriate, policies and legislation,

Have agreed as follows:

Article 1

OBJECTIVE

The objective of this Protocol is to provide for a high level of protection of the environment, including health, by:

(a) Ensuring that environmental, including health, considerations are thoroughly taken into account in the development of plans and programmes;

(b) Contributing to the consideration of environmental, including health, concerns in the preparation of policies and legislation;

(c) Establishing clear, transparent and effective procedures for strategic environmental assessment;

(d) Providing for public participation in strategic environmental assessment; and

(e) Integrating by these means environmental, including health, concerns into measures and instruments designed to further sustainable development.

Article 2

DEFINITIONS

For the purposes of this Protocol,

1. "Convention" means the Convention on Environmental Impact Assessment in a Transboundary Context.

2.   "Party" means, unless the text indicates otherwise, a Contracting Party to this Protocol.

3.   "Party of origin" means a Party or Parties to this Protocol within whose jurisdiction the preparation of a plan or programme is envisaged.

4.   "Affected Party" means a Party or Parties to this Protocol likely to be affected by the transboundary environmental, including health, effects of a plan or programme.

5.   "Plans and programmes" means plans and programmes and any modifications to them that are:

(a) Required by legislative, regulatory or administrative provisions; and

(b) Subject to preparation and/or adoption by an authority or prepared by an authority for adoption, through a formal procedure, by a parliament or a government.

6.   "Strategic environmental assessment" means the evaluation of the likely environmental, including health, effects, which comprises the determination of the scope of an environmental report and its preparation, the carrying-out of public participation and consultations, and the taking into account of the environmental report and the results of the public participation and consultations in a plan or programme.

7.   "Environmental, including health, effect" means any effect on the environment, including human health, flora, fauna, biodiversity, soil, climate, air, water, landscape, natural sites, material assets, cultural heritage and the interaction among these factors.

8.   "The public" means one or more natural or legal persons and, in accordance with national legislation or practice, their associations, organizations or groups.

Article 3

GENERAL PROVISIONS

1.   Each Party shall take the necessary legislative, regulatory and other appropriate measures to implement the provisions of this Protocol within a clear, transparent framework.

2.   Each Party shall endeavour to ensure that officials and authorities assist and provide guidance to the public in matters covered by this Protocol.

3.   Each Party shall provide for appropriate recognition of and support to associations, organizations or groups promoting environmental, including health, protection in the context of this Protocol.

4.   The provisions of this Protocol shall not affect the right of a Party to maintain or introduce additional measures in relation to issues covered by this Protocol.

5.   Each Party shall promote the objectives of this Protocol in relevant international decision-making processes and within the framework of relevant international organizations.

6.   Each Party shall ensure that persons exercising their rights in conformity with the provisions of this Protocol shall not be penalized, persecuted or harassed in any way for their involvement. This provision shall not affect the powers of national courts to award reasonable costs in judicial proceedings.

7.   Within the scope of the relevant provisions of this Protocol, the public shall be able to exercise its rights without discrimination as to citizenship, nationality or domicile and, in the case of a legal person, without discrimination as to where it has its registered seat or an effective centre of its activities.

Article 4

FIELD OF APPLICATION CONCERNING PLANS AND PROGRAMMES

1.   Each Party shall ensure that a strategic environmental assessment is carried out for plans and programmes referred to in paragraphs 2, 3 and 4 which are likely to have significant environmental, including health, effects.

2.   A strategic environmental assessment shall be carried out for plans and programmes which are prepared for agriculture, forestry, fisheries, energy, industry including mining, transport, regional development, waste management, water management, telecommunications, tourism, town and country planning or land use, and which set the framework for future development consent for projects listed in annex I and any other project listed in annex II that requires an environmental impact assessment under national legislation.

3.   For plans and programmes other than those subject to paragraph 2 which set the framework for future development consent of projects, a strategic environmental assessment shall be carried out where a Party so determines according to article 5, paragraph 1.

4.   For plans and programmes referred to in paragraph 2 which determine the use of small areas at local level and for minor modifications to plans and programmes referred to in paragraph 2, a strategic environmental assessment shall be carried out only where a Party so determines according to article 5, paragraph 1.

5. The following plans and programmes are not subject to this Protocol:

(a) Plans and programmes whose sole purpose is to serve national defence or civil emergencies;

(b) Financial or budget plans and programmes.

Article 5

SCREENING

1. Each Party shall determine whether plans and programmes referred to in article 4, paragraphs 3 and 4, are likely to have significant environmental, including health, effects either through a case-by-case examination or by specifying types of plans and programmes or by combining both approaches. For this purpose each Party shall in all cases take into account the criteria set out in annex III.

2. Each Party shall ensure that the environmental and health authorities referred to in article 9, paragraph 1, are consulted when applying the procedures referred to in paragraph 1 above.

3. To the extent appropriate, each Party shall endeavour to provide opportunities for the participation of the public concerned in the screening of plans and programmes under this article.

4. Each Party shall ensure timely public availability of the conclusions pursuant to paragraph 1, including the reasons for not requiring a strategic environmental assessment, whether by public notices or by other appropriate means, such as electronic media.

Article 6

SCOPING

1. Each Party shall establish arrangements for the determination of the relevant information to be included in the environmental report in accordance with article 7, paragraph 2.

2. Each Party shall ensure that the environmental and health authorities referred to in article 9, paragraph 1, are consulted when determining the relevant information to be included in the environmental report.

3. To the extent appropriate, each Party shall endeavour to provide opportunities for the participation of the public concerned when determining the relevant information to be included in the environmental report.

Article 7

ENVIRONMENTAL REPORT

1. For plans and programmes subject to strategic environmental assessment, each Party shall ensure that an environmental report is prepared.

2. The environmental report shall, in accordance with the determination under article 6, identify, describe and evaluate the likely significant environmental, including health, effects of implementing the plan or programme and its reasonable alternatives. The report shall contain such information specified in annex IV as may reasonably be required, taking into account:

(a) Current knowledge and methods of assessment;

(b) The contents and the level of detail of the plan or programme and its stage in the decision-making process;

(c) The interests of the public; and

(d) The information needs of the decision-making body.

3. Each Party shall ensure that environmental reports are of sufficient quality to meet the requirements of this Protocol.

Article 8

PUBLIC PARTICIPATION

1. Each Party shall ensure early, timely and effective opportunities for public participation, when all options are open, in the strategic environmental assessment of plans and programmes.

2. Each Party, using electronic media or other appropriate means, shall ensure the timely public availability of the draft plan or programme and the environmental report.

3. Each Party shall ensure that the public concerned, including relevant non-governmental organizations, is identified for the purposes of paragraphs 1 and 4.

4. Each Party shall ensure that the public referred to in paragraph 3 has the opportunity to express its opinion on the draft plan or programme and the environmental report within a reasonable time frame.

5. Each Party shall ensure that the detailed arrangements for informing the public and consulting the public concerned are determined and made publicly available. For this purpose, each Party shall take into account to the extent appropriate the elements listed in annex V.

Article 9

CONSULTATION WITH ENVIRONMENTAL AND HEALTH AUTHORITIES

1. Each Party shall designate the authorities to be consulted which, by reason of their specific environmental or health responsibilities, are likely to be concerned by the environmental, including health, effects of the implementation of the plan or programme.

2. The draft plan or programme and the environmental report shall be made available to the authorities referred to in paragraph 1.

3. Each Party shall ensure that the authorities referred to in paragraph 1 are given, in an early, timely and effective manner, the opportunity to express their opinion on the draft plan or programme and the environmental report.

4. Each Party shall determine the detailed arrangements for informing and consulting the environmental and health authorities referred to in paragraph 1.

Article 10

TRANSBOUNDARY CONSULTATIONS

1. Where a Party of origin considers that the implementation of a plan or programme is likely to have significant transboundary environmental, including health, effects or where a Party likely to be significantly affected so requests, the Party of origin shall as early as possible before the adoption of the plan or programme notify the affected Party.

2. This notification shall contain, inter alia:

(a) The draft plan or programme and the environmental report including information on its possible transboundary environmental, including health, effects; and

(b) Information regarding the decision-making procedure, including an indication of a reasonable time schedule for the transmission of comments.

3. The affected Party shall, within the time specified in the notification, indicate to the Party of origin whether it wishes to enter into consultations before the adoption of the plan or programme and, if it so indicates, the Parties concerned shall enter into consultations concerning the likely transboundary environmental, including health, effects of implementing the plan or programme and the measures envisaged to prevent, reduce or mitigate adverse effects.

4. Where such consultations take place, the Parties concerned shall agree on detailed arrangements to ensure that the public concerned and the authorities referred to in article 9, paragraph 1, in the affected Party are informed and given an opportunity to forward their opinion on the draft plan or programme and the environmental report within a reasonable time frame.

Article 11

DECISION

1. Each Party shall ensure that when a plan or programme is adopted due account is taken of:

(a) The conclusions of the environmental report;

(b) The measures to prevent, reduce or mitigate the adverse effects identified in the environmental report; and

(c) The comments received in accordance with articles 8 to 10.

2. Each Party shall ensure that, when a plan or programme is adopted, the public, the authorities referred to in article 9, paragraph 1, and the Parties consulted according to article 10 are informed, and that the plan or programme is made available to them together with a statement summarizing how the environmental, including health, considerations have been integrated into it, how the comments received in accordance with articles 8 to 10 have been taken into account and the reasons for adopting it in the light of the reasonable alternatives considered.

Article 12

MONITORING

1. Each Party shall monitor the significant environmental, including health, effects of the implementation of the plans and programmes, adopted under article 11 in order, inter alia, to identify, at an early stage, unforeseen adverse effects and to be able to undertake appropriate remedial action.

2. The results of the monitoring undertaken shall be made available, in accordance with national legislation, to the authorities referred to in article 9, paragraph 1, and to the public.

Article 13

POLICIES AND LEGISLATION

1. Each Party shall endeavour to ensure that environmental, including health, concerns are considered and integrated to the extent appropriate in the preparation of its proposals for policies and legislation that are likely to have significant effects on the environment, including health.

2. In applying paragraph 1, each Party shall consider the appropriate principles and elements of this Protocol.

3. Each Party shall determine, where appropriate, the practical arrangements for the consideration and integration of environmental, including health, concerns in accordance with paragraph 1, taking into account the need for transparency in decision-making.

4. Each Party shall report to the Meeting of the Parties to the Convention serving as the Meeting of the Parties to this Protocol on its application of this article.

Article 14

THE MEETING OF THE PARTIES TO THE CONVENTION SERVING AS THE MEETING OF THE PARTIES TO THE PROTOCOL

1. The Meeting of the Parties to the Convention shall serve as the Meeting of the Parties to this Protocol. The first meeting of the Parties to the Convention serving as the Meeting of the Parties to this Protocol shall be convened not later than one year after the date of entry into force of this Protocol, and in conjunction with a meeting of the Parties to the Convention, if a meeting of the latter is scheduled within that period. Subsequent meetings of the Parties to the Convention serving as the Meeting of the Parties to this Protocol shall be held in conjunction with meetings of the Parties to the Convention, unless otherwise decided by the Meeting of the Parties to the Convention serving as the Meeting of the Parties to this Protocol.

2. Parties to the Convention which are not Parties to this Protocol may participate as observers in the proceedings of any session of the Meeting of the Parties to the Convention serving as the Meeting of the Parties to this Protocol. When the Meeting of the Parties to the Convention serves as the Meeting of the Parties to this Protocol, decisions under this Protocol shall be taken only by the Parties to this Protocol.

3. When the Meeting of the Parties to the Convention serves as the Meeting of the Parties to this Protocol, any member of the Bureau of the Meeting of the Parties representing a Party to the Convention that is not, at that time, a Party to this Protocol shall be replaced by another member to be elected by and from amongst the Parties to this Protocol.

4. The Meeting of the Parties to the Convention serving as the Meeting of the Parties to this Protocol shall keep under regular review the implementation of this Protocol and, for this purpose, shall:

(a) Review policies for and methodological approaches to strategic environmental assessment with a view to further improving the procedures provided for under this Protocol;

(b) Exchange information regarding experience gained in strategic environmental assessment and in the implementation of this Protocol;

(c) Seek, where appropriate, the services and cooperation of competent bodies having expertise pertinent to the achievement of the purposes of this Protocol;

(d) Establish such subsidiary bodies as it considers necessary for the implementation of this Protocol;

(e) Where necessary, consider and adopt proposals for amendments to this Protocol; and

(f) Consider and undertake any additional action, including action to be carried out jointly under this Protocol and the Convention, that may be required for the achievement of the purposes of this Protocol.

5. The rules of procedure of the Meeting of the Parties to the Convention shall be applied mutatis mutandis under this Protocol, except as may otherwise be decided by consensus by the Meeting of the Parties serving as the Meeting of the Parties to this Protocol.

6. At its first meeting, the Meeting of the Parties to the Convention serving as the Meeting of the Parties to this Protocol shall consider and adopt the modalities for applying the procedure for the review of compliance with the Convention to this Protocol.

7. Each Party shall, at intervals to be determined by the Meeting of the Parties to the Convention serving as the Meeting of the Parties to this Protocol, report to the Meeting of the Parties to the Convention serving as the Meeting of the Parties to the Protocol on measures that it has taken to implement the Protocol.

Article 15

RELATIONSHIP TO OTHER INTERNATIONAL AGREEMENTS

The relevant provisions of this Protocol shall apply without prejudice to the UNECE Conventions on Environmental Impact Assessment in a Transboundary Context and on Access to Information, Public Participation in Decision-making and Access to Justice in Environmental Matters.

Article 16

RIGHT TO VOTE

1. Except as provided for in paragraph 2 below, each Party to this Protocol shall have one vote.

2. Regional economic integration organizations, in matters within their competence, shall exercise their right to vote with a number of votes equal to the number of their member States which are Parties to this Protocol. Such organizations shall not exercise their right to vote if their member States exercise theirs, and vice versa.

Article 17

SECRETARIAT

The secretariat established by article 13 of the Convention shall serve as the secretariat of this Protocol and article 13, paragraphs (a) to (c), of the Convention on the functions of the secretariat shall apply mutatis mutandis to this Protocol.

Article 18

ANNEXES

The annexes to this Protocol shall constitute an integral part thereof.

Article 19

AMENDMENTS TO THE PROTOCOL

1.   Any Party may propose amendments to this Protocol.

2.   Subject to paragraph 3, the procedure for proposing, adopting and the entry into force of amendments to the Convention laid down in paragraphs 2 to 5 of article 14 of the Convention shall apply, mutatis mutandis, to amendments to this Protocol.

3.   For the purpose of this Protocol, the three fourths of the Parties required for an amendment to enter into force for Parties having ratified, approved or accepted it, shall be calculated on the basis of the number of Parties at the time of the adoption of the amendment.

Article 20

SETTLEMENT OF DISPUTES

The provisions on the settlement of disputes of article 15 of the Convention shall apply mutatis mutandis to this Protocol.

Article 21

SIGNATURE

This Protocol shall be open for signature at Kiev (Ukraine) from 21 to 23 May 2003 and thereafter at United Nations Headquarters in New York until 31 December 2003, by States members of the Economic Commission for Europe as well as States having consultative status with the Economic Commission for Europe pursuant to paragraphs 8 and 11 of Economic and Social Council resolution 36 (IV) of 28 March 1947, and by regional economic integration organizations constituted by sovereign States members of the Economic Commission for Europe to which their member States have transferred

competence over matters governed by this Protocol, including the competence to enter into treaties in respect of these matters.

Article 22

DEPOSITARY

The Secretary-General of the United Nations shall act as the Depositary of this Protocol.

Article 23

RATIFICATION, ACCEPTANCE, APPROVAL
AND ACCESSION

1.   This Protocol shall be subject to ratification, acceptance or approval by signatory States and regional economic integration organizations referred to in article 21.

2.   This Protocol shall be open for accession as from 1 January 2004 by the States and regional economic integration organizations referred to in article 21.

3.   Any other State, not referred to in paragraph 2 above, that is a Member of the United Nations may accede to the Protocol upon approval by the Meeting of the Parties to the Convention serving as the Meeting of the Parties to the Protocol.

4.   Any regional economic integration organization referred to in article 21 which becomes a Party to this Protocol without any of its member States being a Party shall be bound by all the obligations under this Protocol. If one or more of such an organization's member States is a Party to this Protocol, the organization and its member States shall decide on their respective responsibilities for the performance of their obligations under this Protocol. In such cases, the organization and its member States shall not be entitled to exercise rights under this Protocol concurrently.

5.   In their instruments of ratification, acceptance, approval or accession, the regional economic integration organizations referred to in article 21 shall declare the extent of their competence with respect to the matters governed by this Protocol. These organizations shall also inform the Depositary of any relevant modification to the extent of their competence.

Article 24

ENTRY INTO FORCE

1.   This Protocol shall enter into force on the ninetieth day after the date of deposit of the sixteenth instrument of ratification, acceptance, approval or accession.

2.   For the purposes of paragraph 1 above, any instrument deposited by a regional economic integration organization referred to in article 21 shall not be counted as additional to those deposited by States members of such an organization.

3.   For each State or regional economic integration organization referred to in article 21 which ratifies, accepts or approves this Protocol or accedes thereto after the deposit of the sixteenth instrument of ratification, acceptance, approval or accession, the Protocol shall enter into force on the ninetieth day after the date of deposit by such State or organization of its instrument of ratification, acceptance, approval or accession.

4.   This Protocol shall apply to plans, programmes, policies and legislation for which the first formal preparatory act is subsequent to the date on which this Protocol enters into force.   Where the Party under whose jurisdiction the preparation of a plan, programme, policy or legislation is envisaged is one for which paragraph 3 applies, this Protocol shall apply to plans, programmes, policies and legislation for which the first formal preparatory act is subsequent to the date on which this Protocol comes into force for that Party.

Article 25

WITHDRAWAL

At any time after four years from the date on which this Protocol has come into force with respect to a Party, that Party may withdraw from the Protocol by giving written notification to the Depositary. Any such withdrawal shall take effect on the ninetieth day after the date of its receipt by the Depositary. Any such withdrawal shall not affect the application of articles 5 to 9, 11 and 13 with respect to a strategic environmental assessment under this Protocol which has already been started, or the application of article 10 with respect to a notification or request which has already been made, before such withdrawal takes effect.

Article 26

AUTHENTIC TEXTS

The original of this Protocol, of which the English, French and Russian texts are equally authentic, shall be deposited with the Secretary-General of the United Nations.

IN WITNESS WHEREOF the undersigned, being duly authorized thereto, have signed this Protocol.

DONE at Kiev (Ukraine), this twenty-first day of May, two thousand and three.

ANNEXES

ANNEX I

List of projects as referred to in article 4, paragraph 2

1. Crude oil refineries (excluding undertakings manufacturing only lubricants from crude oil) and installations for the gasification and liquefaction of 500 metric tons or more of coal or bituminous shale per day.

2. Thermal power stations and other combustion installations with a heat output of 300 megawatts or more and nuclear power stations and other nuclear reactors (except research installations for the production and conversion of fissionable and fertile materials, whose maximum power does not exceed 1 kilowatt continuous thermal load).

3. Installations solely designed for the production or enrichment of nuclear fuels, for the reprocessing of irradiated nuclear fuels or for the storage, disposal and processing of radioactive waste.

4. Major installations for the initial smelting of cast-iron and steel and for the production of non-ferrous metals.

5. Installations for the extraction of asbestos and for the processing and transformation of asbestos and products containing asbestos: for asbestos-cement products, with an annual production of more than 20,000 metric tons of finished product; for friction material, with an annual production of more than 50 metric tons of finished product; and for other asbestos utilization of more than 200 metric tons per year.

6. Integrated chemical installations.

7. Construction of motorways, express roads*/ and lines for long-distance railway traffic and of airports**/ with a basic runway length of 2,100 metres or more.

8. Large-diameter oil and gas pipelines.

9. Trading ports and also inland waterways and ports for inland-waterway traffic which permit the passage of vessels of over 1,350 metric tons.

10. Waste-disposal installations for the incineration, chemical treatment or landfill of toxic and dangerous wastes.

11. Large dams and reservoirs.

12. Groundwater abstraction activities in cases where the annual volume of water to be abstracted amounts to 10 million cubic metres or more.

13. Pulp and paper manufacturing of 200 air-dried metric tons or more per day.

14. Major mining, on-site extraction and processing of metal ores or coal.

15. Offshore hydrocarbon production.

16. Major storage facilities for petroleum, petrochemical and chemical products.

17. Deforestation of large areas.

---

*/ For the purposes of this Protocol:

- "Motorway" means a road specially designed and built for motor traffic, which does not serve properties bordering on it, and which:

(a) Is provided, except at special points or temporarily, with separate carriageways for the two directions of traffic, separated from each other by a dividing strip not intended for traffic or, exceptionally, by other means;

(b) Does not cross at level with any road, railway or tramway track, or footpath; and

(c) Is specially sign posted as a motorway.

- "Express road" means a road reserved for motor traffic accessible only from interchanges or controlled junctions and on which, in particular, stopping and parking are prohibited on the running carriageway(s).

**/ For the purposes of this Protocol, "airport" means an airport which complies with the definition in the 1944 Chicago Convention setting up the International Civil Aviation Organization (annex 14).

ANNEX II

Any other projects referred to in article 4, paragraph 2

1. Projects for the restructuring of rural land holdings.

2. Projects for the use of uncultivated land or semi-natural areas for intensive agricultural purposes.

3. Water management projects for agriculture, including irrigation and land drainage projects.

4. Intensive livestock installations (including poultry).

5. Initial afforestation and deforestation for the purposes of conversion to another type of land use.

6. Intensive fish farming.

7. Nuclear power stations and other nuclear reactors[*] including the dismantling or decommissioning of such power stations or reactors (except research installations for the production and conversion of fissionable and fertile materials whose maximum power does not exceed 1 kilowatt continuous thermal load), as far as not included in annex I.

8. Construction of overhead electrical power lines with a voltage of 220 kilovolts or more and a length of 15 kilometres or more and other projects for the transmission of electrical energy by overhead cables.

9. Industrial installations for the production of electricity, steam and hot water.

10. Industrial installations for carrying gas, steam and hot water.

11. Surface storage of fossil fuels and natural gas.

12. Underground storage of combustible gases.

13. Industrial briquetting of coal and lignite.

14. Installations for hydroelectric energy production.

15. Installations for the harnessing of wind power for energy production (wind farms).

16. Installations, as far as not included in annex I, designed:

   – For the production or enrichment of nuclear fuel;

   – For the processing of irradiated nuclear fuel;

   – For the final disposal of irradiated nuclear fuel;

   – Solely for the final disposal of radioactive waste;

   – Solely for the storage (planned for more than 10 years) of irradiated nuclear fuels in a different site than the production site; or

   – For the processing and storage of radioactive waste.

17. Quarries, open cast mining and peat extraction, as far as not included in annex I.

18. Underground mining, as far as not included in annex I.

19. Extraction of minerals by marine or fluvial dredging.

20. Deep drillings (in particular geothermal drilling, drilling for the storage of nuclear waste material, drilling for water supplies), with the exception of drillings for investigating the stability of the soil.

21. Surface industrial installations for the extraction of coal, petroleum, natural gas and ores, as well as bituminous shale.

22. Integrated works for the initial smelting of cast iron and steel, as far as not included in annex I.

23. Installations for the production of pig iron or steel (primary or secondary fusion) including continuous casting.

24. Installations for the processing of ferrous metals (hot-rolling mills, smitheries with hammers, application of protective fused metal coats).

25. Ferrous metal foundries.

26. Installations for the production of non-ferrous crude metals from ore, concentrates or secondary raw materials by metallurgical, chemical or electrolytic processes, as far as not included in annex I.

27. Installations for the smelting, including the alloyage, of non-ferrous metals excluding precious metals, including recovered products (refining, foundry casting, etc.), as far as not included in annex I.

28. Installations for surface treatment of metals and plastic materials using an electrolytic or chemical process.

29. Manufacture and assembly of motor vehicles and manufacture of motor-vehicle engines.

---

[*] For the purposes of this Protocol, nuclear power stations and other nuclear reactors cease to be such an installation when all nuclear fuel and other radioactively contaminated elements have been removed permanently from the installation site.

30. Shipyards.

31. Installations for the construction and repair of aircraft.

32. Manufacture of railway equipment.

33. Swaging by explosives.

34. Installations for the roasting and sintering of metallic ores.

35. Coke ovens (dry coal distillation).

36. Installations for the manufacture of cement.

37. Installations for the manufacture of glass including glass fibre.

38. Installations for smelting mineral substances including the production of mineral fibres.

39. Manufacture of ceramic products by burning, in particular roofing tiles, bricks, refractory bricks, tiles, stoneware or porcelain.

40. Installations for the production of chemicals or treatment of intermediate products, as far as not included in annex I.

41. Production of pesticides and pharmaceutical products, paint and varnishes, elastomers and peroxides.

42. Installations for the storage of petroleum, petrochemical, or chemical products, as far as not included in annex I.

43. Manufacture of vegetable and animal oils and fats.

44. Packing and canning of animal and vegetable products.

45. Manufacture of dairy products.

46. Brewing and malting.

47. Confectionery and syrup manufacture.

48. Installations for the slaughter of animals.

49. Industrial starch manufacturing installations.

50. Fish-meal and fish-oil factories.

51. Sugar factories.

52. Industrial plants for the production of pulp, paper and board, as far as not included in annex I.

53. Plants for the pre-treatment or dyeing of fibres or textiles.

54. Plants for the tanning of hides and skins.

55. Cellulose-processing and production installations.

56. Manufacture and treatment of elastomer-based products.

57. Installations for the manufacture of artificial mineral fibres.

58. Installations for the recovery or destruction of explosive substances.

59. Installations for the production of asbestos and the manufacture of asbestos products, as far as not included in annex I.

60. Knackers' yards.

61. Test benches for engines, turbines or reactors.

62. Permanent racing and test tracks for motorized vehicles.

63. Pipelines for transport of gas or oil, as far as not included in annex I.

64. Pipelines for transport of chemicals with a diameter of more than 800 mm and a length of more than 40 km.

65. Construction of railways and intermodal transhipment facilities, and of intermodal terminals, as far as not included in annex I.

66. Construction of tramways, elevated and underground railways, suspended lines or similar lines of a particular type used exclusively or mainly for passenger transport.

67. Construction of roads, including realignment and/or widening of any existing road, as far as not included in annex I.

68. Construction of harbours and port installations, including fishing harbours, as far as not included in annex I.

69. Construction of inland waterways and ports for inland-waterway traffic, as far as not included in annex I.

70. Trading ports, piers for loading and unloading connected to land and outside ports, as far as not included in annex I.

71. Canalization and flood-relief works.

72. Construction of airports[**] and airfields, as far as not included in annex I.

[**] For the purposes of this Protocol, "airport" means an airport which complies with the definition in the 1944 Chicago Convention setting up the International Civil Aviation Organization (annex 14).

73. Waste-disposal installations (including landfill), as far as not included in annex I.

74. Installations for the incineration or chemical treatment of non-hazardous waste.

75. Storage of scrap iron, including scrap vehicles.

76. Sludge deposition sites.

77. Groundwater abstraction or artificial groundwater recharge, as far as not included in annex I.

78. Works for the transfer of water resources between river basins.

79. Waste-water treatment plants.

80. Dams and other installations designed for the holding-back or for the long-term or permanent storage of water, as far as not included in annex I.

81. Coastal work to combat erosion and maritime works capable of altering the coast through the construction, for example, of dykes, moles, jetties and other sea defence works, excluding the maintenance and reconstruction of such works.

82. Installations of long-distance aqueducts.

83. Ski runs, ski lifts and cable cars and associated developments.

84. Marinas.

85. Holiday villages and hotel complexes outside urban areas and associated developments.

86. Permanent campsites and caravan sites.

87. Theme parks.

88. Industrial estate development projects.

89. Urban development projects, including the construction of shopping centres and car parks.

90. Reclamation of land from the sea.

ANNEX III

Criteria for determining of the likely significant environmental, including health, effects referred to in article 5, paragraph 1

1. The relevance of the plan or programme to the integration of environmental, including health, considerations in particular with a view to promoting sustainable development.

2. The degree to which the plan or programme sets a framework for projects and other activities, either with regard to location, nature, size and operating conditions or by allocating resources.

3. The degree to which the plan or programme influences other plans and programmes including those in a hierarchy.

4. Environmental, including health, problems relevant to the plan or programme.

5. The nature of the environmental, including health, effects such as probability, duration, frequency, reversibility, magnitude and extent (such as geographical area or size of population likely to be affected).

6. The risks to the environment, including health.

7. The transboundary nature of effects.

8. The degree to which the plan or programme will affect valuable or vulnerable areas including landscapes with a recognized national or international protection status.

ANNEX IV

Information referred to in article 7, paragraph 2

1.   The contents and the main objectives of the plan or programme and its link with other plans or programmes.

2.   The relevant aspects of the current state of the environment, including health, and the likely evolution thereof should the plan or programme not be implemented.

3.   The characteristics of the environment, including health, in areas likely to be significantly affected.

4.   The environmental, including health, problems which are relevant to the plan or programme.

5.   The environmental, including health, objectives established at international, national and other levels which are relevant to the plan or programme, and the ways in which these objectives and other environmental, including health, considerations have been taken into account during its preparation.

6.   The likely significant environmental, including health, effects[*] as defined in article 2, paragraph 7.

7.   Measures to prevent, reduce or mitigate any significant adverse effects on the environment, including health, which may result from the implementation of the plan or programme.

8.   An outline of the reasons for selecting the alternatives dealt with and a description of how the assessment was undertaken including difficulties encountered in providing the information to be included such as technical deficiencies or lack of knowledge.

9.   Measures envisaged for monitoring environmental, including health, effects of the implementation of the plan or programme.

10.   The likely significant transboundary environmental, including health, effects.

11.   A non-technical summary of the information provided.

---

[*] These effects should include secondary, cumulative, synergistic, short-, medium- and long-term, permanent and temporary, positive and negative effects.

ANNEX V

Information referred to in article 8, paragraph 5

1.   The proposed plan or programme and its nature.

2.   The authority responsible for its adoption.

3.   The envisaged procedure, including:

   (a)   The commencement of the procedure;

   (b)   The opportunities for the public to participate;

   (c)   The time and venue of any envisaged public hearing;

   (d)   The authority from which relevant information can be obtained and where the relevant information has been deposited for examination by the public;

   (e)   The authority to which comments or questions can be submitted and the time schedule for the transmittal of comments or questions; and

   (f)   What environmental, including health, information relevant to the proposed plan or programme is available.

4.   Whether the plan or programme is likely to be subject to a transboundary assessment procedure.

EUROPEAN UNION

THE EUROPEAN PARLIAMENT   **THE COUNCIL**

Luxembourg, 27 June 2001

1996/0304 (COD)   PE-CONS 3619/3/01
C5-0118/2001   REV 3
LEX 271

ENV   135
CODEC   260

DIRECTIVE 2001/42/EC OF THE EUROPEAN PARLIAMENT AND OF THE COUNCIL

ON THE ASSESSMENT OF THE EFFECTS OF CERTAIN PLANS AND PROGRAMMES

ON THE ENVIRONMENT

DIRECTIVE 2001/42/EC OF THE EUROPEAN PARLIAMENT AND OF THE COUNCIL
of 27 June 2001

on the assessment of the effects of certain plans and programmes

on the environment

THE EUROPEAN PARLIAMENT AND THE COUNCIL OF THE EUROPEAN UNION,

Having regard to the Treaty establishing the European Community, and in particular Article 175(1) thereof,

Having regard to the proposal from the Commission [1],

Having regard to the Opinion of the Economic and Social Committee [2],

Having regard to the opinion of the Committee of the Regions [3],

Acting in accordance with the procedure laid down in Article 251 of the Treaty [4], in the light of the joint text approved by the Conciliation Committee on 21 March 2001,

---

[1] OJ C 129, 25.4.1997, p. 14 and OJ C 83, 25.3.1999, p. 13.
[2] OJ C 287, 22.9.1997, p. 101.
[3] OJ C 64, 27.2.1998, p. 63 and OJ C 374, 23.12.1999, p. 9.
[4] Opinion of the European Parliament of 20 October 1998 (OJ C 341, 9.11.1998, p. 18), confirmed on 16 September 1999 (OJ C 54, 25.2.2000, p. 76), Council Common Position of 30 March 2000 (OJ C 137, 16.5.2000, p. 11) and Decision of the European Parliament of 6 September 2000 (OJ C 135, 7.5.2001, p. 155). Decision of the European Parliament of 31 May 2001 and Decision of the Council of 5 June 2001.

Whereas:

(1)   Article 174 of the Treaty provides that Community policy on the environment is to contribute to, inter alia, the preservation, protection and improvement of the quality of the environment, the protection of human health and the prudent and rational utilisation of natural resources and that it is to be based on the precautionary principle. Article 6 of the Treaty provides that environmental protection requirements are to be integrated into the definition of Community policies and activities, in particular with a view to promoting sustainable development.

(2)   The Fifth Environment Action Programme: Towards sustainability – A European Community programme of policy and action in relation to the environment and sustainable development [1], supplemented by Decision No 2179/98/EC [2] on its review, affirms the importance of assessing the likely environmental effects of plans and programmes.

(3)   The Convention on Biological Diversity requires Parties to integrate as far as possible and as appropriate the conservation and sustainable use of biological diversity into relevant sectoral or cross-sectoral plans and programmes.

(4)   Environmental assessment is an important tool for integrating environmental considerations into the preparation and adoption of certain plans and programmes which are likely to have significant effects on the environment in the Member States, because it ensures that such effects of implementing plans and programmes are taken into account during their preparation and before their adoption.

---

[1]   OJ C 138, 17. 5.1993, p. 5.
[2]   OJ L 275, 10.10.1998, p. 1.

(5)   The adoption of environmental assessment procedures at the planning and programming level should benefit undertakings by providing a more consistent framework in which to operate by the inclusion of the relevant environmental information into decision-making. The inclusion of a wider set of factors in decision-making should contribute to more sustainable and effective solutions.

(6)   The different environmental assessment systems operating within Member States should contain a set of common procedural requirements necessary to contribute to a high level of protection of the environment.

(7)   The United Nations/Economic Commission for Europe Convention on Environmental Impact Assessment in a Transboundary Context of February 25 1991, which applies to both Member States and other States, encourages the parties to the Convention to apply its principles to plans and programmes as well; at the second meeting of the Parties to the Convention in Sofia on 26 – 27 February 2001, it was decided to prepare a legally binding protocol on strategic environmental assessment which would supplement the existing provisions on environmental impact assessment in a transboundary context, with a view to its possible adoption on the occasion of the 5th Ministerial Conference "Environment for Europe" at an extraordinary meeting of the Parties to the Convention, scheduled for May 2003 in Kiev, Ukraine. The systems operating within the Community for environmental assessment of plans and programmes should ensure that there are adequate transboundary consultations where the implementation of a plan or programme being prepared in one Member State is likely to have significant effects on the environment of another Member State. The information on plans and programmes having significant effects on the environment of other States should be forwarded on a reciprocal and equivalent basis within an appropriate legal framework between Member States and these other States.

(8)   Action is therefore required at Community level to lay down a minimum environmental assessment framework, which would set out the broad principles of the environmental assessment system and leave the details to the Member States, having regard to the principle of subsidiarity. Action by the Community should not go beyond what is necessary to achieve the objectives set out in the Treaty.

(9)   This Directive is of a procedural nature, and its requirements should either be integrated into existing procedures in Member States or incorporated in specifically established procedures. With a view to avoiding duplication of the assessment, Member States should take account, where appropriate, of the fact that assessments will be carried out at different levels of a hierarchy of plans and programmes.

(10) All plans and programmes which are prepared for a number of sectors and which set a framework for future development consent of projects listed in Annexes I and II to Council Directive 85/337/EEC of 27 June 1985 on the assessment of the effects of certain public and private projects on the environment [1], and all plans and programmes which have been determined to require assessment pursuant to Council Directive 92/43/EEC of 21 May 1992 on the conservation of natural habitats and of wild flora and fauna [2], are likely to have significant effects on the environment, and should as a rule be made subject to systematic environmental assessment. When they determine the use of small areas at local level or are minor modifications to the above plans or programmes, they should be assessed only where Member States determine that they are likely to have significant effects on the environment.

---

[1]   OJ L 175, 5.7.1985, p. 40. Directive as amended by Directive 97/11/EC (OJ L 73, 14.3.1997, p. 5).

[2]   OJ L 206, 22.7.1992, p. 7. Directive as last amended by Directive 97/62/EC (OJ L 305, 8.11.1997, p. 42).

(11) Other plans and programmes which set the framework for future development consent of projects may not have significant effects on the environment in all cases and should be assessed only where Member States determine that they are likely to have such effects.

(12) When Member States make such determinations, they should take into account the relevant criteria set out in this Directive.

(13) Some plans or programmes are not subject to this Directive because of their particular characteristics.

(14) Where an assessment is required by this Directive, an environmental report should be prepared containing relevant information as set out in this Directive, identifying, describing and evaluating the likely significant environmental effects of implementing the plan or programme, and reasonable alternatives taking into account the objectives and the geographical scope of the plan or programme; Member States should communicate to the Commission any measures they take concerning the quality of environmental reports.

(15) In order to contribute to more transparent decision-making and with the aim of ensuring that the information supplied for the assessment is comprehensive and reliable, it is necessary to provide that authorities with relevant environmental responsibilities and the public are to be consulted during the assessment of plans and programmes, and that appropriate time frames are set, allowing sufficient time for consultations, including the expression of opinion.

(16) Where the implementation of a plan or programme prepared in one Member State is likely to have a significant effect on the environment of other Member States, provision should be made for the Member States concerned to enter into consultations and for the relevant authorities and the public to be informed and enabled to express their opinion.

(17) The environmental report and the opinions expressed by the relevant authorities and the public, as well as the results of any transboundary consultation, should be taken into account during the preparation of the plan or programme and before its adoption or submission to the legislative procedure.

(18) Member States should ensure that, when a plan or programme is adopted, the relevant authorities and the public are informed and relevant information is made available to them.

(19) Where the obligation to carry out assessments of the effects on the environment arises simultaneously from this Directive and other Community legislation, such as Council Directive 79/409/EEC of 2 April 1979 on the conservation of wild birds [1], Directive 92/43/EEC , or Directive 2000/60/EC of the European Parliament and the Council of 23 October 2000 establishing a framework for Community action in the field of water policy [2], in order to avoid duplication of the assessment, Member States may provide for coordinated or joint procedures fulfilling the requirements of the relevant Community legislation.

---

[1] OJ L 103, 25.4.1979, p. 1. Directive as last amended by Directive 97/49/EC (OJ L 223, 13.8.1997, p. 9).

[2] OJ L 327, 22.12.2000, p. 1.

(20) A first report on the application and effectiveness of this Directive should be carried out by the Commission five years after its entry into force, and at seven-year intervals thereafter. With a view to further integrating environmental protection requirements, and taking into account the experience acquired, the first report should, if appropriate, be accompanied by proposals for amendment of this Directive, in particular as regards the possibility of extending its scope to other areas/sectors and other types of plans and programmes,

HAVE ADOPTED THIS DIRECTIVE:

Article 1

Objectives

The objective of this Directive is to provide for a high level of protection of the environment and to contribute to the integration of environmental considerations into the preparation and adoption of plans and programmes with a view to promoting sustainable development, by ensuring that, in accordance with this Directive, an environmental assessment is carried out of certain plans and programmes which are likely to have significant effects on the environment.

Article 2

Definitions

For the purposes of this Directive:

(a)   "plans and programmes" shall mean plans and programmes, including those co-financed by the European Community, as well as any modifications to them:

–   which are subject to preparation and/or adoption by an authority at national, regional or local level or which are prepared by an authority for adoption, through a legislative procedure by Parliament or Government, and

–   which are required by legislative, regulatory or administrative provisions;

(b)   "environmental assessment" shall mean the preparation of an environmental report, the carrying out of consultations, the taking into account of the environmental report and the results of the consultations in decision-making and the provision of information on the decision in accordance with Articles 4 to 9;

(c)   "environmental report" shall mean the part of the plan or programme documentation containing the information required in Article 5 and Annex I;

(d)   "The public" shall mean one or more natural or legal persons and, in accordance with national legislation or practice, their associations, organisations or groups.

Article 3

Scope

1.   An environmental assessment, in accordance with Articles 4 to 9, shall be carried out for plans and programmes referred to in paragraphs 2 to 4 which are likely to have significant environmental effects.

2.   Subject to paragraph 3, an environmental assessment shall be carried out for all plans and programmes,

(a)   which are prepared for agriculture, forestry, fisheries, energy, industry, transport, waste management, water management, telecommunications, tourism, town and country planning or land use and which set the framework for future development consent of projects listed in Annexes I and II to Directive 85/337/EEC, or

(b)   which, in view of the likely effect on sites, have been determined to require an assessment pursuant to Article 6 or 7 of Directive 92/43/EEC.

3. Plans and programmes referred to in paragraph 2 which determine the use of small areas at local level and minor modifications to plans and programmes referred to in paragraph 2 shall require an environmental assessment only where the Member States determine that they are likely to have significant environmental effects.

4. Member States shall determine whether plans and programmes, other than those referred to in paragraph 2, which set the framework for future development consent of projects, are likely to have significant environmental effects.

5. Member States shall determine whether plans or programmes referred to in paragraphs 3 and 4 are likely to have significant environmental effects either through case-by-case examination or by specifying types of plans and programmes or by combining both approaches. For this purpose Member States shall in all cases take into account relevant criteria set out in Annex II, in order to ensure that plans and programmes with likely significant effects on the environment are covered by this Directive.

6. In the case-by-case examination and in specifying types of plans and programmes in accordance with paragraph 5, the authorities referred to in Article 6(3) shall be consulted.

7. Member States shall ensure that their conclusions pursuant to paragraph 5, including the reasons for not requiring an environmental assessment pursuant to Articles 4 to 9, are made available to the public.

8. The following plans and programmes are not subject to this Directive:

– plans and programmes the sole purpose of which is to serve national defence or civil emergency,

– financial or budget plans and programmes.

9. This Directive does not apply to plans and programmes co-financed under the current respective programming periods[1] for Council Regulations (EC) No 1260/99[2] and No 1257/99[3].

Article 4

General obligations

1. The environmental assessment referred to in Article 3 shall be carried out during the preparation of a plan or programme and before its adoption or submission to the legislative procedure.

2. The requirements of this Directive shall either be integrated into existing procedures in Member States for the adoption of plans and programmes or incorporated in procedures established to comply with this Directive.

---

[1] The 2000-2006 programming period for Council Regulation (EC) No 1260/99 and the 2000-2006 and 2000-2007 programming periods for Council Regulation (EC) No 1257/99.

[2] Council Regulation (EC) No 1260/99 of 21 June 1999 laying down general provisions on the Structural Funds. (OJ L 161, 26.6.1999, p. 1.)

[3] Council Regulation (EC) No 1257/99 of 17 May 1999 on support for rural development from the European Agricultural Guidance and Guarantee Fund (EAGGF) and amending and repealing certain regulations. (OJ L 160, 26.6.1999, p. 80.)

3.   Where plans and programmes form part of a hierarchy, Member States shall, with a view to avoiding duplication of the assessment, take into account the fact that the assessment will be carried out, in accordance with this Directive, at different levels of the hierarchy. For the purpose of, inter alia, avoiding duplication of assessment, Member States shall apply Article 5(2) and (3).

Article 5

Environmental report

1.   Where an environmental assessment is required under Article 3(1), an environmental report shall be prepared in which the likely significant effects on the environment of implementing the plan or programme, and reasonable alternatives taking into account the objectives and the geographical scope of the plan or programme, are identified, described and evaluated. The information to be given for this purpose is referred to in Annex I.

2.   The environmental report prepared pursuant to paragraph 1 shall include the information that may reasonably be required taking into account current knowledge and methods of assessment, the contents and level of detail in the plan or programme, its stage in the decision-making process and the extent to which certain matters are more appropriately assessed at different levels in that process in order to avoid duplication of the assessment.

3.   Relevant information available on environmental effects of the plans and programmes and obtained at other levels of decision-making or through other Community legislation may be used for providing the information referred to in Annex I.

4.   The authorities referred to in Article 6(3) shall be consulted when deciding on the scope and level of detail of the information which must be included in the environmental report.

<u>Article 6</u>

Consultations

1. The draft plan or programme and the environmental report prepared in accordance with Article 5 shall be made available to the authorities referred to in paragraph 3 of this Article and the public.

2. The authorities referred to in paragraph 3 and the public referred to in paragraph 4 shall be given an early and effective opportunity within appropriate time frames to express their opinion on the draft plan or programme and the accompanying environmental report before the adoption of the plan or programme or its submission to the legislative procedure.

3. Member States shall designate the authorities to be consulted which, by reason of their specific environmental responsibilities, are likely to be concerned by the environmental effects of implementing plans and programmes.

4. Member States shall identify the public for the purposes of paragraph 2, including the public affected or likely to be affected by, or having an interest in, the decision-making subject to this Directive, including relevant non-governmental organisations, such as those promoting environmental protection and other organisations concerned.

5. The detailed arrangements for the information and consultation of the authorities and the public shall be determined by the Member States.

Article 7

Transboundary consultations

1.   Where a Member State considers that the implementation of a plan or programme being prepared in relation to its territory is likely to have significant effects on the environment in another Member State, or where a Member State likely to be significantly affected so requests, the Member State in whose territory the plan or programme is being prepared shall, before its adoption or submission to the legislative procedure, forward a copy of the draft plan or programme and the relevant environmental report to the other Member State.

2.   Where a Member State is sent a copy of a draft plan or programme and an environmental report under paragraph 1, it shall indicate to the other Member State whether it wishes to enter into consultations before the adoption of the plan or programme or its submission to the legislative procedure and, if it so indicates, the Member States concerned shall enter into consultations concerning the likely transboundary environmental effects of implementing the plan or programme and the measures envisaged to reduce or eliminate such effects.

Where such consultations take place, the Member States concerned shall agree on detailed arrangements to ensure that the authorities referred to in Article 6(3) and the public referred to in Article 6(4) in the Member State likely to be significantly affected are informed and given an opportunity to forward their opinion within a reasonable time-frame.

3.   Where Member States are required under this Article to enter into consultations, they shall agree, at the beginning of such consultations, on a reasonable time-frame for the duration of the consultations.

Article 8

Decision making

The environmental report prepared pursuant to Article 5, the opinions expressed pursuant to Article 6 and the results of any transboundary consultations entered into pursuant to Article 7 shall be taken into account during the preparation of the plan or programme and before its adoption or submission to the legislative procedure.

Article 9

Information on the decision

1. Member States shall ensure that, when a plan or programme is adopted, the authorities referred to in Article 6(3), the public and any Member State consulted under Article 7 are informed and the following items are made available to those so informed:

(a)   the plan or programme as adopted,

(b)   a statement summarising how environmental considerations have been integrated into the plan or programme and how the environmental report prepared pursuant to Article 5, the opinions expressed pursuant to Article 6 and the results of consultations entered into pursuant to Article 7 have been taken into account in accordance with Article 8 and the reasons for choosing the plan or programme as adopted, in the light of the other reasonable alternatives dealt with, and

(c)   the measures decided concerning monitoring in accordance with Article 10.

2. The detailed arrangements concerning the information referred to in paragraph 1 shall be determined by the Member States.

Article 10

Monitoring

1. Member States shall monitor the significant environmental effects of the implementation of plans and programmes in order, inter alia, to identify at an early stage unforeseen adverse effects, and to be able to undertake appropriate remedial action.

2. In order to comply with paragraph 1, existing monitoring arrangements may be used if appropriate, with a view to avoiding duplication of monitoring.

Article 11

Relationship with other Community legislation

1. An environmental assessment carried out under this Directive shall be without prejudice to any requirements under Directive 85/337/EEC and to any other Community law requirements.

2. For plans and programmes for which the obligation to carry out assessments of the effects on the environment arises simultaneously from this Directive and other Community legislation, Member States may provide for coordinated or joint procedures fulfilling the requirements of the relevant Community legislation in order, inter alia, to avoid duplication of assessment.

3. For plans and programmes co-financed by the European Community, the environmental assessment in accordance with this Directive shall be carried out in conformity with the specific provisions in relevant Community legislation.

Article 12

Information, reporting and review

1. Member States and the Commission shall exchange information on the experience gained in applying this Directive.

2. Member States shall ensure that environmental reports are of a sufficient quality to meet the requirements of this Directive and shall communicate to the Commission any measures they take concerning the quality of these reports.

3. Before   * the Commission shall send a first report on the application and effectiveness of this Directive to the European Parliament and to the Council.

With a view further to integrating environmental protection requirements, in accordance with Article 6 of the Treaty, and taking into account the experience acquired in the application of this Directive in the Member States, such a report will be accompanied by proposals for amendment of this Directive, if appropriate. In particular, the Commission will consider the possibility of extending the scope of this Directive to other areas/sectors and other types of plans and programmes.

A new evaluation report shall follow at seven-year intervals.

4. The Commission shall report on the relationship between this Directive and Regulations (EC) No 1260/*1999* and No 1257/*1999* well ahead of the expiry of the programming periods provided for in those Regulations, with a view to ensuring a coherent approach with regard to this Directive and subsequent Community Regulations.

---

*   Five years after the entry into force of this Directive.

Article 13

Implementation of the Directive

1. Member States shall bring into force the laws, regulations and administrative provisions necessary to comply with this Directive before *. They shall forthwith inform the Commission thereof.

2. When Member States adopt the measures, they shall contain a reference to this Directive or shall be accompanied by such reference on the occasion of their official publication. The methods of making such reference shall be laid down by Member States.

3. The obligation referred to in Article 4(1) shall apply to the plans and programmes of which the first formal preparatory act is subsequent to the date referred to in paragraph 1. Plans and programmes of which the first formal preparatory act is before that date and which are adopted or submitted to the legislative procedure more than 24 months thereafter, shall be made subject to the obligation referred to in Article 4(1) unless Member States decide on a case by case basis that this is not feasible and inform the public of their decision.

4. Before **, Member States shall communicate to the Commission, in addition to the measures referred to in paragraph 1, separate information on the types of plans and programmes which, in accordance with Article 3, would be subject to an environmental assessment pursuant to this Directive. The Commission shall make this information available to the Member States. The information will be updated on a regular basis.

---

*   Three years after the entry into force of this Directive.
**   Three years after the entry into force of this Directive.

Article 14

Entry into force

This Directive shall enter into force on the day of its publication in the Official Journal of the European Communities.

Article 15

Addressees

This Directive is addressed to the Member States.

Done at Luxembourg,

For the European Parliament

The President

For the Council

The President

Information referred to in Article 5(1)

The information to be provided under Article 5(1), subject to Article 5(2) and (3), is the following:

(a)   an outline of the contents, main objectives of the plan or programme and relationship with other relevant plans and programmes;

(b)   the relevant aspects of the current state of the environment and the likely evolution thereof without implementation of the plan or programme;

(c)   the environmental characteristics of areas likely to be significantly affected;

(d)   any existing environmental problems which are relevant to the plan or programme including, in particular, those relating to any areas of a particular environmental importance, such as areas designated pursuant to Directives 79/409/EEC and 92/43/EEC;

(e)   the environmental protection objectives, established at international, Community or Member State level, which are relevant to the plan or programme and the way those objectives and any environmental considerations have been taken into account during its preparation;

(f)   the likely significant effects[1] on the environment, including on issues such as biodiversity, population, human health, fauna, flora, soil, water, air, climatic factors, material assets, cultural heritage including architectural and archaeological heritage, landscape and the interrelationship between the above factors;

(g)   the measures envisaged to prevent, reduce and as fully as possible offset any significant adverse effects on the environment of implementing the plan or programme;

(h)   an outline of the reasons for selecting the alternatives dealt with, and a description of how the assessment was undertaken including any difficulties (such as technical deficiencies or lack of know-how) encountered in compiling the required information;

(i)   a description of the measures envisaged concerning monitoring in accordance with Article 10.

(j)   a non-technical summary of the information provided under the above headings.

------

[1]   these effects should include secondary, cumulative, synergistic, short, medium and long-term permanent and temporary, positive and negative effects.

<u>**ANNEX II**</u>

Criteria for determining the likely significance of effects referred to in Article 3(5)

1. The characteristics of plans and programmes, having regard, in particular, to

    –   the degree to which the plan or programme sets a framework for projects and other activities, either with regard to the location, nature, size and operating conditions or by allocating resources;

    –   the degree to which the plan or programme influences other plans and programmes including those in a hierarchy;

    –   the relevance of the plan or programme for the integration of environmental considerations in particular with a view to promoting sustainable development;

    –   environmental problems relevant to the plan or programme;

    –   the relevance of the plan or programme for the implementation of Community legislation on the environment (e.g. plans and programmes linked to waste-management or water protection).

2. Characteristics of the effects and of the area likely to be affected, having regard, in particular, to

 – the probability, duration, frequency and reversibility of the effects;

 – the cumulative nature of the effects;

 – the transboundary nature of the effects;

 – the risks to human health or the environment (e.g. due to accidents);

 – the magnitude and spatial extent of the effects (geographical area and size of the population likely to be affected);

 – the value and vulnerability of the area likely to be affected due to:

   = special natural characteristics or cultural heritage;

   = exceeded environmental quality standards or limit values;

   = intensive land-use;

 – the effects on areas or landscapes which have a recognised national, Community or international protection status.

—————————

Index

Aarhus Convention on Access to
    Information, Public Participation
    in Decision-Making and Access to
    Justice in Environmental Matters,
    1998
  European law 81–82, 279
  horizontal directives 183, 191, 192,
    193, 194–195, 197
  SEA Protocol 2–3, 73, 80–86, 93, 94–95,
    105–106, 281
access to information 83, 84, 86, 190,
  197
  see also information
access to justice
  Aarhus Convention 82–83, 85
  EIA Directive 185–186, 190
  Environmental Information Directive
    191
  Environmental Liability Directive
    196–197
  IEL 63–64
  proposed Directive 193–194
  SEA Protocol 96, 106, 281
  see also Aarhus Convention
accountability 9
action programmes 255–256
advisory jurisdiction 35
Air Quality Framework Directive 256–257
alternatives
  EIA Directive 184–185
  Habitats and Wild Birds Directives 248
  reasonable 219–220, 220–221, 252
  SEA protocol 103, 106
amendments 30, 119, 184
Amsterdam Treaty 163–164

Analytical Strategic Environmental
    Assessment (ANSEA) project 7–8
ANSEA *see* Analytical Strategic
    Environmental Assessment project
arbitration 27, 36–37
Article 11, SEA Directive 239–271
autonomous regimes 40–41, 140,
    273–274, 275–276

baseline data collection 251–252
binding precedent 11, 12
biodiversity conservation 115–133
  see also conservation
Bonn Convention *see* Convention on the
    Conservation of Migratory Species of
    Wild Animals
Brundtland Report, 1987 48
burden of proof 116

CBD *see* Convention on Biological
    Diversity
CFI *see* Court of First Instance
citizens, EU 144
civil emergency 219
civil law legal systems 11–12
CMS *see* Convention on the Conservation
    of Migratory Species of Wild Animals
Commission, EU 141–142, 149–150, 160,
    171, 186–187, 228
common but differentiated
    responsibilities 49, 50, 61
common law 11–12, 33
common market 141
compensation
  Espoo Convention 76–77

Habitats and Wild Birds Directives 247, 249
IEL 50, 54–55, 59–60, 62–63, 86
competence 162, 164–165, 276–277, 278–279
compliance
    Aarhus Convention 86
    conservation conventions 127
    EIA and SEA overlaps 241
    Espoo Convention 78, 79–80
    European environment law 169–173
    international law 36, 64
    SEA Protocol 107–108
    treaties 34
conciliation 37
Conferences of the Parties (COPs) 40–41, 121–122, 127–128, 129
    see also Meetings of the Parties
conferences 29, 48–49, 161
conservation 3, 48, 115–133, 244, 280–282
consistent interpretation 32, 34–35
constitutional aspects 10–11, 13, 38–39, 150–151, 161
consultation 104, 221–223, 254, 281
contentious jurisdiction 35
Convention on Biological Diversity, 1992 (CBD) 59, 125–129
Convention Concerning the Protection of the World Cultural and Natural Heritage, 1972 (World Heritage Convention) 122–124
Convention on the Conservation of Migratory Species of Wild Animals, 1979 (Bonn Convention/CMS) 124–125
Convention for the Protection of the Marine Environment of the North-East Atlantic (OSPAR) 277
Convention on the Protection and Use of Transboundary Watercourses and International Lakes 57, 58
conventions
    see also Aarhus Convention; Espoo Convention
Convention on Wetlands of International Importance, Especially as Waterfowl

Habitat, 1971 (Ramsar Convention) 119–122
cooperation 50, 53–54, 57–59, 62, 145
coordination 126, 240, 251
COPs see Conferences of the Parties
Council of Europe 141
Council of Ministers, EU 141
Court of First Instance (CFI) 146–147
courts 12–13, 39–40, 150
cross-referencing 49, 281
cumulative effects 245, 246, 280
customary law 28, 29, 31, 33, 47, 51–55

decision making
    European law 141, 142–143, 146
    need for laws 10
    project level 87
    SEA Directive 223
    SEA overview 7–8
    SEA Protocol 95, 98, 106–107
    see also Aarhus Convention
definitions
    international law 26
    migratory species 125
    plans and projects 245
    public 105, 185, 192, 281
    SEA Protocol 99
democratic deficit 150–151
designation of sites 243, 245
development consent 188–189, 218, 240, 241, 256, 281
development proposals 120, 123
direct effects
    EIA Directive 189–190
    European law 3, 148–149, 170–171, 274, 275
    Habitats Directive 246
    international law 32, 33, 34, 274, 275
    national law 32, 33, 34
    SEA Directive 208–209
directives
    air quality 256 257
    EIA 183–190, 206, 239, 240–242, 258
    environmental information 190–192
    environmental liability 190, 195–197
    European law 146, 149
    Habitats 166, 243–250, 255, 258, 278

horizontal 183–204
implementation 171–172
nitrates 255–256
proposed access to justice 193–194
public participation 190, 192–193
waste 256, 258
water 208, 250–255, 258
disclosure 191
discretion 51, 102, 184, 187, 188, 226, 246
dispute resolution
  ECJ 140–141, 150
  Espoo Convention 27, 79
  international law 36–37, 39–40, 275
  overlapping jurisdiction 277–278
  SEA Protocol 108
doctrine of binding precedent 11, 12
doctrine of implied powers 28
doctrine of parallelism 165
doctrine of sympathetic interpretation 148
drafts 50, 95–96, 206–207, 221
dualism 33, 274
dual representation 277
due account 76, 85, 106, 193, 223, 281
due diligence 59, 61, 63, 196

EAPs *see* Environmental Action
  Programmes
Earth Charter, 2000 116
Earth Summit, 1992 48, 49
EC *see* European Community
EEC *see* European Economic Community
  Treaty
EIA *see* environmental impact assessment
ELD *see* Environmental Liability Directive
enforcement
  Directive and Protocol comparisons
   281
  EIA Directive 186–190
  European law 3, 149–150, 169–170,
   172–173, 276, 279
  international law 3, 35–37, 63–64,
   274–275, 279
Environmental Action Programmes
  (EAPs) 160–161
environmental impact assessment (EIA)
  conservation conventions 116–117,
   120–121, 127, 128, 129

Directive 183–190, 197, 206, 239,
  240–242, 258
Espoo Convention 74–75, 76, 78
Habitats and Wild Birds Directives 244
IEL 2, 47, 50–51, 52, 53, 54–55, 57, 58,
  62
international and European law
  279–282
relationship to SEA 6, 196
sustainable development 48
Environmental Information Directive
  190–192
environmental level
  damage 54–55, 195–197
  European law 159–182
  international law 2, 47–71, 86, 279
  prevention of harm 50, 51–53, 56–57,
   60–61
  protection 97, 98, 209, 210
  reports 102–103, 104–105, 220, 221,
   281
  significant effects 216–217, 245–246
  structural funds regulations 257–258
  treaties 47, 49–50, 55–60
environmental level, information 192
Environmental Liability Directive (ELD)
  190, 195–197
environmental policy integration (EPI)
  210–212
Environment Title 163–164, 168
EPI *see* environmental policy integration
equal treatment principle 145
Espoo Convention, 1997 2–3, 27, 74–80,
  93–94, 94–95, 108, 279
EU *see* European Union
European Community (EC)
  environmental law 160–162
  EU relationship 138–139
  institutions 140–144, 194–195
  international law 26, 28, 139–140
  overview 138
European Council 141
European Court of Justice (ECJ)
  case laws 146–147
  dispute resolution 140–141, 150
  EIA Directive 187–190
  enforcement 149, 150

environmental law 160, 161, 162,
    172–173
Habitats and Wild Birds Directives 243,
    244, 245–246
proposed access to justice directive
    194
structure 143
European Economic Community (EEC)
    Treaty 138
European law 3, 39, 41, 59–60, 75, 81–82,
    94, 135–285
European Union (EU) 26, 28, 39, 137,
    138–140, 140–144
    see also Commission
evaluation 8–9
exclusion 275–276
exemptions 219, 247–250
external competence 164–165
external relations 276–277

federal states 34
follow-up 224, 253
formality 215
forum shopping 39–40, 277
full effectiveness principle 147–148
fundamental rights protection 211
fundamental rule of treaty law 33–34
future development consent *see*
    development consent
future measures 208

General Assembly, UN 27
guardian of the Treaties 140, 141, 149,
    170, 186
    see also Commission

Habitats Directive, 1992 166, 243–250,
    255, 258, 278
hard law *see* customary law; treaties
harm prevention 50, 51–53, 56–57,
    60–61, 86, 252
health 97, 103, 168, 256, 280
historical level
    Aarhus Convention 81–82
    EIA Directive 183–184
    Espoo Convention 74–75
    European law 137–140, 160–162

international law 25–28, 48–49
    SEA Directive 205–207
    SEA Protocol 94–95
horizontal direct effects 148, 149, 170,
    190, 208
horizontal directives 183–204
human health *see* health

IAIA *see* International Association for
    Impact Assessment
ICJ *see* International Court of Justice
IEL *see* international environmental law
ILC *see* International Law Commission
IMPEL *see* Network for the
    Implementation and Enforcement of
    Environmental Law
imperative reasons 247, 248, 249
implementation
    Aarhus Convention 82, 83–85, 86,
        194–195
    EIA Directive 186–190, 243
    Espoo Convention 79–80
    European law 141, 145, 170, 171–172
    SEA Directive 220, 225–228
    SEA Protocol 107–108
incidental jurisdiction 35
indirect effects 3, 32, 148, 170–171, 189,
    209, 274
individual level 26, 63–64, 144
information
    access to 83, 84, 86, 190, 197
    overlapping jurisdictions 277
    precautionary principle 115, 116
    scientific 52–53
    SEA Directive 221, 222–223, 281
    SEA Protocol 105–106, 281
    see also Aarhus Convention
inquiry 37
institutional level 26–28, 140–144, 161,
    162–165, 194–195
integration
    conservation conventions 126,
        128–129
    European law 145, 167
    SEA Directive 209, 210–212
    SEA performance criteria 8
intergovernmental level 27–28, 40, 161

interim application approval 50
International Association for Impact
    Assessment (IAIA) 8–9
International Court of Justice (ICJ), UN
    27, 28, 34, 35–36, 53
international environmental law (IEL) 2,
    47–71, 86, 279
international law 3, 23–134, 210
International Law Commission (ILC) 27,
    77
international level 147, 164–165, 168,
    191, 273–282
interpretation 12–13, 30, 32, 34–35, 143,
    186, 258

joint procedures 240, 251
judicial level 10–11, 12, 31, 63–64
    see also access to justice
jurisdiction 35, 240–241, 274, 277–279

land use planning 254–255
leadership 165
legal requirements 10–14
legislation
    common and civil law contrast 11
    EIA and wetlands 120
    Espoo Convention 75
    European 140, 142, 144, 163, 164,
        170
    interpretation 12
    SEA Protocol 97–99, 280
legitimacy 38
liability 55, 59, 60, 62–63, 76–77, 169,
    195–197
Lisbon Reform Treaty 137, 139, 151,
    161–162, 164, 276
listing sites/species 122–123, 124–125
local level 218–219

Maastricht Treaty 163–164, 166
mandatory provisions 13, 101, 129–130,
    184
margin of discretion 51, 226
marine environments 277
MEAs *see* multilateral environmental
    agreements
mediation 37

Meetings of the Parties (MOPs) 3, 29, 79,
    80
    see also Conferences of the Parties
member states, EU 144
merits appeal 12
migratory species 124–125
mitigation measures 248, 249, 253
mixed agreements 165, 274, 276–277,
    277
monism 33, 147, 274
monitoring 106–107, 170, 172, 207,
    223–224, 253–254, 281
MOPs *see* Meetings of the Parties
multilateral environmental agreements
    (MEAs) 40, 57, 60, 79, 115–133, 276

national defence 219
National Environmental Policy Act
    (NEPA), US 5, 279, 280
national level
    European law 147–148, 150, 171–172,
        225, 246, 273–282
    international law 32–35, 63, 273–279
    SEA development 5–6
    see also state level
Natura 2000 243, 248
natural law 33
natural resource use 168
negotiation 37
NEPA *see* National Environmental Policy
    Act
Network for the Implementation and
    Enforcement of Environmental Law
    (IMPEL) 170, 172
NGOs *see* non-governmental
    organizations
Nice Treaty 163–164
Nitrates Directive 255–256
non-governmental organizations (NGOs)
    63–64, 118
non-self-executing provisions 50

OECD *see* Organisation for Economic
    Co-operation and Development
option screening 252
Organisation for Economic Co–operation
    and Development (OECD) 61

OSPAR *see* Convention for the Protection
    of the Marine Environment of the
    North–East Atlantic
overlapping jurisdiction 240–241, 274,
    277–279
overriding public interest 247, 248–249

parallelism 165
parliament, European 142–143
participatory principle 50, 54, 58–59, 78
PCIJ *see* Permanent Court of
    International Justice
performance criteria 8–9
Permanent Court of International Justice
    (PCIJ) 34, 35
Plan of Implementation (POI) 49
planning 61, 95, 183–184, 212, 227–228,
    254–255
plans and programmes
    horizontal directives 195
    projects relationships 240–241
    related directives 244, 245, 255
    SEA Directive 206–207, 213–216, 217,
        218–219, 239
    SEA Protocol 97–98, 99–102
    structural funds 257
    see also SEA Directive
POI *see* Plan of Implementation
policy level
    Aarhus Convention 85
    European environmental law 160–162
    SEA development 5–6
    SEA Directive 210–212, 226, 279, 280
    SEA Protocol 97–99, 280
    Water Framework Directives 253
policy, plan and programmes (PPPs) 6,
    78, 83–84, 85, 87, 94, 121
polluter pays principle 50, 55, 59–60, 169
pollution 255–256, 256–257
PoMs *see* programmes of measures
power 10–11, 28, 141, 142, 162
PPPs *see* policy, plan and programmes
precautionary principle
    CBD 126–127
    EIA 116–117
    environmental assessment 115–116
    European environment law 168–169

Habitats and Wild Birds Directives
    245–246
IEL 50, 52–53, 56, 61
liability 196
Ramsar Convention 119–120
SEA Directive 210
soft law 32
preventative principle 169
prevention of environmental harm 50,
    51–53, 56–57, 60–61
primacy principle 147–148
primary law 11, 148
Principle 21, Stockholm Declaration
    60–61, 76
principle of non-discrimination *see*
    participatory principle
priority natural habitats or species 249
private international law *see* international
    law
procedural level
    Aarhus Convention 82–83
    directives effectiveness 243
    EIA Directive 184–186
    Espoo Convention 75–76
    related Directives 251–254, 258
    SEA Directive 213–221, 281
    SEA performance criteria 8–9
    SEA Protocol 99, 281
    self-contained regimes 40
programmes *see* plans and programmes;
    policy, plans and programmes
programmes of measures (PoMs) 251,
    253, 255
projects 87, 188, 216, 240–241, 245, 255,
    258
    see also environmental impact
        assessment
proportionality principle 145, 166–167
proposed Access to Justice Directive
    193–194
protocols 30, 49, 93–113
public definitions 185, 192, 281
public interest 247, 248–249
public international law 25
public participation
    Aarhus Convention 80–86, 83, 84, 85
    EIA Directive 185, 189, 197

Espoo Convention 78
Habitats and Wild Birds Directives
246–247
SEA Directive 221–223, 226, 281
SEA overview 6, 9
SEA Protocol 96, 104–106, 581
Water Framework Directives 254
see also Aarhus Convention
Public Participation Directive 190,
192–193

quality
air 256–257
reports 103, 221
SEA Protocol 107

Ramsar Convention *see* Convention
on Wetlands of International
Importance, Especially as Waterfowl
Habitat, 1971
ratification 29, 30, 34, 50
RBMPs *see* river basin management plans
reasonable alternatives 219–220,
220–221, 252
referendums 144
regulations 11–12, 146, 170, 194–195,
250, 257–258
reporting
EIA Directive 186–187
environmental 102–103, 104–105, 220,
221, 281
Espoo Convention 80
SEA Protocol 106–107
see also reviews
resource manuals 108
responsibility
common but differentiated 49, 50, 61
European law 162–165, 166, 169–170
state 39, 55, 275
responsible institutions 162–165
reviews 12, 80, 107, 186–187, 193, 281
see also reporting
rights 144, 193, 196, 211
Rio Declaration 61, 62
river basin management plans (RBMPs)
251, 253, 254, 255
rule of law 10–11, 186

rules 51

SA *see* sustainability appraisal
scientific information 52–53
scoping 102–103, 184, 219–221
screening 99–102, 104, 106, 213–219,
252, 280
SEA *see* Strategic Environmental
Assessment
secondary law 11, 148–149
secretariats 107
Security Council, UN 26–27
self-contained regimes 28, 39–41, 139
self-executing provisions 50
separation of powers 10–11
shared competences 276–277
shared responsibility 166
significant environmental effects
216–217, 245–246
Single European Act, 1986 163
site designation 243, 245
soft law 29, 32, 47–49, 60–63
SPAs *see* Special Protection Areas
Special Protection Areas (SPAs) 245
stare decisis see doctrine of binding
precedent
state of the art defence 195–196
state level 25, 26, 39, 55, 275
see also national level
state practice 31
see also customary law
statutes 11–12
Stockholm Declaration on the Human
Environment, 1972 48, 60–61, 76
Strategic Environmental Assessment
(SEA) Directive
EIA Directive 183
environmental information access 192
integration principle 167
overview 205–237
Protocol comparisons 94, 102, 106,
108–109, 279–282
relationship to other directives
239–271
Strategic Environmental Assessment
(SEA) Protocol 2–3, 73, 80–86,
93–113, 205, 279–282

strategies 216
structural funds regulations 257–258
subsidiarity principle 145, 164, 166
substantive provisions
    Aarhus Convention 105–106
    conservation conventions 126, 128, 129
    EIA Directive 197
    Espoo Convention 79
    SEA Directive 213, 281
    SEA Protocol 281
supranational level 32–35, 139–140
sustainability 8
sustainability appraisal (SA) 7, 220
sustainable development
    EIA 48, 279
    European environment law 167–168
    international law 49
    SEA Directive 209, 211, 212
    SEA Protocol 97, 98
sympathetic interpretation *see* indirect
    effects
system evaluation 8–9

thresholds 187, 188
tiered approaches 103, 240, 281
transboundary context
    cooperation 50, 53–54, 57–59, 62
    EIA 74, 185
    enforcement 275
    Espoo Convention 74–80
    national jurisdiction 64
    SEA Directive 222–223, 281
    SEA Protocol 99, 281
    treaties 73–74
    World Heritage Convention 122
transparency 38
treaties
    enforcement 275
    environmental 47, 49–50, 55–60
    European 138, 141, 145, 162–165
    guardian of 140, 141, 149, 170, 186
    international 29–31, 33–35
    interpretation 143
    transboundary 73–74
    see also conventions; Lisbon Reform
        Treaty
tribunals 39–40

UN *see* United Nations
unanimity 208
UNCED *see* United Nations Conference
    on Environment and Development
uncertainty 52–53, 101–102
UNCHE *see* United Nations Conference
    on the Human Environment
UNCLOS *see* United Nations Convention
    on the Law of the Sea
UNECE *see* United Nations Economic
    Commission for Europe
United Kingdom 227–228
United Nations Conference on
    Environment and Development
    (UNCED), 1992 48, 49
United Nations Conference on the
    Human Environment (UNCHE),
    1972 48, 49
United Nations Convention on the Law
    of the Sea (UNCLOS) 39–40, 49, 50,
    56–57, 59, 130, 277
United Nations Economic Commission
    for Europe (UNECE) 3, 73–74
United Nations (UN) 26–27, 28, 38

VCLT *see* Vienna Convention on the Law
    of Treaties
vertical direct effects 148, 149, 170, 246
Vienna Convention on the Law of
    Treaties (VCLT) 28, 29–30, 34
voluntary approaches 13, 161, 196

Waste Framework Directive 256, 258
watercourses 55, 56, 57, 58
Water Framework Directive, 2000 208,
    250–255, 258
wetlands 119–122
Wild Birds Directive, 1979 243–250
World Charter for Nature, 1982 62
World Conservation Strategy, 1982 48
World Heritage Convention *see*
    Convention Concerning the
    Protection of the World Cultural and
    Natural Heritage, 1972
World Summit on Sustainable
    Development (WSSD), 2002 49,
    97